STRENGTH FOR THE FIGHT

A History of Black Americans in the Military

BERNARD C. NALTY

THE FREE PRESS
A Division of Macmillan, Inc.
NEW YORK

Collier Macmillan Publishers
LONDON

The Free Press
A Division of Macmillan, Inc.
866 Third Avenue, New York, N.Y. 10022

Collier Macmillan Canada, Inc.

First Free Press Paperback Edition 1989

Printed in the United States of America

printing number

2 3 4 5 6 7 8 9 10

Library of Congress Cataloging-in-Publication Data

Nalty, Bernard C.
  Strength for the fight.

  Bibliography: p.
  Includes index.
  1. United States—Armed Forces—Afro-Americans in
  the military—History.   III. Title: Black Americans in
  the military.
UB418.A47N35   1986   355'.008996073   86-536
ISBN 0-02-922411-X

To
Richard B. Nalty
in
Grateful
Memory

Contents

Acknowledgments

OF ALL THE PERSONS who helped this book take shape, the most important is my wife, Barbara. Besides being a source of encouragement, she joined Elizabeth Nalty, our daughter, in helping with the different jobs that come under the heading of research assistance.

The book originated as a collaboration with Morris J. MacGregor, Jr., who had to withdraw at the outset because of his duties as head of the General History Branch of the Army's Center of Military History. He has nevertheless been extremely generous in sharing his knowledge and in helping obtain research materials that otherwise would not have been available. Another individual who has been especially helpful is Col. Alan L. Gropman, USAF, the author of one of the two official monographs dealing with race relations in the Air Force. His suggestions greatly strengthened my treatment of the racial policies of the Army Air Forces and the U.S. Air Force.

Thirteen volumes of documents, edited by Mr. MacGregor and myself and published in 1977 by Scholarly Resources of Wilmington, Delaware, as *Blacks in the United States Armed Forces: Basic Documents*, served as a major source of information for the book. A variety of other documents, statistics, and photographs supplemented the material in this collection, and several persons have helped make them available. Jerald Anderson, author of *Black Americans in Defense of Our Nation*, an account prepared for the Office of the Secretary of Defense, proved particularly gracious, as did Capt. RitaVictoria DeArmond, USAF, a graduate of the Defense Race Relations Institute now assigned to the Office of Air Force History. Herman S. Wolk, a supervisory historian at the Office of Air Force History, made available copies of the minutes of the Air Board, which he is editing for publication in the near future. Lawrence J. Paszek, the recently retired chief of the Editorial Branch, Office of Air Force History, provided photographs from his own collection. Alfred M. Beck, then of the Center of Military History but later Mr. Paszek's successor, shared the results of his research on the 24th Infantry.

A number of libraries and librarians have helped me obtain books and articles, some of them comparatively rare. The Prince George's County, Maryland, library system deserves my thanks, especially the Hyattsville branch, where a dozen or more staff members proved uniformly helpful during my many visits. The list of librarians who inconvenienced themselves on my behalf includes Frank Pietropaoli, chief librarian, National Air and Space Museum; Capt. Susan Cober, USAF, a historian and librarian for the Office of Air Force History; Pearline H. Seals, a member of the staff of the base library at Bolling Air Force Base, Washington, D.C.; and both Barbara Lynch and Katherine Bowman of the Navy Department Library.

Paul J. Scheips, a senior historian at the Center of Military History, and Ronald H. Spector, now a member of the history faculty at the University of Alabama, generously loaned me books from their personal libraries.

Truman R. Strobridge, with whom I have collaborated on numerous occasions, helped arrange for the copying of several photographs.

I owe a special debt to Joyce Seltzer, the senior editor of this book. Her sense of continuity brought order to an initially chaotic manuscript.

Celia Knight supervised production, including the copy editing, which was done by Hunt Cole.

Such are the persons who have contributed in a special way to any strengths this volume may possess. For the weaknesses I accept sole responsibility.

Abiding Strength for an Unending Fight

SINCE COLONIAL TIMES blacks have made an increasingly important contribution to American military might. At first the black soldiers and sailors were few in number, usually serving in time of emergency and then as auxiliaries. White colonial militiamen might rely on blacks to clear a parade ground or build a blockhouse, but only when threatened by invasion or Indian attack would they trust the black man with musket, ball, and powder. When given an opportunity to fight, black soldiers and sailors did well, whether in the North American wilderness, at sea, or on foreign battlefields.

Helping defeat America's foes did not gain acceptance within the military. Traditionally, when the firing died away, no more than a token number of blacks remained in the ranks. Besides fighting the wartime enemy, black Americans faced a second and far more dangerous foe—racism, which sharply restricted their opportunities within the armed services and in civil society as well. The accomplishments of blacks in combat all but disappeared when examined through the distorting prism of white supremacy.

In "The Warrior's Prayer," written shortly before his death in 1906, the black poet Paul Laurence Dunbar identified the fight against racism as the critical battle where victory would bring not medals and parades, but full citizenship, and said:

> I do not ask that Thou shall front the fray,
>   And drive the warring foemen from my sight;

1

> *I only ask, O Lord, by night, by day,*
>   *Strength for the fight.*

At this time racism was tightening its grip on every aspect of American life, civilian and military, by means of the so-called Jim Crow laws, which sought to enforce racial segregation thoroughly and completely.

Paul Dunbar's heritage made him uniquely qualified to offer this prayer for strength in the fight against racism, for his father had won a personal victory in this struggle. An escaped slave, the elder Dunbar had served during the Civil War in a black regiment recruited in Massachusetts and afterward moved to Dayton, Ohio, where he taught himself to read and write, learned the plasterer's trade, and created for his family a respected place in local society. The father had attained the fullest measure of citizenship then possible, inspiring the son to set for his black warrior the goal of obtaining all the rights due a citizen of the United States.

Racism deprived generations of blacks of these basic rights, in the process imposing artificial limits on their opportunities within the military. Only gradually did Jim Crow relax his hold on the armed services and the other elements of American society. Changing circumstances helped defeat Jim Crow, undermining the unjust code that formed the legal basis for racial segregation in the military and elsewhere. Wars became longer in duration and broader in scope; they demanded greater skill on the part of the combatants and required the support of the entire populace. The recurring need for manpower prevented the armed forces from continuing to indulge in the wastefulness of racism. In this manner, blacks came to participate more fully in the defense of the nation—an evolutionary process that began before there was a United States and continued through revolution, civil strife, and foreign wars.

1

Toward a Black Identity

THE CAPTAIN of a Dutch ship that was short of food and water anchored at Jamestown, Virginia, in 1619 and exchanged twenty blacks, probably captured in the West Indies, for the needed provisions. As agriculture expanded, the demand for slaves like these increased, so that within a generation a profitable trade in human beings had grown up. By the time the North American colonies declared their independence from Great Britain, a half million blacks toiled in bondage, most of them laboring on plantations in Maryland, Virginia, the Carolinas, and Georgia, although Rhode Island had become a center of the slave trade with a large, though transient, black populace.

Introduced against their will into a struggle between whites and Indians, blacks soon contributed to the military strength of Britain's North American colonies. They did so even though most of them were slaves destined for a lifetime of involuntary servitude, replacing in the interest of greater efficiency the indentured servants, many of them whites, who labored in the fields for a specific number of years. Their white owners considered the slaves animals rather than human beings, sullen, devious, scarcely able to communicate—hardly unusual attributes for a person kidnapped from his home, packed into the hold of a ship for a harrowing voyage, and imprisoned in an alien environment. After this shocking introduction, the slaves found themselves involved in a conflict they barely understood. Their earliest military service, circumscribed though it was,

3

marked the beginning of a long and arduous journey toward individuality, freedom, citizenship, and ultimately a comparatively secure place in society.

In the colonial era, the population of British North America consisted of three basic racial groups—Indians, whites, and blacks. Although the white component at times included cruelly treated indentured servants and even a few slaves, the majority were free men—artisans, professional men, mechanics, farmers, and planters—who were confident that they could impose their collective will upon the new continent and its Indian inhabitants. White colonists, determined to create their vision of a shining city on a hill, sought to mold the Indian populace to their will, whether through diplomacy, religious instruction, or force. Certain that its members formed a chosen people, the dominant faction of the white group believed that blacks, even more than Indians, existed for the convenience of the elect.

Despite treaties, preaching, and military campaigns, the semi-nomadic Indians proved hard to control. In contrast, the blacks provided a ready source of labor, fixed in location, its size and the degree of freedom of its members depending largely upon the nature of the work that had to be done. Large farms required vast numbers of laborers, most of them held in permanent bondage; where farms were small and cities large, blacks tended to be few in number and bound for a fixed period, helping an artisan or merchant and his family.

In the agrarian South, therefore, armies of slaves toiled on huge plantations and made up a majority of the non-Indian populace. Where plantations yielded to smaller farms, the proportion of blacks decreased and correspondingly the numbers of people enslaved. In New England, a region of rocky soil and subsistence farming, blacks were fewest. As the plantation owners of the South realized, the greater the proportion of slaves to masters, the more terrifying was the danger of rebellion.

The colonies at various times and in varying degrees experienced the fear or frightful reality of either a slave uprising or Indian warfare. The greater the danger from the black or the Indian, the more necessary it became to enlist the aid of the other. The black American, especially the slave, thus became a counterweight against the Indian. When the tribes, whether justly aggrieved or stirred up by Britain's European enemies, seemed especially dangerous, colonial governments held out various rewards, including freedom, to black slaves willing to help fight the Indian instead of making common cause with him.

Nowhere was this three-cornered conflict among blacks, whites, and Indians sharper than in South Carolina. There the nightmare of

Indian attack, perhaps Spanish-inspired, weighed aga
ter of armed blacks fomenting a slave uprising or ma
cause with the red man against the white. The plan
trolled the colony of South Carolina demonstrated ma
balancing the danger from black slaves, who greatly outnumber
their masters, against the threat of marauding Indians. These colonists offered trade with the Creeks, Cherokees, and others in return
for peace and tribal help in tracking down fugitive slaves. A comparative handful of whites thus drove a wedge between the slave populace, numbering as many as 75,000, and some 60,000 Indians. Had
the two groups joined forces, they might have destroyed a white
population that did not reach 50,000 until after the French and Indian War, which ended in 1763.[1]

The enmity created between blacks and red men enabled South
Carolina authorities to begin as early as 1703 to enlist slaves in the
colonial militia. A law adopted that year promised freedom to any
slave who, "in actual invasion," should "kill or take [prisoner] one or
more of our enemies," and could produce a white person who had
witnessed the deed. Should a slave escape from bondage as the
result of heroism backed by the eyewitness testimony of a white
man, his former master would receive appropriate compensation.
The owner also would be paid if his valuable property was killed or
disabled.[2]

Playing upon black animosity toward the Indians, who in effect
were paid to hunt down escaped slaves, South Carolina set about recruiting a military force divided about equally between free citizens
and slaves. As confidence in this force increased, the colonists began
displaying contempt for their Indian allies. Traders routinely
cheated the back-country tribes, and farmers encroached on land
where tribesmen grazed their cattle. Among the groups thus alienated were the powerful Yamasees, who had recaptured blacks fleeing from bondage, pacified lesser tribes on behalf of the Carolinians,
and delivered captured Indians into slavery. Gradually the members
of the tribe realized that they were hopelessly in debt to unscrupulous white merchants willing to sell Indian women and children as
slaves in order to obtain what the tribesmen owed. Unable to find redress, the Yamasees formed a confederation with the Creeks and
several weaker tribes and on Good Friday, April 15, 1715, attacked
their oppressors.[3]

After the attack, realizing that a Yamasee victory might inspire other Indian tribes, Virginia and North Carolina sent troops,
and the New England colonies furnished supplies. Faced just beyond its borders with the threat of several thousand Indians believed incited by Spanish agents and capable of "inexpressible tor-

tures," North Carolina mustered both blacks and whites, free men and slaves, to meet that threat. Even in this time of peril, however, North Carolina's leaders warned that in issuing weapons "there must be great caution used, lest our slaves when arm'd might become our masters."[4]

South Carolina prevailed, but victory was not the result of outside aid from North Carolina or other colonies or due to the prowess of the militia. Commerce triumphed rather than armed might, for the Cherokees, pressured to join the uprising, instead sided with the whites, whom they valued as trading partners. No match for the Cherokees, the Yamasees and Creeks abandoned the lands they had fought to retain.[5]

Armed slaves fought alongside whites against the common enemy, and presumably some of the black militiamen killed or captured one or more of the tribesmen, furnished the necessary proof, and thus gained freedom. The practice of linking manumission to battlefield heroism had certain disadvantages, however, and these must have been obvious to colonial authorities. A slave, after all, was a valuable possession who would have to be replaced if killed or released from bondage. The payment received for this loss could not compensate fully for the forfeiture of needed skills, the cost of acquiring another slave, and the time required to train a replacement. More ominous for the plantation owner was the relationship established between killing and freedom. Granted that a slave might win freedom by killing on behalf of his owner, would liberty not be more certain if he killed that owner? This consideration may have prompted the warning by the colonial leadership of North Carolina that arming the slaves might make them masters. Such presumably were the concerns that in 1719 prompted South Carolina to amend its militia laws so that a slave who killed or captured one of the enemy received not his freedom but a cash award.

The beat of a drum which echoed across the colony of South Carolina in September 1739 signaled the outbreak of the Stono uprising, the first opportunity to invoke the revised militia statutes. A slave named Tommy rallied twenty or so other blacks, kidnapped like him from villages in Angola at the mouth of the Congo River, and fled toward Spanish Florida, using the drumbeat to rally still others to his cause.The group increased in size, burned some plantation buildings, and killed a number of whites, but it never became a disciplined force. The pursuers, mostly Indians led by whites but not reinforced by loyal slaves, tracked Tommy and his followers and came upon the rebels at rest, singing and dancing in an open field. The slaughter that followed put an end to the mutiny, though not to the desire of slaves to be free.

In this crisis the colony depended upon Indian allies rather than using black militiamen to pursue and defeat the rebels, for a white minority surrounded by slaves had come to find the Cherokee less fearsome than the armed black man. After all, the Indians did not have the easy access to white families that was granted to household slaves. Nonetheless the tribesmen could not be fully trusted.

Despite the declining enthusiasm for issuing weapons to slaves, South Carolina could not ignore this source of manpower in the event the Indians should take up arms against the whites. Only the most trustworthy of slaves would be allowed to serve, however, and for that reason the colony felt confident enough in the decade following the Stono war to revive the old law authorizing freedom in recognition of valor on the battlefield. The policy remained on the law books through the 1750s and beyond, but the government of South Carolina no longer dared to call out the authorized number of blacks, a third of the total militia strength. Indeed, when the white colonists at last grew bold enough to fight the Cherokees, only a handful of carefully chosen slaves helped defeat South Carolina's former allies in a campaign that began in 1759 and continued fitfully over three years.[6]

Other colonies tried to strike a balance between fear of Indian attack and dread of a slave uprising. Virginia represented one extreme, promptly forbidding slaves to bear arms. Not until 1676 did a Virginian dare to arm blacks. This individual, Nathaniel Bacon, was in rebellion against a government that sought to protect the lands of Indian tribes living within the colony. Bacon and the poor white farmers who followed him wanted to seize the tribal holdings, and his offer of freedom to any slave that ran away to join his uprising seemed an effective way of weakening the planter class that ruled Virginia. His tactics reflected desperation rather than concern for the oppressed blacks. The colonial authorities suppressed Bacon's rebellion without resorting to the use of slaves in the armed forces of Virginia. Slaves continued thereafter to be excluded from militia service, although after 1723 free blacks might serve as drummers and trumpeters or wield the pick, axe, and shovel as pioneers, working on field fortifications.[7]

Far to the north, the New England colonies had already faced a threat similar to that which forced South Carolina to enlist slaves, but the citizens living on small farms or in towns lacked the vast pool of involuntary labor upon which to draw. French authorities in Canada, like the Spanish in Florida, could stir up backwoods tribes to attack vulnerable frontier settlements. So real was the threat that the initial reaction of Massachusetts Bay colonists anticipated the policy of the Carolinians, requiring that blacks, free or slave, undergo militia training. But the black populace of New England remained so small during colonial times—roughly 2.5 percent, with the heaviest concentration in the slave trading center of Rhode Island—that it did not have a decisive effect on total military strength. As a result, Massachusetts legislators saw no need to hold out freedom as a reward for the slave serving heroically in the Bay colony's armed forces, although the lawmakers did compensate owners who lost the services of their slaves either temporarily during the period of service or permanently, because of death or disability. Usually the slave surrendered to his master at least half of any money earned while on military duty, sometimes a considerable sum in the case of prize money distributed among the crews of privateers. Unrest stirred the comparatively few New England slaves and apparently persuaded the colonies to amend the militia laws to make the bearing of arms a white monopoly. Local authorities occasionally required free blacks to perform whatever duties the militia commander might decide, but the tasks usually involved improving the drill ground or performing other labor or housekeeping chores.

As in South Carolina, law and practice came to diverge throughout New England. Fear ultimately compelled the southern colony to stop enforcing laws that required military service from trustworthy slaves; in New England, confidence that the slave populace would remain under control, and a persisting shortage of manpower, emboldened the New England colonists to ignore the legal ban on arming blacks. Quite illegally, a Framingham, Massachusetts, militia unit included a slave, Nero, serving as trumpeter when it marched off to King George's War. During that conflict, lasting from 1740 to 1748, companies from New Hampshire, Rhode Island, and Connecticut also had a scattering of blacks in the ranks. Moreover, privateers fitted out in New England to prey on the commerce of England's enemies frequently had black crewmen on board. A slave called Toney cooked for the crew of one of several Boston privateers—including the *Virgin Queen, Shepherd, Providence,* and *George*—that signed on black sailors. Another such ship, the *Revenge,* numbered five blacks in a 37-man crew.

The same pattern of legal exclusion and actual acceptance continued throughout the French and Indian War, fought in the New World from 1754 to 1763. When the New England colonies could not recruit enough whites to maintain the forces needed to protect the frontier, they turned to slaves like Benjamin Negro and Caesar from Rhode Island or free blacks like George Gire of Grafton, Massachusetts, who "became infirm" because of his "hard service in the French War" and eventually received an annual pension of 40 shillings. Like all common soldiers of the time, the blacks tended to be mere entries on a muster roll. Only those like Gire who received pensions or other special recognition emerge as individuals.

The first New England blacks to serve on shipboard or in the wartime colonial militia usually were slaves. Indeed, the first black to die in the service of Massachusetts was a slave, his name unrecorded, whose death resulted in the payment of 20 pounds to his master. Similarly, the seagoing cook Toney who had sailed with the privateers belonged to Samuel Lynde of Boston, and the Framingham trumpeter, Nero, was the slave of a minister living in that town.

Slaves like Benjamin Negro, Caesar, Toney, or Nero had no voice in deciding whether or how they would serve. Their masters either brought them along to war or sent them off and remained at home. Although reliable figures are not available, the number of slaves capable of involuntary military service represented a fairly large segment of a small minority, the blacks of New England. As late as 1790, long after the destruction of the Rhode Island slave trade during the American Revolution, some 7,000 men, women, and children remained in bondage throughout New England. A decade later, about 35,000 slaves lived in the North, most of them in New York and New Jersey.

George Gire, however, had emerged from a new class, the free blacks, who were becoming more numerous along the northeastern seaboard. There the economic underpinning of slavery proved weak, since the nature of the region made large-scale agriculture impossible, even though the area's sea captains and merchants did engage in the slave trade. Ironically, the same religiously oriented society of New England that bought and sold blacks tended to look upon local slaves as unfortunate human beings, though of a somewhat lower type, who would be forced to endure servitude for a fixed period of years rather than indefinitely.

Although the free blacks like Gire exercised a measure of control over their destinies, their presence in the ranks may not have been entirely voluntary. Social pressure prodded them into uniform, as townspeople tended to rid their communities of undesirables. Economic necessity also played a role, for free blacks had difficulty acquiring property or finding jobs. But service with the militia in some cases may also have indicated that at least a few considered themselves members of a society worth defending.[8]

During the period of increasing tension that led to the American Revolution, a black man stepped from anonymity onto the pages of history in Boston. He was Crispus Attucks of Framingham, Massachusetts, probably the same Crispus who had fled from slavery some twenty years before and was described in a circular dating from that time as tall, part Indian, curly-haired, and knock-kneed.

He figured in the Boston Massacre of March 5, 1770, possibly provoking that incident, for an eyewitness claimed that Attucks had attacked a British officer and knocked the musket from the hands of a
grenadier who tried to intervene. Another bystander was equally
certain, however, that the black man had done nothing more violent
than lean upon a walking stick. In either case, the British opened
fire upon their tormentors, and when the smoke cleared, Attucks
and ten others lay dead.[9]

A black American thus took his place in legend, being hailed as a
martyr to the cause of independence. When fighting broke out at
Lexington and Concord, Massachusetts, some five years after Crispus Attucks died, several blacks joined in firing upon the British.
Among them was Peter Salem, like Attucks a resident of Framingham, who had been freed in order to enlist. Another black, Prince
Estabrook, was wounded during the skirmish at Lexington.

Peter Salem also fought in the Battle of Bunker Hill at Boston,
where according to legend he used his long rifle to kill Major John
Pitcairn, commander of the British assault force. Other blacks
fought with equal distinction in the American militia line, which
stood firm while shot and powder lasted, then had to retreat. One of
them, Salem Poore, received a commendation for gallantry from the
officers of his regiment. Another, Cuff Whitmore, exhibited a trait
that became a characteristic of the American soldier, as would be
shown during future wars by the acquisition of samurai swords and
Mauser pistols. He "liberated" a British officer's sword that he later
sold.[10]

In the autumn of 1775, a number of blacks were serving with
New England units in the Continental forces arrayed around Boston. General John Thomas, an American brigade commander, reported that "we have some Negros but I look upon them as equally
serviceable with other men, for fatigue [labor details] and in action."
He added that "many of them have proved themselves brave." Despite the contributions of the black troops, objections to their presence were increasing, in part because of the arrival of troops from
colonies where slavery was entrenched. General Thomas attributed
the attitude to "prejudice" by soldiers of the southern colonies
"with respect to troops raised in this"—the colony of Massachusetts. The prejudice, however, stemmed to some degree from a simple spirit of regionalism, for the southern soldier considered himself
better than any New Englander, white or black.[11]

As General Thomas sensed, pressure was mounting for a purge
of blacks from Continental ranks, but it was not exclusively of
southern origin. Not quite a month before the freed slave Peter Sa-

lem fired his rifle on Bunker Hill, Massachusetts legislators had recommended against accepting slaves for military service, although
free blacks might still enlist. The leaders of the rebellious colony apparently believed that their cause would triumph without the help
of slaves. The war for independence would be a free man's fight.[12]
The heroic defense of Bunker Hill, in which Salem took part, may
have made the rebel leadership even more selective in its recruiting
practices. Horatio Gates, the adjutant general of the new Continental Army, forbade "Officers of the several regiments of Massachusetts Bay forces" to enlist "any stroller negro or vagabond, or person suspected of being an enemy to the liberty of America nor any
under eighteen years of age."[13] For Massachusetts, confident of its
strength, everyone's war was now a free man's war and threatened
to become a white man's war, even though Salem and his fellow
blacks who had already enlisted might remain in the ranks.

Even as the white leaders of Massachusetts pondered the wisdom of enlisting additional blacks, southern plantation owners rejected the idea, for they continued to harbor a fear of arming their
slaves and possibly imperiling a society built upon the involuntary
labor of a black majority. The Continental Congress addressed the
issue in September 1775, defeating a motion by Edward Rutledge of
South Carolina to dismiss all blacks, free or slave, from the Continental Army.[14] Although unwilling to discharge their black soldiers,
most of whose enlistments would soon expire, General Washington
and his principal officers decided to appease the slaveholders and
accept only whites in the future. On October 8, they "Agreed unanimously to reject all slaves, and by a great majority to reject negroes
altogether," a policy that the Continental Congress promptly ratified.[15] The ban on slaves may have reflected economic reality, for
the rebellious colonies, including Massachusetts, normally reim-
bursed those masters whose slaves were killed or crippled.

The action of the Continental Congress applied to the Continental Army, the equivalent of a national force manned and paid for by
levies imposed by congressional action on the states. The individual
states also recruited and equipped militia units, for which they established their own policies. The militia had been the first to fight,
opposing the British before the Continental Army took shape. But as
time passed, the better-disciplined Continentals, enlisted for a
longer period, increased in importance, whereas the militia tended
to function as local defensive forces, mustered to meet a particular
crisis and disbanded when the emergency passed. Because the fighting dragged on, enthusiasm waned, and the states found it increasingly difficult to meet the manpower levies established by Congress,

so that race tended to become less important in recruiting. During the fall of 1775, however, confidence in an American victory ran high; the pool of white manpower seemed adequate for the conflict.

Meanwhile, his excellency, the right honorable John, Earl of Dunmore, the royal governor of Virginia, had come to realize that slaves were willing to fight for their freedom, even though they had to oppose freedom for the colonies in doing so. On November 7, 1775, Lord Dunmore declared "all indentured servants, Negroes, or others free, that are able to bear arms," should they join "His Majesty's troops as soon as may be, for more speedily returning this colony to a proper sense of duty to His Majesty's crown and dignity."[16] Dunmore envisaged the slave quarters of the Tidewater region of Virginia as a source of soldiers, whose unexpected escape from the plantations would cripple an agricultural system dependent upon slavery.

The master class responded with a combination of paternalism and terrorism, in effect offering those misguided enough to take up the offer a choice between forgiveness (with acceptance of slavery) or death. The leaders of the rebellion in Virginia promised amnesty to "all such who have taken this unlawful wicked step," provided they put aside the weapons Lord Dunmore had issued them and promptly surrendered. Any who persisted in what the slaveowners considered mutiny would "suffer death" and forfeit "all benefit of clergy."[17]

Word of the British offer percolated through the slave society, and within two weeks some 500 persons had fled from bondage to gamble their lives on Lord Dunmore. The royal governor promptly organized an Ethiopian Regiment that was about 300 strong when it joined an equal number of white soldiers in defensive positions at Great Bridge, protecting the landward approaches to Norfolk, Virginia. A force of 900 Virginians and North Carolinians stormed the entrenchments on December 11, driving out the defenders and pursuing them into Norfolk. On New Year's Day, Lord Dunmore's ships shelled the victorious rebels, setting fires in the town. The Americans then set ablaze the property of loyalists, and the resulting conflagration all but leveled Norfolk. Following this defeat, a smallpox epidemic struck the Ethiopian Regiment, so that after six months Lord Dunmore could muster no more than 150 escaped slaves. In June 1776, Virginia troops drove Lord Dunmore's men from their base camp on Gwynn's Island at the mouth of the Rappahannock River and ended the threat of a slave rebellion in the Tidewater.[18]

Even as Virginia slaves were risking their lives to gain freedom in the service of George III, black veterans of the fighting around Boston found themselves barred from reenlisting, a result of Washington's October 8 conference with his generals. The very officers who had testified to the courage of Salem Poore at Bunker Hill could no longer accept him in their regiment. Dissatisfaction on the part of blacks seeking to reenlist and white officers who wanted them caused General Washington to reconsider. Another factor may have been the immediate and enthusiastic response to Lord Dunmore's offer and the possibility, remote though it was, that free blacks might find some similar offer almost as attractive. On December 30, 1775, Washington issued a general order in which he acknowledged that "Numbers of Free Negroes are desirous of enlisting" and authorized recruiters to "entertain them," pending approval of such an enlistment policy by the Continental Congress.[19]

Washington called attention to the eagerness of his black veterans to remain in service at a time when the zeal of many of the first volunteers was fading as their enlistments came to an end. Congress responded by permitting blacks to reenlist but retained the ban on new Negro recruits. Nevertheless, the congressional reaction helped hold the Continental Army together at a time when the chill of winter, the boredom of military drill, and the dreariness of camp life were eroding enthusiasm for the Revolution. The decision enabled Salem Poore to remain in the army, fighting at White Plains, New York, in October 1776, and suffering at Valley Forge, Pennsylvania, in the winter of 1777–1778.[20]

Blacks, except for veterans, were thus officially excluded from the Continental Army. The various rebellious colonies followed suit, announcing that they would accept only whites for militia service. Early in 1776, the Massachusetts General Assembly formally adopted such a policy, foreshadowed by the directive of Horatio Gates during the previous autumn. Massachusetts was followed shortly afterward by New Hampshire.[21] Circumstances, however, would soon cause both the Continentals and the militia to ignore the restrictions.

Although barred for the present from enlisting even in militia units (but not from reenlisting in the Continental Army), blacks provided a welcome source of labor for building or repairing fortifications during periods of danger. The American commander in New York, William Alexander, Lord Stirling, whose claim to that title had been rejected by Great Britain's House of Lords, ordered all able-bodied black men to be issued picks and shovels so they could work alongside Continental troops in preparing for the defense of the city, which had to be abandoned to the enemy later in 1776.[22]

Similarly, the South Carolina Committee of Safety resolved that "able-bodied negro men be taken into public service and enrolled and employed, without arms, for the defense of the several batteries" that guarded Charleston. The slaves were, in effect, being leased from their masters for 10 shillings per day, with the owners receiving compensation if their property was killed or wounded. In addition, "suitable rewards" would be given "to those slaves who behave well in time of action."[23] Early in June 1776, when a British attack was expected within days, press gangs were rounding up "every Negro that they . . . [met] in the Streets by Day Light in order to work on an Additional Battery. . . ."[24] This time Charleston beat off the attackers, thanks in part to the fortifications built by the city's slaves; in 1780 the city would not be so fortunate, falling to a British expedition under Sir Henry Clinton.

The pattern of barring blacks from enlisting, though allowing them to use the shovel if not the bayonet, did not apply in the naval service. Danger, discomfort, and separation from home for long periods discouraged recruits, so that a captain would settle for any able-bodied hand regardless of race. At sea blacks served as sharpshooters in Marine detachments, manned guns, joined boarding parties, and took part in forays ashore, in addition to cooking, handling the sails, caulking, and cleaning. A number of black sailors and marines, both slaves and free men, helped sail the ships of the Continental and state navies or joined privateers, risking their lives in return for a share of the profits from commerce raiding. Two unnamed slaves, for instance, were "mariners" under Captain Henry Johnson of the luckless Boston privateer *Yankey*, which captured two British merchantmen only to have prisoners from these ships overpower the American crew and sail to England. Two blacks, Quako Chadwick and John Clarke, graced the muster roll of the Continental sloop *Fly*, while two others, John Cook and a man called Dick, languished for a time in the brig of another Continental warship, *Andrew Doria*.[25]

As the war dragged on, most states found it increasingly difficult to meet recruiting quotas established by Congress for the Continental Army. Recruiters in New England ignored official policy and accepted free blacks or slaves, who might join up voluntarily in the case of free men or involuntarily. One of the volunteers, Luke Nickelson (or Nickerson), a "man of color," enlisted in a Massachussetts regiment and fought at Saratoga in New York, where a British musket ball tore into his thigh. Another black, Cuff Wells, a slave owned by the proprietor of a Colchester, Connecticut, apothecary, enlisted in a regiment raised in that state, became a surgeon's assistant, and "received his freedom because of his service in the Army."[26]

In Connecticut, where legislators were discussing the manumission of slaves, a committee of the general assembly recommended in 1777 that "negro and mulatto slaves judged to be reasonably worthy by the select men of the town" be, in effect, hired from their masters, sworn into the Continental Army, and declared "de facto free." The upper house, which postponed action on abolition, also refused to endorse the committee report, but hundreds of blacks, slaves like Cuff Wells or free men, enlisted nonetheless.[27]

Rhode Island found itself in a more desperate situation than Connecticut, for British troops occupied the town of Newport and enforced a blockade that was strangling commerce, which included the slave trade. General James M. Varnum—a former officer of the Rhode Island militia, now one of Washington's brigadiers, who had assumed responsibility for recruiting Continental troops—doubted that the state's quota of two battalions could be met by drawing exclusively from Rhode Island's white citizens. He therefore recommended late in 1777 that one of the units be recruited from among the slave populace, offering freedom in exchange for military service. George Washington, ignoring the long-standing policy of excluding slaves, acceded to the plan, and the Rhode Island Assembly passed the necessary legislation, requiring that masters receive compensation. Recruiting went so well that some state lawmakers grew fearful of destroying the slave trade that had contributed to Newport's peacetime wealth. As a result, the assembly halted recruiting for the black battalion effective June 10, 1778, not quite four months after enlistments began, but ban or none, the unit maintained an average strength of about 150 men throughout some five years of service.

Recruited and led by Colonel Christopher Greene, the battalion fought in Rhode Island, New Jersey, and New York. After Colonel Greene was killed in a night attack by British cavalry at Point's Bridge, New York, in May 1781, command passed to the lieutenant colonel, Jeremiah Olney. When the battalion, sometimes referred to as a regiment as the Continental Army contracted in size, disbanded at Saratoga in June 1783, Olney paid tribute to the "unexampled fortitude and patience" his men had displayed throughout the "long and severe war."[28]

Meanwhile, James Madison had urged that Virginia abandon its policy of restricting free blacks to service as military laborers, drummers, or fifers and excluding slaves altogether. He advocated an approach to recruiting similar to that which was proving successful in Rhode Island. The arming of freed slaves, he told his uncle, Joseph Jones, "would certainly be more consonant with the principles of liberty which ought never be lost sight of in a contest for liberty; and with white officers and a majority of white soldiers, no imaginable danger would be faced from [the freed slaves] themselves. . . ." The future President did not believe that the taste of freedom would inspire the armed ex-slaves to strike the shackles from other blacks, "experience having shown that a freedman immediately loses all attachment and sympathy with his former fellow slaves."[29]

Madison's arguments did not prevail. Virginia refused to recruit slaves. But authorities turned a blind eye as individual masters offered the service of their chattels so that the owner, or perhaps a member of family, could lay claim to patriotism without having to endure the danger or inconvenience of actual military duty. Because the arrangement was extralegal, once the term of enlistment had ended a master might refuse to honor a promise of freedom. This kind of deceit must have been widespread, since Governor Benjamin Harrison felt compelled in 1782 to take action to protect the rights of returning slaves.[30] Neither did the commonwealth adhere to accepted practice and relegate all free blacks to noncombat tasks, acting as musicians or pioneers, as the law had required for more than a century. Ambrose Lewis, for example, served on two Virginia ships of war, then shouldered a musket in a infantry company, seeing action at Camden, South Carolina, as a private soldier and suffering five bayonet wounds.[31]

Maryland, Virginia's northern neighbor, not only agreed in 1780 to accept individual black recruits but also entertained the idea of raising a regiment of 750 slaves. The prospect of an organized body of armed slaves proved too bold for the legislators at Annapolis, and the plan languished.[32] As in Virginia, Maryland blacks aided the revolutionary cause as sailors or pilots on Chesapeake Bay. Stephen Steward, for instance, employed two slaves as "sailor negros" on boats ferrying troops across that body of water. "They are," their master declared, "as fine fellows as ever crost the sea," worth not less than "two hundred pound" apiece.[33]

In 1779, the South became the decisive theater of war, but the defense of that region initially rested in the hands of North Carolina militiamen enlisted for just nine months. South Carolina's governor, John Rutledge, protested that his state could not raise troops in the usual fashion because so many able-bodied white men had to stand guard against a slave insurrection. He was willing, in these circumstances, to resurrect the earlier practice of recruiting trustworthy slaves, thus creating a force used to discipline and at the same time reducing the danger of a slave uprising "by detaching the most vigorous and enterprising from among the negroes."[34]

The Continental Congress seized upon the idea, recommending that South Carolina join with Georgia in raising a total of 3,000 black troops, who would receive freedom in return for military service. The plan was rejected, however, failing in the South Carolina Council by a vote of eight to one. General Nathaniel Green, upon taking command in the South, tried to revive the idea,[35] but it again perished at the hands of what John Laurens of South Carolina called "the triple-headed monster, in which prejudice, avarice, and pusillanimity were united."[36]

During the crisis of 1779, when South Carolina and Georgia refused to recruit slaves in their own defense, France, now an ally of an independent America against Great Britain, dispatched a 3,600-man expedition to break British power in the southern states. About one French soldier in seven was a black, enlisted in Santo Domingo by the expedition's leader, Charles Hector Theodat, Count d'Estaing. Among the Dominicans was Henri Christophe, an officer's orderly, who later would rule an independent Haiti, carved by rebellious slaves from the French colony of Santo Domingo. Unfortunately, the Franco-American forces could not expel the British from entrenchments before Savannah, Georgia, and in October, faced by the prospect of winter storms, d'Estaing had to withdraw after losing some 600 killed or wounded in a gallant but unsuccessful attack.

The presence of so many blacks serving as soldiers under the flag of France created no unrest among the slave populace of Georgia, thanks to precautions taken by the French commander. Count d'Estaing led a disciplined force and cooperated with the American officers in preventing contact between his troops and local slaves. Since the French were allies, they did not seek—as the enemy general, Lord Dunmore, had done in Virginia—to recruit slaves or otherwise undermine authority. The French general thus prevented the slaves from contrasting his treatment of the blacks in his army with that afforded by the Americans, who officially refused to grant freedom in return for military service (although this practice became common in some areas) and instead forced slaves to work on fortifications.[37]

Meanwhile, Spain had joined France in waging war against Great Britain. From Louisiana, which the Spanish had received from France as the price of an earlier alliance, Bernardo de Galvez led an expedition against nearby British outposts. About 80 free black militiamen from New Orleans served in this 700-man force, which set out to clear the enemy from the banks of the lower Mississippi River. Gathering additional recruits, including Indians and more blacks, de Galvez accomplished his purpose, capturing Baton Rouge at about the time that d'Estaing was failing to seize Savannah. Accepting slaves as well as free blacks to augment his ranks still further, the Spanish commander advanced into West Florida, acquired by the British after the French and Indian War, taking Fort Charlotte at Mobile and Fort George at Pensacola.[38]

Excluding those who fought under the command of de Galvez or d'Estaing, roughly 5,000 blacks served the American cause during the Revolution, with perhaps 1,000 under arms or on shipboard at any given time. The total represented about 2.5 percent of the estimated 200,000 men who at one time or other fought the British. Although most of the blacks entering the service were slaves who entertained the hope of better treatment or freedom, the slave populace, perhaps 17 percent of a national aggregate of 2.5 million persons, remained largely untapped by recruiters.[39]

A majority of the slaves who expected to escape bondage by taking part in the conflict did not cast their lot with the American forces. In fact, the hundreds who fled slavery to join Lord Dunmore's Ethiopian Regiment accounted for a mere fraction of those who gambled their lives on promises made by the officers of King George III. Along with whites loyal to the monarch, as many as 20,000 fugitive slaves left the newly independent United States when hostilities ended, settling in Canada, on British islands in the Caribbean (where an unfortunate few were sold back into slavery), or in Africa.[40]

By the time the American Revolution ended, military service had become a means by which a slave might earn his freedom or a free black enhance his standing in the community, discharge what he perceived as a duty owed his country, or simply satisfy a craving for adventure. Also, the black soldier or sailor, originally the anonymous possession of some white planter, merchant, or professional man, was gradually emerging as an individual. The 5,000 blacks in the ranks or on shipboard acquired an identity; they became men whose names and deeds were worth preserving both to acknowledge their exploits and to inspire future generations.

The Revolutionary War thus lent credence to the belief, which later would become almost an article of faith among blacks, that military service in wartime represented a path toward freedom and greater postwar opportunity. Unfortunately, the conflict also set the pattern, followed for more than a century and a half, by which the American government used blacks in time of crisis and ignored them afterward. Only a handful of blacks succeeded in taking advantage of the mechanism the war provided for betterment. Despite the contributions of 5,000 blacks in the cause of liberty, their freedom was assured only in the handful of states that formally abolished slavery during the war or immediately afterward.

2

Service in Time of Slavery

SERVICE IN THE CAUSE of the American Revolution had earned for some blacks freedom, individual renown, and perhaps a measure of economic security. With rare exceptions, these success stories unfolded in the North, but even there many blacks found themselves victims of prejudice. Regardless of freedom or recent military service on the part of blacks, a majority of whites continued to view them with contempt and fear, considering them lazy but violent, semicivilized if human at all, and given to lust and lying. Much of this picture stemmed from the unique conditions of the peculiar institution—slavery. What slave, after all, would exert himself voluntarily, display initiative, or tell a truth unpleasant to the hearer when the alternatives brought the same reward? The protective mechanisms developed during slavery thus came to be considered the innate characteristics of the entire race.

Convinced of their supremacy, the white citizens of the emergent United States sought to exclude blacks, free and slave, from normal society. This attitude influenced the composition of the new nation's armed forces. At first, Congress believed that a militia, locally recruited and trained, could defend the country against a threat posed mainly by Indian tribes living in the wilderness. The law passed in 1792 that authorized the creation of this force provided for the enrollment of white men between the ages of eighteen and forty-five.[1]

With three exceptions, the states interpreted the law of 1792 as a ban on enrolling blacks. Only North Carolina permitted free blacks to bear arms in the ranks of its militia; South Carolina and Georgia allowed them to serve as musicians or laborers. Gradually the policy of exclusion became complete, as local militia companies evolved into social clubs, not unlike the latter-day volunteer fire departments. Along with white cameraderie, fear contributed to this exclusion of blacks, for the black slaves of Haiti, led by men like Henri Christophe, d'Estaing's wartime orderly, had rebelled against their masters, slaughtering those whites who did not flee Haiti and creating a black republic. If one slave populace could rise up under leaders of its own race, might not another do the same? Some white Americans became concerned that a militia that admitted blacks might bring forth a Christophe capable of rallying the slaves of the South.[2]

The armed forces of the United States followed the policy adopted by the state militias. The Navy, for instance, banned "Negroes or Mulatoes," along with "Persons whose Characters are suspicious,"[3] and Colonel William Ward Burrows, Commandant of the Marine Corps, issued similar instructions, although he permitted the use of black fifers and drummers to attract crowds for recruiters.[4]

What ensued was a struggle between ideal and reality. The artist John Trumbull, described as the painter of the Revolution, might celebrate the real heroism of blacks during that war by including a black armed with a rifle, clearly Peter Salem, in a depiction of the Battle of Bunker Hill done some seven years after the firing died away. His enshrinement of Salem could not, however, ensure that other blacks would have the chance to live up to Trumbull's vision in future wars. The armed forces, whether national or state, were striving toward a vision of their own, a military establishment exclusively white. Would circumstances compel the Army and Navy to accept other Peter Salems, or would racism prevail?

Racial exclusiveness became the order of the day in the Army and the Marine Corps. Enlisting only whites caused no shortage of manpower, since both organizations were small. The Marine Corps initially recruited ship's detachments of about twenty-five men as new frigates joined the fleet and by 1800 numbered no more than a thousand men serving afloat or at barracks ashore. The post-Revolutionary Regular Army at first totaled a few hundred soldiers, expanding beyond 3,000 only to meet the threat of Indian warfare. Ironically, the Army that wanted no more Peter Salems came to be administered by a War Department that included one free black,

Caesar Lloyd Cummings, who served as clerk, messenger, door-keeper, and janitor for the six-man office.[5]

Although the Army and the Marine Corps, for the time being at least, managed to retain their all-white composition, the Navy had to reconsider its policy almost at once. Hard upon the announcement that blacks were not welcome, Navy recruiters began accepting them for service on shipboard. So unattractive was the combination of harsh discipline, dangerous work aloft, long cruises, wormy biscuit, and bad beef that the Navy had to accept almost anyone willing to serve, black or white. Some blacks went to sea during the undeclared naval war with France, 1798–1800, and almost a decade afterward others were serving on the *Chesapeake*, when HMS *Leopard* forced her to strike her colors and removed several sailors, including three blacks, claiming they were British subjects.[6]

This incident typified the British high-handedness at sea that, combined with an American desire to seize Canada, triggered a second war with Great Britain. Hostilities began in 1812, with blacks serving in American warships and privateers, and these men continued to be valuable crew members throughout the conflict. Within a year of the outbreak of fighting, Congress acknowledged a practice of several years' standing, declaring that once the war had ended, native-born blacks would be eligible to enlist (or reenlist) in the Navy of the United States or serve on board privateers.[7]

When the privateer *Governor Tompkins* ran afoul of a British frigate, from which the American ship managed to escape, two black seamen were mortally wounded. One of them, John Johnson, had his leg torn away but continued encouraging his shipmates until he died. The other, John Davis, asked to be thrown overboard since "he was only in the way of others." Wrote Nathaniel Shaler, who commanded the American schooner, "While America has such tars, she has little to fear from the Tyrants of the ocean."[8]

On the Great Lakes, Oliver Hazard Perry welcomed blacks—in fact, any able-bodied person—who could help man the fleet he was building. That armada defeated the British at Put-in Bay on Lake Erie, and the performance of his black sailors pleased the commodore.[9] Perhaps because conditions aboard ship, even on the Great Lakes, were so arduous, the royal Navy also found it inexpedient to reject potential recruits on the grounds of race.

Admiral John Borlase Warren, in charge of His Majesty's naval forces in North American waters, sent an expedition into Chesapeake Bay in 1813 and discovered to his surprise that slaves throughout the region were eager to flee from captivity for the chance to gain their freedom in the service of the king. The mere sight of a British warship riding at anchor was a signal for slaves to escape. If the admiral was pleased at this unexpected harvest of recruits—actually the same sort of response that had greeted Lord Dunmore a generation earlier—slaveowners on the eastern and western shores of the bay grew furious with their disloyal property. Only the whites, British and American, had forgotten Dunmore; he apparently lived in the legends preserved by the slaves, and his memory inspired escape. The Americans laid ambushes to prevent the exodus, disguising themselves either as British seamen, in order to trap escapees, or as slaves so they could lure Warren's sailors within musket range.

From the outset the fugitive slaves asked for weapons, but Warren withheld arms, though he did use the men as guides for raids on plantations in the region. In contrast, Vice Admiral Sir Alexander Cochrane, who took command of the North American station in the spring of 1814, followed Lord Dunmore's example and promptly offered escaped slaves a choice of bearing arms or emigrating as free men to Canada or one of Britain's West Indian colonies. Cochrane's strategy not only brought him recruits but also weakened the foundation of the plantation economy on the shores of Chesapeake Bay. To prevent the loss of agricultural workers, the states of Virginia and Maryland shifted militia units that should have been fighting the admiral's raiding parties to the task of preventing mass escapes.

The British commander in the Chesapeake region, Rear Admiral George Cockburn, established a processing center and training depot on Tangier Island, and soon the former slaves were ready for combat. Under the leadership of Acting Ensign William Hammond, a sergeant in the Royal Marines, some 200 escapees learned marksmanship and close-order drill. This contingent of black marines saw its first action in May 1814, helping storm an American coast defense battery at Pungoteague, Virginia, at the cost of one killed and four wounded.[10]

The British black marines fought at Bladensburg, Maryland, on the outskirts of the federal city of Washington, where the invaders defeated an American force composed largely of militia. One of the few regular units among the defenders was a 500-man battalion of sailors and U.S. Marines commanded by Commodore Joshua Barney. Among the sailors were a few blacks, including Charles Ball, a slave who declared himself emancipated and accompanied Barney's men as a cook. The American seamen and marines made a fight of it, but the ill-trained militia broke, forcing the regulars to retreat.[11]

Cockburn's black marines next joined in the advance into Washington, where the civilian inhabitants apparently were as frightened of a slave insurrection as they were of the invaders. After the occupation of the federal city and the burning of the Capitol and the President's House, the black contingent took part in the unsuccessful attack upon Baltimore that inspired Francis Scott Key to write "The Star Spangled Banner." These 200 or so colonial marines, as they were called, fought so well that their unit became a permanent part of Britain's North American forces, serving in the same battalion with a slightly larger white contingent.

Although the dread slave uprising failed to materialize during the War of 1812, as many as 5,000 slaves fled plantations located along Chesapeake Bay to find refuge with the British. (Ironically, this figure equalled the approximate number of blacks, slave and free, who had fought in American ranks during the recent Revolution.) Still others were turned back by their supposed benefactors, who did not want to be burdened with noncombatants during expeditions inland. Despite the large number of escapees, the total represented at most 15 percent of the total slave populace, a result in part of the strict security measures enforced by Maryland and Virginia authorities, who patrolled roads and landings, kept watch over slave quarters, and inflicted cruel punishment on slaves recaptured while trying to flee to join the British.[12]

The success enjoyed by Admirals Warren and Cochrane in recruiting slaves and of Admiral Cockburn in organizing and training them did not inspire the Americans to accept blacks as soldiers. New York did adopt legislation authorizing as many as 2,000 blacks to enlist—free men of their own volition and slaves with the consent of their masters—but the policy went into effect in the fall of 1814, too late to permit recruiting to begin before the fighting had ended in the Northeast.[13] Indeed, even as the New York lawmakers were acting, Cochrane had decided to attack New Orleans in what promised to be the decisive battle of the war.

During Spanish rule, black militiamen had contributed to the security of New Orleans, taking the field under Bernardo de Galvez to help drive the British from the banks of the lower Mississippi and the shores of Mobile Bay. Later, members of the New Orleans militia, guided by a slave named Chacala, waded far into the Louisiana swamps to capture some fifty runaway slaves who were terrorizing remote plantations. The black troops had thus established themselves as effective and dependable soldiers by the time that Spain, in 1801, agreed to cede Louisiana back to France, and the authorities directed to restore French sovereignty had orders to retain the services of the militia units, both black and white, that the Spanish had organized. In 1803, however, France sold Louisiana to the United

States, so that the black militiamen now had to convince an American governor, William C. C. Claiborne, of their loyalty and usefulness.[14]

Scarcely had Claiborne taken office when Louisiana's "free people of color" who had been "employed in the military service of the late Government" asked to be "in like manner honored by the American Government, to which every principle of interest as well as affection" bound them, and which they promised to serve "with fidelity and Zeal."[15] The new governor accepted the offer, only to run afoul of white opinion aroused by the slave uprising against French authority in the Caribbean. The white citizens of New Orleans branded the local black militia as "wretches who have sucked the blood of the ill-fated inhabitants of Santo Domingo," from which the Haitian republic had been formed.[16] Fear caused by the slave revolution and concern that the free black militiamen of New Orleans, despite their protestations to the contrary, owed allegiance to Spain prompted the territorial government to eliminate black units from the militia list. Governor Claiborne tried to resurrect the organizations, but his argument that it was folly to ignore potentially useful troops failed to sway a legislative council that reflected American racial attitudes rather than those of France or Spain.[17]

Prejudices suddenly became expendable, however, when war broke out with Britain in 1812, and the council promptly authorized the recruiting of free blacks who had paid taxes and for the previous two years had owned property worth $300. The law specified that all militia officers would be white, but within six months of its adoption Governor Claiborne signed a commission that appointed Isidore Honoré, a "free man of color," to the grade of second lieutenant. Like their white counterparts, Honoré and his fellow black militiamen mustered once a month for drill, would serve no more than ninety days' active duty in time of emergency, and would not have to venture beyond the territorial boundaries.[18]

Although the militia could not cross these borders to go to war, the enemy could bring the conflict to New Orleans. In 1814 an invasion armada bound for the city was massing in Jamaica even as Andrew Jackson, the commanding general of American forces along the Gulf coast, prepared to meet the impending attack. As part of his preparations, the general issued a call for additional volunteers, urging all "free colored inhabitants of Louisiana . . . to rally 'round the Standard of the Eagle, to defend all which is dear in existence." Every free black who answered his call, Jackson promised, would receive the same pay, rations, and bounty as white volunteers. To prevent friction from arising between whites and blacks, the general proposed organizing the free Negroes into "a distinct independent battalion or regiment." Besides promoting harmony, the creation of separate units would ensure that the black volunteers retained a unit identity so that in "pursuing the paths of glory" they would receive the undiluted "applause and gratitude" of their fellow countrymen.[19]

Overlooked in the response to Jackson's call to the colors were the existing black militiamen. Faced with the certainty of invasion, Louisiana authorities called out the companies they already had organized. Honore and his fellow soldiers reported for duty on December 12, 1814, four days before the swearing in of the first of the new battalions of black volunteers.

The new battalion consisted of 350 free men of color, who marched off accompanied by their own twelve-piece band. The senior black officer of the unit was Vincent Populus, a militia veteran, who held the rank of major. Within a week, another black major, Joseph Savory, received his appointment from General Jackson and set about raising a second battalion, about 250 strong, also from among the free Negroes of Louisiana. Command of both units rested for the time being in the hands of white officers, Pierre Lacoste leading the first battalion and Louis Daquin the second.

By the time the second battalion went into action a few days before Christmas, Savory had assumed command. His black troops held their ground, helping check a preliminary thrust toward the city. Later, on January 8, 1815, both battalions fought from carefully prepared positions and helped cut down the British regulars during the climactic battle before New Orleans. The Americans won a brilliant but unnecessary victory, unaware that a peace treaty had been signed two weeks earlier.[20]

General Jackson paid tribute to the blacks who had rallied to the defense of New Orleans. "The two corps of colored volunteers have not disappointed the hopes that were formed of their courage and perseverance in the performance of their duty," he declared, singling out Joseph Savory for special mention.[21] Heroism was not enough, however, to save the black militia. White self-confidence reasserted itself, as did the racism that pervaded American life. After all, true Americans need not follow the example of the Spanish or French, themselves lesser peoples, and rely on blacks for their protection. In 1834, a revision of the militia law sounded the death knell of the black militia, which would not be resurrected until the coming of the Civil War.[22]

Nor did the U.S. Army recognize the contribution of the black volunteers to the victory at New Orleans, for whites alone were eligible to serve in the Army's ranks. Once again the government had turned to blacks in time of peril, accepted their aid, and then spurned them. Although barred from enlisting and shouldering a musket, a few blacks, all of them slaves, did serve as laborers at military installations in the South. Since these men did work normally performed by slaves, they were not competing with free labor, and no outcry arose from white workers in the area.[23]

White America remained blind to the military contributions of blacks. William Cooper Nell, a black historian, tried in 1855 to dispel the prevailing ignorance. Unfortunately, his published account of the participation by members of his race in the American Revolution and the War of 1812 could not penetrate the wall of prejudice and change the attitudes of the white majority.[24]

In contrast, the Navy continued to recruit free blacks under the policy affirmed during the War of 1812, for service afloat rarely attracted men able to earn a living in some other way. The forecastle became the haven of many a criminal, drunk, or sexual deviate who could find no refuge ashore. No wonder that any steady, sober individual was welcome, regardless of race. Although it accepted free blacks for service alongside white sailors, the Navy in 1816 barred slaves from shipboard and excluded them from employment at navy yards. The prohibition against slave labor ashore reassured the shipwrights, sailmakers, and other skilled workers who feared competition from unsalaried labor. Afloat, the slave seemed a potential source of trouble—perhaps he would establish a common bond with free blacks in the crew and, while not actually fomenting mutiny, demean the status of every free man in the Navy.[25]

Naval officers did not always heed these restrictions, as William McNally, a white former sailor, testified. He charged that officers on board the USS *Java* had signed on their slaves as crew members and pocketed the pay. This same kind of corruption, he continued, was also taking place at navy yards, where slaves were replacing free workmen.[26]

Even though the number of slaves serving as crewmen could not have been great, black sailors had become so numerous on American warships that intelligent Europeans might well believe, as did three travelers overheard by an American touring the Continent, that all Americans were black and that the naval officers, all of them white, were Englishmen specially recruited by the Navy.[27] There were those, of course, who objected to the racial composition of the various naval squadrons. Acting Secretary of the Navy Isaac Chauncey, who had commanded black sailors in the War of 1812, took note in 1839 of "complaints of the number of blacks and other colored persons entered at some of the recruiting stations and the consequent under-proportion of white persons transferred to ships or naval stations." He imposed a quota on the recruitment of blacks, declaring that in the future the number accepted would not exceed 5 percent of the "whole number of white persons" enlisted "weekly or monthly."[28]

For the representatives of an increasingly militant slaveowning South, the quota was not acceptable. Senator John C. Calhoun of South Carolina, a state which threatened to jail any black sailor who dared step ashore there, tried in 1842 to bar from the naval service all blacks except cooks or personal servants.[29] Although the Senate ignored the heroism of black seamen in previous wars and approved Calhoun's proposal, the House of Representatives allowed the matter to perish, apparently satisfied by assurances from Secretary of the Navy Abel P. Upshur that blacks made up "not more than one-twentieth part of the crew of any vessel."[30]

The Navy's acceptance of blacks testified not so much to a realization of their past contributions in time of war as to the difficulty of recruiting white Americans for service afloat. Since the small Regular Army had less trouble filling its ranks, the War Department remained indifferent to blacks. With slavery emerging as an issue capable of plunging the nation into civil war, the Army's policy of exclusion seemed a minor issue at most. Slavery itself was the critical problem, defended by southern politicians and opposed by abolitionists.

Instead of worrying about blacks in the military or naval service, the abolitionists wanted nothing less than the destruction of slavery, the outlawing of this cruel and immoral institution. Many, but by no means all, of the foes of slavery also advocated the admission of freed blacks into American society with all the rights of citizenship. Blacks were prominent in the abolitionist movement. Escaped slaves swelled the sound of protest; men like Frederick Douglass recounted the treatment they had received while in bondage. Harriet Tubman, herself a refugee from servitude, helped others flee over the so-called Underground Railroad. Contact with escaped slaves who had found refuge among the abolitionists at Cincinnati, Ohio, provided the raw information that Harriet Beecher Stowe refined into *Uncle Tom's Cabin*, the antislavery novel that infuriated southern leaders.

The southern fear of abolitionists reflected an awareness that the slave populace might welcome weapons and encouragement from militant whites like Thomas Wentworth Higginson or from blacks like Douglass, who had come to believe that slavery could end only in violence, and Henry Highland Garnet of New York, who publicly urged the slaves to stand and fight. Slave insurrections were not all that uncommon, even though the rebels had to fight with makeshift or captured weapons. A thousand slaves had marched on

Richmond, Virginia, in 1800, and ten years later five hundred advanced upon New Orleans, although in both instances state authorities easily prevailed. In 1822, a slave betrayed a potentially dangerous uprising planned by Denmark Vesey, a free black living in Charleston. The most shocking of all for the plantation aristocracy was the rebellion led by Nat Turner of Southampton County, Virginia. In August 1831, he gathered about seventy followers and killed some sixty whites, but spared a poor white family that owned no slaves. Again, the authorities suppressed the uprising, and as always vengeance was swift and brutal. In this instance, Turner and his fellow rebels were executed, and a number of sympathizers were either slaughtered or sent to distant plantations. From all this the planters knew that their slaves were neither content nor incapable of organized violence; slavery provided tinder for the abolitionists to ignite.[31]

3

Civil War and Emancipation

OPPOSITION TO SLAVERY helped drive the South to the brink of rebellion. A fanatical farmer, John Brown, sought to destroy slavery in the territory of Kansas, where guerrilla warfare raged between antislavery elements from the North and East and those who were determined to extend slavery westward from Missouri. Blooded in the Kansas fighting, he returned to the East and prepared to strike another blow for abolition. In October 1859, Brown's militancy culminated in a raid, financed by abolitionists from the Northeast, against the federal arsenal at Harper's Ferry, Virginia, in a vain effort to capture weapons and ignite an uprising of the slaves. Brown and his men freed only a mere handful of slaves, and those temporarily, and the first person killed in the raid was not a slaveholder but a free black, Hayward Shepherd, the baggage master at the railroad station. Captured when marines from the city of Washington stormed the firehouse where his band had taken refuge—Frederick Douglass had warned that the low-lying arsenal was a natural trap—Brown was hanged for treason against the Commonwealth of Virginia.

Under pressure from abolitionists and weary of compromise, as manifested by the past practice of balancing new free states with the admission of slave states, the leaders of the South could foresee a steady expansion of antislavery power as territories unsuited to slave-based agriculture entered the Union as states with votes in the Congress. In these circumstances, the states of the plantation South exercised what they considered their legal right to withdraw from the Union. Confident of the world's need for their cotton and the military prowess of their white citizens, they formed a confederation and in the spring of 1861 attacked the federal installations on their territory, beginning with Fort Sumter in Charleston harbor.[1]

The war that resulted at first gave every indication of determining the future of America's blacks without involving them as combatants. Except at New Orleans, where the tradition of free blacks serving as militiamen again surfaced, the enlistment of black soldiers, free or slave, seemed unthinkable. The South, which styled itself the Confederate States of America, feared arming the slaves, and the United States was reluctant to recruit blacks for reasons of statecraft.

According to the plans of the administration of President Abraham Lincoln, the force that would punish seccession and restore the Union would consist of volunteers, militiamen, and members of the small Regular Army. The states were to recruit and organize the volunteer regiments according to quotas established by Congress; the units would then be mustered into federal service for training and combat. Already organized and drilled locally, the state militia units stood ready to serve in Union ranks for ninety days or less; in brief, they remained a source of manpower for a brief emergency, suitable only for local defense in the event of a long war. A good many professional officers of the Army, Navy, and Marine Corps cast their lot with the Confederacy. Therefore, as the Union forces expanded, an increasing number of volunteer or even militia officers joined the remaining regulars as commanders of major units.

At the outset, the North leaped to arms, and the first wave of 75,000 militiamen and perhaps twice that number of volunteers seemed certain to crush the rebellion in a matter of months, probably after a single decisive battle. Confident of a quick victory, the federal government saw no need to take advantage of the eagerness of northern blacks to destroy slavery, avenging the cruelty that some of them had suffered and freeing their brothers still in bondage. Not only did the recruiting of blacks seem unnecessary, but their presence in the northern armies might prod additional states into the Confederacy.

President Lincoln hoped to persuade the border states—Delaware, Maryland, Kentucky, and Missouri—to remain in the Union. In this region, where pro-Union sentiment was strong, slavery was accepted, though practiced on a lesser scale than in the new Confederacy, which stretched in a vast arc from Virginia through Texas. To avoid alienating the border governments and to gain time for enacting some form of compensated emancipation, the President was content that the war to preserve the Union continue to be, for the time being at least, a white man's struggle. Saving the Union took precedence over other considerations, and Lincoln would do nothing that might drive the border states into the Confederacy. As a result, free blacks seeking to enlist in the armed forces of the United States encountered outright rejection, and the abolition of slavery was ignored as a war aim. Typical of the government's attitude during the early months of the war was Brigadier General Benjamin F. Butler's offer of federal troops to help the governor of Maryland suppress a reported (though nonexistent) slave rebellion.[2]

The question of slavery could not be ignored, however, especially when ardent abolitionists like Major General John C. Frémont took command of operations against those who were trying to dissolve the Union. In the sensitive border state of Missouri, Frémont, who five years earlier had carried the banner of the antislavery Free Soil Party in an unsuccessful campaign for the Presidency, began freeing slaves whose masters were active secessionists. Manumission was but one aspect of Frémont's plan to suppress secession in Missouri. There efforts to dissolve the Union triggered an armed conflict that took the form of irregular warfare, with secessionists sniping at Unionists and attacking from ambush as well as fighting the occasional pitched battle. The Union general imposed martial law and proposed to execute captured guerrillas and confiscate all property belonging to rebels, not just their slaves—in short to enforce drumhead justice throughout the state. Frémont's high-handedness—he even sent his wife to Washington to lecture the President on matters of policy—made it easy for Lincoln to disavow the entire program, thus dodging the emancipation issue and avoiding the creation of anti-Union sentiment along the border between North and South.[3]

The freeing of slaves in Missouri, within the context of martial law, could have fueled rebel sentiment in Kentucky, as Lincoln had feared, but to abolitionists the arming of slaves set free in South Carolina seemed a safe enough course. When Brigadier General Thomas W. Sherman was organizing an expedition to capture Port Royal in the heartland of secession, Secretary of War Simon Cameron, a foe of slavery, instructed the officer to arm the able-bodied slaves freed by the invaders and to promise that no liberated slave would be returned to his master. The President, however, decided that public opinion in the North would not yet accept the arming of former slaves. As a result, when Tim Sherman landed on the South Carolina coast in October 1861, he issued a proclamation pledging not to interfere with "social and local institutions," a euphemism for slavery.[4]

Although Lincoln could delay acknowledging that abolition was becoming a war aim, postponing official recognition until the idea became acceptable throughout the North, he could not prevent some commanders from taking advantage of the manpower pool created by refugee slaves. In Virginia, General Ben Butler had begun tapping this resource in May 1861, while commanding officer at Fortress Monroe. The use of these "contrabands of war," as Butler classified the former slaves, became accepted policy within the Union Army's Department of Virginia, and the refugees received pay, clothing, and rations for working as laborers or as servants to officers.[5]

In South Carolina, moreover, Tim Sherman was losing any respect he might have had for local mores, having discovered that "hordes of totally uneducated and improvident blacks have been abandoned by their constitutional guardians." The expeditionary force had to become a welfare agency, administering agricultural and educational programs. Sherman's troops issued clothing to the former slaves, taught them "the rudiments of civilization and Christianity," and employed them as paid laborers on the abandoned plantations.[6]

Commanders whose troops were operating along the border between North and South continued to be circumspect in their dealings with slaves and masters. In Tennessee, for example, Brigadier General Ulysses S. Grant emphasized the importance of turning back fugitives fleeing owners who supported the Union cause. If the slaveholder was a secessionist, however, the refugees could go to work on construction projects, such as the strengthening of Fort Donelson, which Grant's troops had just captured.[7]

The Union Navy, meanwhile, was also encountering refugees from slavery, but these individuals or families arrived a few at a time, seeking sanctuary on ships of the blockading squadron, which sought to seal off Confederate ports from Virginia to Texas. In July 1861, for instance, three boatloads of escaped slaves were picked up by Union warships at the mouth of Virginia's Rappahannock River.[8] In May of the following year, another such group—nine men, five women, and three children—made its way to the USS *Onward*, a unit of the blockading squadron off Charleston. The slave who engineered their escape, Robert Smalls, led his followers on board the steamer *Planter*, fired the boiler, took the helm, and when intercepted by the *Onward*, added his ship, fitted with two guns and carrying four others as cargo, to the Union Navy. Since Smalls and the other adults who helped sail the steamer had, in effect, brought in a prize, Congress passed a private bill enabling them to share one-half the value of the *Planter* and her cargo, dividing $4,584 among them.[9]

A 300-ton sidewheel steamer, the *Planter* was a welcome addition to the Union Navy, and the former Confederate ship served in a series of expeditions along the southern Atlantic coast. Smalls acted for a time as her pilot before moving on to take the wheel of other Union vessels. After her naval career had ended, *Planter* finished out the war as a transport for the Army quartermaster department at Hilton Head, South Carolina.[10]

The Navy found contrabands easy to assimilate. The service had a tradition of enlisting free blacks—forced upon it by 1800 because the perils and discomfort of service at sea discouraged enlistments—and therefore would not exclude potential seamen solely on the basis of race. Racial policies in the Atlantic Blockading Squadron had no impact on the Union loyalist in Kentucky or Missouri who happened to own slaves. As a result, at about the time that Simon Cameron was trying unsuccessfully to arm any slaves who might be freed by Tim Sherman in South Carolina, Secretary of the Navy Gideon Welles encountered no obstacles in granting the commander of the blockading squadron authority to enlist contrabands, granting them full rations but paying them less than the normal wage.[11]

Throughout the war, blacks served in the Union Navy, some of them enlisted under the racial quota established more than two decades earlier, others signed on according to the policy Secretary Welles had adopted in the summer of 1861. Their service, moreover, was not restricted to ships of the blockading squadron, for the rapidly expanding fleet of river gunboats and mortar boats created a sudden demand for seamen. The task of manning these river craft proved especially difficult because of a combination of sickness, which was prevalent along the Mississippi in the summer, demanding physical labor, and the absence of a bonus to attract Navy enlistees. As early as October 1862 Acting Rear Admiral David Dixon Porter began substituting former slaves for white sailors as firemen and coal heavers on the river steamers, "reducing the expenses in that way," since the blacks received lower pay.[12]

Before a year had passed, Porter was recruiting blacks in greater numbers, having decided that "white men cannot stand the southern sun, an exposure to which inevitably brings on the disease of this climate, remittent fever." Although confident that "in many cases of emergency the blacks will make efficient men," the admiral complained that "they are not naturally clean in their persons" and insisted that they be "kept distinct from the rest of the crew." His was an unusual attitude at a time when blacks and whites shared the same mess and hung their hammocks side by side on board seagoing warships.[13]

The number of blacks who served in the Union Navy remains a matter of conjecture. The harried wartime expansion and the loss or sketchiness of ships' muster rolls have forced the Navy to extrapolate from existing records, which indicate that one sailor in four was a black. Assuming that this ratio prevailed at sea and on the Mississippi, as many as 30,000 of the roughly 120,000 wartime enlistees were black volunteers.[14]

Even as the Navy was recruiting perhaps five times the peacetime quota of blacks, President Lincoln came under increasing pressure to let down the racial barrier to service in the Army. Frederick Douglass, the escaped slave who had become a leading abolitionist, asked why his fellow blacks, though good enough to serve under George Washington, could not bear arms in George Brinton McClellan's Army of the Potomac. Radical politicians, who considered freeing the slaves the principal objective of the war, sought to convert the President to their way of thinking. One of them, Governor John Andrew of Massachusetts, predicted a long war in which Union generals would no longer care whether their men's ancestors hailed "from the banks of the Thames or the banks of the Senegal."[15]

The first general to ignore race and attempt to arm black men was David C. Hunter, who tried in the spring of 1862 to form a regiment of contrabands. Impatient for results, he thought nothing of rounding up the able-bodied and declaring them soldiers, with scant regard for their wishes or family responsibilities. His recruiting methods smacked of the press gang, alienating the northern newspapers, and he received no support from Edwin M. Stanton, now Secretary of War, replacing Simon Cameron. Despite Stanton's coolness and the opposition of the newspapers, Hunter managed to maintain one company of ex-slaves, who performed garrison duty at St. Simon's Island off the Georgia coast. The idea of issuing weapons to blacks remained alive, and the Lincoln administration could ignore it no longer. A radical Congress in July 1862 authorized the President to arm blacks, and within two months Mr. Lincoln allowed Brigadier General Rufus Saxton to carry on through normal recruiting methods the work that Hunter had begun.[16]

In the meantime, James H. Lane, a free soil leader and amateur soldier who had been waging guerrilla warfare in Kansas against William Quantrill's Confederate raiders, took advantage of the federal government's changing attitude toward black recruits and commissioned J. M. Williams and H. C. Seamans to sign up those blacks "evincing by their actions a willing readiness to link their fate and share the perils with their white brethren in the war of the great rebellion." Some 500 volunteers came forward, and about half this number underwent sketchy training and marched off into the Rebel-controlled portion of Missouri. At Island Mound, near the town of Butler, an estimated 500 Confederates attacked the leading elements of the black force on October 28, 1862, only to be driven from the field when Captain Williams arrived with reinforcements.[17]

Two months before elements of what became the 1st Kansas Colored Infantry underwent their baptism of fire at Island Mound, General Saxton had imparted new momentum to the project launched by Hunter and at last approved by Secretary Stanton. In spite of competition from the Navy and lingering resentment at Hunter's recruiting tactics, Saxton signed up the men he needed, entrusting them to a recently arrived volunteer officer. The newcomer,

Thomas Wentworth Higginson, an abolitionist clergyman from New England, turned out to be a gifted military leader and a skilled propagandist on behalf of the black solider.

Higginson's infantry regiment, the 1st South Carolina, went into combat early in November, a few weeks after the skirmish in Missouri, taking part in a series of raids along the Atlantic coast in Georgia and Florida.[18] Operations of this sort continued beyond the first of the year, as a handful of ships—among them the *Planter*, which Robert Smalls and his group had presented to the Union Navy—enabled Higginson's troops to use rivers emptying into the Atlantic as avenues of access to objectives in the interior. The armed steamer *John Adams*, on one such incursion, carried a 250-man detachment some 40 miles up the St. Mary's River in Florida, "regarded by the naval commanders as the most dangerous in the department." The expedition returned with some 40,000 bricks, needed for Rebel construction projects and worth a thousand dollars. After advancing up the St. Mary's, the *Planter*, no longer piloted by Robert Smalls, ventured a short distance onto the Crooked River, landing troops to destroy a salt works. In the course of these river operations, which lasted through January 1863, Higginson's black soldiers collided with a detachment of Confederate cavalry while on a night march. Although the horsemen managed to surround the Union force, the former slaves succeeded in breaking out of the encirclement and driving off the enemy.[19]

After Generals Hunter, Saxton, and Lane were organizing these first black units, President Lincoln decided to make the abolition of slavery a formal war aim, taking advantage of changes in the political climate, public sentiment, and the military balance. More radical than the Chief Executive, Congress led the way, approving both the confiscation of slaves owned by Rebels in Union-conquered territory and the arming of blacks. Furthermore, public opinion tended to support the congressional attitudes. Still wary of the immigration of slaves freed in the South and the resulting competition for jobs, citizens of the North were nevertheless veering toward acceptance of emancipation. Even though Delaware, by a narrow margin, had rejected an administration proposal for compensated emancipation and Missouri shelved the same plan, abolitionism was gaining strength, especially in the western counties of Maryland and Virginia.

These considerations in themselves might not have been enough had General Robert E. Lee not invaded the North during the late summer of 1862. A copy of his battle plan, wrapped around three cigars and intended for another Confederate commander, fell into the hands of Union soldiers. Alerted by this intelligence, General Mc-

Clellan's Army of the Potomac turned back Lee's invasion force at Antietam Creek, Maryland. President Lincoln interpreted this bloody victory as a military affirmation of the growing opposition to slavery and issued the Emancipation Proclamation. Invoking his wartime powers, the Chief Executive decreed that slaves held by persons living in areas still in rebellion on January 1, 1863, would be free. This policy guaranteed the eventual abolition of slavery as the Union forces advanced through the South and at the same time encouraged slaves to accelerate the coming of freedom by fleeing their masters and thus draining the labor pool of the Confederacy.[20]

Once President Lincoln had issued this proclamation, the recruiting of black troops underwent revitalization, especially in Louisiana. Some five months earlier, in April 1862, when Admiral David Glasgow Farragut forced his way past the batteries guarding New Orleans, the federal troops that occupied the city discovered black militiamen enrolled for its defense. Governor Thomas O. Moore, after Louisiana seceded from the Union, had organized a militia unit from among the free blacks of New Orleans, the Native Guard. One of the men who answered the call was Jordan Noble, a drummer boy during the 1815 fighting, who now raised a company to serve in the latest emergency. When ordered to abandon the city to Union forces and make a stand elsewhere, the black militiamen refused, for they considered themselves defenders of the city rather than the state. General Ben Butler, in command of the occupying army, interpreted this action as an expression of loyalty to the Union, though the blacks probably felt more loyal to the city than to Louisiana or the United States, and found a place for them in Union ranks. Indeed, he was so impressed with their skill and discipline that he recruited several other companies of free blacks. The Native Guards and these new companies donned the Union blue and by autumn were in action against General Richard Taylor's Confederates in western Louisiana.[21]

Butler limited his recruiting to the more stable elements of the city's black populace—artisans, property owners, mechanics, and military veterans; he ignored the large number of escaped or freed slaves who were finding a haven behind Union lines. The task of turning these refugees into soldiers fell to Brigadier General Daniel Ullmann, directed by the President to raise a regiment from among the contrabands of Louisiana. Before heading south to carry out these instructions, Ullmann interviewed prospective officers, all of them white. Some of these men flatly refused to command black troops—an attitude, Ullmann later would declare, reflecting a pervading racial prejudice that soon manifested itself in the Draft Riots of 1863. These interviewees seemed to share the notion that blacks would be second-line soldiers, little more than military laborers, thus depriving their commanders of opportunities for glory and advancement.

Upon reaching Louisiana, Ullmann discovered that another Union general, Nathaniel Banks, was organizing black regiments into a grandiloquently styled *Corps d'Afrique.* The two soon fell to quarreling because Ullmann considered Banks too sensitive to the interests of former slaveholders.[22] Indeed, a New England soldier described Banks as "trying to sit on two stools," carrying out the Emancipation Proclamation but taking "such a quiet, inoffensive, temporizing stand that its effect is almost nullified."[23] Despite the clash, Ullmann responded with all the black troops he had managed to recruit and train when Banks called for help in a raid on May 27, 1863, against Port Hudson, Louisiana.

Three hastily organized black regiments took their place that day on the "extreme right where the ground was very broken and covered with an exceedingly tangled abatis." Ullmann's troops joined forces with contingents organized by Ben Butler to make "six or seven charges over the ground against the enemy's works," during which the men "were exposed to a terrible fire and were dreadfully slaughtered." Although the assault failed and Port Hudson held out until July, the courage displayed by the black soldiers, Ullmann recalled, "wrought a marvelous change in the opinion of many former sneerers."[24]

Once the Emancipation Proclamation took effect, the systematic recruiting of blacks began throughout the country, from Iowa to Rhode Island. Two regiments—the 54th, raised by Robert Gould Shaw, and the 55th, under N. P. Hallowell—marched to war from Massachusetts, although comparatively few blacks lived there. To take charge of recruiting among the liberated slaves who had found refuge in the Mississippi Valley, Secretary of War Stanton chose the Army's Adjutant General, Lorenzo Thomas. After completing this task in May 1863, Thomas established within his office a Bureau of Colored Troops, which assumed responsibility for administering the existing regiments, some of which received new designations, and organizing new ones.[25]

Some six weeks after the newly formed 54th Massachusetts had paraded through Boston, Colonel Shaw's black soldiers formed up for an attack against Fort Wagner on Morris Island, dominating the ship channel leading into Charleston harbor, South Carolina. Only one avenue of approach to the fort existed, a narrow road bounded by the surf on one side and a marsh on the other, across which the

Rebels had built a formidable earthwork. Even though the terrain channeled the assault in this fashion, General Truman Seymour boasted to General Quincy Adams Gillmore, his commander, that "I can run right over it. I can camp my whole command there in one night."

"If you think you can take it," Gillmore replied, "you have my permission to make the assault. How do you intend to organize your command?"

According to Nathaniel Paige of the New York *Tribune*, Seymour answered, "Well, I guess we'll let Strong lead and put those damned niggers from Massachusetts in the advance; we might as well get rid of them one time as another."

Thus did Shaw's 54th Massachusetts come to lead General George C. Strong's brigade in the assault on Fort Wagner. As Strong's column approached its objective, it came under fire from Forts Wagner, Gregg, and Sumter, and from Confederate batteries on a headland nearby. About 150 of Strong's men were cut down before the actual assault began; then, in the failing twilight, the black soldiers made their charge.

Shaw urged his men over the earthwork and into the fort itself, but as he scrambled over the parapet he was shot dead. Even though the regimental officers were dying one by one, the Massachusetts blacks clung to a part of the fort. Three times Rebel fire cut down the unit's standard bearer, only to have someone else take up the colors.[26] The last man to seize the flagstaff was Sergeant William H. Carney of Company G, who brought the emblem safely back when grapeshot and canister at last drove the survivors from the works.[27] When the firing at last died away, General Strong was dead, and a major had succeeded him in command. The senior officer of the 54th Massachusetts to survive the battle unscathed was a second lieutenant, the nephew of Thomas Wentworth Higginson of the lst South Carolina.[28]

Killed, wounded, or captured during the evening's fighting were half the officers and men of Shaw's regiment. The Confederates, out of hatred for any white man who would lead black troops into battle, threw Shaw's body into a pit, then heaped the dead troops on top of his corpse—a mass grave shared by the dead of a gallant regiment.[29]

Almost a century later, poet Robert Lowell celebrated this gesture of contempt as a tribute, a monument more enduring than bronze, as Shaw's family realized.

Shaw's father wanted no monument
except the ditch,

where his son's body was thrown
and lost with his "niggers."
>   Robert Lowell,
>   "For the Union Dead"

While the 54th Massachusetts was braving enemy fire, its sister regiment, the 55th, dug trenches and built shelters for the Yankee forces on the Union-held portion of Morris Island and elsewhere in the vicinity of Charleston. After performing equally tedious garrison duty in Florida, the black regiment returned to South Carolina, where simmering resentment over inequity in pay was boiling over. The dispute had been heating up over the months and involved more than just the two Massachusetts regiments.

Initially the government had operated on the tacit understanding that black soldiers would serve mainly as auxiliaries, do less fighting than whites, and therefore deserve less pay. Despite assurance from Secretary of War Stanton that blacks would receive the same amount of money as whites of comparable rank, no one enlisting in the U.S. Colored Troops, whether contraband or free citizen, received more than $10 per month. As a result, Sergeant Major Thomas B. Hawkins, who would earn the Medal of Honor with the black 6th Regiment, collected each pay day $3 less than the lowliest private in a white regiment.

Complaints about this injustice reached Secretary Stanton and the President from white officers like Colonel Hallowell of the 55th Massachusetts and General Gillmore, in overall command of the advance upon Fort Wagner, and from black soldiers like Sergeant John F. Shorter and seventy-three other members of Hallowell's regiment. Shorter and his fellow soldiers affirmed their determination "to fight for Liberty justice & Equality," but they had reluctantly concluded that after "thirteen months spent cheerfully and willingly doing our Duty most faithfully," they should either be paid as equals of white soldiers or be discharged from the service. Corporal James Henry Gooding wrote a similar letter reminding President Lincoln that "we are fully armed, and equipped, have done all the various Duties pertaining to a Soldier's life, have conducted ourselves to the complete satisfaction of General Officers, who were, if any, prejudiced *against* us, but who now accord us all the encouragement and honor due us. . . ." The black troops were soldiers, not merely military laborers, and they deserved to be paid "as american SOLDIERS, not as menial hirelings."

Reasoned protests like these brought further promises but no action, so the blacks tried other tactics such as refusing to accept the $10 due them, a gesture of defiance that disrupted War Department bookkeeping and, technically at least, constituted mutiny. The sense of frustration intensified until, in November 1863, Sergeant William Walker, a member of a black South Carolina regiment, persuaded his company to refuse to perform any duty unless the men received pay equal to that of their white counterparts. The regimental commander, Colonel Augustus C. Bennett, told the group that this indeed was mutiny, and when his warning went unheeded, he brought charges that resulted in Sergeant Walker's execution by firing squad. Harsh though it was, this punishment took place at a time when fear provided the customary form of motivation, indiscipline was not to be tolerated, mutiny was unthinkable, and executions were not all that unusual. In a gentler or more enlightened era, military justice might have been less of a contradiction in terms, for the mutiny was actually a nonviolent protest that jeopardized neither the lives of Walker's fellow soldiers nor the unit's operations.

A black artillery unit from Rhode Island, serving in Texas, underwent a similar upheaval that also ended in death. After several men had been sentenced to hard labor for refusing their pay, one of the soldiers threatened a white officer. The lieutenant promptly shot and fatally wounded his assailant, an action endorsed as proper by the regimental commander.[30]

In July 1864, after almost a year of turmoil, Attorney General Edward Bates ruled that blacks who were free men at the outset of the war and subsequently volunteered for military service should receive the same pay as white soldiers. As might be expected from its earlier treatment of the pay issue, the War Department moved slowly to carry out even this partial reform. In the 55th Massachusetts, Colonel Hallowell sped the paperwork forward, drafting a simple declaration for his men to sign. Nevertheless, the additional money did not arrive until September, and in the interim some of the soldiers threatened to stack arms and return to New England. Hallowell convened a court-martial that sentenced five privates, adjudged to be the ringleaders, to hard labor for mutiny. Once the grievance over pay had been resolved, the regiment again took to the field. After campaigning against the defenses of Charleston, it joined the 54th Massachusetts and other black units in storming the Confederate works at Honey Hill, near Beaufort, South Carolina, an attack designed to cut the lines of communication between Savannah, Georgia, and Charleston.[31] (In the ranks of the 55th Massachusetts was Joshua Dunbar, the father of the poet Paul. Apparently the soldier was not discouraged by the broken promises concerning pay and the swift punishment for protest, since the son would celebrate in his poetry the interracial cameraderie of the battlefield.)[32]

Why was the question of pay so important that men would risk imprisonment, even death? First, the few dollars were important in themselves, especially to the black who had left a family in Massachusetts or elsewhere to fight for the abolition of slavery. Three dollars would represent 30 percent of a month's pay. Furthermore, the lower pay became, in effect, evidence of racial discrimination, almost a badge of servitude rather than remuneration for service freely rendered, and therefore a source of fierce resentment.

Resolution of the pay issue for free black enlistees did not end the discrimination against those men who had gone directly from slavery to military service and continued to fight for a mere $10 each month. Not until March 1865 did Congress give force of law to Secretary Stanton's promise to General Saxton that contrabands recruited in South Carolina would be paid at the same rate as white volunteers. Three months later, however, the War Department invoked the kind of legalism resorted to by governments bent on saving money and decided that James Lane, operating independently of Saxton, had never been authorized to offer recruits for his Kansas Colored Infantry more than $10 per month.[33]

The response of black Americans to calls for volunteers, heartening though it was in spite of the agitation over pay, could not satisfy President Lincoln's need for troops. In order to maintain the strength of the Union Army, the federal government turned to conscription. At first, President Lincoln merely empowered any state unable to meet its quota of volunteers to resort to a draft, while calling up some 90,000 short-term militiamen. The most attractive solution to the shortage of manpower proved to be federally run conscription. Draft calls went out early in July 1863, hard upon the victories at Gettysburg, Pennsylvania, and Vicksburg, Mississippi, and at about the same time that the two black regiments from Massachusetts were completing their training.

In anticipation of the draft, large numbers of men volunteered, thus becoming eligible for bonuses. Indeed, the law served mainly as an incentive to enlist, since four wartime drafts produced fewer than 164,000 soldiers, not quite 75,000 of them substitutes obtained by draftees, out of a manpower pool of roughly three-quarters of a million. Besides spurring some men to enlist, the first federal draft call incited others to violence against blacks, whose freedom had become a war aim. The black living in New York City became a convenient scapegoat instead of a human being; he served as a symbol, a means by which white workingmen could protest a law they perceived as unjust.

The violence stemmed from resentment over a provision of the draft law that permitted a man to buy an exemption from military service by paying $300, a sum far beyond the means of the average laborer. The deck seemed stacked against the workingman, who might be forced to leave a family barely able to survive on his wages and shoulder a musket for the lesser sum of $13 per month. Moreover, the emancipation of slaves might ultimately result in competition for jobs, plentiful in wartime but likely to become scarce afterward, and competition meant lower wages for those lucky enough to find work. Anger and frustration gave way to rage, directed not against the wealthy, who could buy exemption, but against blacks, who were near at hand.

Mobs roamed the streets of New York, attacking blacks and setting fires. Ignited by the arsonists was the Colored Orphan Asylum, from which the occupants had fled. As many as 150 black New Yorkers were injured or killed, and thousands joined in an exodus from the city.

The upheaval in New York City prevented the federal government from vigorously enforcing the draft law. This development made the black regiments especially important, even though white youths continued to enter the service. Usually the whites joined regiments raised by the states in order to receive the bonuses offered for military service instead of joining the small Regular Army, which offered no incentive of this sort. The violence that rocked New York did not spread to other cities or infect the military. Since the racial strife remained confined to one city, the recruiting of blacks went forward unimpeded by unusual concern for the safety of friends and family members. Within the Army a sense of shared danger (or relief, perhaps, on the part of white troops that someone else was being shot at) resulted in a kind of comradeship and prevented repetition within the service of the outrages inflicted upon black civilians in New York.[34]

Usually, blacks found greater acceptance in the Army or Navy than in the larger cities. Thomas Wentworth Higginson, for instance, insisted that "as a general thing there is no absolute prejudice amounting to hatred. . . . For three months there has not been a time when I have not had white troops as well as black . . . , and there has never been a complaint; they have mingled in camp and fought side by side with perfect good feeling."[35] On the other hand, Ben Butler acknowledged that some white units would not associate with the black regiments,[36] and too many commanders looked upon blacks solely as laborers, good for digging but not for fighting. "All that is necessary is to give them a chance," said Daniel Ullmann of the effectiveness of blacks in combat, "but this has not been done. Since I have been in command such has been the amount of fatigue work thrust upon the organization [his division of ten regiments] that it has been with the utmost difficulty that any time could be set aside for drill." No military unit could fight effectively unless drilled in tactics and the use of weapons.[37]

Although generals might prove obstinate and relations between racially different units become strained, white soldiers as a rule were willing to put aside their prejudices and grant the black soldier what a New York humorist (and volunteer officer on General Hunter's staff) celebrated in the song "Sambo's Right to Be Kilt." At times the slaughter could be vast and tinged with glory, as at Fort Wagner, or tainted by failure, as at the Crater, before Petersburg, Virginia, where Union engineers sank shafts beneath the Confederate fortifications and detonated explosives planted there. In planning to exploit the blast that formed the Crater, northern commanders sought to avoid charges of expending comparatively inexperienced black soldiers like so many cartridges, as journalist Nathaniel Paige declared had happened at Fort Wagner, and therefore led the way with white troops. Unfortunately, the first men into the Crater moved so sluggishly, perhaps awed by the violent explosion, that the defenders were able to regroup along the rim and fire downward into the assault wave and the black units trying to advance through it. The various elements lost cohesion, discipline collapsed, and the attack failed.[38]

A total of 186,000 blacks wore the Union blue during the Civil War, most of them assigned to infantry regiments, though a few served as artillerymen or with the cavalry. Nor were the chevrons of a noncommissioned officer all that these men could aspire to, for a few earned the sword and epaulets of an officer. The commissioning of these exceptional few served to demonstrate that, as a rule, whites exercised command in the U.S. Colored Troops. Ben Butler, for example, accepted some officers commissioned in Governor Moore's New Orleans milita. The two Massachusetts regiments had a handful of black officers, and Thomas Wentworth Higginson commissioned a few former slaves, though he relied upon white officers and sergeants until his black soldiers had gained experience. In no instance did a black officer command white troops.[39]

Other blacks contributed to Union success without bearing arms. Among them were chaplains and hospital stewards, recruiters and spies. Especially valuable in providing battlefield intelligence were recently liberated slaves. "The Negroes are our only friends and in two instances I owe my own safety to their faithfulness"; so testified Major General O. M. Mitchel, operating in northern Alabama and in constant danger from Rebel cavalry. "I shall very soon have watchful guards among the slaves on the plantations from Bridgeport [Tennessee] to Florence [Alabama]," he reported, "and all who communicate to me valuable information I have promised the protection of my Government."[40] Similarly, in the Carolinas some fifty former slaves volunteered for spy missions, penetrating from thirty to three hundred miles inside Confederate territory to return with information on morale and troop dispositions. One agent was caught and shot to death, one or two disappeared, but the others returned safely despite patrols using bloodhounds.[41] Men had no monopoly on this dangerous work. Elizabeth Bowser, an escaped slave, voluntarily returned to servitude and reported from the household of Confederate President Jefferson Davis. Both Sojourner Truth and Harriet Tubman, veterans of the prewar Underground Railroad, used their knowledge of escape routes to guide Union forces operating in hostile territory. Miss Tubman once led a force of 300 cavalrymen on a raid in South Carolina that freed 800 slaves and destroyed valuable cotton.[42]

Rather than make military use of its own black manpower, except as musicians or slave labor on fortifications, the Confederacy launched a campaign of terror against the Union's Negro troops. The Confederate Congress approved the death penalty for white officers captured while leading black units and decreed that the soldiers themselves would be turned over to state authorities for punishment. This policy, announced in May 1863, ratified existing practices. Indeed, in Arkansas during the previous year, Confederate soldiers had shot black prisoners of war, and similar atrocities occurred elsewhere.[43]

Hatred of armed blacks and fear that they would become the agents of a slave uprising triggered outrages like these. Confederate General Nathan Bedford Forrest, former slave trader and future organizer of the Ku Klux Klan, stood accused of presiding over the slaughter of Union soldiers trying to surrender after the capture of Fort Pillow, Tennessee, in April 1864. A congressional subcommittee more interested in propaganda than accuracy charged that "the rebels commenced an indiscriminate slaughter, sparing neither age nor sex, white or black, soldier or civilian. The officers and men seemed to vie with each other in the devilish work; men, women, and even children, wherever found, were deliberately shot down, beaten, and hacked with sabres; some of the children not more than ten years old were forced to stand up and face their murderers while being shot; the sick and wounded were butchered without mercy, the rebels even entering the hospital building and dragging them out to be shot or killing them as they lay there unable to offer the least resistance." Despite the exaggeration, the report established that Forrest's troops had killed blacks, though probably not whites, who were attempting to surrender.[44]

Within three months of this congressional report, President Lincoln acted to deter, if not future massacres, at least the mistreatment of prisoners of war. He vowed to execute one Confederate officer for every Union commander of black troops whom the Rebels might put to death and to sentence to hard labor one captured southern soldier for every black Union trooper sold into slavery. The threat did not have to be carried out.[45]

In fact, demands to punish blacks in Union ranks and their officers diminished in volume as southern voices began calling for the liberation of slaves in return for military service. Most respected of the advocates of change was Major General Pat Cleburne, who joined several other officers in the Army of Tennessee in recommending this policy. "Satisfy the Negro," Cleburne urged, "that if he faithfully adheres to our standard during the war he shall receive his freedom and that of his race." The general argued that the Confederacy should immediately announce the gradual but complete eradication of slavery, gaining access to a source of military manpower and at the same time removing an issue that kept European nations, which otherwise might seek a counterweight in America to the industrial North, from supporting southern independence through diplomacy and commerce. To Cleburne and his fellow officers, the preservation of the Confederate nation was well worth the price of abolishing slavery.[46]

The plan offered by Cleburne, who would die in action at Franklin, Tennessee, in November 1864, met prompt rejection at the hands of Jefferson Davis. The Confederate President warned that any suggestion of this sort "can be productive only of discouragement, destruction, and dissension."[47] Throughout 1864, the prospect of a Confederate victory grew progressively dimmer, but President Davis nevertheless resisted the arming of slaves, though he was willing to enroll 40,000 of them as military laborers, granting them freedom on completion of their period of service. He flatly refused to abolish the institution of slavery.[48]

A year after Cleburne submitted his proposal, the Confederate Chief Executive at last began facing up to the necessity of arming the black man. Before undertaking so revolutionary a step, the government sought an endorsement from Robert E. Lee, commanding general of the Army of Northern Virginia. Lee agreed to the idea, pointing out that the arming of blacks and the abolition of slavery had become essential conditions for the survival of an independent Confederacy. "If it end in subverting slavery," he told the President, "it will be accomplished by ourselves and we can devise the means of alleviating the evil consequences to both races. I think, therefore,

we must decide whether slavery shall be extinguished by our enemies and the slaves be used against us, or use them ourselves at the
risk of the effects which may be produced on our social institutions."[49]

The Confederacy established procedures for drafting slaves into
the Army, but before the machinery could begin functioning, the Union had triumphed.[50] Carried away perhaps by his enthusiasm for
the admission of blacks to the Union ranks, the black abolitionist
Frederick Douglass had predicted that "the side which first sum-
mons the Negro to its aid will conquer."[51] The Confederacy in the
person of Governor Moore of Louisiana had acted first, but fear of
the armed black man, dread of a slave uprising, and the myth of
white supremacy combined to prevent southern leaders from realizing the military potential of the black populace. Although not the
first, the Union had been more decisive, overcoming initial resistance to organize and train the U.S. Colored Troops.

The Union Army, unlike the Navy, insisted upon grouping
blacks in racially segregated units. The practice began in the South
among liberated slaves, unfamiliar with weapons, who required especially intensive training. An officer serving with Colonel Higginson during the organization of the 1st South Carolina Volunteers declared that there was as much of the soldier visible in the former
slave as there was of an angel in a block of marble awaiting the
touch of Michelangelo's chisel.[52] Segregation prevailed even among
the Massachusetts volunteers—a phenomenon that reflected a lack
of confidence in the black man, a belief (also revealed in the pay
scale) that he would be less a soldier than the white, and a persistent
racial prejudice.

4

Reaction in the South, Action in the West

THE CIVIL WAR effected a social revolution in the South. Not only did slavery perish forever, but a few intelligent and resourceful former slaves became, at least temporarily, men of power and property, leaders in militia affairs and other aspects of government. As Robert E. Lee had feared, the wartime leaders of the Confederacy had proved unable, after the surrender, to maintain the prewar social structure based on slavery. To remind these men of the reality of their defeat, the radical Republican faction within the triumphant federal government for a time stationed black troops in the vanquished South. The radicals, several of them businessmen, included many of those who had pushed for emancipation, the confiscation of the property of Rebels, and the arming of blacks.

Now the radicals sought to punish those who had launched the failed rebellion. Part of that punishment was a military occupation. Since the presence of federal troops in the South was sure to prove temporary, the radicals tried to reshape state politics throughout the old Confederacy, organizing the newly enfranchised freedmen and creating black militia units to support governments that were intended to recast the South in an egalitarian mold.

The radicals had good reason to fear for the future of the social order that the war had fashioned. Scarcely did the firing die away before the prewar white leaders attempted to frame laws to oppress the freedmen. New statutes undermined the rights of blacks to bear arms, compete with whites for jobs, and move freely about. Vagrancy laws could result in the sentencing of blacks to forced labor little different from slavery. The passage of time demonstrated that the great mass of former slaves lacked the political cohesiveness and, with notable exceptions, the skill and education to cope with their white enemies. Also, not every northern white who moved to the defeated South was a selfless idealist determined to help the freedmen; some were unscrupulous opportunists willing to prey upon the black man to line their own pockets. Over the years, a declining number of radical Republicans and a thinning cordon of federal troops (finally removed altogether) protected southern blacks from a return to power by the very men who had fought to keep them in bondage.

As the program of radical reconstruction waned, both North and South sought to normalize sectional relationships within a restored Union. For the South, this meant getting rid of the postwar governments and reducing the military and political power and the social status of their black supporters. Whereas the South sought to eliminate the influence of the North and insofar as possible reverse the results of the recent conflict, the North searched for common interests, largely in economic matters, even at the expense of turning away from the commitment of the radical Republicans to the civil rights of black Americans. Consequently, Republican administrations came to settle for gestures toward blacks, the appointment of individuals to minor jobs like marshal or collector of customs.

A product of the reconstruction South that arose from the ashes of the Confederacy and survived only briefly was Robert Smalls, who during the war had escaped from slavery to join the forces of liberation, bringing with him the steamer *Planter*. Although commissioned an officer in the U.S. Colored Troops, he had fought in the Navy, serving as pilot of the *Planter* and later of the gunboat *Keokuk*. When Confederate resistance collapsed, Smalls was one of several blacks who demonstrated the kind of leadership required to build a new and more nearly egalitarian society in South Carolina.

Smalls promptly identified himself with the Republican party, the political champion of the black man, the Union veteran, and the owners or managers of the nation's businesses and emerging industries. He belonged, after all, to these three constituencies. The onetime slave and soldier had amassed property on the Sea Islands and begun operating a coastal steamer, probably using the prize money he had received for his role in the capture of the *Planter*, so that the "steamboat man," as his fellow blacks called him, became an entrepreneur if not an industrialist.

As long as the radical element controlled the Republican party and that organization guided federal policy, Smalls remained a force to be reckoned with in South Carolina. He served in the state legislature, where he obtained a franchise for the construction of a railroad in which he had a financial interest, and went on to represent his predominantly black congressional district in the House of Representatives. He also became an officer in the state militia, attaining the rank of major general.

Smalls was not unique in his accomplishments during the immediate postwar years. For instance, Oscar James Dunn, who had attained the rank of captain in the U.S. Colored Troops, became the first black elected to statewide office in Louisiana; he served as lieutenant governor to a white, Henry C. Warmouth, who had the reputation of being a "carpetbagger," a northern opportunist who arrived in the South with all his belongings in a single satchel and schemed to make his fortune. Although Smalls and Dunn had been slaves, a number of free blacks rose to prominence in the decade following the war. Francis L. Cardozo set up schools for the freedmen of South Carolina, but with the end of reconstruction he became an outcast and he had to leave the state, moving to the District of Columbia, where he became head of the school system for black children. Another free black, Robert Brown Elliott, moved from the North to South Carolina, where he achieved prominence as an orator, attorney, and Republican politician. Pinckney Pinchback, a free black born in Mississippi, helped General Banks organize the *Corps d'Afrique* in wartime New Orleans and rose to the rank of captain. Chosen senator from Louisiana and later congressman at large, he was each time denied his seat by white supremacists. Hiram Revels, who also helped recruit black tooops during the war, went to Mississippi, served in the Senate from that state, and helped found a state college for blacks, which has become Alcorn University. Several blacks of different backgrounds and talents thus emerged as leaders during the period of reconstruction.[1]

Despite the accomplishments of blacks like these, the attempt by the radical Republicans to eradicate racism from the conquered South ended in failure. The black militia units proved too weak to serve as the underpinning for a new social and political order as the radicals had intended. The militiamen lacked the strength to protect the right of blacks to vote or to ensure that the laws of the reconstruction governments were carried out. Indeed, all these local forces soon disappeared from the old Confederacy, usually amid violence.[2]

In Mississippi, for instance, whites took down the names of black militiamen in "dead books" and fired weapons as the units drilled, successfully pressuring many of the members into quitting. Raiding parties seized the weapons being shipped by rail to black militia units in Florida, South Carolina, and Arkansas. Individual militia leaders were murdered, among them Jim Williams of York County, South Carolina, who was hanged, and Charles Caldwell of Mississippi, lured by a white acquaintance into a cellar to drink to the Christmas season and shot and fatally wounded as he raised his glass. Members of a white paramilitary group attacked the lawfully constituted black militia in Hamburg, South Carolina, firing upon the armory with a cannon, driving the blacks from the building, and murdering five men who could not escape. Whether motivated by a sincere desire to serve his community or merely to bear arms as the white man had done, the black militiaman could not resist such ruthless intimidation, and the organization went into eclipse.[3]

By 1876, with the power of the black militia already badly eroded, the Republicans had begun losing their ardor for the civil rights of the former slaves. A test of their commitment to blacks occurred that year when rival slates of presidential electors clouded the outcome of an election that pitted Republican Rutherford B. Hayes against Samuel J. Tilden. In order to retain control of the White House, the Republican Party pressed its courtship of a new class of southerner, the white businessmen and industrialists who seemed to share common interests with their solidly Republican northern counterparts. As part of the effort to align conservatives of both regions, President Hayes withdrew from the South the last of the federal occupation forces.

In South Carolina and elsewhere, a resurgent white aristocracy took advantage of the federal government's changed attitude to make society conform insofar as possible to the prewar pattern. Reaction ensued, though not thoroughgoing oppression, for the restored leadership for the moment took a paternalistic attitude toward the black man, discouraging outrages against him and extending him certain rights in return for political support. Smalls, for example, no longer served as a militia officer, though he retained for another decade his place in Congress. During his service in the House of Representatives, the state's more rabid ex-Confederates persisted in calling him "the boat thief," a reference to the *Planter* incident. Smalls remained a reliable member of the Republic Party, insisting that its followers, however preoccupied they might be with tariffs and similar issues, wore the mantle of the martyred Lincoln and were the true friends of black Americans.[4]

The same radical Republican minority that had supported the recruiting of black militia units in the South tried also to ensure a place for the black soldier in the post-Civil War Regular Army. Despite the contributions of the wartime U.S. Colored Troops, opposition to black regulars quickly formed. The most successful of wartime leaders displayed no enthusiasm for the proposal of the radicals. General Grant said that although he personally "had no objection to the use of colored troops," he saw them as emergency augmentation for a small, well-trained Army, not as peacetime members of that force.[5]

In spite of the general's attitude of indifference, Senator Henry Wilson, the Massachusetts Republican who headed the committee dealing with military matters, choose to seek the inclusion of black infantry, artillery, and cavalry regiments in the postwar Army.[6] The ensuing debate revealed an abiding belief within the Army that blacks lacked the intelligence to serve as artillerymen. Also affecting the deliberations was the fear of armed blacks that persisted not only in the South but in the former border states as well.

Among the fiercest opponents of the Wilson plan was Senator Willard Saulsbury, a Democrat from Delaware. After reminding his colleagues of the widespread unemployment that had followed the cessation of hostilities, he argued that black troops were not needed. "There are hundreds of thousands of white men who have been engaged in your Army," he told the Senate, "who would gladly accept the place of soldiers in the Regular Army." Since this vast reservoir of white veterans was available, the senator could see no need to recruit blacks unless they were better soldiers than whites, an assumption that he emphatically denied. Black soldiers, he charged, were bullies, given to swagger and menacing gestures, although he offered no concrete evidence to support this stereotype. "What would be the effect," he asked his fellow senators, "if you were to send negro regiments into the community in which I live to brandish their swords and exhibit their pistols and their guns?" Such an action, he answered, "would raise a stench in the nostrils of the people from whom I come."[7]

Senator Wilson and his Republican colleagues prevailed, however, and Congress in the summer of 1866 decreed that the Regular Army should include six black regiments, four of infantry and two of cavalry but none of artillery, even though the wartime U.S. Colored Troops had formed units in all three of the combat arms. As a result of this law, the Army was authorized a total of ten regiments of cavalry, forty-five of infantry, and five of artillery. A subsequent Army reorganization in the spring of 1869 consolidated the four black infantry units into two, part of a reform that eliminated twenty regiments of infantry. The 38th and 41st Regiments became the 24th Infantry (Colored), while the 39th and 40th emerged as the 25th Infantry (Colored). The two regiments of cavalry, the 9th and 10th, retained their original designations.[8]

The decision to raise black regiments did not ensure that an overwhelmingly white Army would accept the members of the new units. Stories circulated that the black soldier was lazy, undisciplined, lacking in initiative, and incapable of doing routine paper-work. Granted that a lack of formal education proved a handicap for most recruits and that few of the men had been required to exercise initiative or demonstrate mechanical skill before entering the ser-vice, the black soldier soon proved himself loyal, brave, and depend-able. The reenlistment rate remained high and desertions few at a time when three recruits out of ten could be expected to go over the hill and less than a fifth of the Army's enlisted men had spent five or more years in uniform. Nor did the black regiments suffer to the usual extent from alcoholism, the great curse of the peacetime ser-vice, a frequent reason for transgressions that led to court-martial punishment and desertion.[9] "By a simple mathematical calculation on the cost of deserters . . . ," said an officer of the 10th Cavalry, "it will appear that in the twenty-three years since the [1866] reorgani-zation of the Army, the Government would have saved ten million dollars on the item of desertion alone, if the Army had been com-posed entirely of 'colored troops.' "[10]

Despite their soldierly qualities, black troops from the outset encountered rejection, discrimination, and contempt. In command of the 10th Cavalry, looked upon as a collection of misfits, was Colo-nel Benjamin Grierson, who was something of a misfit himself. His face scarred from childhood, when a pony had kicked him, Grierson not only lacked the dashing appearance of the cavalry leader but ac-tually hated horses; yet he had been one of the few successful Union cavalry commanders during the Civil War. The first indications of the shabby treatment his regiment would receive came when Grier-son was fitting out the unit at Fort Leavenworth, Kansas, in 1867. The post commander assigned the black troopers a bog as their campsite, complained because tents and uniforms became muddy, and issued an order that none of Grierson's men come within 15 yards of a white soldier. This treatment inspired Grierson to finish his work, order his men onto the trail-worn mounts they had inher-ited, and ride off to duty on the frontier as quickly as possible.[11]

For a dozen years Grierson commanded the 10th Cavalry, lead-ing it through a series of arduous campaigns against such resource-ful foes as the Apache chieftain Victorio and the Cheyenne warrior Black Kettle. During the war with Black Kettle, Grierson's men rode to the aid of Lieutenant Colonel George A. Forsyth, whose scouts were trapped on an island in the dry bed of the Arikara River in Col-orado, just beyond the western border of Kansas. For eight days the scouts, firing from hurriedly dug trenches or from behind dead horses or mules, held off some 700 Cheyenne tribesmen, while two volunteers made their way some 85 miles to Fort Wallace, Kansas, where they found help. When the black troopers reached the island

and broke the siege, they found the defenders "living on horse flesh without salt or pepper." Besides providing food and protection from hostile fire, the dead animals "impregnated the air with a terrible stench."[12]

At times, the men of the 10th Cavalry had to show the same stamina displayed by Forsyth's scouts on the besieged island. Black troopers stationed at Fort Concho, near the Texas panhandle, routinely patrolled the desolate Staked Plain, tracking down Indian war parties. On one such mission, Captain Nicholas Nolan led Troop A into the wasteland in search of Mescalero Apache raiders who had attacked stations on the stagecoach line between San Antonio and El Paso in Texas.

The unit set out in pursuit on July 19, 1877, but encountered no Indians except for a group that had permission to leave their reservation. Although the summer was the driest in years, Nolan's men for several days succeeded in finding water by digging into the beds of arid lakes or streams. By the 27th, however, their luck had run out. A civilian guide set out to look for water but never returned; eight men, loaded down with the command's empty canteens, tried to follow his trail but neither found him nor located the spring he was seeking. The only fresh water available to the cavalrymen was the dew they managed to soak up with their blankets from the coarse desert grass. Nolan's black troopers struggled through the wilderness, trying to retrace their steps to one of the lakes where water lay beneath the dry bed. Men became weak and collapsed; some lost confidence in the captain and struck out on their own. Throats became too dry to swallow bread or beans; indeed, the troopers tried to quench their thirst with urine or the blood of dying horses.

The entire group might have perished in the desert had it not been for the efforts of one man. Private Barney Howard moved from one weak and tired soldier to another, joking with the men and urging them to hold out just a little longer. As it was, four men died, including one whose body was left behind and never recovered, but the others survived without water for eighty-six hours, at last found one of the lake beds, dug through the dry crust, and found drinking water. Once his men had rested, Nolan moved swiftly to restore discipline, pressing charges of desertion against four troopers, including a sergeant, who had left the column and made their way independently to safety.[13]

As if nature and the Indian were not a deadly enough combination, fate sometimes joined the conspiracy against the black troopers. On one such occasion in July 1880, while searching for Victorio's Apaches, Colonel Grierson and his six-man escort came under attack. Nearby elements of the command rode to the sound of firing, however, and a four-hour running battle ensued, in which the Indians fled toward the Rio Grande trying to shake off a detachment led by Corporal Asa Weaver. Thus far luck favored the troopers, but during the fight, one of the cavalry horses bolted, carrying its rider, a private named Tockes from Troop C, into the midst of the Apaches. Instead of trying to leap from his mount, Tockes dropped the reins, drew his carbine, and opened fire "to the right and left." Some months later, a patrol discovered his skeleton. Corporal Weaver's resourcefulness in organizing and leading the pursuit earned him a promotion to sergeant, for his action prevented Victorio from concealing his trail and enabled Grierson to deliver a surprise attack a few days later, when the marauders recrossed the Rio Grande from Mexico.

However well they fought, the men of the 10th Cavalry remained on the outer fringes of the military community. One of the regiment's original officers recalled that "I was once told to take my 'Damned hokes,' and camp outside of the post." This officer also remembered the campaign against the Cheyennes in 1867 and 1868, when the colored men did all the fighting—sustained nearly all the casualties, and the white troops received the commendations.[14]

The 9th Cavalry differed from the 10th mainly in the appearance of its commander, Colonel Edward Hatch, a handsome, soldierly officer, who had served with Grierson during the Civil War. Troopers of both regiments shared the nickname Buffalo Soldiers, bestowed out of respect by their Indian enemies, who saw a resemblance between the hair of the black cavalryman and the hair of the buffalo, an animal considered sacred by the plains tribe. The 9th Cavalry participated in many of the same campaigns as the 10th, facing similar danger and hardships and sharing a common problem in what today might be called community relations.

On the Texas frontier, the black soldier could expect no protection by local lawmen. During January 1870, for instance, a patrol looking for cattle rustlers came under fire from a ranch house. The sergeant in charge, Edward Troutman, led his men off the property, but several gunmen lay in wait for them. Troutman and two others fought their way through the ambush, killing one of their assailants; Privates Moses Turner and Jerry Owsley were shot to death.

Upon learning of the attack, Colonel Hatch rode out with another patrol, arrested nine suspects, recovered the two soldiers' bodies, and retrieved their uniforms and equipment from a shack nearby. A grand jury released eight of the men that Hatch had brought in, and the one actually prosecuted speedily won acquittal. Ignoring the results of a coroner's inquest, the grand jurors returned a murder indictment against Troutman and the other two survivors for killing one of their attackers. Hatch was charged with false imprisonment of the men he had arrested and, along with one of his officers, indicted for burglary in entering the shack to recover property belonging to the two dead troopers. Only a change of venue saved the accused from probable conviction by a local trial jury.[15] Hatch was fully justified in charging that the inhabitants of Starr County, Texas, were attempting to "harass both the Officers and Soldiers" of his regiment and that outlaws from both sides of the border had joined forces to establish "a system of terror . . . to control the county in their interest."[16]

Like the 9th and 10th Cavalry, the black infantry outfits received assignments in the Southwest. The 38th and 41st regiments, before being consolidated and redesignated the 24th Infantry in 1869, were scattered among outposts from Louisiana to New Mexico. William B. Hazen, a brevet major general during the Civil War, commanded the 38th Infantry and Ranald S. MacKenzie, also a wartime brevet major general, led the 41st. Ranald MacKenzie—who would become a formidable Indian fighter, succumb to madness, and leave the Army—retained command of the 24th Infantry until 1870. His replacement was Abner Doubleday, succeeded as colonel in 1873 by Joseph H. Potter, who served for more than a decade before yielding to Zenas R. Bliss.

The result of combining the 39th and 40th regiments, the new 25th Infantry enjoyed greater stability of command, despite a turbulent beginning. The first colonel, Joseph A. Mowrer, died in 1870 as the unit was taking shape at New Orleans. For the next several months, colonels and lieutenant colonels replaced one another in dizzying succession, but in the spring of 1871 Colonel George L. Andrews took the reins, which he held for twenty years.[17]

Indicative of the Army's prevailing attitude toward black troops, whether cavalry or infantry, was the fact that they rarely served at the more desirable military posts. The arrival of one troop from the 9th Cavalry at Fort Myer, Virginia, across the Potomac from the national capital, proved unusual enough to inspire favorable editorial comment from a publication interested in the rights of black citizens.[18] Normally, the reward for extended service on the frontier battlegrounds was transfer to some more peaceful but equally remote cantonment. When commanding the 10th Cavalry, Colonel J. K. Mizner urged that his men be sent from New Mexico to the comparative luxury of Fort Riley, Kansas. Some of the unit's horses did get to Kansas, but most of the men ended up at a fort in distant Montana.[19] After the 25th Infantry had served for a decade along the Rio Grande, the Hayes administration and Secretary of

War George W. McCrary proposed keeping the black troopers on the border while rotating the white officers to less spartan posts.[20]

Pseudo-scientific arguments could be made for retaining the black soldiers in the Southwest. "The race is from the tropics," said Quartermaster General Montgomery C. Meigs, "for their ancestors were not from the Northern or Southern extremities of Africa but from the Torrid Zone almost entirely." As a result, the general concluded, "the Southern climate suits the men and while the officers doubtless need change, that can better and more cheaply be accomplished by transferring the officers to other regiments."[21] If any black unit actually did prefer the wasteland of the Southwest, it would have been the Seminole Indian Negro Scouts, some fifty strong, descendants of slaves who had found refuge with the Seminoles until the Army had expelled that tribe from Florida. The scouts had drifted into Mexico, then returned to the United States to don the Army blue and serve along the border.[22]

"I cannot but think," Meigs warned, "that orders to Dakota will prove to be the death knell of any colored regiment,"[23] but despite his concerns all the black units served in the northern latitudes. The 25th Infantry, for example, moved to Fort Sturgis in what was then the Dakota Territory during the 1880s, and one company of the 24th Infantry spent two years in Alaska at the turn of the century.[24] Similarly, cavalry units served in Wyoming, the Dakotas, Nebraska, Utah, and Montana during the 1890s.

The 24th Infantry remained the longest in the Southwest, serving in the Indian Territory, which became the state of Oklahoma, and then returning to the border as an element of the Army's Department of Arizona. In this regiment as in the other black regiments, the chaplain assumed responsibility for education as well as for the spiritual welfare of his men. Besides teaching subjects like reading and arithmetic to interested soldiers, he conducted services and sponsored a variety of programs designed to combat two related evils, boredom and whiskey. Typical of these efforts were the literary society and debating group sponsored by Chaplain Allen Allensworth. Appointed in 1885 to the 24th Infantry, Allensworth was the second black minister to become a Regular Army chaplain, following by one year Henry V. Plummer of the 9th Cavalry.

Medal of Honor winners were far from rare—black soldiers received seventeen of these awards during the Indian wars—but in May 1889 Sergeant Benjamin Brown and Corporal Isaiah Mays of the 24th Infantry earned theirs for heroism far from the battlefield. Ambushed by bandits while escorting the regimental payroll, both were wounded by the first volley as they tried to remove a boulder blocking the trail. While Brown reorganized his men in the cover of a ditch and exchanged shots with the outlaws, Mays walked two painful miles to get help. The paymaster accompanying the shipment praised the courage and skill of the two soldiers, though heroism could not prevent the highwaymen from making off with more than $28,000.[25]

In 1896, with the Indian tribes pacified, the 24th Infantry left the Southwest to join the other black regiments in a colder climate. Fort Douglas, Utah, became the infantrymen's new home.[26] Ironically, the black soldier, regardless of unit, found that the people of the northern tier of states could at times be as hostile as those in the Southwest. Much of the friction arose from the presence of black prostitutes who set up shop at "hog ranches" near the military posts and inspired loathing and anger among the more respectable elements in the frontier communities. Relations between the soldiers and women were complicated by the fact that blacks sometimes made up less than 1 percent of the permanent residents.[27]

When the black soldier, an intruder despite his uniform, broke the law, retribution was swift as the citizens of Sturgis City and Sun River, Dakota Territory, demonstrated. In each town, vigilantes lynched a black soldier charged with murdering a white civilian. The two killings that touched off the mob violence stemmed from quarrels over women.[28]

Regardless of local attitudes, training had to continue. While stationed in Montana, the 25th Infantry took part in an experiment designed to increase the foot soldier's mobility without converting him into a cavalryman. Lieutenant James Moss in 1896 took command of a bicycle detachment that pedaled from Fort Missoula to Yellowstone Park and back, covering a thousand miles. Over the steepest part of the route, Moss's men maintained a speed of 6 miles per hour, better than twice that of marching men traversing average terrain. Neither mud nor pursuing dogs could stop the soldiers, who sometimes made bone-jarring detours over railroad lines to avoid long hills or toll gates. The following year, Lieutenant Moss led some two dozen volunteers 1,900 miles from Fort Missoula to St. Louis, Missouri. With good reason he praised his cyclists for the "spirit, pluck, and fine soldierly qualities they displayed."[29]

The saga of the black regiments that began with Senator Wilson's bill in 1866 and included the bicycle experiment had faced the threat of abrupt curtailment as long as two decades before Moss led his troops out of Fort Missoula bound for St. Louis. Problems of finding suitable locations for black units, the attitude of those officers who would rather be second lieutenants in white regiments than captains in black ones, and sporadic congressional opposition to black regulars caused General William Tecumseh Sherman, then

Commanding General of the Army, to suggest that "the word 'Black' be obliterated from the Statute Books, that whites and blacks be enlisted and distributed alike in the Army as has been the usage in the Navy for a hundred years." In proposing adoption of the Navy's racial policy, the general called for "men of muscle, endurance, will, courage, and that wildness of nature, that is liable unless directed to result in violence and crime, to combat the enemies of civilization, with whom we have to contend." He added that he considered "the white race the best for this," but he was "willing to take black and white alike on equal terms, certainly a fairer rule than the present one of separating them into distinct organizations."[30]

Could such a rule of fairness have prevailed during the late 1870s, when even its principal advocate acknowledged that he considered whites to be better soldiers? The Congress thought not. A bill introduced to open every regiment to both races went down to defeat, even though its sponsors argued that the 14th Amendment, adopted to ensure equal rights to all, superseded the Army Reorganization Act of 1866 and put an end to exclusion because of race. To the opponents of open recruiting, however, equality was a disguise for racial discrimination, and in this instance the opposition was correct. Had the black regiments disbanded, given the racial attitudes of the time, a recruiter approached by a black and a white of equal character and ability would instinctively have administered the oath to the white man.[31]

While the four black regiments were surviving a challenge to their continued existence, changes encouraging to blacks took place within the Army's segregated structure and elsewhere. For one thing, Congress at long last placed all Civil War veterans on an equal footing insofar as pensions and bonuses were concerned. The distinction between free man and freed slave no longer obtained.[32] For another, W. Hallett Greene, a graduate of New York's City College, became the first black to enlist in the Signal Corps, forced by Secretary of War Robert Todd Lincoln, son of the Civil War President, on a reluctant chief signal officer, the same Brevet Major General Hazen who had once commanded the 38th Infantry, one of the original post-Civil War black regiments.[33] The precedent established with Greene in 1884 enabled blacks to serve as hospital stewards (an assignment open to them during the Civil War) and as commissary or quartermaster sergeants within the black regiments, assignments formerly held on a temporary basis.[34]

At the outset, white officers commanded every component of the black regiments. Although the Army Reorganization Act of 1866 did not establish a racial test, examiners rejected every black veteran of the Civil War who sought to be commissioned in the new units. Not until black cadets began graduating from the U.S. Military Academy would the soldiers of the four regiments be led by officers of their own race.[35]

Of twenty-five blacks appointed to the Military Academy during the 1870s and 1880s, twelve survived the entrance examination, but just three graduated and received commissions. Those who entered the academy faced harassment by a corps of cadets and a faculty that for the most part shared the views of Major General John M. Schofield. While in command at West Point, he reviewed an especially blatant example of hazing involving one of the few black cadets and in doing so denied that racial prejudice was an issue. "The prevailing 'prejudice,'" he suggested, "is rather a just aversion to the qualities which the people of the United States have long been accustomed to associate with a state of slavery and intercourse without legal marriage, and of which color and its various shades are only the external signs." At the root of the problem, Schofield maintained, were those Republicans, whether northern whites or southern blacks, who insisted upon exercising their right as congressmen to appoint blacks to fill vacancies at the academy. "To send to West Point for four years' competition a young man who was born in slavery is to assume that half a generation has been sufficient to raise a colored man to the social, moral, and intellectual level which the average white man has reached in several hundred years. As well might the common farm horse be entered in a four-mile race against the best blood inherited from a long line of English racers." Such were the general's views.[36]

Schofield's homely analogy referred not to the usual social ostracism and petty harassment endured by all of the black cadets, but to a singularly brutal attack upon one of them, Johnson Chestnut Whittaker, who was discovered bleeding, unconscious, and tied securely to his bunk. The general, given his preoccupation with blood lines and illegitimacy, may have known that Whittaker was the descendant of a white slaveholder, a member of the Chesnut clan, which explained the cadet's middle name. Incredibly, in view of the condition in which the victim was found, both an official inquiry and a court-martial decided that Whittaker had written himself a threatening note, inflicted painful wounds to his own face (slitting an ear, for example), and then tied himself to a bunk so securely that those who discovered him had to cut him free. At the prodding of Secretary of War Lincoln, the Chester A. Arthur administration reviewed and reversed the decision of the court-martial. Unfortunately, on the very day the conviction was overturned, the U.S. Military Academy dropped the black cadet for academic deficiencies. Although he did not graduate and receive a commission, Whittaker's two sons were officers during World War I, and a grandson became an officer in World War II.[37]

The first black graduate of West Point, Henry O. Flipper, received his commission in 1879, two years before Cadet Whittaker, a former roommate, was expelled. Lieutenant Flipper joined the 10th Cavalry and quickly demonstrated his competence as an officer, but had served just five years when his career came to an abrupt end. Appointed commissary officer at Fort Concho, Texas, he proved an inept bookkeeper and soon faced charges of embezzlement. He later claimed that his friendship with the sister-in-law of a white fellow officer had aroused jealousies that inspired the charges. Whatever the source, the accusation of embezzlement did not hold up under the scrutiny of a court-martial, but the panel did find him guilty of conduct unbecoming an officer—he had made false statements in a transparent effort to conceal the shortage—and directed that he be dismissed from the service. After leaving the Army, Flipper went on to a distinguished career as an engineer, representing American mining interests in Mexico. He also translated into English the Mexican laws governing land ownership and mining, served as a translator for the Senate Committee on Foreign Relations, and became a special assistant to the Secretary of the Interior. Ninety-five years after his dismissal, he received posthumous vindication from the Army's Board for the Correction of Military Records, which held that the punishment had been too severe and had the record changed to indicate that Flipper had received an honorable discharge.[38]

John H. Alexander, the next black to graduate from the U.S. Military Academy, became a second lieutenant in 1887. He served with the 9th Cavalry in Nebraska and Utah for some seven years and then received an assignment as the Army's professor of military science and tactics at Wilberforce University, a school for blacks in Ohio. While serving there, he died in March 1894 of heart disease.

The next black graduate of the academy, and the last for almost fifty years, was Charles Young, who embarked in 1889 on a long and remarkable career with both regular and volunteer forces. Like Alexander, he served initially with the 9th Cavalry at Fort Robinson, Nebraska, and Fort DeChesne, Utah. In the autumn following Alexander's death, Young became military instructor at Wilberforce and was teaching there when the United States went to war with Spain in 1898.[39]

The hallmark of the black regiments was loyalty. The men did what was expected of them, whether fighting the Apache in the Southwest or taking part in the skirmishing that followed the massacre of the Sioux at Wounded Knee. Their duties sometimes involved law enforcement, as when cavalrymen helped restore order to the warring ranchers of Lincoln County, New Mexico, or among the cattlemen of Johnson County, Wyoming. What passed for labor relations during the nineteenth century came under their purview at least once, for the 25th Infantry helped break a strike by miners at Coeur d'Alene, Idaho. Occasionally the troops did rebel in the face of local hostility or harassment—the average soldier lacked the super-human patience of Johnson Whittaker, Henry Flipper, or Charles Young—shooting up the town of Suggs, Wyoming, to avenge a series of insults or firing into Nasworthy's saloon, near Fort Concho, after a group of Texas Rangers pistol-whipped some black troopers drinking there. The fear that had haunted colonial Americans, the specter of blacks and Indians joining forces, may briefly have revived on the frontier; if so, the threat was nonexistent. In fact, western communities came to accept the black soldier, however grudgingly, as a reliable means of helping suppress the more dangerous Indians.[40]

The toleration of black soldiers in a small town in Nebraska or Wyoming did not signify that members of the Negro race were enjoying all the rights of citizenship. Despite occasional exceptions, by the mid-1890s segregation was becoming the law of the land. In the South, however, a few populist governors fought a delaying action, trying to create a political alliance of blacks and poor whites.

Out of the ruins of the reconstruction era's black militia organizations, such as the one in which Smalls had served, there eventually arose a handful of units that accepted blacks. The units formed one element in the campaign to form an interracial coalition capable of breaking the economic and political domination of the conservative leadership that was now the backbone of the Democratic Party in the South.[41] North Carolina established a company of light infantry (colored) at Charlotte. Alabama's militia rolls contained the names of 190 black infantrymen by the eve of the war with Spain, and Virginia was maintaining companies of black militia at Richmond, Petersburg, and Norfolk.[42]

The emerging white aristocracy of the South, the kind of people that President Hayes had hoped to cultivate two decades earlier, responded to this threat to its ascendancy by using race as a wedge to sunder the new coalition. Since regaining power, the conservative white leaders had taken a paternalistic attitude toward the black man, discouraging random violence by persons whom they characterized as white trash. Some blacks, moreover, were willing to sacrifice a measure of social acceptance and economic opportunity to obtain freedom from the sort of violence that had been visited upon black militia leaders in the 1870s.

The relationship between conservative whites and the black populace now changed. Instead of treating the black as a ward, de-

pendent upon their good will for protection against the white rab-
ble, the conservatives allied themselves with a class they despised to
disenfranchise all blacks (and the poorest of whites who might become their economic and political allies), isolating the black race
from the mainstream of political, cultural, and social life. A series of
statutes, the so-called Jim Crow laws, enforced racial segregation, at
first in the old Confederacy but later throughout the nation, thanks
in part to a series of Supreme Court decisions dealing with voting
rights and public accommodations.[43]

The emergence of Jim Crow at first had little impact on the four
regiments of black soldiers. Stationed at isolated outposts, performing the same duties as any white unit in a similar location, the
troops rarely encountered the blatant forms of racism that were already assuming the force of law throughout the South. This isolation from a burgeoning form of racial discrimination might well explain the high morale and great efficiency of the black units. Indeed,
the post-Civil War era, a period of isolation on the frontier, would
mark the last time that segregated black units could be numbered
among the Army's finest.

5

To Hell with Spain

MESS ATTENDANT John H. "Dick" Turpin, a talented baseball player popular with his shipmates, had been sitting in the wardroom pantry talking with two other black messmen when a convulsion shook the battleship *Maine*. Being trained to wait upon officers, which was becoming the usual assignment for black sailors, gave Dick Turpin an opportunity to save his life. Near the forecastle, where most of the crew was sleeping, an ammunition magazine had detonated. There the loss of life was greatest, whereas some 200 feet aft of the explosion, in officers' country where Turpin was on duty, a man had a chance of escape. Even so, not everyone got away. Before anyone could go to his aid, one of the officers collapsed into the water that was flooding the ship and vanished. Turpin searched for the ladder leading topside, but the shock had torn it away. A rope, however, dangled from an overhead hatch, enabling him to climb to the deck and swim away from the doomed *Maine*.

Of the two fellow messmen with whom Turpin had been talking, Westmore Harris and Robert White, one survived without a scratch. Disoriented and wandering the lower deck, Harris encountered another crewman who was praying to find a way out. The prayers apparently were answered, for the two of them found a passage leading to safety. Unable to escape the interior of the rapidly settling battleship, White died in the wreckage, one of 22 blacks among the 266 persons who perished as a result of the explosion.[1]

Sent to Havana to look after American interests imperiled by the struggle between Cuban rebels and their Spanish rulers, the *Maine* exploded and sank on the night of February 15, 1898. An American court of inquiry attributed the tragedy to the explosion of a mine planted beneath the keel, though recent engineering studies concluded that an accidental explosion on board ship was the cause, and public opinion fixed the blame on Spanish authorities. "Remember the *Maine*, to hell with Spain," proved an effective rallying cry, and in April the United States Congress declared the rebellious island of Cuba free and independent and authorized the President, William McKinley, to use force to drive out the Spanish. A formal declaration of war followed in a few days.[2]

Should black citizens, their rights being stripped away by Jim Crow laws, support a war to bring American-style freedom to Cuba, with its large Negro population? For E. E. Cooper, editor of the Washington *Colored American*, the answer remained an unqualified yes, since he believed that shared adventure and danger—or perhaps shared boredom—in a common cause would contribute to "an era of good feeling the country over and cement the races into a more compact brotherhood through perfect unity of purpose and patriotic affinity." The black soldier, Cooper insisted, would demonstrate his worth, gain the respect of those who oppressed him, and ignite a spark of "comradeship" that would persuade white Americans to "unloose themselves from the bondage of race prejudice." All of this the result of helping defeat Spain.

In contrast, Henry M. Turner, the senior bishop of the African Methodist Episcopal Church in the United States, concluded that any Spanish outrages in Cuba could be no worse than the mistreatment of blacks in the United States. He therefore argued against "rushing into a death struggle" on behalf of America's white oppressors. At his most extreme, the bishop declared that "Negroes who are not disloyal to the United States ought to be lynched."

Bishop Turner was not alone in his views. John Deveaux, a black colonel in the Georgia militia during the brief political alliance between blacks and poor whites, agreed that "whites in quest of wealth" would prey upon the poor in a conquered Spanish empire. A chaplain in the black 9th Cavalry, George W. Prioleau, asked, "Is America any better than Spain? Has she not subjects in her midst who are murdered daily without trial?"

The average black experienced neither Cooper's euphoria nor Bishop Turner's revulsion over the war, and like black volunteers in earlier wars, the black man who sought to avenge the *Maine* responded to a variety of influences. He was fulfilling an obligation of citizenship, however much his rights might be abused. He also welcomed, in varying proportions, the prospect of travel, pocket money, adventure, and an opportunity to prove himself.[3]

Before the war actually broke out, the War Department began ordering the black Regular Army units southward, confident that these troops were naturally suited for service in the tropics. The 25th Infantry left Montana for Key West, Florida, but fresh water was too scarce on the island for so large a unit, forcing the Army to send the black soldiers to Chickamauga Park, Georgia. The 9th and 10th Cavalry joined the 25th Infantry at the Georgia encampment, where the 24th Infantry also arrived after being diverted from its original destination, New Orleans.

Once the four regiments had reached their destination, the War Department faced the task of bringing them to wartime strength and equipping the men for combat. Recruiters had to find 750 additional men for each regiment and sign them up in a matter of days, a task so formidable that volunteers were accepted who could neither read nor write. The new soldiers either brought existing battalions up to authorized strength or formed new ones, in which twenty or so veterans served as a cadre.

The War Department lacked the authority to purchase equipment before Congress declared war. Supply therefore lagged far behind demand, so that many an American soldier, whether black or white, regular or wartime volunteer, failed to receive his basic equipment until training had ended, if then. A new recruit might have a rifle but neither a sling nor a bayonet. He might lack the cup, knife, or spoon that he needed in order to share in one of his regiment's messes.[4]

Even as the Regular Army massed in the southern states, a call went out for wartime soldiers. Adhering to the practice that had evolved during the Civil War, the federal government requested a certain number of volunteers, allowing the states to handle the actual recruiting. In the case of officers, the federal government commissioned the individual, either directly from civil life or in the militia grade to which a state governor had appointed him. When President McKinley asked for volunteers in April 1898, Ohio, Indiana, and Massachusetts offered militia forces including units recruited from among the black populace. In response to a second call, issued in May, the states of Alabama, North Carolina, Kansas, Virginia, and Illinois responded by forming black regiments around cadres provided by the existing militia units.

The existence of these volunteer organizations fueled the fires of patriotism among black citizens. A proposal surfaced suggesting that the President appoint Henry Flipper the colonel of a wartime regiment composed of black militiamen. At the same time, Congress was debating the creation of units made up of volunteers immune to the diseases that American soldiers could expect to encounter in the Caribbean. The acceptance of some blacks in the wartime Army, the growing pressure to recruit others, and the question of immunity to tropical fevers combined to persuade Congress to authorize the recruitment of ten regiments of so-called immunes, five of them (later reduced to four) to be composed of blacks.

The Army that fought the Spanish could thus draw upon three black components. The best trained were the regular regiments—the 9th and 10th Cavalry, the 24th and 25th Infantry—each with a cadre of long-service men, some of them veterans of the Indian wars. The second source consisted of the individuals who had volunteered for the immune regiments. The third comprised the black militia units that hailed from Alabama, Virginia, North Carolina, Kansas, Illinois, Indiana, Massachusetts, and Ohio. Except for recent recruits, members of these organizations had received some military training, but the quality of the periodic militia musters varied markedly from state to state, as did the experience of the officers in command.

Charles Young, one of the three black graduates of West Point, commanded the Ohio unit, whereas Robert L. Bullard, a white officer of the Regular Army, took over the black regiment from Alabama. Among the ranks of the 7th, 8th, 9th, and 10th U.S. Volunteer Infantry—the black immunes—the principal criterion for enlistment other than race, was residence in an area where tropical disease prevailed. The officers, however, did not have to be immune to this sort of fever. They tended to be veteran noncommissioned officers of the Regular Army's black regiments, who took over the platoons and companies, or white regular officers, who filled the staff and senior command positions.

The selection of officers to command black volunteers, whether immunes or federalized militiamen, proved difficult. When the United States went to war, 1st Lieutenant Charles Young, then a military instructor at Wilberforce University in Ohio, was the only black officer in the entire Regular Army who was qualified to lead troops in combat. He took over the 9th Ohio Colored Infantry, assuming the wartime rank of major.[5] Although he did not see action in Cuba, his skills proved so impressive that his commanding officer, Major General J. C. Breckinridge, declared, "Certainly we should have the best obtainable officers for our volunteers and therefore some such men as Colonel Young . . . , whether black or white, must be sought for."[6] In this instance "colonel" referred to the usual rank of a regimental commander, not Young's actual rank.

Young, unfortunately, was the only officer in his unit with mili-

tary experience, for rare was the black militia office₁
Army service at all. In North Carolina, for example,
devolved upon black men successful in civil life. Th₍
member of the state legislature and the lieutenant c₍
and musician whose contact with the military cam
sons serving in the 10th Cavalry. The 23rd Kansas h.. .. ..
officers with enlisted service in the Regular Army, and the governor
of Illinois, who insisted that only blacks serve as officers in the 8th
Illinois, found seven men with previous Army service, granted them
militia commissions, and relied upon them to instruct and inspire
the other thirty-two officers in the outfit.[7]

The policy of commissioning blacks as wartime officers encountered resistance from the outset. This was in part a reaction to the
difficulty in finding men with military experience but principally a
manifestation of the racism that was enshrining Jim Crow in the
statute books. Richard Croxton, a white lieutenant of the Regular
Army selected to command Virginia's black troops, promptly rid
himself of every black officer he had inherited. The unit demanded
the return of its black leaders, refused duty for several days, but ultimately became reconciled to a white command structure. The War
Department refused to accept black captains holding commissions
in the Indiana militia, though first lieutenants were deemed suitable.[8]

Black regulars encountered a new racial hostility when they entered a South where Jim Crow laws legitimized prejudice. Elements
of the 9th Cavalry, for instance, left Lander, Wyoming, in April 1898
to the cheers and good wishes of the citizenry, many of whom
had once been hostile to the presence of black troopers.[9] Townspeople gathered by the tracks and cheers resounded as the train rolled
southward, but once the men reached their new encampments, especially the staging areas at the ports of embarkation in Florida, they
found themselves second-class citizens, forced to endure a more
humilitiating form of racial discrimination than they had encountered in the West.

Captain John Bigelow, who commanded a company of black regulars, claimed that the whites of Florida could have avoided trouble
if they had shown civility in maintaining segregation, but local citizens insisted upon an arrogant style of law enforcement, and the soldiers rebelled at this treatment. In the town of Lakeland, for example, after the proprietor of the Forbes drugstore refused to serve
troopers of the 10th Cavalry, the soldiers began gathering in front of
the building. One of the blacks entered a barber shop, demanded a
shave, and was ordered to leave. White bystanders began shouting
obscenities at the soldiers, who retaliated by shooting up the barber
shop and firing wildly into the air. Before regimental officers ar-

ived and restored order, a stray bullet had killed Joab Collins, one of those that had been insulting the black cavalrymen.

The worst incident occurred at Tampa, shortly before the 24th and 25th Infantry sailed for Cuba. Drunken whites from an Ohio volunteer regiment amused themslves by shooting at a two-year-old black child, and one of the bullets cut through his clothing. When word of this outrage reached their camp, the black infantrymen ran amok, attacking white soldiers and smashing Jim Crow businesses, including brothels. Neither military nor civilian police could restore order, but a regiment of white volunteers from Georgia quelled the riot, inflicting on some thirty blacks injuries serious enough to require hospitalization.[10]

The black volunteers also faced racial discrimination when they answered President McKinley's call to arms. Encamped at Mobile, the 3rd Alabama feuded with the streetcar conductors who enforced segregated seating on their vehicles. A soldier shot and wounded one of these tormentors, causing the regimental commander, Colonel Bullard, to make sure that none of his men carried any sort of weapon off post.[11] The commander's discipline took hold. When the unit was stationed near Anniston, Alabama, townspeople abused some of the black soldiers; the soldiers refused to retaliate, but formed a column of fours and marched back to Camp Shipp. It was, said Bullard, "a wonderful display of discipline and control, the likes of which I never saw before, will probably never see again."[12] No wonder, though, that one of the companies adopted as its mascot an injured crow, which the men nicknamed Jim.[13]

All four of the Regular Army's black regiments took part in the expedition to Cuba. Together with the 1st Volunteer Cavalry, the Rough Riders, organized by Theodore Roosevelt and commanded by Colonel Leonard Wood, the 9th and 10th Cavalry formed one brigade of "Fighting Joe" Wheeler's cavalry division. Now a major general of volunteers, Wheeler had served the Confederacy during the Civil War. Space was at such a premium on board the makeshift transports carrying the invasion force that the cavalrymen had to leave their horses in Florida. As a result, the black troopers had to fight on foot, like their comrades in the 24th and 25th Infantry.[14]

The first Americans ashore in Cuba when the expedition landed on June 22 were members of Wheeler's dismounted cavalry. During the landings at Daiquiri, a boat carrying men of the 10th Cavalry capsized. Several sailors and a captain in the Rough Riders, Bucky O'Neill, plunged into the water, but despite their efforts, two men drowned. Trooper English and Corporal Cobb could not shed their heavy cartridge belts or the blanket roll that each had secured over his shoulder.[15]

After this ominous beginning, one squadron of the 10th Cavalry joined another squadron of regulars from the Regular Army's 1st Cavalry and two squadrons of Rough Riders and "marched on foot fourteen miles and, on the morning of the 24th, attacked and defeated double their number of regular Spanish soldiers. . . ." The entire 9th and 10th Cavalry were with the division on July 1, when it "cheerfully pushed onward" and, according to General Wheeler, "gallantly swept over San Juan Hill, driving the enemy from its crest."[16]

During the fighting on the 24th, which lasted roughly ninety minutes, elements of the 10th Cavalry, regulars of the 1st Cavalry, and the Rough Riders stormed a blockhouse that dominated the slopes of a ridge near the village of Las Guasimas. Taken under fire while advancing across open ground, the volunteers suffered eight killed and thirty-four wounded before the black troopers, along with white soldiers from the other regular cavalry regiment, emerged from a wood and silenced the Spanish riflemen. Actually, casualties among the regulars, eight killed and eighteen wounded, were comparable to those sustained by the volunteers. The Rough Riders might have suffered additional losses, however, had the other troopers not arrived when they did.[17] So said John J. "Black Jack" Pershing, who acquired his nickname while serving with the 10th Cavalry. Assigned as regimental quartermaster, he took part in the fight for Las Guasimas and credited his men with "relieving the Rough Riders from the volleys that were being poured into them from that portion of the Spanish line."[18]

The next objectives of the expedition were the village of El Caney and the two hills, San Juan and Kettle, that together formed the outer defenses of Santiago de Cuba. To the 25th Infantry, which had yet to disembark when elements of the 10th Cavalry were attacking Las Guasimas, fell the task of seizing El Caney. The black infantrymen stormed the village on the morning of July 1, advancing with two companies abreast. Spanish fire raked the Americans as the assault force crossed open ground, but two fresh companies moved forward to sustain the attack. Taking advantage of dry stream beds and other available cover, the men found a depression from which snipers could fire into the enemy defenses, demoralizing the Spanish, who raised a white flag before the Americans could mount their final charge. During the fighting the 25th Infantry lost seven killed and twenty-five wounded, including a captain whose life was saved when Private Conny Gray bandaged the wound and carried the officer to cover, where litter bearers placed him on a stretcher.

The other three black regiments were moving into position for an assault upon San Juan Hill and Kettle Hill, two indistinct knobs on the ridge line that guarded the eastern approaches to Santiago de Cuba. Plans called for the El Caney force, the 25th Infantry, and supporting units, to join in storming San Juan Hill, but stubborn resistance at El Caney disrupted that aspect of an unrealistic scheme of maneuver. A three-pronged attack on the San Juan heights—one thrust by way of El Caney, another across Kettle Hill, and the third bypassing Kettle Hill—proved infeasible because of the effects of distance, dense undergrowth, and hostile fire on the timing of the operation. Spanish gun crews and marksmen found convenient aiming points along the approaches to Kettle Hill—clouds of smoke from the black powder used by American field pieces and an observation balloon that bobbed above the advancing troops. Luckily, shell splinters ruptured the gas bag, which collapsed into a stream, falling slowly enough for the two-man crew to leap to safety.

While infantry advanced on either flank, the cavalry division, commanded by Samuel S. Sumner because Wheeler had fallen ill, had orders to overrun Kettle Hill, advance past a lagoon, and join in assaulting San Juan Hill. Spanish fire, however, stopped the troopers in their tracks. Convinced that the men would be slaughtered where they had taken cover, Theodore Roosevelt, temporarily in command of the Rough Riders, and some company officers of the 9th Cavalry urged the soldiers forward. Discipline and individual initiative soon took hold, and elements of the 10th Cavalry and the other dismounted regiments joined in the assault. All the attacking units lost cohesion, so that a tangle of small groups scrambled toward the Spanish defenders of Kettle Hill.

During the hectic assault, when a bullet cut down the color bearer of the 3rd Cavalry, a white regiment, Sergeant George Berry grabbed the staff and carried that unit's standard as well as the flag of the 10th Cavalry. Sergeant Horace Bivins of the 10th Cavalry, a deadly shot with rifle or pistol, brought forward a battery of Hotchkiss automatic guns and pinned down the defenders of Kettle Hill as the other cavalrymen rushed forward.[19]

All was confusion on the slopes of the hill. Frank Knox, a Rough Rider who would serve as Secretary of the Navy during World War II, became separated from his unit and found himself among the black troopers of the 10th Cavalry, whom he described in the heat of the moment as the bravest men he had ever seen. A contributing factor to this intermingling of units was the severe loss of life among the junior officers. Said John Pershing, "Our losses were 20% killed and wounded—50 percent of the officers were lost, a fearful rate."[20]

The direct attack on San Juan Hill also got off to a confusing start, for the infantry, their approach blocked by the cavalry preparing to storm Kettle Hill, came under fire aimed at the dismounted horsemen. Before the tethered balloon had expired, the observers on board it reported a trail leading past the milling cavalrymen toward the San Juan heights. The 71st New York Volunteers promptly moved forward, only to recoil in the face of enemy fire. "It seemed," said one of the New Yorkers, "that if one stuck out his hand, the fingers would be clipped off. We huddled within ourselves and bent over to shield our bellies. Overhead, a shell burst—like the popping of a blown-up paper bag."[21]

First Lieutenant Charles Taymen, regimental adjutant of the 24th Infantry, and Captain Rafferty of the 71st got the volunteers moving. They now were intermingled with soldiers of the black regiment. One element of the 24th Infantry, Captain Charles Ducat's Company D, rushed across a clearing, regrouped, and stormed San Juan Hill. In this fight Ducat himself was shot in the hip, one of his lieutenants was fatally wounded, and the first sergeant, Merriman H. Ellis, suffered a wound in the foot.[22] As the black soldiers closed with the enemy, Captain Ben W. Leavell's Company A and Company C, under Captain Charles Dodge, encountered a barbed-wire fence, had to cut their way through, and thus became further intermingled with the New Yorkers and with the regulars of the 9th Infantry. Despite the confusion, El Caney, Kettle Hill, and finally San Juan Hill were under American control by late afternoon on July 1.[23]

From the heights above Santiago de Cuba, the black soldiers could look down toward the Spanish naval squadron that had steamed across the Atlantic, sent tremors of fear along the Atlantic seaboard of the United States, and dropped anchor in Santiago Bay. Now that anchorage was untenable, and Admiral Pascual Cervera y Topete decided to attempt to break through the American squadron, superior in numbers and firepower, blockading the port. On Sunday July 3, two days after the capture of El Caney and the two hills, the six Spanish warships steamed boldly out of the bay. Each, in turn, came under the fire of American guns, and within four hours all had sunk or were aground.[24]

One black sailor won the Navy Medal of Honor in Cuban waters, but his act of heroism occurred some two weeks after the battle off Santiago. When a gasket gave way in a boiler in the USS *Iowa*, Fireman 1st Class Robert Penn balanced himself on a board placed flat on a bucket and risked falling into the scalding water that was flooding the boiler room as he extinguished the coal fire. Although Penn was the only black sailor thus honored, five soldiers, all from the 10th Cavalry, received the equivalent Army decoration.[25]

The black regulars now took up positions in the trenches around Santiago de Cuba, which capitulated in mid-July, leaving the island in American hands. Victory coincided, however, with the outbreak of yellow fever, which provided further work for some of the black regulars. In deference to the superstition that the Negro race had a natural immunity to tropical disease, the 24th Infantry received orders to provide work details for the hospital at Siboney, but roughly 50 percent of the 471 officers and men of the regiment who reported for duty there contracted the malady.[26]

Ironically, only one of the four specially recruited regiments of black immunes, the 9th U.S. Volunteer Infantry, actually served in Cuba, arriving after the fighting and remaining as part of the American garrison force. Joining this unit were two black militia regiments, the 8th Illinois and 23rd Kansas.[27] Both these organizations were composed of blacks from the colonel commanding to the newest private. They apparently arrived as the yellow fever was abating, for the elements of the garrison force, both black and whites, did not suffer as severely as the combat forces that had landed in June.

Many of the Kansans devoted almost as much energy to exploring the economic prospects in an independent Cuba free of Jim Crow laws as they did to building bridges and roads or otherwise repairing damage caused by insurrection and war. The absence of a Jim Crow tradition made Cuba seem especially attractive, although the island also boasted fertile soil, a good climate, and towns large enough to accommodate black entrepreneurs. Two Kansans, John L. Waller, a Republican politician, and John T. Vaney, a clergyman, tried to form emigration societies. They could not, however, raise the necessary capital, and the potential members proved reluctant to move to a new society, where Spanish was spoken, that was likely to be dominated by Cuba's neighbor the United States. In short, the black citizens of Kansas preferred a devil they knew to one they did not.[28]

Once Santiago de Cuba had surrendered, American forces landed in Puerto Rico. Among the invasion forces was the 6th Massachusetts, with one company of blacks. That unit, company L, participated in a few skirmishes and had one of its soldiers wounded in the finger. By mid-August Spain had agreed to negotiate a settlement, and the campaign in the Caribbean ended, except for disarming the Spanish troops and arranging passage for them across the Atlantic. The peace treaty gave Puerto Rico to the United States but affirmed Cuba's independence, though the island became in effect an American protectorate.[29]

The United States first took the offensive in the Spanish-held Philippine Islands rather than in Cuba. On May 1, 1898, Commodore George Dewey's American squadron destroyed the obsolete Spanish ships that guarded Manila Bay. When Dewey's flagship, *Olympia*, went into action, John Jordan, a black gunner's mate, was in charge of the crew that fired the first shot.[30]

Like Cuba, Spain's Philippine colony had rebelled, and Dewey hoped to make common cause with the insurgents, led by Emilio Aguinaldo, on the island of Luzon. Once American foot soldiers arrived, however, the United States demonstrated that its policy called for acquisition rather than liberation. The peace treaty with Spain, ratified in February 1899, entrusted the Philippines to the United States; by that time American troops and Filipino insurgents had already exchanged shots. In the view of Aguinaldo and his followers, the United States had replaced Spain as the oppressor.[31]

No American battleship had exploded in Manila Bay to rally public opinion behind the war in the distant reaches of the Pacific. In fact, anti-imperialist sentiment coursed through the nation, affecting even blacks, who, in general, had supported the liberation of Cuba, whose inhabitants they had considered brothers and fellow victims of oppression, in this case by the island's Spanish rulers. By now E. E. Cooper, despite his confidence in the beneficial effect of war upon race relations, had become wary of involvement in the Philippines, warning that it was impossible to Christianize and civilize a people at gunpoint, as President McKinley seemed to be proposing. Said Booker T. Washington, founder of the school for blacks at Tuskegee, Alabama, "Until our nation has settled the Indian and Negro problems, I do not think we have a right to assume more social problems." John E. Bruce, a journalist, predicted that once the pacification of the islands had begun, "liberty will be assassinated in the name of freedom." Consistent with his earlier beliefs, Bishop Turner denounced those who would wage an "unholy war of conquest" against Aguinaldo and his "feeble band of sable patriots."

Bishop Turner, in grouping American blacks with oppressed Asians, sounded a note that would reverberate for generations. More than a half century later, blacks opposed to another war in Asia, some of them also clergymen, stressed the fact that both the Vietnamese and black Americans were victims of white oppression.

The bishop's words struck sparks as soon as he spoke them. Other blacks rallied to him, some of them forming a Black Man's Burden Association—a clever parody of the "white man's burden" popularized by the British poet of imperialism, Rudyard Kipling. Whereas Kipling, along with McKinley and Theodore Roosevelt, spoke of the burden of civilizing dark-skinned peoples everywhere, these black Americans saw only the burden of suffering that was the price of thus being civilized. According to a press report, an officer in the War Department expressed doubt that black troops would fight their "Filipino cousins," and comparatively few blacks were among the hundred thousand or more Americans who served in the islands. Over the years, the black regulars shuttled in and out of the

Philippines, but only two regiments of black volunteers served there, and those for a short time.[32]

Before black opposition to the conquest of the Philippines had crystallized, the McKinley administration invited blacks to take part in the conflict, authorizing the organization of two black regiments, the 48th and 49th Volunteer Infantry. To man the new units, the War Department turned to the existing black outfits, whether Regular Army, volunteer, or militia. Among those who offered their services were five black militia officers of the 3rd North Carolina; all received volunteer commissions, and one of them, David Gilmer, attained the grade of captain and commanded a town garrison in the islands. Theirs was a remarkable vote of confidence in American society, for North Carolina's black militia had received especially ruthless treatment while stationed in Georgia. White citizens had killed four of the soldiers, and for each of the accused a plea of justifiable homicide, accompanied by a racist harangue from the defense lawyer, proved sufficient to sway a local jury.[33]

Early in 1900, not quite a year after fighting broke out between American troops and Filipino insurgents, the two regiments of black volunteers arrived in the islands, joining the black regulars already on the scene. The volunteers left the Philippines in 1901, their term of service having expired. Under an amalgam of black junior officers and white senior commanders and staff officers, the two regiments had by that time fought a number of successful engagements.

In one of the more unusual of these actions, David Gilmer, now an officer in the 49th Volunteer Infantry, came upon a defector who offered to lead a patrol from the regiment to an insurgent encampment. Perhaps because of his training with the 3rd North Carolina, Gilmer knew enough to be suspicious of his guide and had the man change clothes with one of the soldiers. Sure enough, the Filipino came under fire from a forested river bank, but the Americans were able to wade the stream, outflank the position, and capture the ambush party.[34]

During the summer of 1899, some six months before the black volunteers had reached the island of Luzon, the first elements of the Regular Army's black regiments set foot in the Philippines. First came the infantry and later the cavalry. The 25th Infantry rapidly demonstrated its skill, marching throughout the night of November 17–18, 1899, fording several streams in the darkness, and at dawn attacking the town of O'Donnell on Luzon. Surprise was complete, and fortunately so, according to Captain H. A. Leonhaeuser, who led the assault. "The natural and artificial defenses of the town," he reported, "were such that had there been ten minutes' warning of the approach of the column stubborn resistance could have been made."

His black soldiers proved "cool, able, and eager," carrying out orders intelligently and with "no wavering or disorder." The attack by
the 25th Infantry netted 128 prisoners, 11 of whom were released because they were too ill to keep pace with their captors, some 200 rifles, 10,000 cartridges, rice, and miscellaneous military equipment.[35]

Less successful was an attack by a patrol from the 24th Infantry
against an estimated 200 Filipinos entrenched on the opposite bank
of a river. The action began on the afternoon of December 29, 1899,
when an enemy volley wounded Privates James H. Thomas and Kirk
Fowles. A flanking movement then collapsed, according to the regimental commander because of "the fear that many of the men of this
organization seem to have of drowning, few being able to swim."
Not until the following morning did the black soldiers cross the
stream and occupy the trenches that the Filipinos had abandoned. A
search of the area turned up several suspected guerrillas and some
contraband of war, but the main force had vanished.[36]

Upon arriving in the islands, black regulars and volunteers encountered a propaganda campaign urging them desert the army of
oppression. Aguinaldo's pamphleteers raised many of the same
questions that had troubled black critics of the war back in the Un-
tied States. How, the Filipinos asked, could the black soldier believe
that the very government that allowed his brothers to be terrorized
and lynched was promoting justice in the islands? Even a veteran
soldier like John Calloway, the senior noncommissioned officer in
the 24th Infantry, acknowledged the feelings of guilt this propaganda aroused among black soldiers fighting in the Philippines. He
later confessed that he was "haunted by the feeling of how wrong
morally Americans are in the present affair. . . ." Despite the propaganda, no more than five blacks deserted, the most notorious of
them being David Fagen.[37]

Although his record in the United States had earned him promotion to corporal, Fagen somehow ran afoul of his sergeant shortly after his regiment landed in the Philippines. Unable to obtain a transfer out of Company I, 24th Infantry, where he considered himself the
victim of oppression, he deserted in November 1899 and cast his lot
with the oppressed Filipinos. He joined the guerrilla forces of General José Alejandro and within a year had risen to the rank of captain. Although stories circulated that he routinely murdered captured American soldiers, two of his prisoners returned to their units
and reported that they had been well treated. One of the former captives was George Jackson, a private in Fagen's old regiment, and the
other a white graduate of the U.S. Military Academy, Lieutenant
Frederick Alstaetter, who acknowledged that the deserter was a hu-

mane captor, even though he had taken the officer's ring. For two years Fagen commanded Filipino troops, who referred to him as their general, but in December 1901 a bounty hunter brought in a slightly decomposed head, a commission in the insurgent forces bearing David Fagen's name, and Lieutenant Alstaetter's West Point ring. Military authorities decided that this evidence was conclusive proof of the insurgent leader's death and marked the end of Fagen's career—one with unfortunate consequences for two other black soldiers. To discourage other blacks from emulating Fagen, Edmond DuBose and Louis Russel, deserters from the 9th Cavalry, were executed, even though President Theodore Roosevelt, the Rough Rider who had succeeded to that office when William McKinley was assassinated, commuted the death sentences of some fifteen whites found guilty of the same offense.[38]

Long after Fagen was declared dead, the fighting dragged on in the Philippines, especially among the Moslem populace of the southern islands. In August 1906, for example, some five years after a captive Aguinaldo had sworn allegiance to the United States, soldiers of the 24th Infantry, serving alongside members of the recently organized Philippine Constabulary, killed more than fifty rebels on Leyte, near the center of the island chain.[39]

Along with their Regular Army comrades, who were commanded by white officers, black volunteers had served in both Cuba and the Philippines, sometimes under officers of their own race. Yet in spite of the accomplishments of Gilmer, leading black volunteers, or of Young, a Regular Army officer commanding black volunteers, the black officer remained a rarity. When the War Department in 1901 opened the regular officer corps to some 1,100 carefully selected volunteer officers, not a single black received the necessary recommendations and survived the screening process.

Later that year, however, three blacks did achieve commissioned status in the Regular Army. One, John R. Lynch, a paymaster of volunteers, became a regular major in that specialty. (Lynch was no professional soldier; a former slave, he was a self-taught photographer, a businessman, and during reconstruction a three-term Republican congressman from Mississippi.) Another was Benjamin O. Davis, an officer in one of the regiments of immunes raised for service in Cuba; a former enlisted man in the 9th Cavalry, he now joined the 10th Cavalry as a second lieutenant. The third, Corporal John E. Green of the 24th Infantry, passed his qualifying examination to become a second lieutenant in the 25th Infantry. Excluding chaplains, the United States Army now had a total of four black officers— Charles Young, the only black graduate of the Military Academy still on active duty, Lynch, Davis, and Green.[40]

The efforts of black troops in Cuba, Puerto Rico, and the Philippines had little discernible effect on the status of the race in American society, which was understandable in view of the small number involved and the widely separated and distant battlefields. Black regulars and volunteers preparing in the South for combat in Cuba learned that racial prejudice had the force of law, and Jim Crow followed the flag, whether to the Caribbean or across the Pacific. Indeed, white officers in the Philippine Islands tended to group Filipinos and black Americans under the heading of "nigger," though insisting that the trooper of the 9th Cavalry or soldier of the 24th Infantry was a better fighter than any insurgent. In short, the black soldier stationed overseas discovered that transplanted American whites practiced the same kind of discrimination on Luzon or in Cuba that they had in Georgia or Florida. No longer were the black regiments isolated from racism as they had been on the frontier.[41]

If any one person could symbolize the failure of wartime sacrifices to improve the lot of black Americans, that individual was Theodore Roosevelt, second in command of the Rough Riders, Vice President in 1901, and President of the United States after McKinley's assassination. The sound of Sergeant Bivins's Hotchkiss guns had scarcely died away when Roosevelt acknowledged that a black cavalry regiment had fought "one on either side of mine at Santiago." He could, he told a black journalist, wish "no better man beside me in battle than these colored troops showed themselves to be," and he promised that when he wrote his account of the campaign, he would have "much to say about them."[42]

His story—dubbed *Alone in Cubia* in the Irish dialect of humorist Peter Finley Dunne—had little to say about blacks and less that was complimentary. He and his Rough Riders moved to center stage, thrusting into the wings the very men he had recently praised. Anything the black troops had accomplished, he now assured his readers, resulted from the leadership of their white officers. He told of encountering black soldiers who were drifting away from the battlefield and forcing them at pistol point to return to the front lines. Presley Holliday, a sergeant in the 10th Cavalry, challenged this account, which persisted even in the posthumous edition of Roosevelt's book, pointing out that the colonel had actually stopped four troopers on their way to a supply point to pick up ammunition. The very theatrics that appealed to Roosevelt's readers had prevented the men from refilling empty bandoleers. No wonder that during the 1900 campaign mere mention of vice-presidential candidate Roosevelt was enough to trigger protests from black audiences.[44]

6

A Great White Fleet

THE BLACK MAN was not the only object of racial discrimination in the United States. On the west coast, Japanese immigrants were feared and hated. When Japan suddenly emerged as a world power as a result of an unexpected victory over Russia in 1905, the United States became concerned about the future security of the Philippine Islands. The defeat of Russia also lent credence to vague fears on the part of some Americans that the victor might somehow seek revenge on those who tormented Japanese overseas. As a gesture of warning to Japan, President Theodore Roosevelt decided to send the American battle fleet around the world. The armada boasted sixteen battleships, including a new *Maine*. All had entered service since the victory over Spain. The crews, moreover, were to be as impressive as the white-painted ships themselves. No longer would the Navy settle for hard-drinking, brawling salts, however competent in seamanship; the new sailor would be young, well scrubbed, and well behaved. Nor were large numbers of blacks welcome in a fleet that was to demonstrate, for the benefit of an Oriental people, the superiority of the Caucasian race.[1]

For more than a century the U.S. Navy had needed black recruits, accepting them even when official policy barred all save whites. Service aboard ship was dangerous, whether on the Great Lakes or on the high seas. During the War of 1812, for instance, two American gunboats, converted from commercial vessels, were riding at anchor on Lake Ontario when a sudden squall arose. The sleeping crew members barely had time to rouse themselves before storm-driven waves were breaking over the two ships, both of which plunged to the bottom in a matter of minutes. On board one of the doomed craft, the schooner *Scourge*, was at least one black, a youth named Philips, who served as a "powder monkey," carrying explosive charges from the magazine to the guns. Luckily he had been sleeping on deck and was awakened by the thunder in time to save himself.[2]

If the fate of these two warships testified to the danger a sailor faced, the prevalence of drunkenness in the Navy afforded evidence of his boredom. Alcohol became the currency of the naval service, the records reveal, so much so that during the Civil War only three recruits succumbed to the lure of an extra 40 cents per day to serve in the fireroom of the steamship *Monadnock*, whereas seventeen signed on for the promise of whiskey. Even though the grog ration was abolished early in that conflict, the American sailor proved resourceful at distilling spirits or smuggling them on board ship. As late as 1899, the officer in charge of recruiting concluded that some of the Navy's best sailors suffered from alcoholism.

In the sailing Navy, a recruit's very life depended upon his acquiring skill and agility in scrambling aloft to handle the canvas in fair weather or foul. Since the fate of the ship was also at hazard, recruiters preferred to sign up men with seafaring experience. In 1826 the Navy introduced receiving ships where the raw recruit might learn at least the fundamentals of seamanship, but the training tended to be haphazard, so that the new hand continued to learn his duties at sea. Since recruiters emphasized experience, the port cities of the eastern seaboard provided most of the Navy's men throughout the nineteenth century. Norfolk, Virginia, and Baltimore, Maryland, supplied especially large numbers of blacks with the required seagoing background.

Various factors combined to bring blacks into the naval service. The accident of geography contributed to the phenomenon. Recruiters, in their quest for experienced hands, concentrated upon ports that happened to have in their black populace sizable numbers of men who had already served at sea or were willing to do so either to better themselves economically or simply to see the world. A more important consideration was the risk, boredom, and separation from home and family attendant upon the sailor's life. Indeed, service afloat was so unattractive that the Navy could not afford to reject men because of alcoholism or prison records, let alone race. The Navy needed men, and blacks, whose prospects ashore remained poor, were willing to serve. No wonder then that five years after Appomattox one recruit in ten was a black, who could be assigned to any duty that his white counterpart might perform.

In short, the ideal sailor in the days of wooden ships was experienced, agile, quick to obey, willing to endure danger and discomfort, and sober. Any able-bodied man who came close to fulfilling this ideal was welcome in the Navy. Race was a secondary consideration. Although the Army in this same era placed less emphasis on experience, it also sought men with the traits of agility, obedience, endurance, and sobriety. Because blacks remained segregated by law in certain regiments, race was definitely a factor. Blacks who possessed the desired qualities could find a place in either service, but the Navy, not yet burdened by segregation, could assign them as needed. In contrast, the Army had to wait for a vacancy in a specific unit, and these tended to be few, since the black soldier was likely to reenlist.[3]

The policy of the Navy changed for a combination of reasons, the most fundamental of them the enthronement at the turn of the century of Jim Crow in the North as well as the South. With the passage of time, the status of blacks on shipboard came to reflect the diminished condition of their civilian brothers ashore. Jim Crow did not stop at the gangplank. The comments of a white who served in the Navy from 1892 to 1895 reveal attitudes and practices far different from the pre-Civil War period when the two races shared mess facilities and sleeping quarters. Racism was becoming so deeply ingrained in American life that whites would rarely work with blacks unless the authorities enforced a clearcut structure with the white man at the top. Nor would whites bunk with them and eat with them in the close confines of a warship.

"The presence of blacks," this veteran of the new Navy insisted, "was a constant source of dissatisfaction which often broke out in bloody fights." As evidence he cited a "miniature race war" on the USS *Boston*, "ended by the negroes running to the officers for protection," a brawl on board the *Charleston* triggered when "a negro threw a bowl of coffee into a white man's face," and in the old frigate *Independence* "nothing less than an attempt to kill an insolent negro boasting that he could 'lick any white son of a _____ in the ship.'" The person recounting these incidents declared that he had once believed the black man "more sinned against than sinning," until a hitch in the Navy changed his mind. If anyone should advocate racial integration of ships' crews or Army regiments, the ex-sailor challenged, "Let him serve with negroes as I have done; sling a hammock among them on a hot night; eat at the same mess table with them; heave coal for a negro fireman."[4]

As the comments of this former seaman, later an Army officer, suggest, the relationship of the two races on shipboard was undergoing a gradual but radical change during the decades between the Civil War and the conflict with Spain. Accepting the notion that whites would take orders only from a member of their own race, the Navy withheld promotions from blacks so that progressively fewer of them became petty officers. Since assignment within the ship determined messing and berthing arrangements, naval authorities acceded to the racial polarization resulting from Jim Crow practices by concentrating blacks in certain specialties that kept them isolated from the rest of the crew. By the time of the Spanish-American War, more black sailors waited upon white officers, as Dick Turpin did, or tended the fires, like Robert Penn, than manned guns, as John Jordan had at Manila Bay.[5]

Without exception, the officers upon whom Dick Turpin waited were white men, for the Navy resisted commissioning blacks even though it accepted recruits from that race. This had always been so; even during the Civil War, when the U.S. Colored Troops were accepting a few black officers, the Navy offered commissions exclusively to whites, whether wartime volunteers or graduates of the Naval Academy at Annapolis, Maryland. As a consequence of this policy, Robert Smalls, after delivering a Confederate steamer into Union hands, received an appointment as an officer of Army volunteers, even though he spent most of his service afloat. The Navy Department's official reason for spurning an experienced pilot like Smalls was that he lacked appropriate training at either the Naval Academy or a school for volunteer officers.[6]

After Appomattox, a black candidate occasionally received an appointment to the Naval Academy and tested the waters there. The seas inevitably proved stormy, for, as happened within a similarly closed community at West Point, the white midshipmen joined forces to isolate and expel the intruder. Indeed, the arrival of the first black, James H. Conyers of South Carolina, put a vicious edge on the hazing practiced at Annapolis. Conyers survived harassment and isolation but succumbed academically, declining an opportunity for special tutoring.

In September 1873, a few months after Conyers had departed, Alonzo McClennan, also from South Carolina, arrived at the Annapolis institution. A white midshipman brought vague charges of misconduct against the newcomer, who denied his guilt, but the white man's word prevailed, and McClennan would have been dismissed had the Secretary of the Navy not intervened. Other incidents followed, but the black midshipman held firm until, according to McClennan, two faculty members promised to assure him an education elsewhere if he would resign from the academy. He left, studied medicine, and became a successful physician.

Next to enter the Naval Academy was Henry E. Baker of Mississippi. Once he was jumped by several white midshipmen while on the way to class, and another time an officer had to draw a sword to protect him from his classmates. The superintendent decided, however, that Baker's unpopularity stemmed not from racism, but from his use of an "opprobrious epithet" when another midshipman, while sitting in the mess hall pushed a chair into the black youth's leg. Expulsion was automatic, but the Secretary of the Navy again took a hand. Baker, however, refused an offer of reinstatement and became a clerk in the U.S. Patent Office.[7]

Some twenty years after Baker's departure, the superintendent of the Naval Academy faced the possibility that two young blacks, fully qualified to enter the institution, would arrive at Annapolis in the summer of 1897. Captain P. H. Cooper warned Secretary of the Navy John D. Long that a lonely existence awaited any black who entered the academy. "He will not of course be *persona grata* with the other cadets," the superintendent declared, predicting that any such newcomer would "lead a solitary and forlorn existence in social relations." He would, after all, "have no associates of his own color, for he cannot look to the servants and messengers for companionship."[8] Cooper indicated, however, that if the two blacks could endure four years of ritualized isolation and make the necessary progress in the classroom, they would graduate, as Flipper, Alexander, and Young already had graduated from the Military Academy. In fact, neither of the young men reported at Annapolis, and no black would join the register of Naval Academy graduates until 1949.[9]

The exclusion of blacks from the officer corps, total in the Navy and almost so in the Army, represented an interpretation of Darwinism that pointed to the Anglo-Saxon as the noblest product of human evolution. When in 1880 General Schofield compared the white cadet to a thoroughbred racehorse and the black man to a "common farm horse," he was consciously or otherwise giving voice to this belief. Representative of its acceptance among naval officers was Rear Admiral John Grimes Walker's practice of donning gloves when he might have to shake hands with racially inferior members of a Haitian government. The use of natural selection to demonstrate the superiority of a certain race or even an elite group was not unique to the American military or naval services or to Americans in general. Nor was it the result of formal instruction in Darwinian theory at the service academies. It was the product of the application of a half-understood biological theory to social processes, a misalliance used to rationalize such varied phenomena as anti-Semitism and colonialism.[10]

The departure in 1907 of the Great White Fleet—as the force of battleships was known—confirmed the changed status of blacks in the Navy. Many officers in a battle fleet about to set sail on a voyage designed to intimidate Japan had Japanese servants living on shipboard. The Navy Department, suddenly concerned about the possibility of sabotage, ordered these men replaced. The jobs went to black sailors, regardless of the specialty in which they had trained. One officer complained that the blacks, plucked from their normal duties and pressed into service as personal servants, became impudent. Anger caused by the demotion in status from real sailor to sea-going servant may have contributed to a melee between black and white seamen at Cherbourg, France, one of those outbursts in which racial resentments boil up like thunderheads and then subside.[11]

In this steam age the Navy was looking for a new type of sailor, and in this quest recruiters spread their nets wide, enlisting men from rural towns in the eastern states, from the South, and from the Midwest. Experience at sea appeared less desirable than it had during the age of sail, and the sketchy indoctrination provided on a receiving ship was giving way to comprehensive training at recruit depots and on shipboard, as farm hand or grocery clerk learned to operate the machinery and weapons of the steam-driven warship. The Navy wanted young men amenable to discipline and willing to learn, rather than old salts, many of them difficult to discipline, frequently drunk, infected by venereal disease, or given to waterfront brawls.[12] But the Navy not only needed a different kind of enlisted man, it required more volunteers than previously. Whereas 130 men handled the *Andrew Doria*, the Navy's first warship, the flagship *Connecticut* of the Great White Fleet required 827, and the USS *Wyoming*, commissioned in 1912, had a complement of 1,063.[13] The new Navy thus depended upon young, white volunteers whose attitudes reflected the Jim Crow legislation that was taking hold throughout the nation. Thus realities of recruiting, as well as their own pseudo-scientific bias, persuaded naval leaders to turn their backs on the black sailor. Rather than risk alienating potential white recruits, the Navy accepted few, if any, blacks and segregated those in the service from their white shipmates.[14]

Some naval officers found themselves caught between preserving segregation, which they believed had become necessary, and being fair to a race that for generations had produced capable sailors for the fleet. If the Navy was to pay heed to that "prejudice on the part of some men against working alongside, messing with, or billeting near the negro," wrote one such officer, only one solution, other than concentrating blacks in one or two specialties, seemed possible. Lieutenant Commander T. P. Magruder, acknowledging the right of the black citizen to enlist and conceding that he could become a competent and disciplined seaman, proposed setting aside certain ships for Negroes, just as the Army had done with four of its regiments. Except for officers and senior petty officers, the crews would consist of blacks, along with "Hawaiians, Samoans, and Camorros." Such a plan, Magruder argued, would improve opportunities for promotion and ensure that the black sailor would have "more company of his kind and be freed from the prejudice of a few of another color who may not be his superior physically or in the qualifications for the ratings they hold."[15]

Maintaining racially separate ships was too expensive for serious consideration, however. As a consequence, blacks continued to be scattered throughout the fleet, although assigned to a messmen's branch made up of seagoing servants. When 6,000 sailors paraded in New York City shortly before America's entry into World War I, not one black marched among them. In explaining this phenomenon to black leaders, President Woodrow Wilson's Secretary of the Navy, Josephus Daniels, explained that only members of the deck divisions were eligible to participate and that all the blacks serving in the ships were messmen and therefore disqualified.[16]

Except for a few men in the engine rooms, black sailors were waiting table and preparing food for officers. Those very officers preferred Oriental servants, who seemed neater, quieter, less sullen—in short, less threatening than black Americans—but Japanese servants had been expelled in 1907 from the wardrooms of the Great White Fleet. Fortunately for the sensibilities of the officers, America's new Pacific empire soon yielded an acceptable substitute for the departed Japanese, the Filipino messman, and, by the outbreak of World War I in Europe, Filipinos outnumbered blacks in the naval service.[17] Although the hulls of its warships now were painted grey, the U.S. Navy in its racial composition remained a Great White Fleet.

Nor did the demands of World War I affect the racial composition of the Navy. Of some 238,000 enlisted men on active duty in 1919, a few months after the fighting ended but before demobilization began, roughly 6,000 were blacks, not even 3 percent of the total, compared to 5 percent of a much smaller Navy in 1907, the year the battle fleet set sail around the world.[18] There were, of course, no black officers. About two dozen black women served as members of a uniformed auxiliary, the so-called yeomanettes, that performed office work for the Navy. All the black yeomanettes did their typing and filing in a single racially segregated office within the Navy Department at Washington, D.C.[19]

A black who served on a ship based in the United Kingdom during the war discovered that his white shipmates considered themselves duty bound to keep him in his place, that place having been defined by Jim Crow. The sight of a black sailor with a woman not of his own race could trigger a riot. On at least one occasion British civilians, who disliked seeing their women with any American, took off in unsuccessful pursuit of an offending black sailor. In this incident being an American was a greater incitement to violence than being black, but race was the consideration, rather than nationality, when white sailors from the battleship *Texas* reacted in the same way upon seeing a black, in the uniform of the United States Navy, accompanied by a white woman.[20]

The restrictions on the enlistment and assignment of blacks, under way before World War I, continued afterward. By 1919 Jim Crow was master, for in the summer of that year the Navy refused to accept any more first enlistments by blacks. Those already in the service might reenlist, but many of the veterans who had become petty officers and specialized in engine-room duties, or even gunnery, were attaining retirement age and leaving the service. Also, the postwar demobilization was in process, so that many of the vacancies caused by the departure of blacks need not be filled. If essential openings did occur, except among the stewards or messmen, whites were promoted into them. Consequently, by the end of 1941 the Navy had just twenty-nine blacks who were not messmen, and all but six of these had been summoned from retirement to serve during the national emergency.[21]

During the time that new enlistments by blacks were forbidden, the number of black messmen declined rapidly, as did the total in the enlisted force. By 1932, the Navy had just 441 blacks on active duty, about one-half of 1 percent of the small, peacetime service. In the meantime, because so few messmen were needed, the Navy had in December 1930 suspended first enlistments by Filipinos. The demand soon increased, however, for new ships were being designed and built in order to fight the Great Depression, if not a specific armed enemy, by creating jobs in the nation's shipyards.

In seeking recruits for an expanding messmen's branch, the Navy found Filipinos less attractive than before. Congress was planning to grant the islands eventual independence, and even in a transitional commonwealth status the Philippines would prove an uncertain source of recruits if the United States ever should go to war with Japan. Consequently, the Navy in January 1933 announced that it would accept new enlistments from black Americans interested in becoming stewards. Successful candidates, who had signed on at any of a half-dozen southern cities, attended a school at Hampton Roads, Virginia, where they learned their duties.[22]

Many naval officers continued to prefer Oriental mess attendants to the newly trained blacks. The Filipinos enjoyed the reputation of being neater and healthier, less prone to complaining, and likely to eat less food than their black counterparts. The earlier objections to recruiting in the Philippines still prevailed, but the Navy did arrange in 1937 to sign up Chamorros, residents of Guam, an American possession, with an initial quota of ten enlistees per month. Not until after World War II did the Navy obtain the Filipino stewards it had coveted, when an agreement with the Republic of the Philippines, which became independent in 1946, permitted citizens of the islands to enlist as messmen.[23]

Despite recurring objections by those they waited on, the number of black messmen increased about tenfold between 1933 and 1940.[24] The naval expansion begun in response to the Depression intensified with the approach of war. Once again the Navy turned to blacks to perform a task that others shunned. The job it offered was unattractive not because of danger or loneliness, as had been true in the age of sail, but because few Americans wanted to become seagoing servants.

From before the voyage of the Great White Fleet in 1907 until the mobilization for a second world conflict, the Navy followed a racial policy completely at variance with its practices during most of the nineteenth century. When Jim Crow came to define the relationship between the races in civil life, whites no longer would associate freely with blacks, whether on shipboard or elsewhere. Since the Navy had come to need many individuals with the aptitude to operate complicated machinery—instead of the comparatively few veteran hands, black or white, who could work aloft in foul weather—it could not alienate potential white recruits, who had the desired aptitude, by accepting blacks. On top of this, the members of an exclusively white officer corps, confident of the superiority of their race and aware of the poor education received by so many blacks, did not believe that the black man could master steam propulsion or electricity with the facility of the white recruit. At best, the black sailor could function as a seagoing servant, and in that capacity he was judged inferior to the Filipino.

7

A Racial Battleground in Texas

THOSE BLACKS who agreed with E. E. Cooper, the Washington, D.C., newspaper editor, that participation in the war against Spain would bring about a new era in race relations found their hopes betrayed. Jim Crow not only survived the conflict but thrived afterward, manifesting itself in the segregation of the United States Navy and the abolition of the black militia units that had reappeared in a few southern states and answered the call to fight the Spanish.

By the spring of 1906, Booker T. Washington was asking Secretary of War William Howard Taft "if it is legal for any states to refuse to give the colored people any recognition whatever in the state militia and still draw their quota from the public fund to support the state militia." Several states in the South, the black educator reported, had "recently mustered out all of the colored companies."[1] A glance at the latest militia law, enacted in 1903, persuaded Judge Advocate General George B. Davis that the federal government could not intervene in the operation of the newly established National Guard, provided that a state observed the regulations governing the age, citizenship, and training of the militiamen.[2] Some sixty years would pass before the military establishment began concerning itself with the racial composition of the reserve components.

Federal authorities thus stepped aside as the National Guard units formed in the South under the new law systematically excluded blacks from membership. By the time the United States went to war against Germany in 1917, there were some 5,000 black National Guardsmen, but they were concentrated in two regiments, the 8th Illinois, dating from the Spanish-American conflict, and the recently organized 15th New York. Single companies thrived in a variety of places—Massachusetts, Ohio, Maryland, the District of Columbia, and Tennessee—but not a single unit hailed from the deep South.[3]

During the first decade of the twentieth century, the Regular Army underwent expansion to provide the forces needed to defend the empire acquired as a result of the war with Spain. Despite the prevalence of racial discrimination in every aspect of American life, the possibility existed that blacks might find a place in the expanded Army. Or so some prominent blacks believed. Citing the contributions of black troops in previous wars, especially the success of Sergeant Bivins and his battery of Hotchkiss guns at Kettle Hill, Emmett J. Scott, personal secretary to Booker T. Washington at the Tuskegee Institute, chose this bleak time to ask President Theodore Roosevelt that "six of the batteries of Field Artillery and not less than eighteen of the companies of Coast Artillery added by the act of congress, approved January 25, 1907, be recruited with colored men." The average black citizen, Scott insisted, was making "great progress along intellectual and financial lines commensurate with the opportunities which have been offered. . . ." If black soldiers received a chance to serve in the artillery, considered the most mentally demanding of the combat arms, he predicted that they would prove the equal of whites.[4]

Scott's proposal went to the War Department, where it got a mixed reception. Lieutenant Colonel T. W. Jones of the General Staff's Military Intelligence Division surveyed recent census data on black employment and concluded that too few men had civilian skills indicative of success in artillery training. He then submitted a recommendation that begged the question, calling for experimental units, instead of permanent ones, if blacks should be admitted to the artillery.[5]

Although Jones waited cautiously to see which way the wind would blow, Major Cornelis DeW. Willcox spoke out boldly against recruiting blacks for the field or coast artillery, declaring that to do so would "open a running sore that may never heal." The major, himself an artilleryman, denied almost everything that Scott had said, insisting that "white troops alone" had fought all the "really serious battles" in America's past wars and suggesting that blacks had gained their freedom after only token sacrifice. He thus ignored, among other actions, the battles at New Orleans in the War of 1812 and at Fort Wagner in the Civil War, the campaigns against the

Apache and Cheyenne tribes, the storming of the heights defending Santiago de Cuba, and the dangerous but thankless patrolling that had helped pacify Luzon and other of the Philippines. Willcox was willing to concede the black man's courage, though he insisted that this attribute was shared "in common with a vast majority of the rest of the human race."

Courage, moreover, was not enough, for the artilleryman had to be intelligent and mechanically gifted. According to Willcox and the prophets of white supremacy that he cited, the black American lacked precisely these qualities. To prove that the black man was neither intelligent nor mechanically gifted, the Army officer cited studies on such diverse topics as the plantation Negro after emancipation and the supposed racial traits of black Americans, flotsam on a pseudo-scholarly tide that sought to prove the superiority of the white race. Willcox, the soldier, was a convinced racist, but he had the company of respected scholars in that regard.

Impartial census data provided the foundation for the case against training blacks for the artillery, since statistics demonstrated that blacks gravitated into domestic service and farming. Without inquiring whether aptitude and preference or limited opportunities and external pressure dictated this tendency, the Army officer decided that "there can be but one explanation for this: the negro has so far been found lacking in the skill and intelligence needed in the handling of machinery and mechanical appliances." The black soldier was unfit for the artillery because, as Willcox explained, the "modern gun is a machine . . . served and operated by machines, steam and electric." Furthermore, the electrically triggered underwater mine used in coastal defense was "nothing but a complicated machine to secure a certain mechanical effect." Although willing to concede "the probable ability of negroes to learn to shoot guns of larger caliber," he doubted that they could understand their functioning or aim them accurately.

Another argument against assigning blacks to the coast artillery was the prevalence of Jim Crow practices. From Fortress Monroe in Virginia to Galveston, Texas, southern communities were to provide National Guard units prepared to augment the Regular Army garrisons in time of emergency. As long as all coast artillerymen were whites, the local white militiamen could train and serve alongside them, but the introduction of black regulars would force the southern jurisdictions to choose between maintaining segregation and participating in their own defense. Willcox had no doubt that the states of the southern Atlantic and Gulf coastlines would elect to preserve racial segregation. "Whatever value the enlistment of negroes might have in itself," he warned, it could not be "comparable to the value of organizing an efficient local defense over the entire seaboard. . . ."

Apart from the Army's embrace of the Jim Crow philosophy, if any single incident kept the artillery exclusively white, it was the Brownsville riot. Indeed, to clinch his argument against recruiting black artillerymen, Willcox cited the "late disturbance at Brownsville" as an "illustration, if any be needed, of what may be expected in the South if this plan of negro companies be insisted upon." Yet the facts of the disturbance to which he referred proved to be open to acrimonious debate.[6]

In the spring of 1906, the 1st Battalion, 25th Infantry, received orders to proceed from Fort Niobrara, Nebraska, to Fort Brown at Brownsville, Texas, for training with the Texas National Guard. Three years earlier, white Texas militiamen training at Fort Riley, Kansas, had clashed with black soldiers. Since that time amity between the races had further deteriorated, causing the regimental chaplain to predict that Texas would become a battleground for the black troops.[7]

The men of the 1st Battalion were reluctant to serve in Texas, and the city government of Brownsville did not want them. When federal officials in Texas protested the transfer, Secretary of War Taft calmly replied that since racial prejudice had taken root throughout the nation, the arrival of black troops would arouse objections whatever the choice of encampment. The orders stood as issued, and on July 28 the unit arrived near the mouth of the Rio Grande.[8]

Although Cornelis DeW. Willcox, the artillery officer opposed to assigning blacks to the coastal fortifications, would describe Brownsville as "largely peopled with northerners,"[9] the citizens had enthusiastically adopted a code of Jim Crow laws. Whatever Willcox believed, the inhabitants of Brownsville had embraced racism, which was sweeping the entire country, North and South. When the contingent from the 25th Infantry arrived, the men found that most businesses and even the city parks bore signs that forbade the black Americans to enter. Unfounded stories circulated that black soldiers had tried to rape white women, and white men frequently showed their hatred of the recently arrived troops. These actions went beyond mere enforcement of the statutes requiring racial segregation; individual whites punched or threatened black troops who had done nothing to provoke this kind of treatment. Two privates, Newton and Lipscomb, described by their company commander as "very reliable men and very quiet soldiers, very inoffensive in their manner and everything," managed to offend Brownsville's whites, even though they did nothing illegal. As the two members of the battalion were walking past two white women, a customs officer named Tate, the husband of one of the women, suddenly and unjustifiably accused Newton of pushing her and struck him over the head with a pistol. Tate then threatened Lipscomb, who was at worst a bystander. Later, another customs officer, a white man named Baker, encountered another black soldier, Private Reed, who had been drinking in Mexico, and "booted him off the sidewalk into the river"—treatment more vindictive than a drunken white was likely to have received.

To the battalion's white officers, this treatment of black soldiers seemed unexceptional. For example, Captain E. A. Macklin conceded that Newton was "offended" by the blow to the head but insisted that the private was neither injured nor especially resentful nor bent upon revenge. The captain also accepted Reed's smiling assurances that he had deserved to be thrown into the Rio Grande. Similarly, a local policeman, Victoriano Fernandez, one of the Hispanic Americans who made up a majority of the town's populace, could think of no reason why any of the soldiers should harbor resentment about the citizens of Brownsville.[10] Both Macklin and the policeman believed that for a white to kick a black was the natural order of things and that the victim accepted this treatment with good-humored resignation.

On the morning of August 14, a few minutes after midnight, firing erupted in the vicinity of Fort Brown. In the ten minutes that followed, witnesses testified, a group of men numbering between six and twenty fired as many as 150 shots in the three-block area that bordered on the fort. One man was shot to death as he tried to bolt the doors of the bar where he worked. A bullet struck a Brownsville policeman and injured the man's arm so severely that it had to be amputated. Despite the extreme darkness on the street he was patrolling, he identified his assailants as black soldiers. Another civilian suffered a less serious wound, and gunfire narrowly missed several other persons, including members of the family living in the house next door to the Tates.

At the sound of rifle fire, the sentinel on duty at Fort Brown discharged his weapon three times to alert the guard. The sergeant in charge immediately order the bugler to call the garrison to arms, but minutes passed because the soldiers had to break open one of the locked rifle racks as they prepared to repel what some of the men believed was an attack by townspeople. Shots still echoed through the darkness as the battalion formation took shape, but no assault materialized and quiet returned to Brownsville.

The discovery after dawn of cartridges and clips from the Army's new Springfield rifle lying in the streets provided evidence that some of the infantrymen might have been involved in the shooting. The battalion's officers, however, could find no one who would admit knowledge of the incident.

Despite the absence of either confessions or informants, the same troops that Macklin and officer Fernandez thought docile and free of resentment now became murdering brutes in the eyes of the local populace and on the editorial pages of many newspapers throughout the country. Two investigations followed, the first by the commanding general of Army troops in the Southwest and the second by the Inspector General of the Army, E. A. Garlington, who endorsed the earlier finding that the men of the battalion had entered into a conspiracy of silence to protect those who actually did the shooting. As a result, military authorities could not determine who had fired the shots. The old image of the black man as inherently untruthful, and clannish as well, had persisted since the days of slavery. Even an educated and experienced officer like Garlington accepted the myth.

Willing to believe the worst about the black solider, as he had concerning the imagined cowards at San Juan Hill who actually were ammunition bearers, President Roosevelt promptly accepted Garlington's recommendation to punish the criminals, even though there was insufficient evidence to court-martial anyone, by taking administrative action against every enlisted man and noncommissioned officer who might be involved. Except for a handful of men on leave or detached duty, every black soldier in the three companies of the 1st Battalion was dismissed from the Army and barred from further services in the armed forces or civilian employment by the federal government.[11]

Later, in explaining his action, Roosevelt cited two especially striking precedents, both involving Robert E. Lee. According to research done by a former corporal, now a War Department clerk, the first incident had occurred on the eve of the Civil War when Lee, still an officer in the United States Army, had ordered all the men in a company discharged dishonorably when their enlistments ended because he could not discover which of them had committed a murder. A recent newspaper clipping stated, moreover, that Lee had inflicted the same sort of mass punishment on a battalion of the Army of Northern Virginia after soldiers of the unit had shown cowardice in action.[12]

The announcement of the President's decision, delayed until after the 1906 congressional election, shook a black community that had remained loyal to the Republican Party. From Tuskegee, Booker T. Washington gave voice to "the feeling the colored people now have as a whole regarding the dismissal of the three colored companies." He told Secretary of War Taft that "the race is not so much resentful or angry, perhaps, as it feels disappointed."[13]

The fact that Washington spoke out indicated the shock felt by black citizens, for he was gaining the reputation among younger black leaders of always trying to reach accommodation with white authority. The black press was less polite than the founder of Tuskegee, calling for black troops to refuse to reenlist. The first issue of *The Crisis*, the official publication of the new National Association for the Advancement of Colored People, recounted a recent incident in Ohio, where white troops had killed two persons while freeing their fellow soldiers from jail. On that occasion, the accused had received the right to counsel and a formal trial; such legal niceties had been dispensed with at Brownsville.

The victims of President Roosevelt's rough justice had at least one white champion, Senator Joseph B. Foraker, like the Chief Executive a pillar of the Republican Party. Foraker, a veteran of the Civil War, represented businesses like Standard Oil at least as diligently as he did the people of Ohio. He was patriotic, attentive to the desires of the nation's industrialists, and completely out of sympathy with Roosevelt's attempts to regulate business practices. In addition, the senator hoped to gain his party's presidential nomination in 1908.

The Brownsville incident gave Foraker a chance to break Roosevelt's grip on the next nominating convention. Although Democratic state governments employed rigged literacy tests, poll taxes, and outright intimidation to bar blacks from voting in state or national elections, southern blacks could become delegates to the Republican national convention, where they might help decide the party's nominee for President. Before Brownsville, these black delegations seemed certain to back Roosevelt or his hand-picked successor, who certainly would not be Foraker. Despite the President's disparaging remarks about the conduct of black troops in Cuba, which caused his popularity among Negro voters to sag for a time, he was a member of the party of Lincoln and in firm control of a number of federal appointments that could go to southern blacks. The President's treatment of the men of the 1st Battalion, 25th Infantry, might undermine this support, enabling Foraker to emerge as the defender of these soldiers and thus to establish a useful following in time for the convention.

Although the senator was no doubt influenced by his ambition to succeed Roosevelt, as well as his distaste for the President's reformist tendencies toward American business, he also realized that an injustice had been done. Foraker was determined to right the wrong. He therefore proposed that the Senate investigate the

Brownsville affray and the decision of the President to impose punishment without trial.[14]

At the Gridiron Club dinner at Washington, D.C., in January 1907, Roosevelt and Foraker clashed. What traditionally had been an evening of humorous, off-the-record speeches became a violent debate over the President's handling of the Brownsville incident. The senator stressed the lack of due process, paraphrasing remarks by the Chief Executive to the effect that no innocent person—and some of the soldiers obviously were innocent—would ever lack the full protection of the law.[15] Roosevelt lashed out in reply, charging that some of the black troops were "bloody butchers" who "ought to be hung." He further declared that the only reason they had not been executed was "because I couldn't find out which ones did the shooting."[16]

When the Senate Military Affairs Committee completed the hearing that Foraker had sought, a majority endorsed the President's action, though four of the nine senators urged the adoption of an act enabling the President to readmit to the Army, within one year, any members of the 1st Battalion that he decided were innocent.[17] A minority of four senators declared that the evidence upon which the Chief Executive had based his decision did not "sustain the charge that soldiers of the Twenty-fifth Infantry . . . participated in the shooting affray that occurred at Brownsville, Texas, on the night of August 13–14, 1906." Two members of this minority, Senators Foraker and Morgan Bulkeley of Connecticut, also a Republican, went even further, insisting that "the weight of the testimony shows that none of the soldiers . . . participated in the shooting. . . ."[18]

A brilliant attorney, Foraker not only saw discrepancies that others had missed but used them to construct the theory that he and Bulkeley now advanced. The critical items were the clips and cartridges found at about dawn on August 14. Although witnesses reported as many as 150 shots fired, a search of the streets turned up just forty expended cartridges and a half-dozen empty clips. All six of the clips, each capable of holding five rounds, and seven of the cartridges lay in a circle just 10 inches in diameter. Had a rifleman fired the seven shots from his weapon as he stood in one place, the normal pattern of ejection would have scattered the brass over an area roughly twelve times as large.

Examination under a microscope revealed that the other thirty-three cartridges had been fired from four of the battalion's rifles. Three of the weapons belonged to Privates Thomas Taylor, Joseph L. Wilson, and Ernest English, who had returned them to the racks when their company entered the barracks after the night's excitement ended. The following morning an officer inspected these Springfields and found them "perfectly clean and bright, showing no evidence whatever of having been fired during the night." The three men, moveover, had not had an opportunity to clean the rifles before the inspection. A sergeant named Blaney had left the other Springfield behind when he went on leave, and on the morning after the shooting that rifle had reposed in a locked chest in a storeroom, a piece of paper bearing the sergeant's name undisturbed in the barrel.

A close examination of the brass cartridges revealed other irregularities. Three of them showed two indentations at the base, indicating they had failed to fire, been extracted and ejected, reloaded, and then fired. Ammunition had frequently failed to fire and been used again in precisely this fashion at Fort Niobrara, when protective grease had slowed the action of the recently uncrated weapons. Marks on nine other of the rounds revealed that they had been extracted from the chamber and reinserted before firing, as though a range officer had ordered the weapons cleared during target practice and then reloaded—again a procedure that had often been followed at Fort Niobrara. On the streets of Brownsville, however, the rifleman would have had to extract the round slowly and catch it or, if he missed, grope for it on the darkened street, hardly what a terrorist would choose to do.

How did these unusually marked cartridges, many of them traceable to just four rifles, come to appear on the streets of Brownsville? After all, three of the weapons had been spotless just hours after the incident, and the fourth was locked up during the shooting. All four of the Springfields, however, had been fired on the range at Fort Niobrara, and, as Foraker pointed out, the battalion had brought with it to Texas some 2,000 pieces of brass, expended cartridges salvaged at the Nebraska installation and carefully placed in boxes. One container of the casings had rested on the back porch of a barracks at Fort Brown, easily accessible to anyone visiting the post.

Finally, one of the bullets recovered after the fray could not have been fired from a Springfield, and the others could just as readily have come from a Krag or a Mauser, neither of which had been issued to the men of the battalion. The bullets, therefore, were not consistent with the cartridges that had been used as evidence.

On the basis of what he had discovered, Foraker concluded that there had indeed been a conspiracy, not the conspiracy of silence alluded to by the President, but a successful attempt by townspeople owning Krag or Mauser rifles to frame the soldiers and rid Brownsville of the black battalion. A few handfuls of brass had shifted blame from the actual culprits to the men of 25th Infantry. The President, Foraker and Bulkeley argued, should restore to duty any member of the 1st Battalion who swore that he neither had taken part in the outrage nor knew of anyone who had.[19]

Angered by Foraker's challenge, President Roosevelt seized upon the majority report as justification for his action, although he did endorse, as his tenure in office came to an end, an extension of the period in which the President might reinstate any of the soldiers found to be innocent.[20] He also announced that in the year since the committee's investigation two black detectives, William Lawson and Herbert Browne, had obtained a valid confession from Boyd Conyers, formerly a private in Company B.

Foraker could not let this parting statement pass unchallenged. The newspaper publisher William Randolph Hearst had made public letters proving that the senator had been on the payroll of Standard Oil throughout the time that he and his colleagues were debating legislation affecting the corporation. Roosevelt had pounced on his old adversary, using Hearst's revelations to help put an end to Foraker's presidential hopes. The Ohioan, however, was not about to fade meekly into the twilight.

Once again Roosevelt had yielded to impulse, hearing what he wanted to be told. As he had in accepting the stories about Robert E. Lee's use of mass punishment, which turned out to be dubious, the President did not ask for proof. His adversary did. Foraker contacted the peace officer who had been present during the questioning of Conyers. Sheriff E. C. Arnold of Monroe, Georgia, responded that Conyers had denied any wrongdoing, despite a "most severe cross-examination." The story of the confession, declared the sheriff, was "most absolutely false" and a "most willful misrepresentation of the truth."[21]

After the President left the White House, the War Department assembled a board of officers to conduct further hearings under the extension approved by Mr. Roosevelt. In all, 14 of the 167 men who had received dishonorable discharges were reinstated. With the passing of time, the former President may have realized the magnitude of his error; in any event, when he wrote his autobiography, he devoted not one word to his handling of the Brownsville incident.[22]

Apparently President Roosevelt could deal with members of the black elite but simply did not understand the fears and hopes of the black laborer or soldier, or for that matter those of the white workingman. Although he slighted the achievements of black soldiers in Cuba and dismissed the Brownsville garrison, Roosevelt at times made overtures toward the black community, usually dealing with either leaders of national stature or persons trained in professions like education or the law. Upon accepting the vice-presidential nomination, he had consulted with blacks like W. H. Lewis, a football star at Amherst College and a graduate of the Harvard law school. After becoming President, he appointed Lewis an assistant United States attorney and received the lawyer's support for the Brownsville decision. An educated black man bent upon the advancement of his race, Lewis had to choose between retaining a position of influence or sacrificing the good he might accomplish in order to speak out for some common soldiers in far-off Texas. Lewis was one of several blacks with whom Roosevelt had at least occasional dealings. Thomas Goode Jones, like Lewis a black Republican, became a federal judge in Alabama. The appointment of Jones caused no uproar among southern whites, but such was not the case when Booker T. Washington dined at the White House with Roosevelt. The ensuing furor caught the Chief Executive by surprise, and he soon was describing his invitation to the black educator as an impulsive gesture.[23]

Almost seventy years would pass before the United States government rectified the injustice inflicted upon the black soldiers of the Fort Brown garrison. In 1972, possibly in reaction to demands by Augustus Hawkins, a black congressman, the administration of President Richard M. Nixon intervened on behalf of the soldiers. Acting Attorney General Richard Kleindienst asked that the Army correct the inequity. Instead of citing the arguments that Foraker had constructed, the cabinet officer focused upon two points—the likelihood of prejudgment, as indicated when Inspector General Garlington told the Senate committee that he did not consider blacks to be truthful, and the absence of any precedent for mass punishment of this sort. The incidents involving Robert E. Lee, which had been provided to the President, could not be substantiated in the records of the War Department.

By this time, only one member of the Brownsville garrison was still alive, 86-year-old Dorsie Willis, who had made his living since being dishonorably discharged by working as a porter and bootblack. Although the Army's Board for the Correction of Military Records changed his status and that of the other ex-soldiers to honorably discharged, no provision was made for back pay or other compensation. Congress stepped in, however, and passed a private bill granting Willis $25,000 and arranging for him to receive at a Veterans Administration hospital treatment for the infirmities of age.[24]

In general, Texans like the white citizens of Brownsville treated Americans of Mexican descent with arrogance and contempt similar to that lavished upon blacks. White Americans living in isolated towns or on ranches along the border became concerned when Francisco "Pancho" Villa, the Mexican bandit and revolutionary leader, began trying to overthrow his former comrade, Venustiano Carranza, the provisional president of Mexico who now enjoyed the support of the United States. Villa might use the mistreatment of Hispanic Americans, as well as the endorsement of Carranza, to justify forays onto American soil.[25] To the United States government, revenge seemed less likely to motivate Villa than the need for money and supplies to continue his unsuccessful war against Carranza. In recent years the United States had become increasingly worried that chaos in Mexico was an invitation to European or even Japanese penetration. American sailors and marines had landed at Vera Cruz in 1914 to enforce order, and Villa now seemed potentially as dangerous as the forces that had been contending for power during that year. As a result, the U.S. Army received orders to strengthen its border garrisons, even as Mexican rebels launched a campaign that culminated in a night attack upon Columbus, New Mexico. After midnight on March 9, 1916, the Villistas raided the town, killing fifteen Americans, seven of them soldiers, and wounding thirteen, including five civilians. The attackers, however, lost more than seventy men killed or captured, for the Columbus garrison recovered from its initial surprise and pursued Villa's force a short distance into Mexico.[26]

A week later Brigadier General "Black Jack" Pershing led some 5,000 men across the Rio Grande to locate and scatter the Villistas, thus putting an end to the threat of further attacks. While the Carranza regime hesitated, at first seeming to agree to the expedition and then objecting, Pershing moved southward. Included among his troops, which ultimately numbered 15,000, were the black soldiers of the 10th Cavalry, led by Colonel William C. Brown.[27]

The black regiment spent the rest of March trying unsuccessfully to run Villa to ground. Not until early April did Colonel Brown's command encounter the enemy, a group of Villistas that opened fire from the adobe buildings of the Aguas Calientes ranch and pinned down the regiment's advance guard. Brown immediately ordered Charles Young, the black graduate of West Point who was now a major, to prevent Villa's men from breaking contact and fading away.

Major Young led two troops of horsemen up a hill overlooking the ranch, then ordered his detachment to dismount and open fire. Meanwhile, the colonel ordered the machine-gun unit, led by Captain Albert E. Phillips, to fire over the heads of Young's troopers into the valley. Upon Brown's command, Young ordered his men to mount up, form a single rank, and, pistols at the ready, trot down the slope. The machine guns cut loose, and the defenders fled from the approaching riders. The skirmish had little effect on the course of the so-called Punitive Expedition, but it did mark a tactical innovation. The charge at Aguas Calientes was the first time that American troops had attacked with the support of overhead machine-gun fire.

En route from Aguas Calientes to the town of Parral, the 10th Cavalry learned that another regiment, the 13th Cavalry, had been ambushed. The black troopers broke camp at once and rode to the rescue, sounding bugle calls unique to the American Army— officers' call and a call to attention—as they approached Santa Cruz de Villegas, where a squadron of the 13th Cavalry had dug in. Legend has it that Major Frank Tompkins, commanding the besieged unit, told the leader of the relief force, "By God, Young, I could kiss every black face out there."

"If you want to, you may start with me," Major Young replied.[28]

Tompkins and his men had taken refuge at Santa Cruz de Villegas after advancing to Parral and being driven off by the garrison. Some 600 Mexicans, presumably members of Carranza's armed forces, had opened fire, killing two of Tompkins's cavalrymen and triggering a response in kind that may have claimed as many as forty Mexican lives. Carranza's army apparently considered the Americans, rather than the Villistas, to be the real enemy.[29]

Mexican demands that the Americans withdraw from the country inspired President Woodrow Wilson to take advantage of a National Defense Act, adopted in June 1916, to mobilize the National Guard and begin sending the federalized units to camps along the border. In the meantime, he sought to avoid either a loss of national prestige or a violent confrontation with the increasingly hostile Carranza government as he gradually extricated the Pershing expedition. The armed clash that Wilson did not want took place nonetheless, and it involved the 10th Cavalry.[30]

As the various National Guard units were reporting for duty, two understrength troops of the 10th Cavalry formed a composite group, totalling just eighty-two officers and men, and undertook a reconnaissance mission. General Pershing relied upon Captain Charles T. Boyd to scout the countryside beyond the town of Carrizal. Although Pershing later declared that he wanted the troopers to avoid a fight, both Boyd and the other company commander, Captain Lewis Morey, interpreted the general's instructions as orders to fight their way through the town if necessary. On June 19, 1916, when a Mexican garrison barred the way, Boyd directed the troopers to dismount and advance.

Fire from Mexican machine guns checked the Americans at an irrigation ditch and killed Boyd, who already had been twice wounded. Corporal John Jeter crawled to the fallen officer, discovered that he was beyond help, and removed from the captain's body all maps and papers that might have been of use to the enemy. The corporal then returned to a wounded man, a sergeant named Lyons, to whom he had been giving first aid. A Mexican patrol rode up; Jeter opened fire and drove them off, though not before they had put three bullet holes through his clothing. The corporal attributed his escape to the hand of God; in fact, he later exchanged his saddle for the pulpit, forsaking the cavalry to become a minister.[31]

Meanwhile Captain Morey, himself wounded, ordered the troopers to fall back, but he had difficulty extricating his command. Although reports of American casualties varied, Boyd and as many as twelve others perished, ten to twelve were wounded, and twenty-three or twenty-four men were taken prisoner, a total that probably included some of the wounded. Captain Boyd's attack had resulted in a sobering defeat, but Carranza's men, who probably lost at least seventy-five killed and wounded, most of them victims of long-range rifle fire, lacked the strength to exploit their success and do battle with Pershing's main force.[32]

National Guard units were now converging on the border, lending authority to Wilson's demands that Mexico release the prisoners taken at Carrizal. Although resistance to the United States no doubt enhanced Carranza's popularity, he did not want war. As a result, he not only agreed to free the captives but also offered to enter into negotiations with the Americans.

President Wilson, too, was under pressure to end the intervention, for war was raging in Europe and the likelihood of American involvement was increasing. Relations between the United States and Germany had come to depend upon German respect for the neutral shipping that plied the Atlantic. The Chief Executive could not afford to become bogged down in Mexico when the United States might yet be drawn into the World War if German submarines should sink American merchantmen or passenger liners.[33]

Several months of negotiation restored peaceful relations between the United States and the Carranza government. Pershing's command started northward in January 1917, and the last American soldiers crossed the Rio Grande on February 5. Villa remained in the field, however, harrying his Mexican adversary, though the rebel chieftain's influence and power were declining, the result of his failure to defeat Carranza or stand up to the better-trained Americans of the Punitive Expedition. In June 1919, Villa tried to recoup his fortunes by attacking Juarez, across the Rio Grande from El Paso, Texas. The assault forces enjoyed early success, but Carranza's men rallied and contained their enemies in one part of the city.

American troops, including black riflemen of the 24th Infantry, stood poised around the Texas city in the event the fighting crossed the Rio Grande. The Villistas, their plans frustrated by the Mexican garrison, began firing onto American territory, and the 24th Infantry, together with cavalry units, retaliated, crossing into Mexico, attacking behind accurate fire from howitzers, and routing Villa's men. Pancho Villa lived until 1923, but his power in northern Mexico had been shattered.[34]

In January 1917, as the Punitive Expedition packed up and withdrew from Mexico, Germany decided to launch a campaign of unrestricted submarine warfare designed to bring Britain and France to their knees. Although the undersea campaign in the Atlantic would claim neutral ships among its victims and might therefore bring the United States into the conflict, Germany's leaders believed that help from the United States could not arrive in time to save the European allies. President Wilson had already made the maritime rights of neutrals a potential cause of war and could not ignore the sinking in mid-March of three American merchant ships within twenty-four hours. Congress on April 6, 1917, heeded his call to arms and declared war.[35]

With Villa still at large—his defeat at Juarez lay some two years in the future—the United States had to keep a fairly large force on the border regardless of events in Europe. Indeed, some six weeks before America's entry into the World War, British intelligence intercepted, decoded, and made public a message in which the German government sought to enlist Mexican help in the event of war with the United States. Following an American defeat, Germany promised Mexico would get back the southwestern United States, territory wrested from Mexico some seventy-five years earlier.[36]

One of the units sent to the Southwest was the 3rd Battalion, 24th Infantry, which in July 1917 received an assignment some distance from the border. The black soldiers of this organization were to set up a temporary encampment on the outskirts of Houston, Texas, and provide guards during the construction of nearby Camp Logan, a base where National Guard troops were to train. Following the declaration of war on Germany, the battalion received a draft of new recruits, but it soon lost twenty-five veteran noncommissioned officers chosen for a training course designed to produce black junior officers. The departure of these experienced men had a serious impact on an outfit in which the white officers were of varying quality. The battalion commander, Lieutenant Colonel William Newman, had proved himself a conscientious leader, but with few exceptions the company officers showed scant interest in their men and spent as little time as possible at the camp.

By Texas standards, Houston exuded racial harmony. Some 30,000 blacks, roughly 23 percent of the populace, lived in the city. Although concentrated in clearly defined areas, they supported more than eighty churches, were wealthy enough to sustain their own merchants and professional men, and carried on an extensive social life that included an annual celebration of the end of slavery in Texas. The black community functioned almost independently of the dominant white society. Contacts between the two races were few and usually between black employee and white employer. But, as in other large towns throughout the South, there was one continuing source of friction—a galling Jim Crow law that required segregated seating on a streetcars. For two years, beginning in 1903, Houston blacks had boycotted the transit company in an unsuccessful attempt to force the authorities to abandon this hateful policy.

If Houston's racial climate was mild for a city in Texas, it was harsh compared with California or Wyoming, where the 24th Infantry Regiment had served after returning from a second assignment in the Philippines. The soldiers resented the Jim Crow practices, and like the blacks living in the city, the recently arrived troops focused their anger on the segregated streetcars. Men of the battalion defied the motormen charged with enforcing Jim Crow seating, removed the screens separating the white and colored sections, and threatened to derail the cars.[37]

In addition, troops from the 24th Infantry had to put up with racist insults from the white workmen who were building Camp Logan. Besides being called "niggers," the soldiers could drink only from water cans labeled "colored." "This word 'nigger,'" an Army inspector later reported, "appears in practically every disorder reported, and with the same result; a display of anger on the part of the soldier, with profane and abusive language and threats of vengeance." Since the Houston police habitually used the term, often as the prelude to a beating, the troops harbored an abiding resentment against those who enforced the law.[38]

Colonel Newman's advice to respect the law and obey the police fell on deaf ears. Perhaps not even the strongest of leaders could have prevented a clash between the black soldiers of the 3rd Battalion and the white citizens of Houston, but Newman did not have the chance. He received a new assignment and entrusted the unit to Kneeland S. Snow, recently promoted to major, who had spent about six months with the 24th Infantry.[39]

On the morning of August 23, 1917, one of the soldiers happened upon Lee Sparks, a member of the Houston police force, who was beating a black woman he was arresting. When the soldier objected, Sparks clubbed him and had him taken to jail, under arrest for interfering with a lawman in the performance of his duty. Next on the scene was Corporal Charles W. Baltimore, one of a group of military police who patrolled Houston to steer their black fellow soldiers away from trouble. Baltimore, though not on duty, asked Sparks about the other soldier from the 3rd Battalion, and the policeman responded by beating him and, when the corporal ran, firing at him, then pursuing him into a nearby house and arresting him.

Captain Haig Shekerjian, battalion adjutant, arranged for the release of the two soldiers and persuaded the chief of police to suspend Sparks for the unprovoked attack on Baltimore. The captain and the battalion commander explained to the senior noncommissioned officers that Baltimore and the other man were free and that Sparks was being disciplined. This news, however, did not calm the black soldiers. Snow took steps to restrict the men to camp, but, as an investigating officer later reported, neither he "nor any of the officers of his command appeared to have had the slightest suspicion of an outbreak," until some of the men began passing out ammunition, loading their weapons, and heading toward town. Leading the group was a sergeant who earlier had warned Major Snow of possible "trouble with the men."[40]

Among the hundred or more armed soldiers marching into Houston was Corporal Baltimore. His presence in the mob testified to the failure of the regiment's white officers to understand their men. Not even Captain Shekerjian, considered one of the most competent of the lot, could put himself in the place of a young black man, bruised and humiliated by an unjustified and brutal attack. Although descended from a persecuted minority—he was born in Turkey of Armenian parents—the adjutant had spent his childhood in Connecticut, graduated from West Point, and embarked on a comparatively successful military career. As a result, despite his genuine concern for his black soldiers, he now shared to a great extent the insensitivity of America's racial majority. He simply did not realize the depth of Baltimore's resentment, the desire for revenge that lurked beneath the young corporal's calm exterior. The captain apparently felt that for a black man to be beaten by white authorities was so much the natural order of things that it would not possibly stir the victim to mutiny.[41]

In a two-hour rampage, the mutineers killed fifteen whites or Hispanic Americans and wounded twelve, one of whom later died. Some of the dead were victims of stray shots; others were calmly murdered, as the troops advanced upon the police station nearest the battalion's bivouac. Although Sparks was not among the victims, four of his fellow officers were shot to death and a fifth sustained fatal wounds.

A white officer of the Illinois National Guard, Captain Joseph Mattes, was riding in the rear of an open touring car when he encountered the rioters. He leaped to his feet and tried to halt the rampage, but the black soldiers saw one of the hated Houston police in the automobile and in the darkness may have assumed that the captain and the three enlisted men with him also were members of the force. A deliberately aimed volley of fifty shots killed Mattes and the policeman and wounded two of the three soldiers.

Four of the mutineers lost their lives. One suffered a fatal wound during an outbreak of random firing before the troops left the bivouac area. One succumbed to gunshot wounds inflicted by white citizens, even though a National Guard officer succeeded in bringing him to a military hospital. Another was mistaken for a policeman by his fellow rioters and shot to death. Finally, Vida Henry, the very sergeant who had warned Major Snow of trouble and then taken command of the mutineers, killed himself, thus resolving the conflict between his sworn duty and what he apparently saw as his obligation to his fellow blacks.[42]

After the riot, the entire battalion was sent to Columbus, New Mexico, to join the rest of the regiment. There military investigators found that 156 men had missed roll calls held during the rioting and had presumably taken part in the mutiny. Unwilling to resort once again to mass punishment, Army prosecutors offered grants of immunity, obtained testimony, and amassed enough evidence to charge sixty-three persons with mutiny in time of war, as well as premeditated murder. A court-martial, which convened at Fort Sam Houston, San Antonio, Texas, found fifty-four men guilty of both crimes and sentenced thirteen of them to hang; the others were ordered confined at hard labor for the remainder of their lives. Five men went free, and four, judged guilty of lesser crimes, received prison sentences of at least two years. On the morning of December 22, 1917, three days before Christmas and two hours before the government announced the court's decision, Charles Baltimore and twelve other men were hanged from a common gallows in an isolated part of Camp Travis, adjacent to Fort Sam Houston. The timing represented an effort to minimize the reaction to the execution, whether by resentful blacks or the jubilant whites who believed that justice had been done. Black newspapers reacted with charges of military lynching, but the white press in the North and the South endorsed the punishment.

A second court-martial, also held at Fort Sam Houston, meted out justice to fifteen men charged with leaving their posts at Camp Logan, where they were standing guard, to take part in the mutiny. This proceeding convicted five soldiers of desertion and murder, ordering them hanged, and found the other ten guilty of lesser crimes that carried sentences of from seven to ten years at hard labor.

In the meantime, the Army was gathering evidence to try another forty soldiers. This last proceeding, which came to an end in March 1918, resulted in eleven sentences of death. Twelve men were judged deserving of life imprisonment, fourteen received lesser periods of confinement, two were acquitted, and the charges against one man were dropped.[43]

As a result of a new policy adopted because of protests by blacks following the December executions, President Wilson had to review the sixteen cases in which the defendants faced the death penalty as a result of the second and third courts-martial. Secretary of War Newton D. Baker advised the Chief Executive that "many members of the colored race" had responded to the thirteen earlier hangings with a "formidable petition" urging clemency for the others. Letters from blacks all over the country, he observed, were pleading that no more of the soldiers be executed. Moreover, a grant of clemency would please a segment of the populace that was "giving . . . repeated evidence of patriotic devotion . . . both by their service in the Army and their purchase of Liberty bonds. . . ." Black America seemed to have recovered from the first hangings and the secrecy that had surrounded them; "the execution of these new death penalties, it is said, would come as a shock and reopen an old wound." Secretary Baker therefore recommended the death penalty only for those persons guilty of murdering a specific individual—all five of the soldiers from Camp Logan and one of those condemned by the third court-martial.[44]

Mr. Wilson accepted Secretary Baker's advice, and six more of the mutineers died on the gallows in September 1918. For about five years the National Association for the Advancement of Colored People campaigned to obtain the release of the imprisoned rioters. The government resisted, however, reducing sentences or granting releases a few at a time, so that the last of the men to be freed served twenty years in the Leavenworth, Kansas, federal penitentiary.[45]

Locally, the Houston riot triggered savage repression of blacks, even though the civilian populace had taken no part in the violence. Policeman Lee Sparks—whose "brutal, unwarranted, and unjustified attack" on Charles Baltimore had, in the opinion of an Army investigator, contributed to the uprising—went his bloody way. During 1917 he shot two blacks to death while making arrests; indicted for murder after the first incident, he was acquitted by a trial jury in a matter of minutes.

The men of the 24th Infantry were gone, but black National Guardsmen of the 8th Illinois remained at Houston. Soon they were defying the Jim Crow seating regulations on city streetcars, causing the War Department to withdraw the unit in order to break the cycle of oppression and reaction. The murderous attempt to teach Houston a lesson had claimed the lives of sixteen whites and twenty-three blacks but left race relations in the city in the worst state since emancipation.[47]

As events would prove, the consequences of the Houston riot extended far beyond the city itself and were discernible twenty years later. The mutiny sent the same kind of shock through the Army that Nat Turner's rebellion had inflicted upon pre-Civil War southern society. The War Department had to overhaul its plans and avoid large concentrations of black combat troops. Military leaders also became concerned about the loyalty of American blacks in the aftermath of the hangings. In order to ensure black support for the war against Germany, the Army came to accept troops that it rather would not have had, find assignments for them that would separate them from whites, assign them to comparatively small units, and thus minimize the possibility of other riots like the outburst at Houston. The distrust of blacks lingered beyond World War I, and self-proclaimed patriots, like the members of the newly reconstituted Ku Klux Klan, would cite complaints in the black press of the wartime mistreatment of black soldiers as proof of disloyalty. As late as 1940, during mobilization for a second world conflict, racists were still citing the mutiny at Houston in warning against the malicious provocations of black activists.

8

World War I:
The Results of Closing Ranks

DESPITE THE HANGINGS of the Houston mutineers, some educated blacks believed that World War I afforded an opportunity to break the cycle of white discrimination, black violence, and white repression by demonstrating a willingness to fight for the United States. Some of the more outspoken leaders, men who had protested the executions that followed the riot at Houston, looked upon wartime military service as a vehicle for the betterment of the entire race. As late as the summer of 1918, W. E. B. DuBois, who argued that educated blacks (in his phrase the "talented tenth") should lead the struggle for equality, was urging his fellow blacks, "while the war lasts, to forget our special grievances and close our ranks shoulder to shoulder with our own white fellow citizens and the allied nations that are fighting for democracy."[1]

Not every black leader echoed the optimism voiced by DuBois. A. Philip Randolph, who would become a bold and successful spokesman for black Americans, pointed out that Crispus Attucks had died in 1770 but slavery had persisted for another century. Blacks had fought in the Revolution and all subsequent wars, but the sum of their sacrifices still had not brought full citizenship. He did not believe that this latest conflict would produce different results as far as his race was concerned.

The Navy and Marine Corps were not at all interested in having blacks fight shoulder to shoulder with whites. Following the policy established by William Ward Burrows in 1798, the Marine Corps continued to exclude blacks. Indeed, marines pressed into service as stevedores in France complained of having to work with "niggers"— American members of Army stevedore battalions—instead of fighting Germans, which they considered suitable work for white men. Most of the blacks serving in the Navy were stewards, except for a scattering of veterans, some of them recalled from retirement, who had learned other specialties.[2]

Prior to the Houston riot, the Army proposed to use blacks and saw no problem in attracting them to the recruiting office, although too large an influx could arouse opposition among congressmen from the South. In the words of Major General Tasker H. Bliss, assistant to the Chief of Staff, "The negroes seem to take naturally to military service and at this moment at the snap of a finger we could recruit all of our colored regiments to war strength and plenty more." To do so, he realized, would require the cooperation of the southern congressional delegations that might balk at the prospect of a future, five or six years hence, when the "entire negro population" of their region "will have been trained to arms."[3]

Despite the comments of General Bliss concerning the military aptitude of blacks, the War Department proved reluctant to accept them. The pseudo-scientific racism of the period contributed to this wariness, as did the practical difficulty of absorbing a large number of black recruits while maintaining segregated training and housing facilities. Immediately after the declaration of war, the Army did attempt to bring all its regiments to full strength through voluntary enlistment, accepting some 650,000 recruits, but taking just 4,000 of them to fill out the four black units.

The enactment of selective service legislation, which contained no provisions regarding race, brought large numbers of blacks into the Army, not because the administration of the law was color-blind, but because blacks were not represented on draft boards. With their future in the hands of whites willing, if not eager, to ship them out of the community, blacks had little hope of avoiding military service unless they failed to meet the physical or mental standards. In all, more than 2 million black registrants produced 367,410 soldiers, roughly 13 percent of the total number of draftees.[4]

On August 1, 1917, General Bliss approved a plan to find assignments for the first group of blacks to be drafted, some 75,000 men. Sixteen new infantry regiments would absorb 45,000 of them, while the others would join "special units," serving as bakers, drivers, or laborers.[5] After three weeks—indeed, on the day following the Houston mutiny—the policy suddenly seemed "too dangerous."

In a study begun before the violence in Texas but submitted and approved afterward, a committee of three members of the General

Staff persuaded Secretary of War Baker to withdraw his approval of the plan to train the sixteen regiments of black infantry. General Bliss, Brigadier General Joseph E. Kuhn, and Colonel P. D. Lochridge concluded that sixteen regiments were too many, for blacks and whites would have to train at the same cantonments, at times in nearly equal numbers. "If either or both get out of hand . . . ," the committee warned, "nothing short of a national calamity would be the result."[6] Shortly after the three generals completed their deliberations, a new policy emerged. In the aftermath of the violence at Houston, the War Department would organize one black division—four infantry regiments rather than sixteen, plus field artillery and other integral elements—and allow it to train as little as possible with weapons before shipping it overseas for further instruction. All black draftees not assigned to this division would serve in noncombat units. Besides making limited use of the blacks obtained through selective service, the division would serve as a symbol of involvement in the war behind which black Americans, angered by the executions in Texas, could rally.[7]

Some three months before the rioting at Houston, Secretary of War Baker suggested that the Army War College, which functioned at the time as a policy planning agency, investigate the possibility of training black junior officers to help lead the units being formed from the pool of black draftees.[8] General Kuhn, who headed the War College Division of the General Staff, endorsed the idea. "That colored officers should not be assigned to white organizations requires no argument," he observed, "yet it is believed that there are many colored men of good character who, with training, would make suitable company officers for the colored organizations forming part of the contemplated drafted force." Despite his willingness to accept black junior officers, Kuhn believed that blacks made better soldiers under white leadership; white field grade officers—majors through colonels—would make up for the black lieutenants and captains. He also invoked what in later years became a recurrent theme—that the use of blacks was "more of a political than a military question," implying, as would be done early in World War II, that politics required some sacrifice in military efficiency.[9]

The Wilson administration could not ignore the enthusiasm being shown by educated blacks to join the war effort. College men tended to agree with DuBois that wartime service could become a path to equal rights, although a few saw the irony of calling upon blacks to fight abroad for the rights denied them at home.[10] Typical of the attitude among black college students was a declaration by a committee of undergraduates at Howard University, Washington, D.C., who pointed out that "the Negro has had no chance to fight under his own leadership" and urged that officer candidates "pour into . . . camp in overwhelming numbers." Describing the officer training program as "the greatest opportunity since the Civil War," the committee warned that a "terrible responsibility" faced educated blacks, for the government had "challenged the Negro race to prove its worth, particularly the worth of its educated leaders."[11]

Idealistic and serious young men like these began discharging their self-imposed responsibility at Fort Des Moines, Iowa, where the War Department in June 1917 opened an officer training school for blacks. Plans called for 1,250 men to undergo instruction, 1,000 of them civilian volunteers or enlisted members of mobilized National Guard units. The Regular Army's four black regiments would provide the remainder, 250 noncommissioned officers, including a draft that deprived the 3rd Battalion, 24th Infantry, of a stabilizing influence shortly before the Houston riot.[12]

The creation of a black division with newly commissioned black junior officers should have renewed the War Department's interest in Charles Young. Now a lieutenant colonel, he had led troops into combat during the Punitive Expedition into Mexico, and in the war with Spain he had demonstrated his skill in training, organizing, and disciplining large bodies of inexperienced recruits. Unfortunately, Young became a victim of Jim Crow, sacrificed to the symbol of racism with the approval of President Wilson.

A white officer of the 10th Cavalry, First Lieutenant Albert S. Dockery, had complained that as a southerner, he found it distasteful to take orders from a black superior. Alerted to Dockery's plight by Senator John Bell Williams of Mississippi, the President promptly sided with the junior officer, suggesting that the Secretary of War transfer the lieutenant to a white regiment.[13] Had the Chief Executive not intervened, Secretary Baker might have rejected the appeal for special treatment. Dockery, he believed, should "either do his duty or resign," since there was "nothing else we can do about it." Once the President had intervened, Baker agreed to the transfer.[14]

Secretary Baker and General Bliss soon discovered, however, that they would have to do something even more distasteful than transfer the lieutenant. Additional members of the Senate, apparently approached by other white officers of the 10th Cavalry who feared that Young would assume command of the regiment, brought pressure to bear against the veteran black soldier. After toying with the idea of transferring the lieutenant colonel to Fort Des Moines, where he would command officer candidates of his own race, the Secretary of War found a more devious solution that avoided, on the surface at least, the racial question. Young was transferred to the retired list on the grounds of medical disability, a finding that astonished him. To demonstrate the soundness of his health, he rode on horseback from his home in Ohio to Washington, D.C., but to no avail. Instead of taking command of a regiment or major installation and almost certainly pinning on a brigadier general's star during the Army's wartime expansion, he received orders to report as a military adviser to the adjutant general of the state of Ohio.[15]

Unable to convince the War Department that he was fit enough for active duty, Young remained on the retired list until five days before the hostilities ended. With Germany on the verge of collapse and the Army about to return to its prewar size and rank structure, he received command of a training camp in Illinois. After the war, while serving as military attaché in Liberia, he went on leave to Nigeria, contracted a tropical fever, and died. In his career he had trained black troops for combat and led them in action, but the fear that he might command whites prevented him from wearing the stars of a brigadier general or contributing to victory in the World War.[16]

Although he shelved Young, the Secretary of War did accept a black assistant, Emmett Scott, who was to provide advice on racial matters. The War Department looked upon the appointment as a concession to black Americans, a symbol more than anything else, and rarely heeded his counsel. Scott failed, for example, to reverse a policy that discouraged the promotion of blacks beyond the grade of captain. An associate of Booker T. Washington, he was committed to working for equal treatment, but he sought to do so by erasing the image of the Houston riot, with its murders and executions, which he felt had aroused fear among whites and thus served to justify repression. Better to work quietly than to risk stirring up further resentment on the part of the white majority.[17]

Secretary Baker's War Department had committed itself to organize one black division, manned largely by draftees, and as many small, noncombat units as might be necessary. The various companies and platoons of the division would be led by graduates of the training course at Fort Des Moines, who would function under the close supervision of white senior officers. This combat organization was the 92nd Division, organized in November 1917. The four black regiments of the Regular Army remained scattered among isolated outposts along the Mexican border or served in the Philippines or Hawaii. Possibly because of the violence at Houston, these units served mainly as a source of noncommissioned officers or officer candidates for the 92nd Division and for another black division that the War Department discovered it would need.

The additional black division, set up in December 1917, absorbed the mobilized black National Guard units—the 8th Illinois (withdrawn from Houston not long after the riot) and outfits from

New York, Connecticut, Maryland, Massachusetts, Ohio, Tennessee, and the District of Columbia. Once again the Army had to accommodate a large number of blacks, these at least partially trained, without doing violence to racial segregation. Designated the 93rd Division (Provisional), this organization had its full complement of four infantry regiments but lacked the usual trains (quartermaster, ordnance, transportation, and the like), artillery regiments, or engineer components. To fill out the two brigades, which the infantry regiments formed, the War Department used blacks drafted from the state of South Carolina.[18]

The number of men assigned to combat units totaled some 42,000, but this represented a bucketful drawn from the vast reservoir of black manpower created by the draft. The total in these organizations amounted to just 11 percent of the 380,000 blacks serving in the wartime Army.[19] The vast majority of the 42,000 combat soldiers, perhaps 90 percent, served overseas with the 92nd Division or the 93rd Division (Provisional). The others manned the four understrength regiments—the 9th and 10th Cavalry, the 24th and 25th Infantry—in existence since shortly after the Civil War. An additional eight infantry regiments, authorized in May 1918 to help absorb future draft calls, had not taken shape when hostilities ended.[20]

The other black soldiers—some 89 percent of the total and some 80 percent of the 200,000 who served in France—reported to hastily established service units.[21] (The other 20-odd percent were the 42,000 combat troops.) Typical of these were the quartermaster labor battalions, whose members, often under the supervision of white officers and noncommissioned officers, unloaded ships at ports in France or loaded cargo vessels on the east coast of the United States. Black officers eventually began serving in some of these units, but the freshly commissioned lieutenants tended to be men who had either failed the course of instruction for artillery or proved excess to the needs of that branch. When black officers joined a labor battalion, the white noncommissioned officers were withdrawn and transferred to organizations where they would be taking orders from officers of their own race. In the heyday of Jim Crow, the idea that a black could supervise whites was utterly unthinkable.[22]

The training of black combat units proved at best uneven. The components of the National Guard units assigned to the 93rd Division (Provisional) consisted of officers and men who had served and trained together at least since President Wilson had called them to the colors and in some cases for months or even years before mobilization. Much of this experience had consisted of armory training, however, and when the four regiments went to France, they had to learn the tactics of trench warfare. During this combat indoctrination, the regiments might receive guidance from a succession of French officers, each of whom had different tactical concepts. The disruptions of normal training caused by transfers of instructors could be severe. Indeed, according to an American liaison officer, the provisional division's 370th Infantry, after one month of instruction in France, had neither dug trenches nor taken part in target practice nor engaged in tactical exercises.[23]

No better trained were the draftees of the 92nd Division, who received their introduction to military service at seven widely separated cantonments, sometimes under the supervision of inexperienced junior officers or noncommissioned officers. Upon arriving in France, elements of the division underwent a front-line indoctrination lasting no more than a week and in some instances as little as a few hours. Far from producing the kind of "blooded" division that senior commanders considered the most effective, this brief introduction to combat, carried out under French direction, probably served only to show the officers and men how woefully unprepared they were for actual warfare.[24]

Whether training to fight or to serve as laborers on roads or docks, the black soldier encountered racial discrimination both in the United States and in France. While the 92nd Division was preparing at Camp Funston, Kansas, for combat overseas, its commanding general, Major General Charles C. Ballou, formerly an officer of the 24th Infantry and commandant of the training course at Fort Des Moines, imposed restrictions on his draftees that regulars would have found hard to accept. In the spring of 1918, when one of his black sergeants was refused admittance to a civilian-run theater and responded with angry words, Ballou issued a bulletin that placed blame for the incident not on the theater manager, but on the victim of the Jim Crow practices. According to the general, "the row should never have occurred and would not have occurred had the sergeant placed the general good above his personal pleasure and convenience." Although the sergeant was legally right in seeking admission and the manager legally wrong in barring him, the noncommissioned officer was "guilty of the greater wrong in doing *anything*, no matter how *legally* correct, that will provoke race animosity." He urged his men to "place the general interest of the Division above personal pride and gratification," to avoid "every situation that can give rise to racial ill-will," to attend "quietly and faithfully to your duties," and to avoid those places "where your presence is not desired."[25]

Whereas the prewar regulars had tended to form an isolated and disciplined community, the draftees of Ballou's division had ties to various towns and cities. Relatives learned of the general's attitude, and a flurry of protest erupted that was reported in the black press.[26] Churches and other organizations joined in sending resolutions of protest to Secretary of War Baker, and a group of black editors called for an end to Jim Crow travel restrictions, the suppression of lynching, and acceptance of the negro as a full partner in the war effort—in short, "acceptance of help where help is needed regardless of the color of the helper."[27] Such was the background of the appeal by W. E. B. DuBois that his fellow blacks forget their special grievances, close ranks with whites, and endure "gladly and willing, . . . eyes lifted to the hills."[28] But by the summer of 1918, a number of predominant blacks no longer shared DuBois's enthusiasm for the war or appreciated any longer the efforts of Joel T. Spingarn, a white who had been the first president of the National Association for the Advancement of Colored People and had led the fight to gain for blacks the opportunity to become Army officers. An undercurrent of resentment stirred the black populace, a result of the executions of the Houston rioters and the treatment black draftees were receiving in the wartime Army. Groundless stories circulated that Spingarn, a major in the wartime military service, had joined DuBois in selling out the black race to the Wilson administration.[29]

Ultimately, DuBois himself became disillusioned, principally because of the treatment black troops received overseas. General Pershing's expeditionary headquarters set the tone, advising members of a French military mission how to deal with black Americans. "We must," the members of this mission concluded, "prevent any pronounced degree of intimacy between French officers and black officers. We may be courteous and amiable with these last, but we cannot deal with them on the same plane as with the white American officers without deeply wounding the latter." In addition, French officers were to moderate their praise of black troops, especially in the presence of white Americans, and prevent "the local cantonment populations from 'spoiling' the Negroes." Especially to be discouraged were "any public expressions of intimacy" by white women toward black men, a sight that white Americans—and French officers who had served in the nation's African colonies—found offensive.[30]

Since black troops comprised less than 3 percent of General Pershing's combat strength, his headquarters could, without undue military risk, devote more energy to monitoring their behavior than to preparing the men for trench warfare. The War Department expected little of its black soldiers, looking upon the 92nd Division as a means of ensuring that American Negroes would continue to support the war effort. As for the men of four infantry regiments that made up the 93rd Division (Provisional), the Army's high command believed they could best serve as laborers on the lines of supply in France or as replacements for casualties suffered by the other black combat organization, the 92nd Division.[31]

The commanding general of the 92nd Division, Charles Ballou, admitted that his unit performed poorly, as its detractors had predicted. In doing so, he placed the blame upon the junior officers and men, blacks whom he considered obedient, content, and able to endure hardships, though lacking in initiative and easily panicked. He conceded, however, that the War Department had erred in its choice of white officers. The black rifleman needed firm leadership, Ballou maintained, preferably from white officers, but certainly not from the kind of white all too frequently assigned to the division—the comparatively senior officer who remained "rabidly hostile to the idea of commissioning blacks." Ballou insisted that some blacks, though "in no great numbers," could become competent officers, and he objected to lowering standards in order to obtain the desired 1,250 black officer trainees. The 92nd Division, which he had so confidently taken overseas, might have lived up to his expectations, he believed, if the Army had stressed quality rather than numbers in commissioning blacks and assigned white officers not poisoned by racial prejudice.

The very few blacks who could meet the standards demanded of white officers should, Ballou declared, have the same chance as whites for promotion. The War Department, he insisted, had made a serious mistake in reserving the senior grades for white officers, since this policy had deprived even the best black captains or first lieutenants of any hope of advancement. The general who had led the 92nd Division throughout most of its existence remained a study in contradictions, paternalistic in his attitude even as he demanded that black officers prove themselves. On the other hand, he argued that blacks were "entitled to equality of opportunity"; on the other, he believed that "the average negro" was a "rank coward" in night combat, "the natural result of environment and education," a condition that left the black soldier dependent upon white leaders, like Ballou, who understood him.[32]

Serving with the French during the Meuse-Argonne offensive, September 26 to October 5, 1918, the 92nd Division performed sluggishly, remaining mainly in reserve where it provided depth to the assault until the front narrowed and the Americans no longer were needed. So disappointing did General Ballou find his unit's performance that he decided to rid himself of the least capable of his officers, going so far as to demand that thirty of them, each a recently commissioned black, be court-martialed for cowardice. Trials of this sort were not unusual in wartime, and in his own mind the general was being color-blind, absolutely impartial, merely applying the same standards to blacks as to whites. The courts-martial, however, were composed exclusively of whites, for he believed that blacks would protect one another, placing race before justice.

Four officers had already been found guilty and sentenced to death (subsequent to a review that reduced the punishment to imprisonment) when the 92nd Division passed under the control of the American Second Army, commanded by Robert L. Bullard. Now a lieutenant general, Bullard was formerly an officer in the 3rd Alabama Volunteer Infantry, a black regiment mustered into service to fight the Spanish. As much a believer in white supremacy as Ballou, Bullard had created a notable cohesiveness among his black soldiers some twenty years earlier. He now hoped to do the same for the 92nd Division, an impressive accomplishment should he succeed, for General Pershing had long since given up on the unit.

Bullard's first action was to confer with the black junior officers and sound them out, as best a general could, about Ballou's campaign to punish cowardice. He came away convinced that these lieutenants and captains accepted the need for proceedings of this kind but bitterly resented the absence of blacks from the boards.

Bullard's attempt to improve communication may have helped. Whatever the reason, in the closing days of the war one brigade of the 92nd Division gained ground against the Germans, cutting its way through barbed wire, beating back counterattacks, and even going to the aid of an adjacent French unit halted by the strong defenses. Unfortunately, the other brigade continued to behave as Pershing and his staff expected, moving too slowly for the army commander and causing Bullard to lose patience with the entire division, request that it be withdrawn from his Second Army, and replace Ballou as its commander.

That the one brigade fought competently on this occasion was truly remarkable. From Pershing all the way down the chain of command, only Bullard thought that blacks might fight well, and his attitude reflected confidence in his own ability to lead rather than in the soldiers under his command. Little was expected of the blacks fighting in the American Army. They were trained accordingly, and they responded by performing pretty much as the white generals expected.[33]

Ballou, for one, blamed the black soldiers of his division for ruining his military career. Although he continued to insist that at least some blacks could perform competently as officers, he argued against creating in any future war the kind of division that, he believed, had failed him. Black draftees should receive assignments to labor units for an initial screening. Those who showed genuine aptitude might be transferred to transportation, quartermaster, ordnance, or similar service units. Only the "very best of the material" could aspire to serve, whether as officers or enlisted men, in infantry, artillery, or engineer regiments.[34]

Similarly, Bullard resented the fact that the 92nd Division had not responded more enthusiastically to his efforts at rehabilitation. Following his successful tour of duty in command of the 3rd Alabama, he had penned a glowing tribute to the black soldier: "By character more submissive to discipline, by nature more good-humored and happy, from social position more subordinate, from previous habit of life more accustomed to yield respect to superiors, from poverty more used to plain food, fewer clothes and comfort, the average negro volunteer comes to the colors with more of the first urgently needed qualities of the soldier and readier for service than the white. He ought in all reason to make and I believe he will make an sudden emergency soldier *par excellence.*"[35] That emergency had arisen, black Americans took up arms, and Bullard revised his opinion. "If you need combat soldiers," he now wrote, "and especially if you need them in a hurry, don't put your time upon Negroes."[36]

Neither Ballou nor Bullard had direct contact with the other black combat unit sent to France. The first elements of the 93rd Division (Provisional) began arriving in France in December 1917, at a time when the French were desperate for troops, their army still recovering from the widespread mutinies of the previous spring. Since he had no use for the additional Negro infantrymen, General Pershing was delighted to hand them over to his hard-pressed ally.[37] Colonel William Hayward, the white commanding officer of one of the regiments in the provisional division, accurately described the status of his unit when he wrote to a friend, "Our great American general simply put the black orphan in a basket, set it on the doorstep of the French, pulled the bell, and went away."[38]

Perhaps the best of the American black units to fight the Germans, Hayward's 369th Infantry had evolved from the 15th New York, hardly a typical National Guard outfit. In command was the son of a Republican senator from Nebraska, a former officer in that state's militia, and, after moving to New York City, a successful attorney active in state politics. Indeed, a Republican governor, Charles S. Whitman, asked him to organize a regiment from among New York's blacks.

Hayward (whose son, Leland, would become an actor's agent, a successful theatrical producer, and an organizer of large-scale flight

training in a future world war) was obviously no ordinary National
Guard officer. He apparently respected his black troops; in any
event, he did not spare himself in looking out for them. When the
regiment mustered to report for federal service, he took a turn ladling food into mess gear to make sure the men were fed. In addition, he made skillful use of his political friends in building unit morale, arranging for the governor to present the colors of the 15th
New York and persuading an industrialist to buy instruments for
the band.

The other officers were mostly whites, either National Guard officers who had transferred from other states or socially prominent
New Yorkers recently graduated from Ivy League universities. In
persuading young blacks to enter the enlisted ranks, the colonel
called upon a celebrated black entertainer, Bert Williams, who had
himself been a militia officer in his youth. Hayward's best recruiting tool, however, proved to be the regimental band, led by a talented black musician, James Europe, who recruited instrumental-
ists from as far away as Chicago. Despite its band, its dynamic
colonel, and its several well-connected officers, the regiment was
not permitted to take part in the farewell parade of the New York
National Guard division, of which the unit was nominally a part.

In France, after exchanging their original title of 15th New York
for the designation of 369th Infantry, the "Men of Bronze," as Hayward's soldiers styled themselves, traded their equipment for
French weapons and other gear and underwent a brief indoctrination in trench warfare. Like the other three regiments of the provisional division, the New Yorkers served as a component of the armies of France.[39] As such, between July 1918 and the armistice of
November 11 the regiment fought itself to exhaustion.

Understrength when it landed in France, the 369th Infantry
rarely received replacements for the officers and men killed or seriously wounded. During the fighting, only two drafts of new men
arrived—300 on the eve of a German attack in mid-July 1918 and 600
just before an Allied offensive in late September. The methods of assigning replacements proved almost as debilitating as the effect of
sustained combat. Both groups appeared without advance notice,
and the officers who marched the newcomers to the regimental sec-
tor returned almost immediately to the rear, leaving Hayward with
untrained mobs that included men who had never donned a steel
helmet or gas mask. Nor did the colonel and his officers have an opportunity to train these replacements, for the regiment remained on
line for six months, with interruptions for rest and reorganization
totaling just two weeks.

The impossible task of assimilating raw recruits while in sustained combat against a determined enemy all but destroyed the 369th Infantry, a victim not of German fire but of the indifference, verging on contempt, displayed by Pershing's headquarters. Untrained men, adrift among junior officers and noncommissioned officers who were utter strangers, could not fight well. During the battles of late September and early October 1918, although "a large percentage of the personnel of the regiment conducted itself in a most heroic manner," Colonel Hayward charged that "large numbers of enlisted men . . . conducted themselves in the most cowardly and disgraceful manner. . . . stealing away in the night, throwing away their equipment, lurking and hiding in dugouts, and in some cases traveling many, many kilometers from the battlefield." The failure of the replacements, whom he termed a disgrace to the "regiment, the Negro Race, and the American Army," imposed an especially heavy burden upon the officers and veteran soldiers, who responded willingly but at a disproportionate cost in killed and wounded. Thoroughly frustrated by the conduct of the drafts that an uncaring headquarters had thrust upon him and powerless to change official attitudes, the colonel railed against the untrained replacements, sounding a call for courts-martial and executions, precisely what a disappointed General Ballou had advocated for his division.[40]

Casualties, exhaustion among the survivors, and the failure of the expeditionary force to provide adequate replacements were undermining morale in the 369th Infantry, as Hayward pointed out to no avail. Contributing to the problem was the attitude of Pershing's headquarters toward decorations. On several occasions, the French officer commanding the division with which the Men of Bronze were serving sought to reward the heroism of black soldiers, but the American Expeditionary Force usually failed to cooperate. Pershing's staff did, however, make an exception for two men, Sergeant Henry Johnson and Private Needham Roberts.

The two soldiers did precisely what General Ballou later insisted the black infantrymen could not do: they not only fought courageously at night but showed great initiative and self-reliance, since they were defending an isolated outpost forward of the main trenches. In May 1918, when the unit was receiving its introduction to warfare on the Western Front, a German raiding party in quest of prisoners attacked the observation post occupied by the two black soldiers. Although both Johnson and Roberts were wounded, they refused to surrender, fighting back with rifle fire, hand grenades, and even a bolo knife. These two men broke the barrier against decorations for members of the 93rd Division (Provisional), receiving the French *Croix de guerre*. Other blacks would receive the *Croix de guerre*, and American Distinguished Service Crosses, but a disproportionate share of the awards went to white officers.[41]

Despite his outburst against the ill-trained replacements who reached the unit overseas, Hayward shared a bond of respect with the men, like Johnson and Roberts, whom he had recruited for the old 15th New York. He pulled political strings that enabled his men to stage a victory parade through the streets of New York City, marching to the music of James Europe's band. The bond between the colonel and his men survived the passage of time. When their former commander died of cancer, as a second world war was nearing an end, some fifty surviving Men of Bronze formed a guard of honor at the funeral.[42]

The other regiments of the provisional division, also attached to French units, went into action after the 369th and, like Colonel Hayward's outfit, inspired concern among Regular Army officers over whether French villagers would accept the black Americans. The fears proved groundless. Colonel T. A. Roberts inspected all four regiments shortly before they entered sustained combat and found the troops clean, well disciplined, and correct in their behavior toward civilians. Some of the towns where the men had taken up quarters, usually in private homes, seemed tidier and more orderly than other villages nearby that housed white soldiers, whether French or American. Not only did the peasants and townspeople welcome the black Americans; French commanders expected a useful contribution from the four regiments.

These French officers were not disappointed. The 371st and 372nd Infantry, like the 369th, played a prominent role in the Meuse-Argonne fighting during September and October 1918. This bitter, often hand-to-hand struggle cost the three regiments some 2,500 casualties. The 370th Infantry fought alongside French troops in the Oise-Aisne offensive, September 15 to November 11; its casualties numbered 665 killed and wounded.[43]

The French had been confident and their confidence was rewarded. In contrast, the American high command placed no faith in these black units. General Pershing's headquarters had misgivings about the leadership of the regiments in the 93rd Division (Provisional), the worries focusing upon the possible need to rely on black officers, especially as replacements for whites who might be wounded. Not even the 369th Infantry was exempt. Shortly before the regiment entered the lines for ninety-one consecutive days of combat, an inspector was repeating unfounded rumors that "all discipline and morale had gone to the winds" during a brief time that Colonel Hayward had been hospitalized.

Of the other three regiments, only the 371st Infantry enjoyed continuity of leadership. Colonel Perry L. Miles, a white officer of the Regular Army, led the organization throughout training and combat. The 370th Infantry was less fortunate, having experienced the shock of having its black colonel, Franklin A. Dennison of the 8th Illinois, relieved because of ill health. This justification, though it may well have been true, called to mind the recent shelving of Charles Young. Dennison's replacement, T. A. Roberts, became the first white ever to command the black regiment of the Illinois National Guard, thus incurring the ill will of his black officers. In the 372nd Infantry, Glendie Young, the unit's first commander, had nothing but contempt for black officers and discriminated openly against them in the assignment of quarters. His successor, Herschel Tupes, proved more even-handed, though he shared the pervasive concern about the competence of black junior officers and promptly convened boards of whites to weed out the undesirables.[45]

After the battles of September and October 1918, Pershing's headquarters tried unsuccessfully to regain control of at least three of the black regiments serving with the French in order to use the men as laborers. The possible exception in this plan, which the French high command rejected because it needed troops, was to have been the 371st Infantry, which oddly enough resembled in composition the elements of the ill-starred 92nd Division.[46] Made up of black draftees, with no leaven of National Guard members, the 371st had been organized by white officers. Nor was there any special rapport between the men and these senior officers, who at times displayed the insensitivity to the self-esteem of black soldiers that was typical of the time. For example, when ex-President Taft visited the regiment in training at Columbia, South Carolina, the troops did not demonstrate their military prowess; instead a hastily organized choir sang spirituals for the distinguished guest.[47]

Why did the four black regiments, three composed mainly of National Guardsmen and the fourth made up of draftees, serve commendably with different French divisions, fighting on despite a lack of recognition, untrained replacements, and indifference on the part of Pershing and his staff? Why did they perform well while the 92nd Division was faring so poorly?

According to Colonel Vernon A. Caldwell, who had commanded black soldiers in Cuba, in the Philippines, and with the 92nd Division in France, the answer was obvious. "I think," he replied when the Army War College asked his opinion on the role of the black soldier, that "our past policy of massing them by themselves has not been wise." What he had experienced in France convinced him that "colored troops will do much better when they are associated as component parts of white organizations." He therefore proposed following the example of the French, though on a lesser scale, assigning a company or battalion of blacks, led insofar as possible by black officers, to every infantry regiment, instead of assigning black regiments to white divisions. The adoption of Caldwell's plan would doom the four black regiments in existence since shortly after the Civil War, but the colonel believed that any future war would be fought not by the Regular Army, but by an Army drawn from the nation at large. In organizing such a force, the black segment of the populace would represent "an important military asset," to be blended with white Americans into a harmonious and effective whole.[48]

Colonel James K. Parsons, who had once served as a white officer in General Bullard's 3rd Alabama, went even further in his reply to the War College survey. He suggested that no combat units at all be manned exclusively by blacks, recommending instead that black soldiers be assigned as individuals throughout the Army's combat arms at a ratio of about one to every ten whites. Such a policy would place some 2,000 blacks in a typical division, about 300 in an infantry regiment, and roughly twenty in a rifle company. As a result, Colonel Parsons believed, combat casualties would be distributed fairly between the races, thus avoiding racial tensions within the populace at home. No black, however, could exercise command over whites; in order to obtain promotion to a command assignment, the officer or noncommissioned officer would have to transfer to an all-black support or service unit.[49]

Judging from the responses to the survey made by the War College, those who advocated even a small measure of racial integration found themselves out of step with a majority of their fellow officers. Segregation persisted until the armistice and afterward. Black pioneer battalions, field engineers by training, performed the unpleasant task of reburying in military cemeteries the American war dead who had been temporarily interred at battlefield sites. While this work went on in France, some combat veterans returned to the United States, sailing in ships so rigidly segregated by race that the lone black officer assigned to one of them had to eat his meals in isolation after some 400 whites had eaten theirs. The 367th Infantry of the 92nd Division provided a detail to load coal into the bunkers of the USS *Virginia*. After finishing this dirty and exhausting job, the men were to load their gear in the battleship for the passage westward across the Atlantic. Upon learning of the plan, the ship's executive officer declared that no black soldier had ever embarked in an American battleship and vowed that none ever would. The *Virginia's* captain backed up his subordinate; a tug then brought the black troops ashore, their commander carrying a letter commending them for the "good conduct and high state of discipline" they had exhibited while filling the warship's bunkers.[50]

Black America had gone to war in the hope of earning equality, but not even 750 battle deaths and some 5,000 wounded could abolish a system of institutionalized injustice based solely on race. Failure to buy full citizenship with blood and suffering brought disillusionment and alienation. DuBois, the advocate of taking part in the war effort, went to France in quest of the truth concerning the treatment black soldiers had received during the conflict. Upon his return, he printed a series of documents that detailed how these men had fared in training, in combat overseas, and during their return from France. His collection included, among other things, a letter from Colonel Allen J. Greer, Ballou's chief of staff, to Senator Kenneth D. McKellar, in which the Army officer told the Tennessee Democrat that the soldiers of the 92nd Division had been "dangerous to no one but themselves and women." DuBois also revealed the treatment of the men who had coaled the USS *Virginia* and documented other instances of racial prejudice.[51]

Besides angering DuBois, the treatment of black soldiers angered the "talented tenth" for whom he served as spokesman. The idealistic and educated black who had answered the call of a DuBois or a Spingarn was certain to take offense at the day-to-day humiliation experienced in a segregated Army. As Colonel Tupes of the 372nd Infantry reported, with apparent surprise, the best of his black junior officers had "displayed conspicuous courage in action but revealed inclinations to cause trouble over race distinctions."[52] Charles H. Houston, a black wartime officer who became a successful attorney, later declared that his "experience in the World War" left him "so bitter that I have never even applied for a service medal."[53] Nor could Noble Sissle have forgotten the treatment he receive at Spartanburg, South Carolina, while stationed nearby. Already a successful musician and music arranger on Broadway, he later would help launch the career of a young singer named Lena Horne. When he tried to buy a newspaper in the lobby of a hotel reserved for whites, he was beaten for his impudence.[54]

The United States Army, though desperate for flight instructors with combat experience, brusquely rejected a black American who had flown as a pursuit pilot in the French Foreign Legion. Eugene Jacques Bullard, a refugee from Jim Crow, found social acceptance in France and therefore enlisted shortly after war broke out. Of the five or ten expatriate blacks to join the Legion at the time, he was the only one to become an aviator.

After recovering from severe wounds sustained while fighting as an infantryman in the Legion, Bullard volunteered for flight training. He learned to manipulate the throttle of a *roleur*, a clipped-wing monoplane incapable of flight, taxiing it in a straight line on the grass surface of the airfield at Avord, near Tours. He graduated to flyable trainers, the so-called *cages à poules*, or chicken coops, and in the summer of 1917 joined a pursuit squadron. Rebuffed in his attempt to transfer to the American air service, an organization exclusively for whites, he still wore the uniform of France on November 7 of that year, when he shot down a German triplane fighter, the second aerial victory he claimed and the first verified by witnesses.

His career as a sergeant pilot ended after about six months, the result of a quarrel with a French officer. Although the precise details have blurred, a racial insult was at the root of the incident. Unlike the average citizen of France, many of those who had exercised authority in the colonies believed themselves innately superior to blacks or Asians. Bullard's downfall occurred after he either demanded that a colonial officer return his salute or punched a lieutenant who had served in the colonies, when the lieutenant tried to prevent him from boarding a truck carrying men on leave back to their units. Since the American had boxed professionally, a blow struck in anger may well have been what earned him an immediate reduction in rank and transfer back to the infantry, where he served until the armistice.[55]

Far from bringing racial amity, the war heightened the barriers that separated the races in the United States and caused growing resentment among blacks. No longer did DuBois speak of ignoring grievances, of closing ranks with white Americans, of eyes lifted up to the hills. With violence against blacks spreading throughout the nation, he thus summarized the condition of his race: "They cheat us and mock us; they kill us and slay us; they deride our misery. When we plead for the naked protection of the law . . . , they tell us to 'GO TO HELL!'" His advice now was "TO YOUR TENTS, O ISRAEL! and FIGHT, FIGHT, FIGHT for Freedom."[56]

9

Oppression, Indifference, and a Surge of Activism

AT A BEACH on Chicago's lakefront on a hot summer day in 1919, white youths began throwing rocks at some blacks, sons of newcomers from the South who had found wartime jobs in local factories, who were swimming in waters that formerly had been used exclusively by whites. Seventeen-year-old Eugene Williams drowned, apparently after being hit by a stone. Black adults demanded that police arrest a white who had thrown at the victim, but Chicago's white officers would not accept the word of blacks and did nothing. The victim had not been hit, in fact, but the result was the same; the hail of stones kept him from swimming to shore until he became exhausted, could no longer keep himself afloat, and drowned.

The drowning of Eugene Williams touched off a violent and destructive race riot. Blacks tried to avenge the death, and whites gave vent to the pent-up hatred caused by competition for jobs and housing, as well as for recreational space alongside Lake Michigan. The bloodshed and burning lasted one week, and the National Guard continued to patrol the city for another. The casualties totaled 23 blacks and 15 whites killed, 342 blacks and 178 whites injured. Arsonists burned the homes of a thousand persons, most of them Lithuanian whites living near the stockyards. The value of the property destroyed by rioters amounted to a quarter million dollars.[1]

The violence was not unique to Chicago but erupted in several cities with a large black populace and in some where blacks formed a tiny minority. A mob at Omaha, Nebraska, lynched a rape suspect, in the process setting fire to the new Douglas County court house and assaulting the mayor. The citizens of Duluth, Minnesota, took three blacks suspected of rape from the city jail and hanged them.

The nation's cities in 1919 were primed for conflict between whites and blacks. The black migration to the northern cities, which began before the United States entered World War I, continued during the conflict, and blacks took over industrial jobs vacated by white northerners who had gone to war. When hostilities ended, white veterans returned to claim their prewar jobs, blacks also left the service and began seeking employment, and the wartime pace of production slowed abruptly. Urban employers realized that they could play off one group against another, cutting wages and firing those who complained. Competition for jobs fed racial animosity in the cities, rapes and other interracial crimes (whether real or rumored) intensified the hatred, and violence followed, as white mobs tried to restore order of a Jim Crow variety even in the national capital. The Red Summer of 1919, stained with the blood of hundreds of blacks killed or injured in some thirty race riots, demonstrated once again that wartime service could not of itself touch the conscience of white Americans and earn full citizenship for the black minority.

Indeed, the black soldiers and the comparative handful of black sailors who served during the World War returned to find Jim Crow entrenched more solidly than before. Demogogues like James K. Vardaman of Mississippi urged that every town and village in the state form vigilante groups to keep watch on the "French-women-ruined negro soldiers" and prevent them from sating their lust with white southern womanhood. Theodore G. Bilbo, the governor of Mississippi, refused to take action against lynching, which he considered the just and inevitable fate of any black man who might rape a white woman. In 1918, mobs killed fifty-eight blacks accused or convicted of various crimes; the total in 1919 reached seventy-seven, ten of them former soldiers. One returning veteran, still in uniform, was beaten to death in Georgia, not because he had been accused of rape or murder, but because he had vowed, while in jail for ignoring a "whites only" sign, never to yield to Jim Crow.[2]

President Wilson, preoccupied with his role as an international peacemaker and in failing health, looked out upon an America torn by racial violence and kept insisting that the sacrifices blacks had made during the recent war would bring civil rights, though not social equality. Empty words from a man whose administration had imposed segregation on the federal work force. For blacks, closing ranks in wartime brought disappointment, frustration, and a wave of repression that confirmed the dominance of the white majority.

This was a time of madness. The recent Bolshevik revolution in Russia, among other factors, inspired downtrodden American laborers to unionize and challenge their employers, resorting to violence if necessary. Meanwhile, federal and local authorities, including the Attorney General of the United States, A. Mitchell Palmer, battled the Red tide that they believed was engulfing the country. For the hysterical superpatriots, including the members of a resurgent Ku Klux Klan, all labor unions, "foreign" religions like Roman Catholicism or Judaism, and all ethnic groups were suspect, especially black Americans. When black newspapers protested the treatment that black soldiers had received in wartime, the Klan and its apologists cited this as irrefutable proof that the entire race had succumbed to Bolshevik subversion.[3]

Once the violent postwar oppression had spent itself, white America tended to display indifference tinged with suspicion toward black citizens, an attitude reflected by the armed forces. Still wary after the recent violence, blacks gave little thought to the armed forces. On the one hand, blacks hardly figured in the military planning for the admittedly remote possibility of another war. On the other, the only military issue that interested black Americans during the immediate postwar years was the occupation of Haiti, a nation created by former slaves who rebelled against their French masters.

Since 1915 the U.S. Marine Corps had, in effect, been running the country, maintaining order with rifle and bayonet, while American experts controlled the nation's finances. Blacks like James Weldon Johnson, a poet and lyricist who had held minor diplomatic posts during the Roosevelt and Taft administrations, objected to the occupation on two counts. First, it served as an extension of American racism by denying that blacks could govern themselves; second, white marines seemed all too willing to use violence against the Haitians.

On the latter point some Marine officers agreed, conceding that too many local "bandits" were being "shot while escaping." Johnson and his allies of both races helped bring about an investigation that curbed the unnecessary violence but did not put an end to the occupation, which lasted until 1934. Over the years, the marines developed an amused contempt for the Haitians, an application of Jim Crow attitudes to the local scene, as evidenced by the tune selected by a Marine band when the President of Haiti left the capital on a trip. The white musicians played "Bye Bye Blackbird."[4]

A number of officers within the War Department shared the instinctive kind of racism shown by the marines in Haiti, as became apparent when the Army began studying the future of the black soldier. The investigation dealt with all three components of the Army—the regulars, the National Guard, and the organized reserve—and also embraced mobilization plans for a future war. The four black regiments of the Regular Army posed a special problem, for laws adopted shortly after the Civil War decreed, in effect, that a certain number of units had to be made up of blacks whether the regular force waxed in strength or waned. Once World War I ended, the Army went into a numerical decline, which raised the possibility that the black regiments would form a disproportionately large share of the peacetime military establishment.

The War Department in 1919 took its first tentative steps to deal with the matter, imposing restrictions on the enlistment of blacks in the infantry or cavalry. The new policy discouraged first enlistments but accepted reenlistments, sometimes by men with wartime service in any unit, at other times only by those who had been serving with the unit they wished to rejoin.[5]

The simple, if devious, solution was to make one of the black regiments a mere headquarters, with no troops actually assigned. Such a plan surfaced, underwent consideration, and sank in a maelstrom of complications. The Army Reorganization Act adopted after the Civil War and then modified had merely fixed the number of black regiments at four. Reducing one unit to a headquarters company could have circumvented the law had another consideration not intervened. The decisive complication was the Army's current racial policy. Neither cavalry regiment could be reduced in this fashion because some 400 troopers of the 9th Cavalry were due to return from the Philippines. Since their unit was scheduled to remain in the islands, the 10th Cavalry would have to absorb the returnees, thus making one of the infantry regiments the likely candidate for reduction to token strength. Plans called, however, for the two black infantry regiments to form a brigade in the event of war. Elimination of either the 24th or 25th Infantry would mean that one black and one white regiment would serve in the same infantry brigade, an unthinkable occurrence in a segregated Army.[6]

Stymied by practice if not by law, the Army retained the four black regiments throughout the 1920s, from time to time abolishing a company or converting a combat unit into a service or housekeeping unit without changing the designation. As a result, black soldiers driving trucks or serving as post maintenance men might be carried on the rolls as machine gunners or riflemen, members of a cavalry or infantry regiment stationed hundreds of miles away. This practice worked reasonably well in terms of bookkeeping. Congress in 1926 approved a gradual increase in the strength of the Air Corps without a corresponding change in the overall size of the Army, but for four years, the War Department balanced the manpower accounts by diverting vacancies from white units to the all-white air arm. In 1931, however, the supply of these vacancies ran out and it became necessary to shift openings from the black regiments to the Air Corps, a branch of service that excluded blacks.[7]

The administration of President Herbert Hoover tried unsuccessfully to draw a veil of secrecy over the raiding of black units for manpower spaces to be filled by whites. Scheduled to be sacrificed on behalf of the Air Corps were the 10th Cavalry and 25th Infantry. Vacancies in both units would go unfilled until they became collections of small and widely scattered housekeeping detachments, regiments in name only. Upon learning of the plan, Walter White, secretary of the National Association for the Advancement of Colored People, protested what amounted to the substitution of white airmen for black soldiers or cavalry troopers. Robert R. Moton, the principal at the Tuskegee Institute, joined in arguing the case for the black regiments, a defense that the War Department rejected out of hand.[8] General Douglas MacArthur, the Chief of Staff, insisted that the Army was not attempting to disband any of the black regiments, but was merely trying to equalize between white and black units the burden of providing manpower for an expanding Air Corps. Black organizations, after all, were not unique in being divided among two or more military posts.[9] Despite the general's assurances, the 10th Cavalry was bearing the brunt of a policy that prevented it from functioning as a combat unit. For three years the regiment was unable to take part in routine maneuvers, but the War Department insisted that spending long periods as labor or service troops was not unusual, even for soldiers in white units.[10]

Nor did the Army see any injustice in barring blacks from the Air Corps. Segregation, conceded Major General George Van Horn Moseley, MacArthur's principal assistant, determined how the Army would use its manpower, and this was both legal and proper. Except for rare instances in the medical service and quartermaster corps, all organizations remained segregated by race, with no blacks serving in white units or whites in the black ones that had been authorized by Congress immediately after the Civil War. The Air Corps, Moseley continued, had emerged only recently as a combat arm, and Congress had made no provision for black squadrons. Indeed, congressional action, unlikely though it seemed, might not of itself be enough to create black aviation units. After all, Moseley asked, could enough educated and technically skilled black men be found to operate a unit that normally attracted college-trained individuals as pilots and persons with great mechanical aptitude or experience to maintain and service the aircraft? Obviously, the general thought that such men were not available.[11]

Spokesmen for the nation's blacks contested the general's belief. Besides lobbying for the preservation of the four black regiments as combat organizations, they sought elimination of the racial barriers that kept the Air Corps exclusively white. They had little success. The black regiments remained combat outfits in name, if not in fact, but the air arm steadfastly refused those applicants who were not white men. As late as the spring of 1939, with the outbreak of war in Europe some six months away, black citizens were unable to gain this objective.[12]

Although the fate of the Regular Army regiments aroused concern among black newspapers and civil rights organizations, for most of the 1930s blacks, and whites as well, were most concerned with survival, for unemployment, bank failures, and farm foreclosures had crippled the economy. The Great Depression, beginning in 1929 and dragging on for much of the following decade, spawned a series of federal programs, elements of President Franklin D. Roosevelt's New Deal, designed to care for the unemployed and put them to work. For a poor family, admission to such a program could mean not only the recapture of lost pride but sustenance and life itself. Impressed by the efforts of the New Deal on the behalf of the poor and helpless, black Americans abandoned the party of Lincoln and rallied behind Franklin Roosevelt. In some areas, especially in the Northeast, civil rights organizations, the black press, and church groups campaigned for the elimination of racial barriers in the local administration of federal programs and enabled blacks to gain greater access.

One of the programs of economic assistance that loomed large in American life had strong military implications. This was the Civilian Conservation Corps, in which jobless young men enrolled to work on parks and similar projects in return for food, shelter, clothing, medical care, and a small salary. In charge of the various semimilitary camps were officers and noncommissioned officers of the regular armed forces and officers of the reserve components. Because the law specified that race would not be a factor in carrying out the program, at the outset a few encampments housed men of both races. Blacks, however, were not represented in proportion to their share of the populace eligible to enroll. Furthermore, the racially integrated camps soon disappeared, as administrators reorganized the corps according to race and began accepting blacks only to replace others of the same race who had left the program.

The vestiges of racial integration thus vanished, but spokesmen for black Americans tried nevertheless to broaden the racial composition of the leadership within the segregated organization. Despite reasoned arguments by Emmett Scott, now an official at Howard University, that blacks in the corps should have, if not black administrators, at least chaplains and doctors of their own race, the War Department remained adamant in opposing the assignment of blacks to positions of responsibility. Not until 1935, when President Roosevelt insisted that black medical officers and chaplains be called up from the reserve, did any of them receive assignments to the segregated camps. Even so, fewer than twenty of these officers were on duty at any one time, although the number of black units peaked at some two hundred. The typical black reservist seeking duty with the Civilian Conservation Corps suffered the fate of one applicant in the Middle West whose progress on the list of candidates inspired a white officer to write, "The Negro officer has been like a frog getting out of the well. He has never come to the top."[13]

As the Depression waned, the emerging black activists who had helped to benefit from the various programs of the New Deal—members of the black press, civil rights organizations, and some church groups—took an active interest in the treatment and assigned role of black servicemen. During 1938, for instance, the *Kansas City Call* focused attention on racial discrimination at Fort Leavenworth, Kansas, where soldiers of the 10th Cavalry, who functioned as the post labor pool, and their families could not use swimming facilities, clubs, and a restaurant that admitted the whites stationed there. The efforts of the newspaper, backed by anonymous complaints to the War Department, had little effect, however, save to inspire an official investigation that glossed over the matter.

The inquiry acknowledged that blacks had been denied access to or granted limited use of various facilities. A "tacit understanding" for example, barred blacks from the restaurant at the post exchange, for otherwise those persons "including the officers and their families whose patronage accounts for the bulk of the business done by the restaurant" would go elsewhere, forcing the establishment to close. Also, blacks attending the post theater had to use the latrines at a 10th Cavalry service club across the street. Although the investigator recommended the construction of separate but equal facilities on bases accommodating both black and white units—an unlikely prospect given the funds available in 1938—he insisted that "the enlisted men of the 10th Cavalry are well taken care of, happy, contented, and possess a high state of morale." What seemed to an outsider to be racial discrimination actually resulted, he insisted, from just and necessary measures adopted "to insure that the limited recreational and athletic facilities available for the enlisted personnel be utilized in such a manner as to prevent any untoward incident due to the intermingling of white and negro soldiers."[14]

Another black newspaper, the *Pittsburgh Courier*, launched an offensive against the Army's racial policies, urging the removal of the barriers that made the Air Corps and other technical branches of the service exclusively white. The verbal barrage laid down by Robert L. Vann, the journal's editor, contained some sensational statements, among them a charge that foreign-born white spies could enter the armed forces more easily than a loyal, native-born black, even though "no American Negro, soldier or civilian, has ever been suspected or convicted of betraying his country."[15] Despite the hyperbole, Vann's statement accurately characterized the War Department's conviction that white officers and soldiers were innately better than blacks, a prejudice that implied, if it did not openly declare, that any white recruit was preferable to any black.

Among the *Courier*'s goals was the establishment of an all-black division within the peacetime Army, the best way to ensure the continued presence of blacks in the service. In pursuit of this objective, the newspaper caught the attention of Representative Hamilton Fish, a New York Republican, who had been a white officer of the 369th Infantry during World War I. By expressing an interest in the *Courier*'s efforts, Representative Fish made sure that the War Department would take the matter seriously, though not necessarily react favorably. And indeed, the official attitude remained unchanged; there would be no such division. The Army, however, failed to advise Fish or the newspaper's editor that it did not intend to organize any black unit larger than a regiment, even in the event of war.[16]

Excluded from the War Department's reply to Representative Fish was any reference to a problem that troubled the Army from the armistice in 1918 until the German invasion of Poland in 1939. What should be done with the large number of blacks—National Guardsmen, reservists, volunteers, and possibly draftees—who would enter the service in case of another war? One part of the puzzle consisted of the few black National Guard units that still survived—the 369th Infantry in New York, an understrength 8th Illinois, and the units in Massachusetts, Ohio, Maryland, New Jersey, and the District of Columbia that made up the 372nd Infantry. Of the sixteen National Guard divisions called for in the 1922 wartime mobilization plan, all were white, and as late as 1937 the largest black unit to be called to the colors was the independent regiment, fleshed out with scattered battalions and companies and unaffiliated with any state or regional division. The War Department, in effect, left the racial composition of the National Guard to the individual states. Thanks to indifference at Washington and prejudice in the state capitals, less than 2 percent of the combined strength of the Regular Army and National Guard consisted of blacks as the 1930s drew to a close.

Its units skeletal cadres in most instances, the federally administered organized reserve had just one black regiment, the 428th Infantry, with headquarters in the District of Columbia. Colleges like Howard, Wilberforce, and Prairie View A&M in Texas continued to produce black reserve officers through the Reserve Officer Training Corps, and some 350 of these graduates could be found on the rolls of a variety of reserve units. Unfortunately, reserve organizations lacked the glamour and tradition of the four Regular Army regiments or the political importance of a National Guard outfit in a state like Illinois or New York. As a result, neither civil rights organizations nor black newspapers paid much attention to the reservists and the limited opportunities available to them for training and promotion.

By 1940, with war raging in Europe and the United States on the verge of mobilizing, the Army endorsed a basic policy of accepting blacks according to their proportion of the populace in a given corps area and assigning them in the same proportion to combat and service or support units. Officially accepted or not, the policy had little impact on mobilization schemes for a possible war. After a cursory examination of the racial composition of the nine corps areas into which the country was divided, War Department planners assigned tentative quotas to each of them and came up with a wartime Army that would be roughly 6 percent black, even though blacks made up almost 10 percent of the population. Moreover, the vast majority of blacks accepted into an expanded Army would serve as infantrymen or as laborers in quartermaster units. None could enter the Air Corps or the Signal Corps, even though the first black to enlist in the latter branch had done so some fifty-five years earlier.[17]

While the War Department struggled with mobilization plans that avoided the question of unrestricted black participation in a future conflict, Adolf Hitler had come to power in Germany, defied the terms of the Treaty of Versailles that had ended World War I, rearmed his nation, and embarked on a course of aggression that would result in a second worldwide conflagration. Hitler's National Socialist Party, the Nazis, preached a form of racism that extolled the so-called Aryan race and branded other peoples, especially Jews, as less than human. A similar spirit of racial supremacy motivated the Japanese, convinced of their innate superiority, who were attempting to make China an economic vassal.

Aware of the danger posed by Germany and Japan, President Franklin D.Roosevelt in October 1937 called for a quarantine of the aggressor nations. The occasion of his proposal was the sinking by Japanese airmen of a clearly marked American gunboat patrolling the Yangtze River in China. Although public opinion in the United States and the other western democracies was not yet ready for concerted action, the President's call dramatized the likelihood of a war against Germany and Japan.

Charles Houston, a veteran of the Fort Des Moines officer training course in World War I and now special counsel for the National Association for the Advancement of Colored People, congratulated the Chief Executive for "warning the United States of the danger it faces in common with the rest of the world on account of the strife and warfare stirred up by the aggressor nations." He then pointed out that if war should come, the "loyalty and support" of blacks, who made up perhaps 10 percent of the populace, would be "indispensible to the United States." The attorney warned, however, that "the Negro population . . . will not again silently endure the insults and discriminations imposed on its soldiers and sailors in the course of the last war."[18]

The points that Houston was making—that the next war would require a truly national effort and that the United States could not rally the black populace while practicing racial discrimination—began gradually to percolate in the consciousness of American policy makers. Tacitly or otherwise, the elimination of racism promised to become one of the aims of any war against Japan or Germany. Influential whites therefore began to challenge racism in the United States, seeking as Houston had to purge the nation of the same evils that it might have to fight in Europe or the Orient.[19]

At times, the efforts of blacks to achieve greater opportunities and the full rights and obligations of citizenship found allies in unexpected quarters. In 1939, for instance, Senator Harry Schwartz, a Wyoming Democrat who numbered a comparative handful of blacks among his constituents, enlisted in the long and thus far unsuccessful campaign to remove the racial barriers that controlled access to the Army Air Corps. He persuaded the Congress to include black institutions among the schools to which the Secretary of War might loan government-owned equipment for aviation instruction. Although the program thus established offered only primary flight instruction, the graduates would form a manpower reservoir that the Air Corps could tap in time of emergency.

Ignoring the senator's intention that civilian pilot training would enable blacks to become Army airmen, the Air Corps tried to interpret the new law as narrowly as possible. The Army's air arm made no move to accept men trained by civilian instructors at a variety of black institutions, including the Tuskegee Institute. Of the first hundred blacks to begin primary flight training, ninety-one graduated, but not one was accepted for further instruction at an Army school. The racial barrier remained in place, even though Major General Henry H. Arnold had assured Congress that the Air Corps, which he headed, could enroll the successful black trainees in basic and then advanced courses. As late as December 1939, more than six months after the enactment of the law containing the Schwartz amendment that admitted blacks to the civilian pilot training program, the Army air arm continued to turn away qualified black applicants for flight training, explaining that it had no segregated units in which they could serve.[20]

Conditioned by years of broken promises, the blacks who had been campaigning for equal access to every branch of the armed forces placed little faith in General Arnold's assurances that he would observe the spirit of the Schwartz amendment, but they did not stop trying. If anything, they stepped up their efforts. In September 1939, two weeks after the fighting began in Europe, Walter White, speaking for the National Association of Colored People, urged President Roosevelt "to use the utmost powers of your high office to remove the barriers to full participation by qualified Negroes in every branch of the defense forces of the government."[21] Charles Houston, Roy Wilkins, and Robert Vann also fought to obtain for blacks the opportunity to serve in the Air Corps.

And these were not all. At Harlem airfield in Auburn, Illinois, two black aviators, Chauncey E. Spencer and Dale L. White, rented an elderly Lincoln-Paige biplane for a flight to Washington, D.C. They hoped to lobby Congress for the admission of blacks to the Army air arm and to stimulate interest in aviation among the young people who might someday take advantage of a change in War Department policy. Near Sherwood, Ohio, a broken crankshaft forced them down in a farmer's field. They succeeded in making repairs, however, and flew to Morgantown, West Virginia, where the airport manager ordered them to leave before dark. They took off for Pittsburgh, Pennsylvania, arriving there after sunset. Since they had neither radio nor landing lights, they had to follow a transport onto the runway, which had been illuminated for its arrival. In doing so, they violated aeronautical regulations governing the separation between aircraft, but, as the federal inspector at Pittsburgh had to admit, it was a brilliant demonstration of flying skill and the only way they could have landed safely. When they reached the nation's capital, White and Spencer impressed legislators like Harry S. Truman, a Missouri Democrat, and Everett M. Dirksen, a Republican from Illinois, when the two fliers related how they had been forced to risk their lives because a white airport manager would not allow blacks to remain overnight on his premises.[22]

Neither Walter White's direct appeal to the President nor the far more dramatic lobbying efforts of Dale White and Chauncey Spencer could by themselves persuade the executive branch or the Congress to take action against racism in the armed forces. War was drawing near, however, and the war seemed likely to be a great struggle for national survival, a conflict in which black participation would be necessary. France surrendered in June 1940, leaving Hitler the master of Europe. With Italy now a belligerent, the United Kingdom stood alone, menaced by Germany and also by an ambitious Japan that coveted British colonies like Hong Kong and Malaya. In these circumstances, the President asked for a draft law, even though the United States still enjoyed a precarious peace.[23]

During the summer of 1940, debate on the proposed Selective Service Act gave blacks and their allies an opportunity to express their views before Congress and the nation. Among those who testified was Rayford W. Logan, a member of the Howard University faculty, who was serving as chairman of the Committee on the Participation of Negroes in the National Defense, a group of civil rights activists, both blacks and whites, formed to lobby for an end to racial discrimination in defense employment and in the military services. Logan demanded that "Negro citizens . . . be given equal opportunity to participate in the national-defense program, civil as well as military; . . . to be trained for work in national-defense industries and . . . to serve in the naval and military services of this country in proportion to their numerical strength in the whole population." He then pointed out that at this time the Army had just five black officers—three chaplains and two officers in the combat arms, Colonel Benjamin O. Davis and his son, Benjamin, Jr., a first lieutenant. Moreover, although blacks made up perhaps 10 percent of the populace, they comprised less than 3 percent of the Army. Finally, the educator and civil rights activist charged that the Air Corps had frustrated Senator Schwartz's plan for training blacks as military aviators.[24]

Charles Houston, speaking on behalf of the National Association for the Advancement of Colored People, harkened back to his own service in France during World War I. How, he asked, could black soldiers be expected to serve without complaint in the Vosges Mountains, while their relatives and friends were being oppressed and even lynched in the United States? The world, he declared, was changing. Everywhere downtrodden races were asserting themselves. Could the United States ignore this movement and, by embracing racial segregation at home, oppose a worldwide struggle for a kind of democracy that ignored race?[25]

Although Representative Paul Kilday of Texas congratulated Logan for seeking on behalf of blacks the opportunity to serve the nation,[26] a number of legislators objected to including in the draft law a clause prohibiting racial discrimination. To do so, charged Senator Tom Connally, would constitute knuckling under to a few blacks "who want continually to agitate, disturb, stir up discussion, and raise the devil about what they speak of as their political and social rights." This kind of activity, the Texas Democrat warned, had produced outrages like the Brownsville and Houston riots in which disciplined regulars, rather than easily influenced draftees, had succumbed to the schemes of "agitators, social climbers, and others."[27]

Despite Connally's arguments and warnings by others of the perils of mixing the races, Congress voted to give blacks the opportunity for military service that their spokesmen had demanded. The members refused to alienate a large and increasingly vocal minority in time of national emergency, and they also sensed the danger of being tarred by provable accusations of racism when the likeliest enemy, Nazi Germany, preached a racism of its own. Therefore, when the Selective Service Act became law in mid-September 1940, it specified that there would be no racial discrimination in the interpretation or execution of the new legislation.

The Selective Service Act also stated, however, that no one would be inducted unless he met a prescribed mental and physical standard and adequate housing and other facilities were available for him. To men like Charles Houston, their suspicions sharpened by service in a segregated wartime Army, it seemed that the War Department might evade the ban on racial discrimination by juggling mental or physical requirements or declaring that separate accommodations for blacks were not available.[28] In seeking some more specific assurance, black leaders enlisted the support of their most valuable white ally, Eleanor Roosevelt, the wife of the Chief Executive. Since her husband had assumed office in 1933, Mrs. Roosevelt had sought greater participation by blacks in the various programs established to combat the economic effects of the Great Depression. She had, moreover, been generally successful, thanks to the efforts of like-minded administrators handling the programs that made up the New Deal.

She did not, of course, always prevail. The President, for example, resisted proposals that he ask Congress for legislation to make lynching a federal crime, an item high on the agenda presented by Walter White on behalf of the National Association for the Advancement of Colored People. Nor would Mr. Roosevelt, as late as 1940, agree to deliver a special radio address to the convention of the civil rights organization that Mr. White represented.

Now another black leader was raising her strong and expressive voice to call for Mrs. Roosevelt's support for a series of actions relating to the armed forces. Mary McLeod Bethune, president of Bethune Cookman College, an institution in Florida for blacks, described various instances of racial discrimination and told of her concern that the War Department would resurrect its policies of World War I and divert most blacks into labor units. To prevent this, she recommended that Secretary of War Henry L. Stimson choose as his assistant an outstanding black citizen, someone more independent and vigorous than Emmett Scott had been during the previous conflict.[29]

In September 1940, Mrs. Roosevelt persuaded her husband to meet with some of the black leaders. The President, along with Assistant Secretary of War Robert P. Patterson and Secretary of the Navy Frank Knox, conferred with three representatives of the black community—Walter White, T. Arnold Hill, formerly of the Urban League, a civil rights organization, and A. Philip Randolph, who headed the union of Pullman car porters. After raising the possibility of racially integrated military units, a suggestion that met a polite, if unenthusiastic, reception, the three men presented a memorandum that called first of all for a stronger commitment to preventing discrimination in carrying out the selective service program. This document also sought the admission of blacks to the Army Air Corps and the other technical services, the expansion of their role in the Navy, and the acceptance of black women as nurses and Red Cross aides. The memorandum proved too radical for Secretary Stimson, who had never accepted the commissioning of blacks, let alone any other reforms. Upon learning of the meeting, he grumbled privately that black politicians were trying to force President Roosevelt to adopt antidiscrimination policies that he believed would prove as ill-considered as President Wilson's decision to appoint black officers during World War I.[30]

What seemed ill-considered on September 27, when the meeting took place, became increasingly necessary as the 1940 presidential election approached. Roosevelt, after all, was seeking an unprecedented third term, a break with tradition that was certain to alienate some of his earlier supporters. The Republican candidate, Wendell L. Willkie, had declared himself an enemy of racism, had won the endorsement of Robert Vann's *Pittsburgh Courier*, and seemed to be making inroads into the black electorate, threatening to tap what had become a source of votes upon which Mr. Roosevelt could depend. Most of those blacks actually permitted to vote had defected from Republican ranks during the Depression, and the President could not risk their reverting to their former allegiance. He needed the votes of enfranchised northern blacks, whose leaders were beginning to appreciate the benefits of bloc voting. As a result, the President on October 9, 1940, announced a revised racial policy for the armed services.[30]

By formally endorsing a program actually drafted by his civilian advisers, although with his encouragement, the Chief Executive agreed that the number of blacks in the Army would correspond in general to their percentage of the populace. In addition, he made other pledges to black Americans, promising that they would be eligible to serve in the Army Air Corps and other branches of the military service, be eligible for officer training, and have access to civilian jobs at Army posts and other installations. These reforms, however, were to take place within the framework of racial segregation, for Mr. Roosevelt refused "to intermingle the colored and white enlisted personnel in the same regimental organizations" because separate units "had proven satisfactory over a long period of years, and to make changes now would produce a situation destructive to morale and detrimental to the preparation for national defense."[31]

The President had hoped to effect a compromise that would appease his black critics, neutralize Willkie's influence among black voters, and avoid upsetting white racists in the Army or on Capitol Hill. As far as the black community was concerned, his plan achieved results that were mixed but on the whole pleasing to him. When the *Pittsburgh Courier*, the National Association for the Advancement of Colored People, and the other newspapers and civil rights organizations had first begun campaigning for admission to flight training, an otherwise racially segregated Army might have been acceptable, provided only that blacks could enter the Air Corps. By the fall of 1940, however, almost a decade after the effort began, these same voices were challenging the very concept of separating the races within the military service. But despite the changing attitude among the leadership, the President's action seemed a dramatic breakthrough to many of the individual black voters whose support he needed.

To consolidate the advantage thus gained, Roosevelt responded during the week before the election to the remainder of the agenda presented by Walter White, Hill, Randolph, and Mary McLeod Bethune. The White House announced that Colonel Davis had been nominated for promotion to brigadier general, the first black ever to achieve that rank. He soon pinned on his star. General Davis went into retirement in July 1941 after more than forty years of service, but was recalled for the national emergency and served until 1948. At the same time that Davis's promotion was announced, Secretary Stimson revealed that he had selected a Civilian Aide on Negro Affairs, a position similar to that held by Emmett Scott during World War I. Chosen for the new office was William O. Hastie, dean of the Howard University school of law, an official of the National Association for the Advancement of Colored People, and a federal district judge for the Virgin Islands.[32]

The President's actions helped him win a third term, but his attempt to compromise with segregation failed to satisfy some of the black leaders whose support Mrs. Roosevelt hoped to retain. The issue was jobs, for the promise of equal opportunity for employment at military reservations did not ensure access to the burgeoning defense industries. Again Walter White and others approached Mrs. Roosevelt, who arranged for Sidney Hillman, a white union official who headed the labor division of the Office of Production Management, to discuss the subject with Robert C. Weaver, who administered federal job training efforts for blacks. Weaver also served with Mary McLeod Bethune and others as an unofficial adviser in the first lady's "black cabinet," the informal group that helped shape Mrs. Roosevelt's racial attitudes and indirectly those of the administration. Unfortunately, the meeting between Weaver and Hillman brought no agreement and confirmed how difficult it would be to persuade employers voluntarily to hire persons without regard to race.

The lack of progress emboldened A. Philip Randolph to organize a march on Washington, scheduled for July 1, 1941, to demand equal opportunity for jobs generated by the defense program and, in addition, an end to racial discrimination within the armed forces. Randolph and the other organizers of the march persisted in the face of the legal and logistical difficulties of massing in the capital and conducting the demonstration. Nor were they deterred by the prospect of offending an administration, however helpful thus far, that was urging cancellation of a march that could prove politically embarrassing.

The threat of the march, which could loosen the bonds the Chief Executive had just established with the black community, and insistent lobbying by Mrs. Roosevelt and others persuaded the President to respond to the grievances that Randolph was voicing. Even Secretary Stimson, confident of the superiority of the white race, felt that concessions had to be made, not out of any sense of justice but because he had come to believe that Randolph and the other leaders were trying to head off a communist takeover of the civil rights movement. Out of the White House came an order requiring fair employment practices in fulfilling defense contracts and establishing a Fair Employment Practices Commission to monitor compliance with the directive. The march never took place; the threat of confrontation had obtained what persuasion had failed to gain.[33]

By September 1941, three months before the Japanese attacked Pearl Harbor and both Germany and Italy declared war upon the United States, the Army was accepting far more blacks than the anticipated 9 or 10 percent of all recruits. One volunteer in seven was a black, as were 25 percent of those drafted or awaiting induction. With war looming on the horizon, the Army was actually postponing the induction of black draftees and reducing the quota for enlistments by members of that race. These moves served several purposes. They brought the percentage of blacks entering the Army more nearly into line with overall population figures and also gained time to build the barracks and other facilities needed to ensure racial segregation. Finally, the resulting delay enabled the War Department to transfer from the four black regiments of the Regular Army the veterans needed to lead and train the new black recruits. Without an experienced cadre, drawn from this source, chaos could result.[34]

Early in 1941 the efforts of almost ten years had paid off, as the Army air arm accepted its first blacks. Flight training commenced at Tuskegee Institute, mechanics and other technicians enrolled in courses at Chanute Field, Illinois, and nine so-called aviation squadrons took shape at bases from Virginia to Louisiana. But men assigned to these squadrons, mostly draftees, performed routine housekeeping duties such as driving trucks, working as janitors, tending lawns, or performing minor maintenance on buildings and runways. Already Judge Hastie was complaining to General Arnold, the Commanding General of the Army Air Forces, as the Army air arm was now designated, that the members of the aviation squadrons divided their time between trash collecting and close-order drill. Nothing they did required much in the way of military, let alone technical, training.[35]

When war broke out in December 1941, segregation remained securely entrenched despite the concessions made by the Roosevelt administration. Acutely aware of discrimination at home, blacks no longer thought in terms of obtaining civil and political rights by shedding their blood on behalf of the country and thus gaining the gratitude of white Americans. More closely unified than ever before, black Americans were willing to fight, but they saw a domestic enemy as well as an overseas one. Borrowing British Prime Minister Winston Churchill's "V for Victory" symbol, they publicly called for a "double V" campaign aimed at defeating America's foreign enemies while at the same time overcoming racism in the United States. Instead of assuming goodwill on the part of white authority, they sought to trade military service for measurable progress toward full citizenship, at times accepting promises, if reasonably confident the pledges would be honored, but continuing to press for civil rights, economic opportunity, and a useful role within the military.[36]

10

The Army's Black Eagles

DURING THE industrial and military mobilization immediately preceding the Japanese attack on Pearl Harbor and America's involvement in World War II, spokesmen for the nation's blacks had concentrated on three issues—equal opportunity for jobs in defense industries, impartial administration of the new draft law, and an opportunity for qualified blacks to learn to fly. The emphasis on flying reflected the fact that aviation had captured the imagination of American youth by means of motion pictures like *Ceiling Zero* and *Test Pilot*, comic strips like "Smilin' Jack," and radio serials like "Jack Armstrong" and "Captain Midnight." Young whites could easily identify with models like Roscoe Turner, the dapper racing pilot, the incomparable Charles Lindbergh of New York-to-Paris fame, or Eddie Rickenbacker, the leading American fighter ace of World War I.

Blacks, too, had their pantheon of aerial heroes, including Dale White and Chauncey Spencer, who had flown from Chicago to Washington to demonstrate for a disbelieving officialdom that blacks could learn to fly. Other inspirations for young blacks were Charles A. "Chief" Anderson, the first of his race to hold a commercial pilot's license, and Albert E. Forsythe, a practicing physician, who made several long-distance flights in the early 1930s. Another of the group was a woman, Willa B. Brown, who operated a flying school near Chicago. She was one of the few women, white or black, to combine business and aviation in this manner. With few exceptions, the black fliers were all but unknown to white Americans. Although White and Spencer had lobbied on Capitol Hill, they had not become celebrities. Chief Anderson was believed to have ready access to General Arnold, the commander of the Army air arm, not because of their shared interest in aviation, but because Anderson's father had once worked for Arnold's parents.

In making their flight to Washington, White and Spencer had hoped to kindle enthusiasm for flying among blacks. They succeeded so well that pilot training attained a disproportionate significance for blacks, becoming a symbol of achievement. Whatever its perceived importance, the numbers actually involved were small compared with the total number of blacks in the Army. The subsequent effort to provide more nearly equal treatment throughout the entire service affected many more persons, black and white, than did the introduction of blacks into the Air Forces.

The two black airmen lent impetus to a program of civilian pilot training for blacks, and this in turn, despite Arnold's misgivings, exerted pressure on the Army to train at least a token number of black aviators. A plan to establish a military pilot training center at Glenview, Illinois, collapsed when the Navy decided to acquire the site for its own use. Nevertheless, by the time the Japanese attacked Pearl Harbor, the Army Air Forces was supervising the instruction of a few black air cadets at the Tuskegee Institute. The actual training was conducted by a group of black civilian pilots under the direction of Chief Anderson. A white officer functioned as overall commander from the outset, white instructors arrived when the program expanded, and a white command structure rapidly took shape.

Segregation prevailed throughout the training cycle. Cadets who completed primary training at the Alabama institution remained there for the subsequent stages of instruction. They entered basic training, an introduction to military flying, then advanced training, which combined aerobatics and gunnery, and finally joined the 99th Pursuit (later Fighter) Squadron, based at the Tuskegee Army Air Field, to undergo combat training. The air base, in short, was a world all its own.

The black cadets had a unique status. They were in the Air Forces, subject to its rules and regulations, but they were not full-fledged members of the service. They could, for example, make practice landings at Maxwell Field, Alabama, or some other base, but they were not welcome to take their meals there or remain overnight. Scheduling and the efficient use of planes and facilities yielded before the unremitting pressure of racism.

The attrition rate among black aviation cadets—those men undergoing flight training but not yet commissioned officers—proved unusually high, 50 percent or more in classes numbering from seven to thirteen students. The director of training, Captain Noel Parrish, attributed this percentage of failures, roughly twice that of a typical class of whites, to the fact that enthusiasm alone served to admit to the aviation cadet program some blacks of mediocre intellectual accomplishments or marginal physical condition. Mrs. Roosevelt, after all, was taking a personal interest in the project, so classes had to be assembled quickly, without the intensive screening to which the Army routinely subjected white applicants.[1]

To local whites, whether farmers or inhabitants of nearly towns, the black fliers were a source of bafflement. In Alabama blacks plowed behind a mule or picked cotton; they rarely drove automobiles and certainly did not fly airplanes. In Montgomery, for instance, a civilian asked Second Lieutenant Charles DeBow if he was "one of those new colored fliers over at Tuskegee." When the young officer acknowledged that he was, the bewildered citizen asked, "What do you boys want to fly for anyhow?" Not only were all blacks "boys" but for one of them to aspire to anything grander than being a teacher at a segregated school seemed almost a violation of the natural order.[2]

If the white townspeople could not understand why "you boys" wanted to fly, the War Department seemed reluctant to believe that DeBow and the others could actually learn to do so. Secretary Stimson, for one, expected the black pilots to make little or no contribution to victory over the Axis powers. He looked upon the program as a concession to a politically active minority rather than a useful element in the nation's war effort. He had written off the black officers trained at Fort Des Moines in an earlier war as failures, an embarrassment to themselves and the service, and he believed the black aviators also would fail.[3]

The black pilots themselves were acutely aware of the fragile nature of the Tuskegee experiment. They knew that the air arm had been reluctant to admit them to training and that the whites of Alabama viewed them with a mixture of fear and curiosity. They realized that their failure would be interpreted as further proof that blacks could not compete in the white man's world. When the Curtiss P-40 fighter flown by Mac Ross caught fire in midair, the lieutenant parachuted safely, but as he disentangled himself from the harness, he wondered if the loss of his plane would convince the War Department authorities that blacks could never become competent aviators. An investigation revealed, however, that the accident resulted from engine overheating rather than pilot error. Ross was thus absolved, but Jim Crow continued to look over his shoulder and those of the black civilians and servicemen who worked on the planes at Tuskegee.[4]

Gradually the 99th Fighter Squadron took shape as black airmen completed training and joined the unit. Although a handful of old-timers from the 24th and 25th Infantry received transfers to Tuskegee to indoctrinate the enlisted clerks in the mysteries of Army administration, there were no veteran black pilots to take over the segregated organization and pass on the lessons of combat flying that required years to learn. As a result, Captain Parrish suggested basing rank upon evidence of the ability to lead men rather than on seniority, although such evidence was admittedly hard to obtain.

The War Department refused, however, to make an exception to the usual practice and ignore the comparative date of rank of the officers in this one unit. In fact, the Army authorities had already decided that the senior officer, Captain Benjamin O. Davis, Jr., a graduate of West Point and the son of the Army's only black general, would command the unit. He was a professional soldier, his character tempered in the crucible of the Military Academy, where no one spoke to him except in the line of duty, and he had five years of commissioned service. His superiors assumed that he would learn to fly, and he did, although his instructors sometimes complained that he banked his biplane trainer with the kind of square turn seen on the parade ground at West Point. He proved an ideal choice, as well as a logical one, even though he was not as skillful a flier as George S. "Spanky" Roberts and some of the others, for he understood Army procedures, what was expected of an officer, and how to motivate others.[5]

During the formative months of the Tuskegee experiment, Judge Hastie, the special adviser on racial matters, had been urging change upon the War Department. As early as the autumn of 1941, after ten months as civilian aide to the Secretary of War, he had become convinced that "existing Negro tactical units" should be "integrated into higher units and combat teams, with a view to their utilization to the greatest military advantage."[6] Although willing to accept some of Hastie's recommendations, such as improving recreational facilities for blacks or appointing black morale officers for segregated organizations, the Army Chief of Staff could not endorse so radical a solution to the racial problems of the service. In commenting upon the judge's proposal, General Marshall warned, "first that the War Department cannot ignore social relationships between negroes and whites that have been established by the American people through custom and habit; second that either through lack of educational opportunities or other causes the level of intelligence and occupational skill of the negro population is considerably below that of the white; third that the Army will attain its maximum strength only if its personnel is properly placed in accordance with the capabilities of individuals; and fourth, that experiments within the Army in the solution of social problems are fraught with danger to efficiency, discipline, and morale."[7] Winning the war was Marshall's obsession, and rightly so. He would insist upon fairer treatment for blacks, but only within the framework of segregation, for he felt that to abandon segregation would disrupt the fabric of the Army, alienate civil society, and make victory all the more difficult to attain.

Eventually, the wartime Army would engage on a small scale in the kind of "experiments" that Hastie recommended and Marshall abhorred, but for the time being the judge's triumphs were few. He concentrated upon the Army Air Forces, objecting to the organization of aviation squadrons, which, he charged, served "no specific military need" and "would never have existed except for the necessity of making some provision for Negro enlisted men in the Air Forces." The wall of segregation that Hastie hoped to batter down by assigning small units of blacks to larger ones made up of whites did crack, however. At Chanute Field, Illinois, where so few blacks were undergoing technical training that separate facilities proved infeasible, men learned in the same classes without regard to race. "The results were excellent," Hastie reported. "The men did well."

At Tuskegee, in contrast, racial segregation remained in force, even in the base medical facility. The hospital staff consisted of general practitioners with neither experience nor training in aviation medicine, for they were the only black physicians available. With few exceptions, notably Captain Parrish, white officers at the airfield had no contact with blacks except during duty hours. Instead of avoiding the black officers, Parrish became a member of their club and habitually dined there. Otherwise, segregation raised a barrier between the races. Although Captain Davis had assumed command of the fighter squadron, black officers were not taking over the base itself, which remained in the hands of whites.[8]

Especially annoying to Hastie was the decision, despite the apparently successful integration at Chanute Field, to establish segregated classes for the comparative handful of enlisted clerks and typists and for the black officer candidates who would serve in nonflying specialties. His annoyance might have become wrath had he known that Congressman Pat Cannon, representing Miami Beach, Florida, where leased resort hotels already housed Air Forces officer candidates, had convinced federal authorities that any hotel where black trainees might live would forfeit its white clientele and face postwar ruin. Swayed by this argument, the Army Air Forces tentatively selected Jefferson Barracks, Missouri, as the site of an officer candidate school for blacks. No wonder that the judge chose early in 1943 to resign from the War Department to continue his fight for equal opportunity. Replacing him was his assistant, Truman K. Gibson, Jr., a black attorney from Chicago.

In submitting his resignation, Hastie acknowledged that progress had been made in certain areas; blacks after all were flying, if not flying in combat. "At the same time," he told Secretary Stimson, "I have believed that there remain areas in which changes of racial policy should be made but will not be made in response to advocacy within the Department but only as a result of strong and manifest public opinion." The subjects crying out for change included segregation in post theaters, the isolation of blood plasma according to the race of the donor, and the general pattern of racial discrimination imposed upon the Army, especially the Air Forces. These injustices, he believed, involved "questions of the sincerity and depth of our devotion to the basic issues of the war"; correcting them would "have an important bearing, both on the fighting spirit of our people and upon our ability as a nation to maintain leadership in the struggle for a free world." Since his efforts within the War Department had accomplished all they could, he chose to become "a private citizen who can express himself freely and publicly," seeking to influence the populace as a whole rather than the military hierarchy.[9]

The instinctive reaction of the Air Forces to Judge Hastie's resignation was to defend its existing policies. Major General George E. Stratemeyer, General Arnold's chief of staff, acknowledged that the aviation squadrons (separate) would not exist had the air arm not been forced to accept black draftees. Stratemeyer did not admit openly that the squadrons served as a dumping ground for the recently inducted blacks, who as a rule scored poorly on the Army General Classification Test. The officer insisted that any enlisted man, regardless of race, spent some time doing odd jobs around an air base—the kind of labor that seemed to be all that members of black aviation squadrons did. He also maintained that "intelligent negroes" could earn transfers to technical training courses or officer candidate school. In fact, the poor test scores would disqualify the vast majority from receiving this kind of instruction. As for the racially integrated classes at Chanute Field, the general said that these were the exception; segregation, as practiced at Tuskegee, was the rule and would remain so.

Included in the defense were a few concessions, one of them of great symbolic importance to black Americans. Basically, all that

Stratemeyer promised was a slight broadening of opportunity within the existing racial policy. Black doctors, for example, would receive appropriate training in aviation medicine, and there would be no separate school for the comparatively few black officer candidates. What delighted blacks and made Hastie's gesture of resignation seem worthwhile was a pledge that the 99th Fighter Squadron would see combat.[10]

Initially, the War Department had not intended to use the squadron in battle. Noel Parrish, promoted to lieutenant colonel and placed in command at Tuskegee, had discussed possible future assignments with Secretary of War Stimson and Robert A. Lovett, Assistant Secretary of War for Air, only to discover that they had formulated a vague idea of sending the black aviators to Liberia, once a refuge for freed American slaves, where Charles Young had served briefly as military attaché. There the squadron, despite the limited range of its fighters, would search for German submarines preying upon convoys along the west coast of Africa.

Several factors ruined the plan. For one thing, the government of Liberia was reluctant to accept American troops, white or black, because of the possible impact of their comparatively high salaries and the inevitable military construction on the nation's fragile economy. For another, Judge Hastie resigned, causing the Air Forces to relent and promise that black pilots could serve in combat overseas. The decisive consideration, however, was the Allied invasion of North Africa and the subsequent need for tactical fighters there, which forced the Army to use the black fliers against the Germans and Italians.[11]

Although lacking any leavening of experienced pilots (the unit commander, after all, had trained alongside the others), the 99th Fighter Squadron underwent no systematic indoctrination when it arrived in North Africa. Only one officer made a genuine effort to teach the newcomers to fly the Curtiss P-40 in actual combat. He was Colonel Philip G. Cochran, who had become a training specialist for Major General John K. Cannon, the commander of the tactical air forces in the theater of operations. Fighter and light-bomber squadrons, hastened through the training cycle in the United States, reached North Africa poorly prepared for combat. Normally, Cochran took over as combat leader, while the squadron commander handled routine administration, during a final indoctrination that paired the least experienced pilots in the outfit with those who had the most flying hours to form two-plane teams. If necessary, Cochran would assign officers from other units to increase the leaven of experience. Assigned by General Cannon to shepherd the 99th through its indoctrination, the colonel discovered that the unit had no veterans and operated under a policy of racial segregation that prevented transfers from white squadrons. The best Cochran could do was assign a few blacks to fly with white units willing to accept them, and even this violated the rules enforcing segregation.

During the brief period that Cochran was able to work with the Tuskegee airmen, he discovered that they were precise fliers, able to maintain a tight formation but weak in aerial navigation, and, like white pilots with similar experience, hard pressed to combine crisp aerobatics with accurate gunnery. Over the wasteland of North Africa navigation proved difficult for everyone, but the blacks may have faced a special handicap. The possibility of making cross-country training flights in the United States depended upon finding bases with separate facilities where the blacks could eat and sleep.

Segregation was hard on the black aviators, and because of segregation they were hard on themselves. The men of the 99th Fighter Squadron realized that they represented all of black America, that they were on trial before a Jim Crow jury eager to convict the entire race of incompetence and cowardice. As a result, every member from Davis to the newest clerk-typist felt unremitting pressure. For pilots especially the tension could become unbearable, causing embarrassment, even anguish, over minor mistakes that any flier who had logged a comparable number of hours might make. And unfortunately, Cochran's program of training and confidence building had to be cut short, for he received orders to the United States and thence to Burma, where he achieved fame as the leader of the air commandos, striking far behind Japanese lines.[12]

In North Africa, the black squadron joined the 33rd Fighter Group, composed of veterans of the earlier fighting there. Unfortunately for the new arrivals, some 40 percent of its white fliers hailed from the South, a sizable enough minority to establish the racial attitude of the organization. Consequently, the whites tended to treat the 99th Fighter Squadron as something of a joke, to expect nothing of the Tuskegee airmen, and to ignore them at meetings prior to combat missions. Instead of receiving precise information on routes, targets, and enemy defenses, members of the black squadron like Spann Watson were allowed to tag along, provided they kept out of the way. The whites called them "boys" and treated them as such, like children who were tolerated as long as they inconvenienced no one.

These "boys" did not hang back as expected. They put themselves in harm's way, flying their first combat mission over the island of Pantelleria in the Mediterranean Sea on June 2, 1943. One month later, First Lieutenant Charles B. Hall became the first American black to score a verified aerial victory since Eugene Jacques

Bullard, flying for the French, had downed a German triplane during World War I. Hall's victim was a Focke-Wulf Fw 190 that he destroyed while he was patrolling between Sicily and Tunisia.[13]

Slowly the black aviators rounded into shape. Many, however, had lower scores on aptitude tests and were in poorer physical condition than their white counterparts, so progress by the end of the Sicilian campaign in the summer of 1943 proved too slow to suit white commanders. "Based on the performance of the 99th Fighter Squadron to date," reported Colonel William W. Momyer, commander of the group to which the organization was attached, "it is my opinion that they are not of the fighting caliber of any squadron in this Group. They have failed to display the aggressiveness and desire for combat that are necessary to a first-class fighting organization." Particularly galling to Momyer was a request by Davis, then a major, to allow the 99th to stand down for three days during the Sicilian fighting so the pilots could rest. As far as the group commander was concerned, the black airmen could fly skillfully enough but lacked the discipline and motivation to succeed in aerial combat.

Colonel Momyer's superior, Brigadier General Edwin J. House, agreed that the Tuskegee experiment had failed, declaring that "the consensus of opinion seems to be that the negro type has not the proper reflexes to make a first-class fighter pilot." The general therefore proposed taking the P-40s away from the squadron and re-equipping it for coastal patrol missions, the sort of work it would have done had it gone to Liberia. House also requested that no more black fighter squadrons be sent overseas.

Major General John K. Cannon endorsed the views of these subordinates, advising the senior airman in the theater, Lieutenant General Carl Spaatz, that the pilots of the 99th Fighter Squadron lacked stamina—apparently his interpretation of the request for a period of rest during the Sicilian campaign—as well as aggressiveness and discipline. General Spaatz then put the finishing touches on the dismal evaluation, remarking that no squadron had "a better background of training," even though the only combat indoctrination was that provided by Colonel Cochran.[14]

Normally such a series of condemnations would have resulted in a unit's transfer or disbandment, but the fate of the 99th Fighter Squadron had political ramifications. As a result, the War Department placed the future of the organization in the hands of its Advisory Committee on Negro Troop Policy, headed by Assistant Secretary of War John J. McCloy. Its members included the directors of personnel for the Army Air Forces, Army Ground Forces, and Army Service Forces, with General Davis serving as the black representative. Judge Hastie had not been a member; in fact, he had not been consulted when the agency was formed in 1942. His absence probably reflected the desire of the War Department to strengthen military control over matters relating to black troops. The official attitude changed, however, and Truman Gibson, Hastie's successor, became a member of the McCloy committee.

As the inquiry by the committee got under way, General Davis, the father of the squadron commander, recognized the seriousness of the complaints and looked to Lieutenant Colonel Parrish for an explanation. In outlining for McCloy and the others the reasons underlying the behavior that had inspired Momyer's assessment, Parrish pointed out that all the pilots in the 99th had begun training at roughly the same time; there were no old hands to pass along the tricks of aerial combat, and segregation prevented the group commander from shifting aviators from the black unit for seasoning with one of the white squadrons. Even what Cochran had done, allowing a few of the black pilots to fly along on missions conducted by white units, bent the existing rules to the breaking point.

Benjamin Davis, Jr., who had returned to the United States to take command of a new fighter group made up of blacks, appeared before the committee to explain further the effect of racial segregation on the pilots and ground crews of the 99th Squadron. He conceded that Colonel Momyer, who had delivered the judgment that led to the committee hearing, was an airman of proven competence. In his own defense, the former commander of the squadron repeated the points that Parrish had made and revealed that he had asked for the period of rest because his unit had fewer pilots than white squadrons—twenty-six compared to thirty or thirty-five—and that replacements proved slow in arriving because so few blacks were being trained. In order to keep the same number of planes in the air as in a white organization, the black aviators had to fly more hours. Given the pressure under which the blacks operated—and which Cochran had observed in North Africa—the intensity of operation caused unusual fatigue. Moreover, since the incident during the Sicilian campaign, the 99th Fighter Squadron had gained experience and improved in both flight discipline and aggressiveness.[15]

Davis was correct in reporting that his old unit was improving. Under his guidance and the leadership of his successor, Spanky Roberts, the stepchild of the 33rd and then the 79th Fighter Group became the equal of the other tactical fighter units serving in the Mediterranean. The squadron sharpened its skill at dive bombing and strafing, supporting both French colonial and American troops and occasionally attacking shipping. Over the Anzio beachhead on January 27 and 28, 1944, the 99th aided an embattled Allied landing force

Washington Crossing the Delaware by Emanuel Leutze. This mural includes a black soldier (third rower from left) of Colonel John Glover's regiment of New England fishermen. Several blacks, among them Prince Whipple and Oliver Cromwell, crossed the icy stream with Washington that Christmas night in 1776. (*The Metropolitan Museum of Art, Gift of John Stewart Kennedy, 1897. [97.34]*)

The crew of the gunboat *Mendota* in 1864. This picture demonstrates the fact that during the Civil War large numbers of blacks, both freemen and freed slaves, entered the Union Navy. *(National Archives)*

Members of the 25th Infantry at Fort Snelling, Minnesota, during the 1880s. The soldiers wore the Prussian-style spiked helmet adopted by the United States Army at that time. The four black regiments of the post-Civil War regular army normally served at posts in the northern plains or southwest desert, far from the principal cities of the East or South. *(National Archives)*

A sketch of a black trooper of the 10th Cavalry serving on the western frontier (ca. 1888). Despite a thoroughly segregated existence at isolated outposts, where the principal recreation might have been educational programs arranged by a black chaplain or the favors of black prostitutes camped nearby, the reenlistment rate among black troops remained high. *(National Archives)*

BERTH DECK COOK'S.
U.S.S. Ossipee.

Sailors on board the USS *Ossipee* in 1887. By the turn of the century, the racial composition of the Navy had begun changing. When this picture was taken, blacks had not yet been relegated to the mess deck and engine room. Here whites as well as blacks prepared and served food. *(U.S. Navy)*

Forgotten Heroes, Fletcher Ransom's re-creation of the charge by black cavalrymen up what came to be called San Juan Hill in 1898. Once the smoke of battle cleared, Theodore Roosevelt overlooked the efforts of the black troopers and claimed for himself and the Rough Riders a lion's share of the credit for defeating the Spanish entrenched there. *(National Archives)*

"Men of bronze," members of the 15th New York Infantry (redesignated the 369th Infantry), which served with the 93rd Division (Provisional) during World War I. They used French weapons, wore French uniforms—including the distinctive helmet that inspired the shoulder patch of the 93rd Infantry Division in World War II—and fought alongside French troops, receiving better treatment than the black soldiers who wore American uniforms and served beside their fellow countrymen. *(National Archives)*

Men of the 367th Infantry, presenting arms at New York City (ca. 1917). These soldiers had just returned from France, where they had served in the 92nd Division. Handicapped by haphazard training, indifferent leadership, and the demoralizing effect of racial segregation, this regiment did not perform as well as those that served exclusively with the French. *(National Archives)*

Lieutenant Colonel Charles Young (left) with two other cavalrymen. This outstanding officer almost certainly would have become the Army's first black general had he not been placed on the retired list in 1917, ostensibly because of ill health. To demonstrate the absurdity of this claim, he rode on horseback from his home in Ohio to Washington, D.C., but to no avail. He was not restored to duty until immediately before the armistice, when the possibility of his becoming a general had passed. *(Library of Congress)*

Joe Louis, the heavyweight boxing champion, flanked by members of the 332nd Fighter Group as he posed before one of the unit's P-51s in 1944. (*Office of Air Force History*)

"Separate but equal" swimming pool, operated during the summer of 1942 for black enlisted men at Fort Sam Houston, Texas. By the end of the war, official policy had changed, requiring commanders to grant access, regardless of race, to most recreational facilities. *(U.S. Army)*

Military police detachment at the Tuskegee Army Air Field (1943). The black MPs were a source of friction with local white officials. To prevent violence by whites infuriated by the sight of blacks carrying guns, Colonel Noel Parrish, the base commander, insisted that men assigned to patrol nearby towns leave their weapons at the guard room. *(U.S. Army)*

Brigadier General Benjamin O. Davis, Sr., on an inspection tour of Europe in 1944. General Davis is shown interviewing a black sergeant, James W. Furman, and his white commanding officer, First Lieutenant John Arnold, a native of Mississippi. According to the then current belief, southern whites knew how best to "handle" blacks and so were chosen to command them. *(U.S. Army)*

Stewards and officers from the escort carrier *Copahee*, which ferried Army aircraft during 1944. The officers were white; the stewards included a few Orientals as well as blacks. The three chief stewards at the center of the second row are shown wearing uniforms different from petty officers in other specialties. *(National Archives)*

Black soldiers of the racially segregated 25th Regimental Combat Team moving toward the front lines on Bougainville in the Solomon Islands (April 1944). In this theater of operations, senior commanders tended to introduce black regiments to combat by attaching reinforced battalions to white organizations. *(U.S. Army)*

Black sailors by the destroyer escort USS *Mason* (1944), which put to sea with white officers and a crew composed largely of blacks. Although *Mason* performed capably enough, the Navy soon began assigning only small numbers of blacks to a variety of ships, thus providing greater opportunity for promotion, transfer, or training in a greater number of specialties. *(National Archives)*

Benjamin O. Davis, Jr., as a lieutenant colonel, peering from the cockpit of a plane (1944). The son of the officer who became the Army's first black general, the younger Davis survived the hostility of his classmates to graduate from the U.S. Military Academy. After learning to fly at Tuskegee Army Air Field, he became a skillful commander of a fighter squadron and later a group. He eventually attained the rank of lieutenant general in the U.S. Air Force. *(U.S. Air Force)*

A naval construction battalion on Guam toasting the end of World War II. As the picture shows, the Seabee unit's officers and noncommissioned officers, in the foreground, are whites and the enlisted laborers blacks. *(National Archives)*

Army soldiers in Korea (September 1952). This racially integrated crew is shown preparing to fire a white phosphorous projectile at Chinese positions in Korea. *(U.S. Army)*

Mess attendants on the battleship *Wisconsin* during the Korean War. The attendants' uniforms, patterned after waiters' attire, caused resentment among the blacks serving in that military specialty. *(U.S. Navy)*

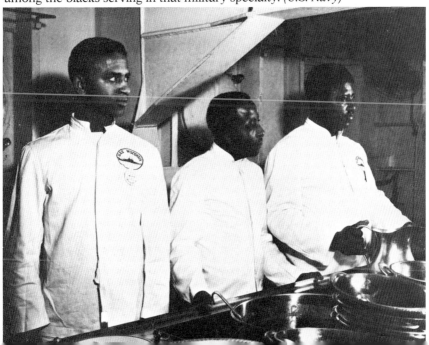

Three soldiers giving first aid to a fellow serviceman wounded by fragments from a mine in Vietnam (April 1968). During combat, shared pain and danger ensured cooperation between whites and blacks. The racial clashes among the troops were a rear-area phenomenon. *(U.S. Army)*

Soldiers in the wilderness of South Vietnam (August 1971). At the time this photograph was taken, Platoon Sergeant John Martindale was issuing hurried instructions to his men as their unit prepared to set up a defensive perimeter. *(U.S. Army)*

Scene near Khe Sanh (1968), during a lull in the fighting. A spontaneous gesture, like the offer of a cigarette, could provide more credible evidence of the success of racial integration than all the speeches and statistics emanating from the Pentagon. *(U.S. Marine Corps)*

Daniel James, in 1975 a lieutenant general and the vice commander of the Military Airlift Command, at the controls of an Air Force transport. He became the first black to don four stars, and he eventually became the commander-in-chief, North American Air Defense Command. *(U.S. Air Force)*

Samuel L. Gravely, the first black to hold flag rank in the U.S. Navy. Commissioned as a reserve officer during World War II, he served in a submarine chaser manned exclusively by blacks. He left the service after the war but then returned as a regular officer. *(U.S. Navy)* by downing a dozen German planes. Proof of the progress made by the black airmen was the decision made by General Spaatz in January 1944 to accept additional fighter squadrons made up of blacks. Spaatz had changed his mind since the previous summer. In addition, the 99th Fighter Squadron earned two Distinguished Unit Citations, one for the invasion of Sicily and the other for the fighting in Italy.[16]

By the time the war in Europe ended in May 1945, the black 332nd Fighter Group—made up of the 99th, 100th, 301st, and 302nd squadrons—was escorting bombers deep into Germany. The fighter pilots could boast that no bomber entrusted to them had ever been lost to German interceptors, even though the enemy employed the latest-model Fw 190s and Messerschmitt Me 109s, along with the revolutionary jet-powered Me 262 when that aircraft became available. First Lieutenant Roscoe Browne, flying a North American P-51D, downed one of the jets, and two members of the group shot down three Fw 190s or Me 109s on a single mission—Captain Joseph Elsberry on July 12, 1944, and First Lieutenant Clarence D. "Lucky" Lester just days later. The discipline and aggressiveness shown by the black pilots assigned to protect the bombers bound for Germany resulted in the award of Distinguished Unit Citations to three of the group's squadrons, the 99th (its third such decoration), the 100th, and the 301st. The Tuskegee airmen downed 108 enemy planes and shared another kill with a white pilot.[17]

Despite their success, the aviators trained at Tuskegee considered themselves the "Lonely Eagles" (a variation on Charles Lindbergh's nickname, the Lone Eagle, which the press had bestowed upon him). Lonely they were, isolated from the rest of the air arm by barriers of racial segregation, their accomplishments largely unknown even among black civilians. They were pleased, therefore, when the War Department agreed to make a documentary about them, a film that created real enthusiasm among black audiences.[18] From a technical standpoint the motion picture was skillfully done, with stock footage of aircraft in combat blended with scenes of blacks in training at Tuskegee. An actor turned soldier, Ronald Reagan, provided a moving narration. Yet, popular though it was at the time, in retrospect the documentary is something of an embarrassment, invoking patriotic sentiment to avoid explaining the contradiction of racially segregated units fighting to destroy the racist Nazis.

Although the 99th Fighter Squadron managed to make its way into the mainstream of the air war, where it was joined eventually by the other units that made up the 332nd Fighter Group, the Army Air Forces sent blacks overseas to carry out duties only indirectly connected with the romance of military aviation. At about the same time that the black fliers reached North Africa, black truck drivers and laborers were arriving in the United Kingdom to patch roofs, roads, and runways at air bases. Because of segregation, only enough blacks became mechanics, radiomen, or other kinds of technicians to support the black squadrons. Although now assigned to components of the Air Service Command, the military laborers performed may of the same duties as the men of the initial aviation squadrons, units that Judge Hastie condemned as having no purpose except providing a place to assign black enlisted men.

In the United Kingdom, a source of racial friction that had arisen among sailors there during World War I now reasserted itself, among the enlisted airmen in the labor units. As one white southerner wrote his parents, "I alone have seen 5 instances of niggers with white women. . . . The English must be pretty ignorant. I can't see how a white girl could associate with any negro." Local girls saw nothing wrong with dating blacks, although many American whites, not all of them southerners by any means, found this intolerable. Because of a deeply felt need to save English women from the blacks, whites, especially military police, were ready and willing to beat up black fellow servicemen, and oppression bred resentment among blacks.[19] On June 24, 1943, the rapidly growing sense of resentment erupted in violence.

Alerted by American officers that blacks were creating a disturbance, white military police arrived in front of a pub in the village of Bamber Bridge, Lancashire, and began making arrests of men who were wearing field jackets instead of military blouses or were otherwise out of uniform. The police were certain that the villagers resented the presence of blacks and appreciated the efforts to protect English womanhood, but this was not the case. The English men, both civilians and soldiers on leave, sided with the blacks, giving vocal support for the defiance of authority. Confident that the sight of a pistol would cow the blacks into submission, one of the military police drew his weapon, but a black noncommissioned officer talked him into putting it back in the holster, and the white military police drove away.

The two military policemen returned with two more and again tried to make arrests, this time trying to frighten the blacks with shouts, cursing, and the brandishing of billy clubs. Instead of scattering or giving up, the blacks fought back with bricks and bottles until the military police opened fire, seriously wounding two members of the air service detachment.

The uninjured blacks returned to their quarters, reported in dramatic fashion that the white soldiers had gone on a rampage, and urged their fellow blacks to grab their weapons and fight back. The white officers could not regain control. The commander was away, his executive tried but lacked experience, and the only officer able to calm the group was the public information officer, a black second lieutenant named Edwin D. Jones, who had been with the unit a few days.

At this point a detachment of military police arrived with an armored car, all the evidence that many of the blacks needed to convince them that the whites were going to attack the compound and slaughter those inside. Members of the service unit took up their weapons. Some prepared to repel an assault, which never came; others went out into the night, setting up roadblocks or commandeering trucks and driving aimlessly over roads, shooting at whites. The firing died away before dawn, and by midafternoon on the 25th, the blacks and all but four of their rifles were accounted for. There had been no deaths, but three blacks, one military policeman, and one white officer of the service detachment had been wounded by gunfire, and two military policemen beaten.

Two separate courts-martial tried the blacks believed to have taken part in the shootings or beatings. The first of these proceedings found four blacks guilty of various charges, and the second convicted twenty-eight defendants. Reviewing authorities took into account the racial slurs used by the military police, as well as their willingness to resort to violence, and reduced the sentences so that no one spent more than thirteen months in confinement and all returned to duty, even though four were to have received dishonorable discharges and others of the group up to seven years in a military prison.

Another mitigating factor was the behavior of the officers of the detachment. No more than three of them tried to assert authority. Lieutenant Jones, by addressing the men as fellow blacks, had some brief success, but the acting commander, Major George C. Heris, could not restrain what he later termed "a mob frenzy." The third officer was wounded when he drove around a roadblock set up by mutinous members of the command. The other officers failed to exercise leadership of any description. Two of them refused to look after the two blacks shot by the military police when the riot began, another reportedly was drunk, and three others abdicated their sworn responsibilities and made no effort to calm the men. Service units of this sort tended to be dumping grounds for the least competent white officers, though there were exceptions.[20]

Indifferently trained and led, likely to be set upon by military police for real or fancied violations of Jim Crow practices—even where Jim Crow as yet was alien—the black enlisted man faced an existence even more disheartening than that of the Lonely Eagles. The pilots, after all, shared the excitement of flying and the danger of combat; the men wielding shovels or paint brushes had no such compensations. Racial segregation within the air arm began to soften, however, as the war progressed, shedding some of its manifestations while retaining its essential viciousness.

This change did not constitute recognition of the heroism of blacks in aerial combat or on the battlefield, but represented a reaction to a series of racial outbursts resembling the violence at Bamber Bridge. Assistant Secretary of War John J. McCloy, the head of the War Department's advisory body on racial matters, urged that the Army modify the thoroughness of racial segregation, pointing out that what had failed in 1917 would not possibly succeed in 1943. He believed that commanders should pay close attention to a worsening racial climate, citing recent "riots of a racial character at Camp Van Dorn, Mississippi; Camp Stewart, Georgia; March Field, California; Fort Bliss, Texas; Camp San Luis Obispo, California; and Camp Breckinridge, Kentucky."[21]

General Marshall heeded McCloy's words, calling for "continuous and vigorous action to prevent incidents of discrimination and the spread of inflammatory gossip," along with "positive preventative measures to spike an impending outbreak." Such a policy, Marshall believed, depended upon an attitude on the part of commanders that refused to allow "the improper conduct of either white or negro soldiers, among themselves or toward each other." This even-handed discipline was also to prevail in relations "between soldiers and the civilian community." Although the Chief of Staff emphasized discipline, he insisted that "adequate facilities and accommodations will be provided negro troops," an attempt, at best, to apply the veneer of equal treatment upon the reality of racial segregation.[22]

Granted that the kind of discipline advocated by General Marshall would not right the fundamental wrong of racism, it could curb the worst excesses. "I do not believe," Truman Gibson commented, "that racial attitudes which have been firmly entrenched over a period of years can be changed in a short time by any general statement." The civilian aide to the Secretary of War remained hopeful, however. He pointed out that the immediate task consisted less of changing basic attitudes than of making sure that "all soldiers engaged in a common task should be treated as soldiers, regardless of race." By exercising discipline, commanders could ensure that black servicemen received, at the very least, civil treatment from other troops, whether on a military reservation or in town.[23]

In seeking to bring about such treatment, the McCloy committee battled the tide of segregation, occasionally making some headway. Instrumental in its efforts were the two civilian aides, Judge Hastie and his replacement, Truman Gibson—along with General Davis. The committee succeeded in obtaining a number of concessions from the War Department, some of them all but unthinkable before the war. Indeed in July 1943 the Adjutant General, James A. Ulio, issued orders on behalf of General Marshall that every soldier, regardless of race, would enjoy equal access to recreational facilities, a far cry from the situation that prevailed at Fort Leavenworth in 1938, when a detachment of black cavalrymen had been barred from clubs and swimming pools.[24]

Recreational facilities on military bases, a category that included officer's clubs, were especially important to blacks, who rarely had free access to restaurants, bars, theaters, or the like in nearby communities. In the Army Air Forces, the officers' club loomed especially large; the proportion of officers to enlisted men in the air arm was half again as great as in the Army as a whole. There existed, moreover, a regulation dating from 1940 that opened the clubs to all officers, but at the time it was written, the Air Corps had yet to begin training pilots at Tuskegee. Although the Army Air Forces no longer felt bound by the rule, which clearly approved the admission of blacks, the black officer could easily familiarize himself with its content, and he was likely to demand full compliance. Thoroughly fed up with segregation, for which admission to the club became a convenient symbol, and looking forward to civilian life after the war, he was quite willing to risk his temporary military career to attack racial discrimination. The kind of man selected to become a pilot and leader of men was highly unlikely to submit to a clearly illegal policy.

A number of senior airmen simply did not believe that blacks were capable of anger, let alone effective action. As late as the fall of 1943 white officers of the Air Service Command, which included a large number of blacks, among them those who had rioted at Bamber Bridge, could devote part of a conference to a serious discussion of the need to keep the child-like black man from becoming frightened, "as under this condition he can do, or will do, nothing." Officers were to flatter their black troops and kid them along, not really expecting anything of them, much as some white fliers had treated Spann Watson and the other Tuskegee airmen. This attitude prevailed at a time when Truman Gibson, who had replaced Judge Hastie as special civilian aide to the Secretary of War, was warning McCloy of the evil that could be done by the wrong kind of white officer, the "fatherly masters" convinced of the "primitive and child-like qualities of their Negro soldiers."[25]

The issue of admission to membership in officers' clubs soon demonstrated that the educated black, far from being child-like, could organize and use regulations to his advantage. At Selfridge

Field, Michigan, a recently organized black unit, the 477th Bombardment Group (Medium), was training. Colonel William L. Boyd, the base commander, ignored both the 1940 regulation and the more recent directive by the adjutant general and refused to admit the unit's black officers to the club. He went so far as to begin construction of a separate facility for blacks, which he submitted as evidence that members of both races were receiving equal treatment. He did not call attention to the fact that as long as blacks were stationed there, he insisted that whites serving in the Women's Army Corps have an armed escort when walking anywhere on the base.

The violation of War Department policy was obvious to anyone willing to look at the facts. Truman Gibson prodded Assistant Secretary McCloy, pointing out that the kind of discrimination practiced by Boyd was illegal outside the gates, according to Michigan law. An investigation followed, and the colonel received a reprimand. Both Boyd and the group were transferred.

Reassigned ultimately to Freeman Field, Indiana, the group remained in the First Air Force, still commanded by Major General Frank O'Donnell "Monk" Hunter, the former leader of American fighter forces in Europe and Boyd's superior. "Negroes," Hunter once told a black reporter, "can't expect to obtain equality in 200 years and probably won't except in some distant future." The general, a native of South Carolina, endorsed what Boyd had done and resented his subordinate's being reprimanded. What was even more ominous for the 477th, Hunter had concluded on the basis of conversations with senior officers at Army Air Forces headquarters that General Arnold's directive of May 1944 that the air arm would follow War Department policy and grant equal access to clubs and other facilities was a gesture to appease the Roosevelt administration and need not be followed.

No wonder, therefore, that Colonel Robert R. Selway, Jr., the group's white commander, proposed to invoke the same racial policies that had got Boyd in trouble. Early in 1945, when the 477th received word of the move to Freeman Field from Godman Field, Kentucky, where it had made a temporary home after leaving Selfridge Field, Selway announced that there would be two officers' clubs at the new location, separate but equal. Race, he assured his black aviators, had nothing to do with his decision; one club would be for trainees and the other for instructors and members of the permanent party at the airfield. The fact that all trainees were black and all the instructors white did not escape the notice of his command, and muttering began among the blacks. Selway then consulted General Hunter, who assured him that this policy was perfectly acceptable as long as race was not mentioned as a consideration. If the black officers objected, Hunter said, "I'd be delighted for them to commit enough actions . . . so I can court-martial some of them."

The officers of the 477th granted Hunter his wish. They had been excluded from positions in which they might command whites, they had been denied promotions for that reason, and now they were being barred from the existing club, its dining room and bar, while a separate facility was being built. They knew all too well that their use of a separate club would be an acknowledgment of inferiority, and they were officers and airmen performing the same duties as their white counterparts. Rather than accept second-class status, they challenged authority.

Four black officers tried to enter the club on the evening of April 5 but left when military police, posted there by Colonel Selway, told them they were not welcome. Next came a group consisting of nineteen officers who insisted upon being arrested. Before the club closed for the night, sixty-one blacks were under arrest, three of them for trying to shoulder their way through a cordon of military police at the entrance.

Within the Air Staff there was strong sympathy for Hunter. He was a veteran flier, who had been replaced in England, not because he had done a bad job, but because he lacked the kind of airplanes to do a good one. Without long-range fighters he had been unable to provide an escort for bombers ranging deep into Germany, and he had shared the blame for the resulting heavy losses. But granted that some of his peers may have supported Hunter because of the circumstances under which he had been summoned home, a good many senior officers shared his views on blacks.

That Hunter and Selway intended to ban blacks from the club at Freeman Field was obvious from the start; the only question was how to disguise their purpose. Upon learning of their action, Major General Laurence S. Kuter, Arnold's Assistant Chief of Staff for Plans, suggested applying the distinction between instructors and trainees to officer's clubs throughout the First Air Force. The McCloy committee cut through the semantic camouflage and advised the Secretary of War that the Army Air Forces was trying to return to a discredited policy of separate but equal. The resegregation of officers' clubs or other recreational facilities could not be tolerated. When Hunter's chief of staff, Brigadier General Edgar E. "Pop" Glenn, heard that the McCloy committee had taken a hand, he was nonplussed. He had never heard of the Assistant Secretary of War, had no idea of his duties, and assumed that he was some sort of black agitator. The fact that Glenn had been serving in China might explain, though not excuse, his ignorance.

The policy advocated by Hunter, Selway, and others was thus

reversed. The Army Air Forces, however, had to deal with the blacks involved in the incident at Freeman Field. Of the sixty-one officers arrested, only the three who attempted to push past the military police went to trial. The defendants—Lieutenants Roger C. Terry, Marsden A. Thompson, and Shirley R. Clinton—turned out to be permanent party, members of the maintenance unit that kept the base in operating order, and not trainees at all. Since members of the permanent party had a right to use the club, this fact destroyed the distinction upon which Selway's policy had been built and with it the prosecution's case. Two of the black officers were acquitted, and Lieutenant Terry was fined $150 for shoving the Freeman Field provost marshal.

In the meantime, General Arnold decided that the 477th should be shaken up and its training intensified for an early deployment to the Pacific. The war in Europe had ended, and General MacArthur indicated that he would accept the black airmen, even though his air commander, General George C. Kenney, recommended against sending them. Benjamin O. Davis, Jr., now a colonel, and other black veterans of the fighting against Germany replaced Selway and his cadre of white officers. Japan yielded, however, before the group was ready for combat.[26]

Efforts by the War Department to ensure better treatment for blacks on military reservations could be subverted in various ways by diehards on staffs or holding important commands. At times racism manifested itself in pettiness, as at the Lincoln, Nebraska, Army Air Field, where blacks slept on wood-and-canvas cots and whites on steel cots with springs and mattresses.[27] On the other hand, a sensitive commander like Noel Parrish, who attained the rank of colonel after taking over at Tuskegee, could improve the lot of blacks in the Army Air Forces. Despite his effort, however, the trainees there experienced demoralizing boredom as they acquired the skills they would never use. Openings simply did not exist for them, since the total number of black squadrons never exceeded eight, four fighter and four medium bombardment, organized into two groups, the 332nd Fighter and the 477th Bombardment, only one of which, the 332nd, served overseas. Although a visit from Lena Horne, who had just launched her career in motion pictures, might briefly relieve the tedium, the lot of the men at Tuskegee remained frustrating indeed.

Because of these circumstances, the air base took on the aspect of a black outpost surrounded by hostile whites. Any incident might trigger violence, and given the attitude of Alabama authorities, who had sworn to uphold the hated Jim Crow laws, such an incident seemed certain to occur. When Tuskegee town police arrested a soldier from the airfield for drunkenness, a black military policeman drew his gun and, though he had no authority to do so, took the man back to base to face military charges. Infuriated by the humiliation of being held at gunpoint by a black man, the town's law officers waited for the military policeman to return, arrested him, and beat him badly enough to put him in the hospital.

Soldiers from the airfield were on their way to town to avenge the beating when Parrish intercepted them and persuaded them to return to their quarters. The colonel then arranged a shaky truce between the Tuskegee airmen and white authorities in the neighboring towns. In return for promises that the local police would treat his men fairly, Parrish made sure that his military policemen no longer carried guns. The local whites could tolerate a black exercising power over others of his race, but they feared and hated the armed black who might conceivably turn against them.[28]

Other incidents demonstrated the difference that a conscientious commander could make. In the southwestern United States, the commanding general of the Second Air Force, St. Clair Streett, scattered black servicemen among all his installations to minimize the demoralizing effect of racial segregation. He further insisted that his subordinate commanders avoided practices that smacked of racism and try to promote cordial relations between black airmen and the citizens of communities near Army air bases.[29]

Through their own efforts, black airmen had triumphed over German pilots overseas and American racists at home. In aerial combat, the graduates of the Tuskegee training center had ranged as far as Berlin, fought the latest jet aircraft, and lost to enemy interceptors not one of the bombers they escorted—an inspiring war record. At home, the nonviolent resistance at Freeman Field foreshadowed future events. At the Indiana base, black officers, in using the regulations to right a wrong, relied on legal advice supplied by the National Association for the Advancement of Colored People. After the war, the same civil rights organization would provide the attorneys who invoked the basic law of the land to overturn a succession of Jim Crow laws that barred blacks from participating in many aspects of American life.

11

Integrating the Fighting, Though Not the Army

THE PROBLEMS THAT confronted blacks in the Air Forces were basically the same as those encountered elsewhere in the Army, for at the onset of war the same racial policy prevailed in the ground forces and service forces as in the air arm. Like the Air Forces, the rest of the Army tried to improve the treatment of blacks while preserving racial segregation. Black troops eventually received generally free access to recreational facilities on military bases, and black units went overseas to fight the Germans and Japanese as well as to form a pool of military labor. This much the Air Forces did, and the Army as a whole would not have gone further had it not run short of infantrymen and been forced to integrate the fighting, if not the service itself.

The air arm and the rest of the Army had established manpower objectives believed adequate for the defeat of the Axis powers. During 1944, however, the Air Forces realized that it had a surplus of men, cut back on recruiting and training, and, along with the Army Service Forces, began transferring men to the Army Ground Forces, especially the infantry. The War Department had calculated too finely in determining how many combat divisions it would need, deciding upon a hundred but reducing the total to ninety. The absence of any margin for error caused the reshuffling of troops within the Army and raised the question whether the service could continue to divert blacks into just two of the combat divisions fighting Germany and Japan.

As during World War I, blacks were eligible to become reserve officers. During the emergency preceeding the outbreak of war, a handful of blacks were attending officer candidate schools along-side whites. Because so few blacks, perhaps one in twenty, could score well enough on the Army General Classification Test to apply for officer training, and fewer actually applied and gained admission, the Army saw no need to set up a segregated school as it had in 1917. The number of black candidates increased after the United States entered the war and the volume of inductees expanded; nevertheless, considerations of test scores and health restricted the number of blacks who could enter officer training.

Even so, more blacks were pinning on the gold bars of a second lieutenant than the existing black combat units, principally the 92nd and 93rd Infantry Divisions and the 2nd Cavalry Division, could absorb. Since the War Department continued to insist officially that the black soldier preferred to serve under a white officer—racist mythology insisted that blacks resented success in others of their race and had a natural respect for white authority—whites occupied the key command and staff assignments, while the black officers not needed to lead small units became specialists in personnel matters, assistants to white staff officers, and the like. One result of this policy was the creation in large combat organizations of two command structures, one black and the other white, each lacking communication with or trust in the other.[1]

White commanders had little confidence in the comparatively well educated black officers and less in the black draftees, who tended to score poorly in the general classification test, a result of inferior schooling, and also to suffer the consequences of inadequate diet and lack of medical care. As in the Air Forces, the black enlisted man encountered attitudes that varied from indifference to hostility, with rare instances of genuine understanding.

If one phrase could summarize the Army's attitude toward blacks, it might well be "You know how niggers are." These words prefaced explanations by white officers that blacks could not be believed, that they had to be cursed at and hounded, and that they were oblivious to racial slurs, "nigger" for one. Many white officers did not credit blacks with intelligence, let alone hopes or ambitions or indeed feelings of any sort. As a result, these insensitive commanders made no effort to discover the state of morale within their units, confident that a stirring speech or a pat on the back by a white man would be enough to motivate the black soldier. Most of the time, they were the kind of leaders who deliberately avoided contact with those they led.[2]

The policy of segregation, which resulted in this divisiveness, was pursued to absurd lengths. Fort Huachuca, an isolated outpost in the Arizona wilderness, boasted not only separate officers' clubs but two hospitals, one staffed by blacks for blacks and the other operated by whites for white patients. The Army did, however, try to compensate for racial segregation and for the remote location by assigning educational specialists and encouraging visits by touring shows, especially those featuring black performers.[3]

Isolated outposts like Fort Huachuca posed special difficulties for blacks. The nearest cities were all but inaccessible to soldiers, who could not have private automobiles, and those with the time and money for the long trip by bus might encounter Jim Crow seating, especially in the deep South, and strict racial segregation upon arriving at the destination. No wonder that prostitution flourished, as it had under similar circumstances at the "hog ranches" of the frontier Army—though the problem during World War II was not, of course, confined to one race.[4]

Segregation was not the sole manifestation of racism. In April 1941, during the prewar mobilization, a black soldier, Private Felix Hall, his hands bound behind him, was found hanging from a tree at Fort Benning, Georgia. Post authorities at first tried to call the death a suicide, but the black troops knew that one of their number had been lynched. They were unable, however, to discover who murdered him, whether servicemen or civilians who had made their way onto the vast reservation.

The Tuskegee fliers had experienced an intense pressure to excel despite hostility on the part of white airmen; the black infantry or engineer trainee sent from his home in the North to a post in the South endured even greater tension—the fear of being lynched for violating the unfamiliar rules of a Jim Crow society. Not surprisingly, the young black, poorly educated and uprooted from all that was familiar, could develop chest pains or shortness of breath out of fear that he would be sent to Georgia or Mississippi and hanged or shot.[5]

Fear also helped unite black soldiers, however, and the indignities of segregation bound them together in anger. Therefore, when Assistant Secretary McCloy warned the Army of the need to face its racial problems, he could point to a series of recent clashes between whites and blacks. In several instances, white military police had triggered the violence by enforcing both Army regulations and Jim Crow customs, and doing so in a style so arrogant that at times it bordered upon the suicidal. At Fayetteville, North Carolina, in the summer of 1941, white military police from Fort Bragg boarded a bus loaded with black soldiers, most of whom had been drinking, and tried to quiet the unruly troops by flailing away with truncheons. Instead of cringing before authority, the angry blacks fought back, one of them snatching a pistol from a military policeman's holster and opening fire. The ensuing exchange of shots left one black and one of the military policemen dead and three blacks and two whites wounded.[6]

One of the incidents mentioned by McCloy involved white military police from Camp Van Dorn, Mississippi, who were trying to enforce uniform regulations among black troops angered by being transferred from the more open society of Phoenix, Arizona. A fight broke out between the black soldiers and military police. The local sheriff arrived on the scene of the disturbance, a black soldier bolted from this enforcer of Jim Crow, and the lawman shot him to death. The black soldiers, members of the 364th Infantry, armed themselves and tried to break out of camp, charging a riot squad of black military police, who opened fire and wounded one man. The regimental commander and the chaplain managed to gain control, although the search for hidden weapons continued for several days.[7]

The lot of the black foot soldier did not consist of unrelieved oppression. As Colonel Parrish and General Streett had demonstrated in the Air Forces, a sympathetic officer could make a difference. At Camp Lee, Virginia, for example, a Georgia-born graduate of West Point, Brigadier General George Horkan, defused a potentially explosive situation. Black soldiers returning from passes to Petersburg faced the choice of returning to camp in the crowded Jim Crow section of one of the few available buses or walking the 10 miles. Resentment over this blatant discrimination was building until Horkan found a way to bypass the segregationist laws of the Commonwealth of Virginia. He arranged with the local transit company to operate Army buses, distinct from the usual public conveyances, exclusively for soldiers, who would be seated in order of boarding rather than by race.[8]

Racial tension was bad enough, however, for General Marshall to insist that commanders "prevent incidents of discrimination" of the kind that had led to racial violence.[9] He was not abolishing racial segregation, which remained the official policy. Indeed, the War Department insisted that separation of the races was desired by most whites and accepted by most blacks, however much the latter hated the practice. Nonetheless, segregation was undergoing modification. No longer could theaters, exchanges, or recreational facilities be reserved for a particular race, although they could be restricted to a particular unit. Army policy would not be violated, therefore, if a black battalion had a segregated exchange, reserved for its own members, and possibly a segregated theater.[10]

The change in policy did not effect a social revolution within the Army. Because black troops usually occupied self-contained cantonment areas, they tended to use their own theaters or exchanges for reasons of convenience. The fact that they could make use of a recreational facility anywhere on post proved a boon to black morale, however, precisely because a manifestation of Jim Crow was thus removed.

At some posts, commanders tried to frustrate even this measure of racial integration by making it difficult for blacks to travel outside their own areas to make use of facilities elsewhere on the reservation. On the other hand, a cooperative commander could ease tensions, if not create racial amity. At Fort Lewis, Washington, for instance, blacks and whites collaborated in the production of a show and played on the same athletic teams. These efforts paid off by lowering the rate of unauthorized absences and courts-martial among black soldiers. In contrast, those posts that tried to maintain segregation in recreation and entertainment encountered demonstrations not unlike the one at Freeman Field.[11]

While the question of modifying racial segregation to permit equal access to theaters or exchanges was thus being resolved, the War Department came to grips with the problem of employing black troops overseas. During the disheartening months after the destruction of the American battle fleet at Pearl Harbor, the nation's allies (and, for that matter, the government of the territory of Alaska) were proving reluctant to allow black soldiers on their soil, concerned for various reasons about racial friction involving their citizens. In return for some fifty destroyers, built for World War I but needed to fight German U-boats in the current conflict, Britain had leased to the United States bases in various possessions in the Western Hemisphere. Colonies like Bermuda and Trinidad adamantly opposed the stationing of blacks at the American bases there. Australia, apparently the ultimate objective of the rampaging Japanese, feared that it would be inundated by a tide of black American soliders. Venezuela and Panama had the same misgivings. The overall military situation was so perilous, however, that the United States could not always yield to these concerns.

The possibility that Japan might isolate Australia caused the War Department to scrape together whatever forces it could to defend the supply line stretching from Hawaii to Australia by way of Samoa, the Fiji Islands, and New Caledonia. The hurriedly improvised contingent included the black 24th Infantry, which garrisoned Efate in the New Hebrides. Once the Allies had launched their counteroffensive, the regiment became a labor pool, rather than a combat team, its black soldiers unloading ships at various ports and manhandling supplies.[12]

The threat to the Panama Canal and the perimeter of outlying bases leased from Great Britain caused the Army to send to Trinidad the black 99th Antiaircraft Artillery Regiment. The presence of a French aircraft carrier at Martinique, a colony controlled by the government at Vichy, caused concern among American planners. Since the Vichy regime collaborated with the Germans, who occupied much of France, the possibility seemed to exist that the carrier's American-built planes might attack the canal or some other important target. The new base at Trinidad lacked antiaircraft protection and the black unit was available, so the War Department ignored the wishes of British colonial authorities and sent the 99th.[13]

The arrival during May 1942 of large numbers of American soldiers, both black and white, had a shattering impact upon life in Trinidad. White troops quarreled with local blacks, and prostitution flourished; but worst of all from the British point of view, the American blacks exhibited a self-assurance that promised to infect the islanders. Fear that colonial authority might thus be subverted caused British officials to ask that the black troops be withdrawn. The Department of State agreed, and the War Department in 1943 replaced one minority with another, substituting Puerto Rican soldiers who did not fit easily into an English-speaking Army because so many of them were fluent only in Spanish.[14]

As the war continued, except for the Tuskegee airmen, blacks in the Army seemed increasingly unlikely to see combat. The 24th Infantry moved cargo, and the 99th Antiaircraft Artillery Regiment got no closer to the war than Trinidad and remained there only briefly. Another large black unit, the 2nd Cavalry Division, arrived in the North African theater of operations only to be disbanded to provide men for service units. Walter White, who visited the former cavalrymen in Morocco, told the McCloy committee that he had never seen "more depressed troops." Apparently they did not understand that, as McCloy phrased it, "There are times when you have to cannibalize"—taking men from one unit and feeding them into another. The change of assignment, the assistant secretary assured White, came about because the soldiers were cavalrymen, members of an obsolete combat arm, rather than because they were black.[15]

Disbandment of the cavalry division coincided with the conversion in January 1944 of two black artillery battalions, organized from the old 8th Illinois, to engineer combat battalions, a change that seemed to indicate that the men would build roads or bridges instead of firing barrages. Alerted by an association of black veterans of World War I, Representative Hamilton Fish told his fellow congressmen that "it is astonishing that after 26 months of World War No. 2 virtually no Negro units have been engaged in combat except the Ninety-Ninth Pursuit Squadron and a few antiaircraft units." After calling attention to the record of the 93rd Division (Provisional), in which he had served as an officer during World War I, he demanded to know why, "since the educational standards of colored people have improved in the past 25 years," Secretary Stimson appeared to insist that most blacks could not master modern weapons. "Fourteen millions of loyal Americans," the white legislator declared, "have the right to expect that in a war for the advancement of the 'Four Freedoms' their sons be given the same right as any other American to train, to serve, and to fight in combat units in defense of the United States in this greatest war in its history."[16] (The Four Freedoms, offered as goals by President Roosevelt, were freedom of speech and religion and freedom from want and fear.)

In the meantime, Truman Gibson, the new civilian aide to the Secretary of War on matters affecting blacks, had realized that Fish and other Republicans would hammer away at the administration's reluctance to use blacks in combat as the 1944 presidential election approached. He therefore urged, late in 1943, that "some negro units" be sent against the enemy.[17] In addition, Eleanor Roosevelt, disturbed by reports of low morale among black service troops stationed in the British Isles, had suggested that "the colored people . . . be given a chance to prove their mettle."[18] Because of these pressures, the War Department by early 1944 was considering plans to dispatch more black units overseas, though not necessarily to use them in combat.

The most influential of the government officials was Assistant Secretary McCloy. He was aware of the bitterness that had surfaced in the black press, the charges that Stimson considered blacks too stupid to fight (at most a slight exaggeration of his views) and that the armed forces were engaging in a conspiracy to keep blacks from serving overseas. McCloy had watched and listened as the morale of blacks had plummeted, a demoralization reflected in their newspapers. Mired in despair, editorial writers were demanding a revolution in race relations, the eradication of Jim Crow. The white assistant secretary firmly believed that the Army had to make use of America's black citizens, whom he described in the cold-blooded terms of the administrator as a potential military asset. The opportunity to serve overseas, he was convinced, would create a sense of purpose among blacks, raising the morale of servicemen and civilians.

Even as Representative Fish, Mrs. Roosevelt, Mr. McCloy, and Mr. Gibson were recommending that black units be permitted to meet the test of combat, another black unit was en route to the far Pacific. The advance echelon of the 93rd Infantry Division sailed from San Francisco in January 1944, and by the end of February its

25th Infantry was at Guadalcanal in the southern Solomons, its 368th Infantry was at Banika in the Russells group, and its newly constituted 369th Infantry was at New Georgia in the central Solomons, All were garrison troops, however, for the fighting had moved to the island of Bougainville in the northern part of the Solomons chain.[19]

While these three regimental combat teams were arriving in the combat theater and taking over as security and labor troops on captured islands, the McCloy committee on March 2, 1944, advised Secretary Stimson that "it is the feeling of the Committee that colored units should be introduced in combat at the earliest practicable moment." Compelling reasons supported the argument for prompt action. "With so large a portion of our population colored," McCloy said, "with the example before us of the effective use of colored troops (of a much lower order of intelligence) by other nations, and with the imponderables that are connected with the situation, we must, I think, be more affirmative about the use of our negro troops." If the Army's reluctance stemmed from a genuine lack of proficiency on the part of black soldiers, McCloy suggested that the solution lay in improving training methods rather than barring a certain class of citizens from service on the battlefield. The Secretary of War yielded and on March 6 sent a statement incorporating McCloy's ideas to Lieutenant General Joseph T. McNarney, the Army's Deputy Chief of Staff.[20]

Black troops were now in position to begin carrying out the policy that the War Department was thus fashioning. The soldiers of the 1st Battalion, 24th Infantry, no longer functioning as stevedores, were serving along with white soldiers of the 129th Infantry as a reserve for the XIV Corps on the island of Bougainville. When word arrived in the theater that the Army wanted blacks introduced promptly into combat, the battalion was building fortifications to add depth to the positions manned by the 37th Infantry Division. Because the unit was readily available, General Millard F. Harmon, the commanding general of Army forces in the South Pacific theater, could commit it to combat almost immediately. On March 11, the battalion joined the 148th Infantry of the 37th Infantry Division, and that night the black soldiers saw their first combat, beating off a Japanese counterattack. The troops proved steady under fire, if somewhat trigger-happy, but when it came time to advance, they found that patrolling in the jungle tested both their own initiative and the ability of their leaders to read maps.[21]

The next ground unit to see combat was the 25th Infantry, the other of the black infantry regiments dating from the Army reorganization after the Civil War. In this conflict, as already noted, the 25th

Infantry formed an element of the 93rd Infantry Division, which had fought alongside French units during World War I. To commemorate its service in the earlier conflict, the division adopted a shoulder patch depicting a French steel helmet of that era.

Reinforced to fight as a combat team, the 25th Infantry arrived at Bougainville on March 28. Each of its three rifle battalions joined a regiment of the Americal Division (made up of Americans in New Caledonia) to participate in an offensive, supported after a time by black artillerymen. The advance, described as an attempt to improve the American perimeter, may have served as much to test the black troops as to forestall a possible Japanese attack.

As Colonel Vernon Caldwell had suggested after the previous war, the blacks fought well when serving with larger white units. Only one company encountered difficulties, briefly giving way to the panic common among troops new to jungle warfare. That outfit, Company K of the 25th Infantry's 3rd Battalion, lost cohesion when the patrols moving ahead into the rain forest lost contact with each other and with the company commander. The Japanese ambushed the leading elements of one platoon, which triggered indiscriminate firing that convinced the ambush victims that they were surrounded. Meanwhile, at the rear of the column, some troops not actually under fire panicked and ran because of the intense action up ahead, much of it shooting at shadows, and the absence of information on what was happening.

A handful of veteran Japanese, at the cost of perhaps two dead, had killed an officer and nine enlisted men and wounded twenty other Americans. The regimental officers attributed the setback to the inexperience of their men and the skill of the Japanese at using the jungle to best advantage, and veteran soldiers would not have been shaken so badly by the ambush. The black troops tended, however, to blame their white officers, saying they had not prepared Company K or led it well enough. The soldiers took note that the dead officer was black and claimed, without justification, that he had died trying to rally the men after the white officers had run away. The incident also inspired the rumor, untrue but widely believed among white soldiers, that the 93rd Infantry Division had broken under fire.

What happened to Company K was not all that unusual. A white unit, the 169th Infantry, underwent a grimmer ordeal during the fighting on New Georgia in the summer of 1943. Some 700 men, one-fifth of authorized regimental strength, had succumbed to combat neurosis during three months of fighting. The sounds of the jungle at night—the cries of strange birds, the noise of land crabs scuttling along, even the wind in the trees—gave rise to tensions that ultimately rendered men unfit for combat, sometimes causing them to panic when the Japanese opened fire. Even the wildest rumors seemed credible to tired and frightened men, some of whom reported seeing Japanese in black robes wielding long-handled metal hooks to drag Americans from their foxholes into the jungle night. The jungle, not race, caused inexperienced American soldiers to break down.

Except for this one incident involving Company K, the black soldiers of the 25th Infantry displayed steadiness, even heroism. Private Wade Foggie, for instance, became the first member of the 93rd Division to earn the Bronze Star when he blew up three Japanese pillboxes with rounds from his rocket launcher, killing ten of the enemy. Stephen H. Simpson, Jr., a medical aid man, braved the jungle night to care for a wounded soldier, whom he helped bring back to his battalion's lines after sunrise. Wounded in the neck during an ambush, Private Isaac Sermon kept firing his automatic rifle, killing at least three Japanese before he lost consciousness. Sermon lived to receive the Silver Star.

Following the fighting on Bougainville, the 25th Infantry and the two other regiments, the 368th and 369th Infantry, that made up the 93rd Infantry Division served mainly as garrison troops, taking over from the assault forces at islands like Biak, Morotai, and Mindanao and occasionally clashing with diehard Japanese. On Morotai, elements of the 25th Infantry tracked down and captured Colonel Kisou Ouchi, one of the highest-ranking Japanese taken prisoner during the war. Sometimes, as at Morotai, the black soldiers of the 93rd had to hunt down and kill or capture Japanese still holding out long after the objective had been declared secure; at other times, their job consisted of unloading ships or cleaning up the debris of war. Despite occasional combat, which fulfilled War Department policy, much of what these troops did was manual labor of the sort their fathers might have performed for General Pershing in France during the previous world war. However necessary or capably performed, the work done by this division often proved wearisome and went unrewarded.[22]

In contrast to the components of the 93rd Infantry Division, the 24th Infantry received official recognition for its service as the garrison force on Saipan and Tinian in the Marianas Islands. On Saipan in particular, the men of the regiment conducted themselves in what a War Department survey group considered a superior manner. At the beginning of May 1945, after more than five months on the island, black troops were patrolling the jungle, fighting almost daily skirmishes and killing or capturing Japanese, who continued to resist almost a year after the American landings. Because of the sustained action, members of the Saipan garrison became eligible for both the combat infantryman's badge and a battle star for their campaign ribbon.[23]

At the time the 93rd Infantry Division was entering combat in the Pacific, the other black infantry division, the 92nd, was completing training prior to seeing combat in Europe. The 370th Regimental Combat Team led the way for the 92nd Infantry Division, arriving at Naples, Italy, on July 30, 1944, and entering the Allied lines early in the following month. After a brief indoctrination, the black unit moved forward in an attack that rapidly became a pursuit, for the Germans had begun falling back to a prepared defensive line and, for the time being, were fighting a rear-guard action. The easy advance sent confidence soaring but scarcely tested the black troops or their leaders; worse yet, the German retreat contributed to a certain carelessness, especially in staff planning.

German opposition soon revealed the weaknesses of this vanguard of the 92nd Infantry Division. Early in October, after Major General Edward M. "Ned" Almond had assumed personal command of the 92nd Combat Team, as the further reinforced 370th Regimental Combat Team was now called, the black troops encountered the carefully prepared defenses of the Gothic line. This obstacle consisted of a series of fortified hills north of Florence that stretched from the vicinity of La Spezia on Italy's west coast to Pesaro on the Adriatic. Here German resistance intensified, magnifying the weaknesses of the attacking combat team. The white officers exercising command blamed their black soldiers when the advance bogged down, charging that the men tended to panic, but the troops claimed that the sluggish performance resulted from the fact that some platoon leaders and company and battalion commanders were indecisive, lacking confidence in themselves or their units.[24]

The arrival in Italy of the balance of General Almond's division soon confirmed the existence of serious weaknesses within the organization, failings that stemmed from a mutual lack of confidence between black soldiers and their white leaders. To a greater extent than artillery, engineer, or support elements, the newly arrived 365th and 371st Infantry had further been weakened by the transfer of some of their better officers and men to the 370th before it sailed to Europe. Centrally, segregation, which the War Department believed would ensure efficiency, fostered mistrust and resentment, eventually crippling the division.

The impact of racial segregation had made itself felt during training and grown more severe as the months passed. In the summer of 1943, Brigadier General Benjamin O. Davis, Sr., and Truman Gibson visited the division at training sites in Texas and Arizona and issued the first warnings. They came away convinced that General Almond was overlooking "the human element." Although "an exceptionally able officer," Almond was emphasizing "mechanical perfection in the execution of training missions" at the expense of maintaining "racial understanding between white and colored officers and men." The division's commanding general and his white offers tended to blame all the organization's problems on black newspapers and the unit's black officers. Gibson and Davis did concede that some black officers were "totally unfit for command" and recommended the elimination of these individuals, but the two men also warned that "there is a feeling of resentment against the white officers as a group by colored officers and enlisted men."[25]

In commenting upon these findings, General Almond charged that Davis and Gibson had been deceived by complaints from malcontents. Despite a variety of ugly incidents—a car carrying white officers had been the target of a volley of rocks, for example, and someone had struck a white officer with a shovel as he slept in his tent—the commanding general denied the existence of any resentment based on race. Ignoring the fact that his troops had recently booed him during a division baseball game, he insisted that morale was high and discipline intact.[26]

Resentment did exist, regardless of the general's denial. An inspection of the 92nd Infantry Division, conducted in December 1944, revealed that "racial sensitivity is strongly evident in the typical Negro officer, while distrust of a Negro's capabilities is present but less evident in the typical white officer." After making this observation, the white inspector, a mere major examining the policies of a major general, declared that "these attitudes do not appear to interfere with the work at hand." Specifically endorsing the "integrity, ability and impartiality of the Generals and policy-making officers whose decisions affect the 92nd Infantry Division," the major gave voice to one of the recurring excuses used to mask the effects of racism on military efficiency. "Racial antagonism," he said, "becomes less and less apparent the closer one gets to the foxholes. Like all non-essentials, it is discarded when lives are in danger."[27]

The inspector was trying to find excuses for General Almond. The deferential attitude of the junior officer was certainly understandable in view of the disparity in rank and the low regard that much of the Army's leadership had for the black soldier. In fact, racial segregation and its consequences hamstrung the division, inflicting more serious damage to its effectiveness than did the enemy.

Other factors, also related to the War Department's racial policies, contributed to the division's sluggish performance. In drawing up plans for replacements, Army personnel experts overlooked the

possibility that black troops might sustain losses as a result of pro-
longed combat, and when casualties did occur, suitable replacements were not available. Desperate measures became necessary,
such as shipping out soldiers who had been absent without leave
when their elements of the division had sailed or turning to men
whose psychological tests had indicated they they were unlikely to
adjust to military discipline, let alone the stress of combat.[28]

In evaluating the record of the 92nd Infantry Division, Truman
Gibson took note of the poor quality of replacements and the overall
educational level of the troops, lower than in comparable white organizations, as factors undermining the unit's performance. He returned, however, to the point the inspector had tried to ignore—
racial attitudes. These, he believed, had caused the division's
problems. White officers had no confidence in black soldiers and
disliked being assigned to lead them; the blacks became aware of
this attitude, resented it, and felt they had no stake—other than personal survival—in the success of the division.[29]

The difficulties of the 92nd Infantry Division required drastic
measures ranging from stopgap reorganization to a degree of racial
integration. To reduce the need for replacements, the organization
acquired a fourth black regiment, the 366th Infantry, a collection of
mobilized National Guard outfits that had been guarding Army Air
Forces bases in Italy. Finally, Lieutenant General Mark W. Clark,
who commanded American forces in the region, decided to restruc-
ture the division to include nonblack units. He did not, however, go
so far as to break up the division and parcel out the black regiments,
the kind of action that Judge Hastie had proposed for all black
troops before his resignation. Under General Clark's plan, two of the
original regiments, the 371st and 365th Infantry, occupied defensive
positions under control of IV Corps of the American Fifth Army,
while the 366th became the division reserve behind the two new regimental combat teams, the 442nd and the 473rd. The 442nd Regimental Combat Team was made up of Japanese-Americans; the
473rd, was a white outfit that consisted mainly of retrained antiaircraft artillerymen. Reconstituted after spending more time in combat than any other of the division's original regiments, the 370th Infantry took its place in the battle line, alongside the 442nd and
473rd.

This step toward racial integration, more a desperate gesture
than genuine reform, came too late. During the final weeks of the
war in Italy, soldiers of the two new regimental combat teams, the
whites and the Japanese-Americans, did most of the fighting on the
division's front. Although elements of the 370th Infantry fought well
at times, the influx of ill-trained replacements that it had recently
absorbed prevented it from achieving its potential.[30]

The smaller black combat units, regimental combat teams at the largest, consistently proved more effective in combat than the 92nd Infantry Division. Especially successful, whether in Europe or in the Pacific, were the artillery outfits that supported white infantrymen or tankers. In the European theater, black artillerymen fired concentrations that helped break out of the Normandy beachhead, punch through the German forces encircling Bastogne in Belgium, and cross the Rhine River. The 969th Field Artillery Battalion, for example, received a Distinguished Unit Citation for its contribution to the defense of Bastogne, an action it fought while detached from its parent headquarters and serving as a component of a white organization.

Black antiaircraft outfits also saw action guarding the outposts in the Pacific and protecting American troops in Europe. The defense of Hawaii against aerial attack rested throughout much of the war in the hands of the 369th Antiaircraft Artillery Regiment, formerly the 369th Infantry of the New York National Guard, the celebrated Men of Bronze who had fought so well during World War I. (A new 369th Infantry, formed since the outbreak of war, was serving in the Pacific.) In Europe, the 452nd Antiaircraft Artillery Battalion, firing 40-mm cannon, shot down its first German plane in August 1944 during the drive across France and its last deep inside Germany in April 1945.

The first black ground unit to receive the Distinguished Unit Citation during World II was another of the smaller outfits, a platoon from Company C, 614th Tank Destroyer Battalion. Firing from the cover of a draw, the platoon lost about half its men killed or wounded but succeeded in driving off a German force that had checked the advance of the 411th Infantry toward the town of Climbach, Germany. After the platoon leader, Lieutenant Charles L. Thomas, was carried wounded to an aid station, Technician Fifth Grade Robert W. Harris displayed initiative as well as courage in driving a truck loaded with ammunition across an open field to keep the unit's guns in action.[31]

Another black unit decorated for distinguished service was the 761st Tank Battalion. Initially assigned to the 26th Infantry Division, the black tank unit supported elements of a half-dozen divisions as it fought its way from France through Germany into Austria. Throughout this sustained action, during which the armored outfit normally provided companies or platoons that served with infantry regiments or battalions, the men of the 761st amassed a record that earned them a long-delayed Presidential Unit citation. The exploits of these soldiers might have gone unrewarded except for the efforts of several black veterans of the unit and one of their white officers, David Williams, whose history of the battalion caught the attention of Senator Richard Stone, a Democrat from Florida. At the senator's urging, Secretary of the Army Clifford Alexander, the first black to hold that office, and Secretary of Defense Harold Brown reviewed the record of the unit. Upon the recommendation of these two officials, President Jimmy Carter in January 1978 at last authorized the long-overdue award.[32]

Throughout the fighting in Europe, some commanders routinely mingled black and white artillery battalions and attached black tank or tank destroyer elements to white organizations. Not until late 1944, however, did the need for infantry replacements become so acute that black platoons were incorporated into white rifle companies. Army planners had calculated carefully the number of troops necessary to defeat Italy, Germany, and Japan, but when the thrust across France ended in stalemate along Germany's borders, casualties mounted rapidly. Furthermore, early in December 1944 the enemy counterattacked in the Ardennes region, killing or wounding some 50,000 Americans during the first week. After a month of fighting, American forces had suffered more than 125,000 casualties, victims of either enemy fire or the savage winter weather.[33]

In the hurried search for replacements, divisions waiting in the British Isles for future commitment to the battle for Germany were stripped of junior officers and trained infantrymen, as were the rear echelons in France. Finally, Lieutenant General John C. H. Lee, who was General Dwight D. Eisenhower's deputy responsible for the logistical support of American forces in Europe, concluded that "a limited number of colored troops who have had infantry training" should receive "the privilege of joining our veteran units at the front. . . ." Given to luxury, insofar as wartime conditions permitted, ever imperious, and reluctant to consult others, he was called "Court House" (from the map abbreviation C. H.) by his peers, but his subordinates when out of earshot, insisted that J. C. H. stood for Jesus Christ Himself. Acting now with his customary independence, Lee did not consult the theater commander before calling for black volunteers, whom he proposed to assign "without regard to color or race to the units where assistance is most needed." White and black troops, therefore, would "fight shoulder to shoulder to bring about victory."[34]

Opposition surfaced immediately. Upon learning that Lee intended to introduce blacks into rifle companies currently manned exclusively by whites, Lieutenant General Walter Bedell Smith, Eisenhower's Chief of Staff, objected to this departure from official policy. Smith was concerned that abandoning segregation in these special circumstances would encourage the black press and the various civil rights organizations in their attempt to banish racial segregation from the entire Army. Also opposed to the idea was Lieutenant General George S. Patton, Jr., who had no good words for any black unit. Not even the 761st Tank Battalion could impress him, despite its accomplishments, for he was convinced that blacks lacked the reflexes for armored combat. As for assigning black riflemen to infantry outfits, he warned that southern-born white soldiers would object to serving alongside blacks.[35]

Because of the sensitivity of this issue among his senior officers and, potentially at least, among civilians back in the United States, General Eisenhower sought to obscure the issue. Although fully aware that the need was for blacks—suitable white soldiers already were being rushed from the rear areas to combat units—the supreme commander insisted that Lee call for volunteers of both races, emphasizing the opportunity to fight rather than the promise of racial integration. As Eisenhower desired, Lee modified the announcement to extend the call to arms "to all soldiers without regard to color or race." Lee did, however, insist publicly that "in the event that the number of suitable Negro volunteers exceeds the replacement needs of Negro combat units, these men will be suitably incorporated in other organizations. . . ."[36]

The call for volunteers, preferably graduates of basic infantry training, went out on the day after Christmas 1944. Since the sources of white manpower in the theater had already been tapped, the response came from black units. Within two months some 4,500 blacks had signed up, roughly half of whom completed a course of instruction and joined the thirty-seven rifle platoons that were formed. Led by a white lieutenant or sergeant, each unit totaled some sixty men, about 50 percent over normal strength to provide a ready source of replacements for battle casualties.[37]

General Eisenhower did not insist that Patton accept the blacks, and none of the platoons joined the combat divisions of the Third Army. Major General Alexander M. Patch, commander of the Seventh Army, which had invaded the Mediterranean coast of France and advanced northward, accepted the volunteers but chose to group three or four platoons to form companies of blacks, a decision that had the effect of perpetuating segregation. Unfortunately, the first division to receive such a company had just rid itself of a black tank destroyer battalion of questionable competence; the division's officers, as a result, were convinced from the outset that blacks could not become combat soldiers. Benjamin O. Davis, Sr., acting as an adviser to Eisenhower on the use of black troops, persuaded Patch to persevere in the experiment, and subsequent companies performed capably with different divisions. Lieutenant General Jacob M. Devers, Patch's immediate superior, suggested assigning the blacks in platoons rather than companies, as General Lee had intended, but the war ended before Patch could respond.[38]

The black platoons proved overwhelmingly successful, especially with the divisions of the First Army. Not only did the newly trained riflemen fight well, they earned the respect of whites in the units they joined. A survey of white company officers and platoon sergeants in the outfits that blacks had joined yielded results that might have surprised General Patton. Of the 250 persons interviewed, none of the officers and just 1 percent of the noncommissioned officers said that blacks had performed "not so well," whereas 84 percent of the officers and 81 percent of the sergeants, an overwhelming majority, indicated that the volunteers had done "very well." the blacks, these replies revealed, had performed as well as white troops, and, more important, the two races had cooperated without the friction that had become almost routine between the black enlisted men and white officers of the 92nd Infantry Division. The officers and noncommissioned officers involved in the experiment that General Lee had inspired believed that the assignment of black platoons to rifle companies should become the normal practice if blacks were to serve as infantrymen. In sharp contrast, junior officers and sergeants assigned to divisions where no black volunteers had served remained overwhelmingly opposed to fighting in the same rifle company with black soldiers.[39]

In calling for black volunteers from service units, Court House Lee had tapped a reservoir of underused manpower, for the Army had channeled members of that race, whether volunteers or draftees, into noncombat tasks. During 1942, for example, with the Army accepting both volunteers and inductees, roughly three whites entered combat units for every one assigned to a service outfit that was not a part of the Army Air Forces. At the same time, seven blacks joined ground service organizations for every three that began preparing for combat. In December of that year, the President directed that both the Army and Navy rely on the draft to fill their ranks. Once the nation's manpower administrator, Paul V. McNutt, had put an end to separate draft calls for the two races, the number of blacks entering the Army increased, though the war had almost ended before the proportion of black inductees reflected the racial composition of the total populace. Looking ahead to this change in the racial make-up of the service, General Marshall, the Chief of Staff, approved a policy of diverting blacks, many of whom had scored poorly on the general classification test, to service units in order to release whites, with higher average test scores, for duty with combat organizations.[40]

A variety of black service outfits performed essential noncombat duties throughout the world. Engineers, for example, helped build a strategic highway through the wilds of Alaska and Canada; indeed, they made up a third of the 10,000 construction troops that worked on the project. In Asia, the principal construction effort was the building of a road from Ledo in Assam, through northeastern Burma, into China. The task required a labor force that included 15,000 Americans, 60 percent of them black engineers. In Europe, three-fourths of the truck companies were manned by black drivers, mechanics, and administrative clerks. These motor transport units operated the so-called Red Ball Express, carrying fuel, ammunition, and other cargo from the French coast to the armies advancing upon Germany. The line between service and combat sometimes disappeared, as happened at Leyte in the Philippines, when a burning Japanese bomber crashed into a ship being unloaded by black soldiers of a port battalion, or during the race across France, when an ordnance company outpaced the infantry to collide with and overwhelm a sixty-five-man German rear guard.[41]

Besides using blacks to replace white soldiers in service units, thus freeing troops to serve in combat, the Army for the same reason employed women in certain kinds of jobs, mainly administrative or clerical. Some 4,000 blacks volunteered for the Women's Auxiliary Army Corps (later the Women's Army Corps); 120 of them completed officer training at Fort Des Moines, the Iowa post where black men had trained for commissioned service in World War I. Although assigned to the same school as white officer candidates, the black women lived in separate barracks and ate at segregated tables.

Once they entered the Army, some of the black women found themselves performing duties far different from the tasks assigned to white members of the Women's Army Corps. At Fort Breckinridge, Kentucky, for instance, blacks discovered that freeing a man for combat required neither technical nor clerical skills, for their jobs consisted of sweeping the floor of a warehouse, ladling out food at a service club, or surviving the heat and humidity of a quartermaster laundry. At Fort Devens, Massachusetts, the blacks worked in mess halls, whereas whites typed in offices. Only one group of black women served overseas, a postal battalion, commanded by a black officer, Major Charity Adams, that arrived in England early in 1945.

A few black nurses, some 500 in a corps of almost 50,000 served in the wartime Army. At first they received assignments to hospitals where they could care exclusively for black patients, but this policy had to be abandoned. The crisis came in the United Kingdom. At a time when few black soldiers had been hospitalized, the nurses had to care for German prisoners of war, duty that aroused so much resentment that the chief surgeon for the European theater of operations had to agree that they would care for Americans, regardless of race.[42]

While black men and women were carrying out these various duties, Assistant Secretary McCloy's advisory committee helped persuade the War Department to publish a pamphlet, *Command of Negro Troops*, designed to help white officers understand the black soldier. The booklet warned against the use of derogatory terms or racial jokes, pointing out that "a safe rule on jokes is to avoid those which are dependent on the traditional ideas of the white man concerning Negro characteristics." Another useful piece of advice called attention to the fact that "officers who act on the theory that little can be expected of Negroes will naturally get little out of them," for the soldier would do his best to justify this expectation. The manual acknowledged that "the idea of segregation is disliked by almost all Negroes and hated by most" but insisted that no remedy was possible. "The Army accepts no doctrine of racial superiority or inferiority," the authors intoned. "It may seem inconsistent, therefore, that there is nevertheless a general separation of colored and white troops on duty," but this segregation was "a matter of military expediency, and not an endorsement of beliefs in racial distinction." Whatever the justification, the results were the same, imposing a hated system on blacks on the grounds that it was accepted by society at large.

This pamphlet provided the framework for a field manual, issued by the Army Service Forces. Along with offering general principles like "Keep your men informed," "Set high standards," and "Care for your men," the publication urged leaders to appeal to the pride of the black soldier, to respect black culture, and to avoid thinking in terms of stereotypes. Perhaps the most valuable portions of the manual were the sections dealing with the role of blacks in American life, their special problems of health and education, and the contributions of black soldiers in past wars.

As in the case of *Wings for This Man*, the film about the Tuskegee airmen, Truman Gibson and the McCloy committee helped persuade the War Department to undertake a similar project, *The Negro Soldier*, dealing with blacks throughout the service. Produced by Frank Capra, a veteran of Hollywood in uniform for the duration of the conflict, this documentary approached its subject with respect and was generally well received, although it could not come to grips with the issue of segregation. A poll of soldiers who saw the film revealed that less than 5 percent of whites and 3 percent of blacks thought that it conveyed a false impression.[43]

No such efforts sought to soften the racial prejudices of white society as a whole. Progress toward greater racial equality proved painfully slow beyond the gates of military reservations. W. L. Dawson of Chicago, a black congressman who had served as an officer during World War I, complained of the humiliation inflicted upon servicemen of his race traveling by bus or rail. He reported that they frequently could not find seats in the railroad coaches or in the sections of buses to which they were restricted. They also had to endure such manifestations of Jim Crow as waiting rooms and rest rooms designated for "colored only." A systematic attack on racism in interstate travel, however, would have to await the heroism of the Freedom Riders, almost twenty years in the future.

Another source of complaint was the treatment received at Red Cross clubs, especially in the United Kingdom. Officials of the organization failed to respond when General Davis called their attention to instances of racial discrimination at various locations. Certain facilities designated "colored staffed" would definitely accept blacks; elsewhere the reception might be hostile, even though in theory any soldier was welcome at any club.[44]

The American Red Cross proved openly more race-conscious in its administration of the blood plasma program than it did in operating its clubs. Ironically, the blood program owed its very existence to the efforts of a black physician, Charles R. Drew of the Howard University medical school, a pioneer in the collection and storage of blood for transfusions. Blood banks admitted blacks only reluctantly and kept plasma from these donors isolated from that drawn from the veins of whites. The excuse was that the possibility of accidentally receiving plasma from a black donor might deter injured whites from agreeing to blood transfusions essential for their survival.[45]

Throughout the war the Army clung to segregation as tenaciously as it could, only gradually yielding on such points as overseas duty, service in combat, and access to recreational facilities on military bases. The pressures that caused these changes in policy took various forms, like the riots at Fayetteville, North Carolina, between white military police and black troops, or Camp Van Dorn, Mississippi, triggered when a local white lawman killed a black soldier. As much as the violence itself, the resulting bad publicity prompted the Army to reconsider its segregationist policy. The growing political strength of blacks in the northern cities helped prod the administration and indirectly the War Department, as did the efforts of powerful or influential persons, including Mrs. Roosevelt. Unlike the first lady, Secretary of War Stimson had scant sympathy for the aspirations of blacks, but his assistant, John Mc-

Cloy, realized that segregation bred dissatisfaction and inefficiency. McCloy therefore worked willingly with Truman Gibson, General Davis, and others, to ease the harshest aspects of racism. Only once did the Army on its own initiative expand the opportunities open to black soldiers, and that occurred late in the European war when Court House Lee arranged for black volunteers as desperately needed infantry for the final offensive into Germany.

The War Department's policy of racial segregation, which yielded ever so slightly to military necessity, prevented the kind of widespread association that might have fostered mutual understanding and tolerance. Some contact did occur, however, and as indicated by the white reaction to Frank Capra's *The Negro Soldier* it might affect race relations in the future. Whatever the prospects for tomorrow, when the war ended racism remained deeply ingrained in American society.

Economic competition was a factor. As had happened during the previous conflict, blacks left the rural South to seek jobs in defense industries in the North. During the first two years after it went into effect, President Roosevelt's executive order requiring fair employment practices by defense contractors helped open an estimated 53,000 jobs to black citizens. The migration attendant upon the search for well-paying jobs created tensions not unlike those that had helped trigger racial strife following World War I.[46] Broader opportunities and higher pay enabled blacks to compete with whites for scarce housing and to make use of parks and other public places of amusement or recreation that had formerly been tacitly reserved for whites. At Detroit, Michigan, for instance, an attempt to establish public housing for the families of black workers on the fringes of a Polish neighborhood contributed to the tension that erupted in violence in the summer of 1943 at a municipal park on Belle Isle in the Detroit River. By the time federal troops restored order, twenty-five blacks and nine whites lay dead. The efforts of black defense workers to move into white portions of Buffalo, New York, aroused opposition, but threats and insults stopped short of physical violence. In New York City's Harlem, blacks rioted upon hearing a false report that a white policeman had killed a black soldier. Six persons died there, all of them black.[47] Since the Army tried to discourage violence against blacks, the racial climate in the service may have been somewhat more tolerant than among certain segments of the white civilian populace.

Questions of justice did not motivate the Army. It could not ignore violence for the same reason that it refused to embark upon racial integration, except in an emergency and then on a limited scale—either phenomenon might undermine discipline, alienate at least a segment of the populace, and impede the war effort. Blacks serving in the wartime Army did not receive the same treatment as whites or enjoy comparable opportunities for training, advancement, and assignment. During the war the Navy, events would prove, was making a more ambitious, though incomplete and short-lived, effort to attain equality of treatment and opportunity.

12

The Naval Service in World War II: Policy and Reality

LIKE THE ARMY, the Navy entered World War II as a racially segregated service, but blacks and whites were kept separate in a different fashion. The Army tried to maintain a specific number of units manned by blacks but commanded by white officers, organizations that were largely self-contained and capable of being housed or employed in a manner that would minimize contact with white soldiers. In contrast, the Navy enforced segregation by occupation. Black sailors, therefore, might serve with whites in a large warship, but with rare exceptions all the blacks prepared and served food or waited upon the ship's officers. Because they performed the same duties, the blacks could easily be segregated, eating and sleeping together separate from the rest of the crew. Except for the very few men with long years of service who had acquired other specialties, blacks were barred from the general service, loosely defined as comprising those occupational specialists—gunners, electricians, radiomen, machinists, and the like that sailed a ship or enabled it to fight.

Again like the Army, the Navy would modify its racial policy to meet the demands of war, but directives did not alter reality. By the time World War II ended, Navy regulations called for a greater mingling of the races and closer cooperation between black and white sailors than the Army demanded of its soldiers. Yet regardless of the rules, the Navy enlisted few blacks, assigned the largest concentration of blacks to ladling out food, and failed to provide the same degree of integration into ships' crews that had been common in 1845 or even 1895. Since the turn of the century the Navy had restricted the role of black sailors and deliberately ignored the fact that in the age of sail blacks had clambered aloft alongside whites, hung their hammocks in the same forecastle, and eaten their meals side by side with white crew members.

The Navy Department adhered to its new racial policy except to experiment briefly and unsuccessfully with small ships manned by Samoan or Filipino crews and commanded by white officers. So few members of racial minorities, blacks included, possessed the skills needed to sail a modern ship that the Navy's General Board—a body roughly comparable to a general staff—concluded that racially segregated ships were not feasible. Advocates of this scheme for manning ships with natives of these Pacific islands assumed that Samoan or Filipino fishermen could adapt as readily to the steam-powered gunboat as black merchant seaman in the era of sailing ships had adjusted to manning warships. Life at sea was no longer so simple, but the plan did not acknowledge this complexity, for it proposed training the Filipinos and Samoans at sea instead of in the formal schools where white seamen learned their basic skills.[1]

The new Secretary of the Navy, Frank Knox, who took office in 1940, followed the racial policy that had evolved within his department. A veteran of the Rough Riders, he had seen the Army's black cavalrymen in action, and he now suggested that black Americans could make their greatest contribution to national defense by enlisting in the Army's black regiments. To thrust blacks into the overwhelmingly white Navy, except as cooks or food servers, would prove cruel rather than kind, Knox insisted, suggesting that members of the racial minority would find themselves in a competitive situation where they were certain to fail.[2]

The beneficiaries of the Secretary's kindness were not pleased to be spared possible humiliation, and their spokesmen so advised the President. In September 1941, one year after a meeting with prominent blacks on the topic of racial segregation in the defense effort, Roosevelt tried to explain to a similar group why the Navy could not accept blacks except as messmen or stewards. The audience wanted the Navy to enlist their fellow blacks for general service, whether in engine room or gun turret, but the service flatly refused. The President now offered a compromise, a suggestion that might well have been taken as an insult except for the great respect that black leaders had for the Chief Executive and his wife. The proposal called for the Navy to take a first step toward ending racial segregation by assigning "good Negro bands" on board battleships, so that blacks and whites could learn to get along as shipmates.[3]

The black spokesmen who met with the President in September 1941 represented the crest of a rising wave of opposition to the Navy's racial policies, and because of this opposition Secretary Knox appointed a committee to review the role of blacks in that service. The uniformed representatives of the Navy and Marine Corps on the committee saw no need to change the existing policy, but another member of the committee, Addison Walker, dissented sharply. A special assistant to Assistant Secretary of the Navy Ralph A. Bard, Walker suggested assigning blacks to a few patrol craft, tenders, or similar auxiliary vessels. Under the guidance of white instructors, the crewman would learn every skill necessary to operate the segregated craft. Walker proposed his plan as a means of easing racial friction, which he considered a serious impediment to a smoothly functioning Navy. The majority, however, opposed any experiment that might upset the status quo and thus reduce efficiency and Walker's proposal generated scant interest within the naval hierarchy.[4]

While the committee was producing two reports, one by the majority and Walker's dissent, the Japanese attacked Pearl Harbor. On that morning Dorie Miller, a steward on the burning battleship *West Virginia*, dragged the wounded captain from the exposed bridge, then manned a machine gun, and, even though he had no formal training with the weapon, shot down two attacking aircraft. Despite his heroism, which earned him the Navy Cross, and his obvious skill with the machine gun, he was still waiting upon officers when he died in the sinking of the escort carrier *Liscome Bay* on November 24, 1943.[5]

Those blacks who sought to enlist in the Navy and avenge Pearl Harbor encountered rejection, except for the few who found vacancies in the stewards' branch. Understandably, the National Association for the Advancement of Colored People complained to the White House, and the President responded by referring the matter to the Fair Employment Practices Commission, established in June 1941, even though that agency had been created to deal with racial discrimination by defense contractors. The committee did address the topic, and its chairman, Mark Ethridge, recommended that the Navy accept blacks for general service, though on a segregated basis, much as Walker had advised.[6]

Mr. Roosevelt, having obtained the endorsement of the Fair Employment Practices Commission, now suggested, as only a President can suggest, that Secretary Knox find some duties for blacks to perform besides waiting on table at officers' messes. Knox then called upon the General Board to devise a plan to absorb 5,000 black recruits. The board, however, refused to remove the existing racial barriers.[7]

During the deliberations of the General Board, one officer, Rear Admiral Charles P. Snyder, the Inspector General, advocated the sort of approach that Walker had recently proposed—the establishment of segregated units in a variety of specialties. The admiral included music among these suggested fields, for he believed the "colored race is very musical," and aviation because the Army was training a black fighter squadron. Snyder's plan got nowhere, since the board rallied behind General Thomas Holcomb, Commandant of the Marine Corps and a vigorous advocate of the status quo. According to the Marine officer, "the negro race had every opportunity now to satisfy its aspirations for combat in the Army—a very much larger organization than the Navy or Marine Corps—and their desire to enter the naval service is largely, I think, to break into a club that doesn't want them."[8]

"The General Board," that organization reported, "regrets that it is unable to comply with . . . [the directive] which requires submission of a plan for taking into the Navy 5,000 men of the colored race, not in the messman branch." The existing policy should remain in effect, unless the Chief Executive specially directed otherwise. "If in the opinion of higher authority, political pressure is such as to require the enlistment of these people for general service, let it be for that."[9]

Clearly, the General Board in mentioning general service hoped to frustrate the President's plan by suggesting a policy—the acceptance of blacks for every enlisted specialty—that went far beyond what Mr. Roosevelt had in mind. The tactics, however, proved transparent and ineffectual. "The President is not satisfied with the alternative suggested by the recent decision of the General Board," Secretary Knox told his policy makers. "He thinks that some special assignments can be worked out for negro enlisted men which would not inject into the whole personnel of the Navy the race question."[10] Although aware of the President's dissatisfaction, Knox still envisaged some form of expanded opportunity that would not disturb racial segregation.

During March 1942 the General Board again addressed the question of opening new specialties to black enlistees, this time approaching the topic in a somewhat more cooperative spirit. The board listed a half-dozen categories of jobs that might be opened to blacks but warily avoided actually opening any of them, making it clear that the Navy would yield reluctantly to a decision by "high authority that social, economic, and other considerations require the enlistment of men of the colored race in other than the messman branch." In short, the naval leadership wanted civilian leaders to accept the full blame for the disorders and decline in efficiency that the General Board believed would result from any tinkering with the current racial practices.

According to Vice Admiral Walton R. Sexton, the board chairman, those units that would "offer the least disadvantages and the least difficulty of accomplishment as a wartime measure" included service units in the naval shore establishment and the Marine Corps; yard craft and similar non-combat auxiliaries; shore-based local defense forces in the various naval districts; seagoing cutters or port security detachments of the Coast Guard, which became a component of the Navy in wartime; naval construction battalions; or composite combat battalions of the Marine Corps. (In this context, "composite" simply meant manned by blacks.) When submitting this list of possibilities, the admiral recommended that "wide latitude be granted the several administrative authorities as to rate of enlistment, method of recruiting, training and assignment to duty and that progressive experience determine the total number to be enlisted."[11]

President Roosevelt, an Assistant Secretary of the Navy during World War I and alert to the ways of the naval bureaucracy, interpreted this recommendation as an escape clause, an "Ethiopian in the woodpile" he called it, demonstrating what a later generation might consider appalling insensitivity. Whether or not he displayed callousness in doing so, the President intervened on behalf of American blacks, cautioning Secretary Knox that the two of them should determine exactly how much latitude the admirals would have.[12] Roosevelt had spiked his cabinet officer's guns, treating him as an ally against an obdurate General Board instead of as one of the opposition.

Thanks to the President's prodding, the Navy began accepting blacks for "general service in the reserve components of the U.S. Navy, the Marine Corps, and the U.S. Coast Guard." Assignment to the reserve indicated that the sailor, Coast Guardsman, or marine would serve for the duration of the war, rather than for a fixed period of enlistment. The recruiting of messmen would continue, but effective in June 1942, some 277 blacks might enlist each week for general service. The Navy thus intended to accept some 14,000 blacks for general duty in one year of recruiting, a total not quite three times the number of messmen in uniform when the expanded effort began.[13]

Through persistence, President Roosevelt had succeeded in changing the Navy's racial policy. The pressure he exerted was intended to bring greater numbers of blacks into the service in a broader variety of specialties, thus making progress toward increasing opportunities in the Navy, as black leaders had urged in September 1940 and again a year later. Reality diverged from policy, however. The Navy's new policy did not attract large numbers of black volunteers, a lack of response that naval officers attributed "in part to Negroes' relative unfamiliarity with the sea or large inland waters and their consequent 'fear of the water.' " The reasons certainly were more complex and included poor physical condition and educational attainment, compared with white volunteers, and possibly a preference for the Army based on a lurking suspicion that the black sailor, whatever his nominal specialty, would end up waiting on table. Whatever the causes, by February 1943 blacks made up just 2 percent of the Navy's enlisted force. Of the 26,000 black sailors, some 18,000, or roughly two-thirds, were messmen, 6,000, or not quite one-quarter, were in the general service, and the remaining 2,000 served in naval construction battalions as Seabees.[14]

In February 1943, when it began obtaining recruits through the draft, the Navy tried to keep the monthly quota of blacks for general service at about 1,200. Secretary Knox explained that some 1,200 blacks for general service, along with 1,500 messmen, represented the maximum number the service could accept each month without resorting to racially mixed crews, an innovation that even the President opposed.[15] At this juncture, Paul V. McNutt, the manpower administrator, warned the armed forces that the ban on racial discrimination in administering the draft law would compel the Army and Navy to accept inductees not according to race but in the order called.[16] In the meantime, Mr. Roosevelt was having doubts about the Navy's commitment to a policy of accepting blacks for general service instead of using them exclusively as stewards or Seabees.

"Most decidedly," the President told Knox, "we must continue the employment of negroes in the Navy, and I do not think it in the least bit necessary to put mixed crews on the ships." The Chief Executive warned of public resentment if the armed forces did not accept blacks in proportion to their share of the populace. The Army had not yet met this goal, since slightly less than 10 percent of its inductees were blacks, but the Navy's performance was far worse. "You know the headache we have had about this," he reminded the Secretary, "and the reluctance of the Navy to have any negroes"— carefully avoiding mention of the fact that Knox himself had given voice to this sentiment. Mr. Roosevelt then concluded, almost conspiratorially, "You and I have had to veto that Navy reluctance, and I think we have to do it again."[17]

Having enlisted Knox as his ally, the President prevailed over the admirals, although his victory was incomplete. The proportion of blacks in the service never approached their share of the nation's populace; the total hovered slightly above 5 percent of the total enlisted strength. But a bit more than 10 percent of the sailors drafted during 1943 were blacks, some 78,000 out of 740,000. More striking was the fact that this figure represented almost two and one half times the number of black recruits in 1942. The increase resulted less from Presidential pressure than from a new manpower policy of apportioning black draftees between the Army and Navy. The naval service had no choice but to accept all the inductees assigned it.[18]

In theory, acceptance for general service opened the doors to a variety of specialties. In fact, blacks who were not servants for officers or food handlers tended to be laborers, either in construction battalions or in units made up of stevedores, ammunition handlers, or maintenance men. As was happening in the Army, where trained infantrymen unloaded ships, resentment grew among the blacks who had been assigned to these menial jobs even though their education or proven skills qualified them for more demanding work.

By the summer of 1943, therefore, signs of unrest began surfacing even among those black sailors not assigned to the messmen's branch. A naval construction battalion, for example, protested segregated quarters on the troop transport carrying them overseas. At the Naval Ammunition Depot, St. Julien's Creek, Virginia, reports that the audience at a radio broadcast would be seated in Jim Crow fashion resulted in a riot. The Navy Department's response to the increasing tension between the races was to create an agency to monitor the enlistment and assignment of black sailors.

Organized in August of that year, this agency, the Special Programs Unit, could easily have become a bureaucratic appendix, an organ of the department with no really vital function. That it did not was a tribute to four officers—Lieutenant Commanders Donald O. VanNess and Charles E. Dillon, their immediate superior, Captain Thomas F. Darden, and Lieutenant Commander Christopher S. Sargent. Although not a member of the Special Programs Unit, Sargent proved an implacable foe of racial segregation and, in effect, led a crusade to integrate the navy. A reserve officer assigned to the Bureau of Naval Personnel, this wealthy and well-educated individual had made numerous contacts among wartime government officials while a member of a law firm headed by Dean Acheson, later to become Secretary of State. Because he was in, though not really of, the Navy, Sargent could use these acquaintances to circumvent normal channels of communication, thus influencing service policies to a greater degree than his rank would indicate.[19]

Despite the Navy's grudging acceptance of blacks and its organization of the Special Programs Unit, the service offered only limited opportunities throughout 1943. Moreover, a policy of exclusion prevailed in the three broad categories of nursing, women volunteers, and commissioned service. Not even a shortage near year's end of some 500 nurses could persuade the Navy to accept qualified black women. Nor could they join the WAVES (Women Accepted for Volunteer Emergency Service) or the equivalent organizations of the Coast Guard and Marine Corps. No black naval officer actually served on active duty, and only a dozen were training at various colleges for commissions in the Naval Reserve. Although Camp Robert A. Smalls, the facility at the Great Lakes Naval Training Station where black recruits received their initial indoctrination, carried the name of an escaped slave who fought gallantly during the Civil War, the command structure was dominated by whites, some of them liberal on racial matters. The officer in charge was a white graduate of the Naval Academy, Commander Daniel Armstrong, whose father had founded a college for blacks, the Hampton Institute in Virginia.[20]

The policy governing the acceptance of women changed, though slowly. As early as April 1943, Secretary Knox was insisting that the possible enlistment of blacks in the WAVES was "under constant review,"[21] and that same month Rear Admiral Randall Jacobs, chief of the Bureau of Personnel, recommended an experimental program that would admit to the enlisted ranks a few "carefully selected Negroes . . . , the number to increase gradually," and offer commissions to a "few highly selected Negro women."[22] Although he "tentatively approved" the concept, Knox directed that planning continue.[23] Here the matter rested when Knox died in April 1944.

The new Secretary of the Navy, James V. Forrestal, resurrected the idea that Admiral Jacobs had proposed and advised the President that the Navy was ready to accept 10 black women as officer candidates and 240 enlistees. Although segregation would prevail, in some parts of the country whites and blacks might share the same mess hall, and everywhere all the separate facilities would be "equal, if not identical."[24] Yet another delay ensued, however, on this occasion because the President postponed a decision until he had returned to Washington after a meeting in Hawaii to adopt a strategy for the defeat of Japan.

Whatever his intentions, the Chief Executive failed to act after his return to the White House. The project remained in limbo until the exclusion of black women from the WAVES became a political issue, raised by Thomas E. Dewey, governor of New York and President Roosevelt's opponent in the 1944 presidential election. During the campaign, Dewey charged the Roosevelt administration with racial discrimination in barring blacks from the Navy's women's auxiliary. Four years earlier, Wendell Willkie had introduced a similar issue, and the prospect of losing black votes had helped persuade Roosevelt to broaden opportunities for members of that race within the armed services. Dewey's words had the same kind of impact; three weeks before the election, the Navy announced that the WAVES would accept black enlistees and officer candidates.[25]

Even so, the battle was not yet won. Recruiting proceeded so slowly that the Navy was unable to form a segregated training company as planned, and the Bureau of Personnel entertained the idea of canceling the entire project. Had Captain Mildred McAfee, the director of the WAVES, not ignored protocol and insisted that Secretary Forrestal himself make the decision, her organization might well have remained exclusively white. As it was, the Secretary of the Navy agreed that the black recruits should train alongside whites, rather than wait until their numbers made segregated training feasible.[26]

Blacks thus obtained access to the WAVES, though the volunteers numbered just two officers and seventy-two enlisted women. Black women did not respond enthusiastically to a call issued in the summer of 1944, at a time when prospects for victory, at least in Europe, were brightening. The Coast Guard's women's auxiliary admitted two blacks, and the women marines none at all. Of almost 11,000 Navy nurses who served during the war, just 4 were blacks.[27]

Secretary Knox, though he had resisted until his death the admission of black women into the WAVES, had come to accept the prospect of black men serving as officers in the Navy Reserve. At first he had opposed the idea, insisting that black officers would not be needed until there were large numbers of sailors of the same race for them to command. Indeed, he told those blacks seeking commissions in the Navy to apply instead to the War Department, which maintained black regiments even in peacetime.[28] The influx of black draftees that began in 1943 deprived Knox of his main argument and left him vulnerable to the logic of Adlai E. Stevenson, one of his assistants, who persuaded the Secretary to yield. As a result, on January 1, 1944, sixteen black enlisted men entered a segregated officer candidate school at the Great Lakes Naval Training Station. Although all of them successfully completed the course, only twelve received commissions, a purely arbitrary number adopted by the Bureau of Personnel for reasons never explained. Of the remaining four, one became a warrant officer, and the others reverted to enlisted status.

The members of this first group to receive reserve commissions included Dennis D. Nelson, later the author of a study on the Navy's racial policies. Joining the twelve were a handful of specialists, such as dentists or chaplains, and the graduates of officer training programs on college campuses. Among the college-trained officers were Samuel Gravely, the first black ever to attain flag rank (Commodore or admiral), and Carl Rowan, journalist, television news commentator, government official, and for a time the U.S. Ambassador to Sweden. In all, some sixty blacks would receive Navy commissions during the war.[29]

During the final months of Secretary Knox's tenure, the Special Programs Unit was campaigning for an opportunity to demonstrate that blacks, far from being inherently afraid of the sea, could operate a modern warship. Admiral Ernest J. King, the Chief of Naval Operations, agreed to such an experiment. Ironically, the foes of racial segregation like Christopher Sargent had thus succeeded in bringing about the organization of all-black crews.

Under the command of white officers and petty officers, black seamen manned the destroyer escort USS *Mason* and a submarine chaser, *PC 1264*. As black officers and noncommissioned officers with the necessary skills became available, they reported on board these ships and the four other segregated patrol craft that saw service during the war. From the standpoint of nautical skills, the black crews performed capably, especially the men serving in the *Mason* on the North Atlantic convoy route, but the experiment came to an end. The new Secretary of the Navy, James Forrestal, sided with those who believed that racial integration would result in a more efficient use of manpower than segregation could.[30]

A long-time member of the Urban League, one of the nation's major civil rights organizations, Forrestal agreed with those, like Sargent, who had concluded that segregation simply did not work afloat or ashore. The Knox policy had been to concentrate blacks in jobs ashore. The new Secretary reversed it out of practical rather than ethical considerations, for reasons of morale and efficiency rather than right and wrong. The new Secretary of the Navy had come to realize that segregation demoralized sailors of both races. "The Negroes resent the fact that they are not assigned to general service billets," he declared, "and white personnel resent the fact that Negroes have been given less hazardous assignments ashore." Although the Navy was substituting women volunteers for men in a number of specialties in the shore establishment, the men thus released for technical training or combat assignments were white sailors. Unable to serve at sea except in a few segregated ships, any black replaced by a WAVE was eligible because of his race for a severely limited number of jobs that actually contributed to victory over the Axis powers. Most of the vacancies continued to be in the steward's branch or the Seabees. Nor could black seamen replace whites due to return to the United States after long periods with combat ships of the fleet, for blacks could serve only in certain small ships. The result was idle or under-utilized black sailors. To introduce some degree of reason into the chaotic use of scarce manpower, Forrestal proposed an experiment of his own, a program to employ blacks, in a ratio of one to ten whites, in the crews of large fleet auxiliaries. If the plan proved successful, he intended "to extend the use of Negroes in small numbers, to other types of ships as necessity indicates."[31]

At Forrestal's direction, the Bureau of Naval Personnel selected twenty-five ships—oilers, ammunition ships, cargo vessels, and the like—in which blacks would serve. The number of ships was trifling in a wartime fleet that numbered some 75,000 ships and landing craft, including 1,600 auxiliaries of all types. The blacks might function in any of more than a dozen fields—for instance, as boiler-room firemen, yeomen pounding away a typewriters, seamen, or even pharmacist's mates—although the total in each field would be small. Some of the Navy's blacks had already completed the required training, others would have to attend service schools, learning their skills alongside white trainees, and still others would join their ships directly from recruit training and learn while on the job.[32]

This limited form of racial integration, which took effect in the summer of 1944, proved a resounding success. Emboldened by the results of a survey of the commanding officers of those fleet auxiliaries in which black sailors were serving, the Bureau of Naval Personnel in March 1945 proposed applying the policy to all such ships. After all, in the words of Admiral Jacobs, the "absorption of the small number of Negro personnel in the auxiliary vessels has been accomplished without due complications." As a result, he intended "to assign Negroes gradually to all auxiliary ships of the Fleet," provided only "that the number so assigned to any one ship should not exceed 10% of the allowed general service complement." Admiral King promptly approved the plan, which was being carried out when the war ended.[33]

The transition from total racial segregation to this limited degree of integration proved uneven at best. Throughout the period of transition, a number of units remained segregated, for the comparatively few fleet auxiliaries could not absorb all the black sailors who wanted to serve at sea, and the fast carrier task forces actually fighting the war accepted blacks only as stewards or messmen. During 1944 and 1945, three serious racial incidents occurred in segregated black organizations stationed ashore—among stevedores at Port Chicago, California, laborers on Guam, and Seabees at Port Hueneme, California—adding strength to the argument that racial integration brought racial amity. As Fleet Admiral Chester W. Nimitz, the Commander in Chief, Pacific, pointed out, by isolating black sailors the Navy was encouraging them to exchange stories of injustices they had suffered, to dwell upon these grievances, and ultimately to defy the authority they found oppressive. Racial integration provided a means of interrupting the powder train of emotion that might ignite violence between blacks and whites. Again, the principal motive of the advocates of integration was efficiency rather than morality.[34]

One racial explosion, a mutiny by black sailors, followed the detonation in July 1944 of hundreds of tons of ammunition at Port Chicago, California. The blast tore apart two ships and killed some 300 persons, 250 of them blacks assigned to a segregated labor unit that was loading ammunition on board the vessels. Fifty of the survivors refused to resume this dangerous work, which they believed had been assigned them because of their race. A court-martial convicted them of mutiny and sentenced them to prison, but the black press and the civil rights organizations campaigned successfully to have the men returned to duty.[35]

Guam was the scene in December 1944 of a riot between black sailors, again members of a segregated noncombat unit, and white marines. Harassment of the blacks by marines had become so flagrant that by mid-December the island commander, Marine Corps Major General Henry L. Larsen, felt compelled to intervene. He reminded his men that "the present war has called together in our service men of many origins and various races and colors. . . ." All of them, he said, "are entitled to the respect to which that common service is entitled." However eloquent, his statement had no effect. Violence broke out late in December when, in rapid succession, an off-duty Marine Corps military policeman, who was white, fired at some black sailors but hit no one; a white sailor shot and fatally wounded a black marine in a quarrel over a Chamorro woman; and a black sentry mortally wounded a white fellow marine who had been harassing him. The black sailors at the island's naval supply depot heard a garbled report that white marines had killed one of their number, a misunderstanding that led to a riot and the arrest of forty-three of the Navy men.[36]

During the ensuing court-martial, Walter White, who was touring the Pacific as an unofficial observer, participated in the defense.

He qualified for this role even though the doctor of laws degrees that he held were honorary, bestowed by Harvard and Atlanta universities in recognition of his contributions in the field of civil rights. The efforts of White and the Navy lawyers assigned to defend the black sailors rights could not win acquittal for any of the accused, but the National Association for the Advancement of Colored People pursued the case through the appeals process and ultimately to the White House. These efforts resulted in the release from prison of all those involved. Reviewing authorities decided that the harassment the black sailors had undergone at the hands of white marines had contributed to the riot and thus diminished the guilt.[37]

Unlike the violence on Guam, the third of the major disturbances was an example of peaceful resistance to racial discrimination. In March 1945, the men of a black Seabee battalion at Port Hueneme, California, refused food for two consecutive days but continued to report for duty, thus avoiding arrest for mutiny. The attendant publicity triggered an investigation that resulted in the replacement of the battalion commander, the principal objective the sailors had been seeking. Veterans of one overseas tour, these blacks had refused to tolerate racial bias on the part of this Mississippi-born officer in selection for promotion and the assignment of quarters.[38]

The discontent that surfaced in California and on Guam inspired Forrestal to follow the example of the War Department and appoint a civilian adviser on policy toward black servicemen. His choice was Lester B. Granger an official of the Urban League, who took office in March 1945. Granger's first task was to conduct a personal survey of racial attitudes and practices throughout the Navy, a tour of inspection that covered 50,000 miles, lasted six months, and involved tactful persuasion of a few officers still clinging to the old ways.[39]

Final evidence of the Navy's abandonment of segregation appeared during the summer of 1945. In June, the Bureau of Naval Personnel directed that inductees report to the nearest recruit training center, regardless of race. The only exceptions were men classified as illiterate, who would attend a special school at Camp Peary, Williamsburg, Virginia.[40]

In December of that year, with victory won, Forrestal acted to prevent the sort of discrimination on board Navy transports that had aroused such resentment among black troops returning from France after World War I. "In their attitude and day to day conduct of affairs," the Secretary of the Navy declared, "Naval Officers and Enlisted men shall adhere rigidly and impartially to Naval Regulations in which no distinction is made between individuals wearing the Naval uniform or the uniform of any of the Armed Services of the United States, because of race or color."[41]

The racial policies fashioned for the Navy also applied to the U.S. Coast Guard. Created in 1915 through a merger of the Revenue Cutter Service and Life Saving Service, the Coast Guard functioned in peacetime as a part of the Treasury Department. Transfer to the Navy occurred in November 1941, during the emergency that preceded American involvement in the conflict.

In peacetime the Navy and Coast Guard had treated blacks in similar fashion. In the era when black sailors helped man the nation's warships, one of the most famous skippers in the Revenue Cutter Service was Michael A. "Hell-Roaring Mike" Healy, whose mother was a mulatto slave, the wife of her master, a Georgia plantation owner. The Life Saving Service accepted black surfmen, and the Light House Service, not absorbed into the Coast Guard until 1939, had enlisted black light tenders, both slave and free. During the age of sail, when the Navy welcomed blacks, the Coast Guard's predecessors were doing likewise, and when the Navy began diverting them into service as mess attendants, the Coast Guard followed along. For the Coast Guard, the change in racial policy became embodied in service regulations during 1922, when new recruiting instructions specified that blacks enlisting for the first time had to become stewards. The old-timers already serving in other specialties received transfers to segregated stations. Among those who enlisted under the rules requiring black recruits to train as stewards was Alex P. Haley, who signed on in 1939, became a journalist when opportunities for blacks broadened, and after leaving the service wrote *Roots*, an exploration of the genealogy of his family, which earned him a Pulitzer Prize.[42]

In wartime the Coast Guard proved less conservative than the Navy concerning race. When the Navy's General Board, reacting to prodding from President Roosevelt, met in January 1942 to consider, though unfavorably at the time, the possibility of expanding the opportunities for blacks, the Coast Guard representative, Commander Lyndon Spencer, declared that "the problem has got to be faced." While the Navy fought a delaying action, Spencer pledged that the Coast Guard, although it was "not anxious to take on any additional problems at this time," would definitely accept more black recruits. The new men would join the few that already were serving as stewards, on light tenders, or in a variety of ratings on buoy tenders or similar craft maintaining navigational aids on the Mississippi River.[43]

Within ten days of the meeting of the General Board, Rear Admiral Russell R. Waesche, Commandant of the Coast Guard, began making good on the promise Spencer had made. The Commandant realized that the naval service could not ignore the President's wishes, and as a result he approved a plan for accepting 500 blacks and employing them in a variety of duties. Roughly 300 would serve on tenders, small cutters, and similar vessels, while the remainder joined port security detachments. The new men, moreover, would have the opportunity, in due course, to become petty officers.[44]

Waesche was not advocating racially integrated crews; the black Coast Guardsmen would serve under white officers and, for the present at least, white petty officers. The impact of the blacks would not be great, since the new recruits and the handful already on duty would amount to less than 2 percent of the the enlisted force. Even so, Admiral Sexton, chief of the Bureau of Naval Personnel, objected to the assignment of blacks to the crews of cutters or other vessels because segregation might prove difficult to maintain on shipboard. Despite Sexton's warning, however, Secretary Knox sided with the Commandant of the Coast Guard, and in the spring of 1942 the first class of 150 volunteers began training in a racially segregated company at the Manhattan Beach, New York, Coast Guard station.

When voluntary enlistment gave way to selective service, the Coast Guard had to find useful work for ten times the number of blacks that Admiral Waesche had anticipated. Of the 5,000 who served as wartime Coast Guardsmen, more than 60 percent were members of the stewards' branch, performing the same duties as the Navy's messmen. The others served in a variety of specialties, both afloat and ashore.[45]

One of the Coast Guard stewards, serving in the cutter *Northland* during 1942, demonstrated such skill with machinery that he was transferred to the engine room. Even though he passed the necessary examinations and was actually doing the required work, he could not become a machinist because, at the time, there were no vacancies for blacks in that specialty. Experiences like this convinced one of the cutter's officers, Carlton Skinner, that his service could not afford, "from sentiment or prejudice," to employ men "below the limits of their capacity." Lieutenant Commander Skinner conceded that "the Negro group as a whole, due to various reasons of environment, nutrition, lack of schooling, *etc.*, would not have the same capacity as the white group." Nevertheless, individual blacks clearly did have greater ability than specific persons in the white group. To hold back capable men like the steward who aspired to become a machinist was an injustice to the victim and a disservice to the Coast Guard. A small number of racially segregated ships would not give blacks the opportunity they deserved; the answer lay in allowing blacks to serve in any specialty for which they might qualify.

A sudden offer of equal opportunity would not be enough, Skinner realized, unless adequate preparations were made to condition blacks to accept the offer and whites to extend it without reservation. At present, whites, especially officers, tended to see black Coast Guardsmen as servants rather than seamen, and the blacks could not help being suspicious of an unexpected reversal of policy. To Skinner, the attitude of the officers seemed likely to make or break the plan. He believed that equal opportunity, leading eventually to racially integrated crews, could succeed provided a ship's officers proved sympathetic to the endeavor. Racial friction and minor breaches of discipline were certain to occur after the new policy took effect, and the ship's captain and his executive officer would have to "take the time and trouble to make it work and not report failure when the first problem developed."

Confident that he was the sort of officer who could make racial integration work, Skinner volunteered his services. Since the Coast Guard was going beyond the goal of expanding the role of blacks within the framework of segregation, which President Roosevelt had established for the Navy as a whole, Admiral Waesche accepted Skinner's, offer, in November 1943 assigning him to command the *Sea Cloud*, a weather ship based at Boston, which was to be manned by an integrated crew. Under Skinner's leadership, the two races got along harmoniously, with as many as four black officers and a hundred black seamen in a total complement of about two hundred.[46]

Despite the success of the *Sea Cloud*, which conferred upon Skinner the status of an expert on race relations, the Coast Guard operated only one other ship, the patrol escort craft *Hoquiam*, with a genuinely integrated crew. Small numbers of blacks did serve on various vessels, and a few black women entered the SPARS, a wartime auxiliary that derived its name from the contraction of "Semper Paratus," the Coast Guard motto. In April 1943, about a year before the Navy commissioned its first black, Clarence Samuels accepted his commission in the Coast Guard. This former warrant officer became the first black to command a Coast Guard vessel when he took over first a lightship and later the cutter *Sweetgum*. And all in all, the Coast Guard succeeded in finding useful and suitable work for the black inductees who entered the service by means of the draft.[47]

In contrast, the Marine Corps fought a determined rearguard action against the encroachment of blacks upon an organization that had been exclusively white since its post-Revolutionary revival in 1798. When the Commandant, General Holcomb, realized that he could resist no longer, he agreed in February 1942 to accept a thousand blacks, though he refused to scatter them among existing units and instead concentrated them in a single organization. Chosen to receive most of the black recruits was one of the recently authorized defense battalions, which consisted of coast defense batteries and antiaircraft artillery.

To ensure segregation, General Holcomb proposed to funnel all blacks through a single training facility, with their unit gradually taking form as the men completed the courses of instruction. He was, he wrote, "of the opinion that, if it becomes necessary to enlist negroes in the Marine Corps above the minimum number, such enlistments should be accomplished only after the minimum number has been enlisted and equipped, and their training has progressed to such a point that they are ready for field service. In this manner the Marine Corps could continue to utilize the facilities in a part of the area of the Marine Barracks, New River [North Carolina], with the least possiblity of injecting the race question." Insofar as possible, black marines would train and serve in isolation.[48]

That portion of Camp Lejeune, as the New River base came to be called, set aside for the black recruits was the Montford Point camp, where the first group of volunteers reported in the late summer of 1942. The drill instructors assigned there were white noncommissioned officers who, if not eager for blacks to join the corps, were not overtly hostile to the idea. As for the trainees who entered boot camp at Montford Point, they had survived careful scrutiny by recruiting officers and included college men and a few persons with prior service. Among the old-timers were Gilbert "Hashmark" Johnson, a veteran of the 25th Infantry and later a Navy messman, and John T. Pridgen, formerly a trooper in the 10th Cavalry. Because of the selectiveness of the recruiters, a number of the boots rapidly became acting assistants and later full-fledged drill instructors.[49]

The unit that General Holcomb envisaged took shape during the spring and summer of 1943. Initially called the 51st Composite Defense Battalion, though the world "composite" soon was dropped, the organization sailed for the Pacific in February 1944. After standing guard without incident over different islands in the Ellice and Marshalls groups and seeing no combat, the battalion returned to the United States in the fall of 1945, after hostilities had ended.[50]

While the 51st Defense Battalion was training at Montford Point, the Selective Service System became the normal source of manpower for all the services, and the Marine Corps had to come to grips with the possibility that as many as 10 percent of future inductees could be blacks. To accommodate these men, the Commandant proposed to assign as many men as possible to defense or special infantry battalions, while diverting the others to duty as messmen, stevedores, security guards, or truck drivers. Whatever his assignment, the black marine would serve in a segregated unit with white officers and, until a sufficient number of blacks acquired the necessary experience, white noncommissioned officers as well.[51]

As it turned out, comparatively few of the 20,000 blacks who entered the Marine Corps actually served in combat battalions as originally planned. In fact, only two such units were formed, the 51st and 52nd Defense Battalions. Instead, the vast majority reported to the fifty-one depot companies and twelve ammunition companies, established by the Marine Corps, or to a 1,400-man messman's branch. Ironically, the combat outfits did less fighting than the depot or ammunition companies that unloaded and distributed munitions and other cargo during amphibious landings on islands like Saipan, Guam, and Iwo Jima.

At Saipan, for example, Private First Class LeRoy Seals became the first black marine killed in action. On Guam, Private First Class Luther Woodard earned the Silver Star when he discovered the footprints left by a half-dozen Japanese, followed the trail to the place where the diehards were hiding, and killed at least one of them. He returned later with five other members of his ammunition company and attacked the survivors. In all, some 8,000 black stevedores and ammunition handlers braved Japanese fire on the Pacific beachheads.

No black became a Marine Corps officer during the war nor were any blacks admitted to the women's reserve. Four college graduates, one the holder of a master's degree and all of them noncommissioned officers, entered officer candidate school in April 1945, but none of them graduated. Not until November 10, 1945, did Frederick Branch accept a commission as a second lieutenant in the Marine Corps Reserve, thus becoming, on the 170th anniversary of the founding of the Continental Marines, the first black officer in the history of the corps.

The blacks who entered the wartime Marine Corps may at times have been dismayed by the reception they received. Having survived the physical and emotional shocks of boot camp, they encountered racial attitudes typical of an organization that had prided itself on being exclusively white. During an off-the-cuff speech to black trainees at Montford Point, the commanding general of Camp Lejeune made some remarks that members of the audience still found offensive a quarter century afterward. In effect, he said that he had not realized how serious the situation was until he saw "you people in our uniform." The speaker was General Larsen, whose subsequent plea for racial understanding at the time of the violence on Guam, no doubt reflected his real beliefs more accurately than the informal comments made at Montford Point. What he probably intended as a joke boomeranged, serving only to remind the blacks that they remained aliens in a white man's organization. Nor did the men of the 51st Defense Battalion warm to a commanding officer who habitually addressed groups of enlisted men as "you people." A phrase that he had used throughout his thirty-five years of service in an all-white corps suddenly became offensive.

Despite sources of friction like these, race relations within the wartime Marine Corps remained correct, if not really cordial, reflecting a courtesy born of discipline rather than genuine camaraderie. Whatever the source, a kind of bond formed among marines, regardless of race, especially when dealing with outsiders. Whether the result of this tenuous solidarity or for some other reason, the black marines stationed on Guam did not side with sailors of their own race who were being harassed by white marines.[52]

By actually integrating the races on board some ships, the Navy and Coast Guard had shown that it might be possible to do more than offer greater opportunity within the framework of segregation, the modest objective originally established by President Roosevelt. Nevertheless, the number of racially integrated ships remained comparatively small, although the total was increasing when the war ended, and at that time all were auxiliaries rather than combat ships. Moreover, compliance with racial policy was spotty among units and installations ashore. The Army, until the closing months of the war, had tried to strike a balance between segregation and military efficiency, but casualties among infantrymen in Europe finally tipped the scales, forcing the integration of the battlefield, if not the Army. The Marine Corps did no more than the minimum expected by the Chief Executive and did that grudgingly.

The emerging signs of political cohesion among those blacks able to vote persuaded President Roosevelt to yield to his better instincts and respond favorably to the demands of Walter White, A. Philip Randolph, and others that blacks have greater opportunities in the armed services. The Chief Executive exerted pressure on the service secretaries, and they, in turn, influenced the uniformed leadership in varying degrees. He could not, however, respond wholeheartedly and without reservation to the appeals of the black leaders, for he felt he needed the suppport of both the oppressors and the oppressed, of hard-line southern Democrats like Theodore Bilbo and of recently registered black voters in the northern cities. This belief shaped his basic wartime policy of easing the impact of segregation in the armed forces without uprooting the policy itself. The question now arose whether the return of peace would encourage the armed services to resurrect their prewar ways, institutionalize the modified wartime racial practices, or pursue those changes to their logical, conclusion—racial integration.

Granted that certain black units had proved disappointing and that lapses of discipline had occurred, it was not yet clear how the postwar armed forces would react to these shortcomings. After World War I the Army, for example, had accepted glib generalizations that blamed inherent racial characteristics for the failure of some black units and ignored the examples of success. During that era, supposedly serious students of military affairs had claimed that blacks would not fight at night or were child-like by nature and given to panic. Perhaps now, a quarter of a century later, the services would at least study wartime operations carefully and impartially, delving into such topics as motivation, self-image, and esprit de corps in order to discover the real reasons why the black soldier or sailor could excel in some circumstances and fail in others.

13

A Postwar Transition

IF ANY ONE INCIDENT symbolized race relations in the United States at the end of World War II, it was the fate of Isaac Woodard. A recently discharged sergeant, still in the uniform of the U.S. Army, he boarded a bus for the trip from Fort Gordon, Georgia, to his home in North Carolina. He had served for three years, including fifteen months in the South Pacific, but the segregation he had encountered in the service had been largely impersonal and nonviolent, a by-product of the functioning of the military machine. In the South of 1946, he encountered brutality, deliberate and cruel. The uniform meant nothing to white authorities determined to demonstrate their superiority over the black man.

At a stop in South Carolina, the bus driver cursed Woodard for taking so long to use the "colored only" rest room. When the bus stopped at the next town, the driver summoned a local sheriff and demanded the arrest of the ex-serviceman. The charge was drunkenness, even though Woodard did not drink. In making the arrest, the lawman beat the prisoner with a blackjack, and someone, either the sheriff or a policeman, thrust the end of a nightstick into his eyes. Denied medical care, locked overnight in a cell, the former sergeant was found guilty and fined $50. When Woodard at last reached an Army hospital at Spartanburg, South Carolina, doctors found his corneas so badly damaged that he was permanently blind.

The incident might have remained yet another forgotten example of random violence against blacks, but in this case there was an outpouring of sympathy, shock, and assistance. The response stemmed in part from the efforts of the National Association for the Advancement of Colored People, which saw to it that the blinding of Isaac Woodard received wide publicity. That a veteran in uniform could be assaulted while en route to visit his family for the first time in almost a year and a half caught the conscience of many a white American, northerner or southerner. The civil rights organization raised enough money to provide a small pension for the victim.[1]

Donations of money made up only a part of the response, however. Foes of racism like actor Orson Welles denounced the atrocity, and the incident also influenced the thinking of a Missouri-born politician who had succeed to the Presidency in the spring of 1945 upon the death of Franklin D. Roosevelt. Harry S. Truman was shocked by the outrage in South Carolina. "My God!" Truman told Walter White, "I had no idea it was as terrible as that. We've got to do something."[2] Within a short time the new President would act.

In the meantime, the blinding of Isaac Woodard was having an effect on the administration of justice in the state of South Carolina, or more precisely upon one of judges who administered justice there. The jurist was J. Waties Waring, already something of an iconoclast after divorcing his wife of thirty-two years, a native of Charleston, and marrying a divorcee from Detroit. Influenced by his new wife, he began questioning the justness of racial segregation. Doubt had already begun surfacing when, in late 1946, he presided over the trial of Sheriff Linwood L. Shull of Batesburg, South Carolina, who admitted striking Woodard with a blackjack but denied blinding him.

Because the victim had been traveling on an interstate bus, the case came under the jurisdiction of the federal court, where Waring was a judge. When the trial began, he discovered that the United States attorney in the district had made no effort to find witnesses to substantiate Woodard's claim that the sheriff had violated a law, adopted during reconstruction by a radical Congress, that protected the civil rights of black Americans. An inquiry by the Federal Bureau of Investigation had already failed to turn up any evidence against the policemen who might have been involved. The defendant swore that he had acted in self-defense after Woodard attacked him, Shull's attorney made an appeal to racism that the judge cut short, the jury found the sheriff not guilty, and the courtroom erupted in cheers. Waring was aghast. The federal prosecutor had made no attempt to present a case. The victim had been denied a hearing, let alone justice.

The judge became an implacable foe of Jim Crow. In one case he gave the state of South Carolina a choice among three alternatives:

admit a qualified black applicant to the state's only law school; bar the candidate and shut down the existing law school; or establish a law school at the state college for blacks. South Carolina chose to create a law school at Orangeburg, where the institution for blacks was located, and appointed a professor in that subject, but neither established a curriculum nor set up a library. In another case, Judge Waring ruled that the Democratic Party of South Carolina could not operate as a private club; specifically, he struck down a "loyalty oath" requiring all Democrats to support racial segregation.[3]

The blinding of Isaac Woodard and the consequences of that outrage revealed three aspects of race relations in the immediate postwar years. The first and most obvious was random violence against blacks, and the second was legal action, initiated by or on behalf of an individual black, in generally sympathetic federal courts. Not every lawsuit succeeded, however, especially when all-white juries were involved. The possibility of failure, accompanied by the danger of retaliation, lent emphasis to the third aspect—the need for active intervention by the federal government to protect the basic rights of black citizens. Before long, President Truman and his successors would seek an end to violence and greater equality of treatment and opportunity.

For the present, however, violence captured the headlines. The attack upon former sergeant Woodard was an extreme example of the intimidation that was occurring throughout the South. In Tennessee, for example, another black veteran would have been beaten, perhaps killed, had a white sheriff not intervened to hold a mob at bay. The black man's crime: upon learning that a white merchant had cheated his mother, the veteran demanded a settlement, and when refused he struck the store owner.

The black veteran, having been treated with some measure of respect while in uniform, would not show the deference expected of him by white racists. He became a force for change, and when perceived as such he faced violence from those intent upon upholding segregation. Yet, despite the beatings and deaths, prospects for blacks were beginning to improve.[4]

Disheartening as the action of the prosecution and jury in the Woodard case had been, the law was changing. The subsequent judicial decisions of J. Waties Waring, outrageous enough in the view of his fellow white South Carolinians to bring social ostracism and a flood of hate mail, formed part of a judicial revolution that had begun before World War II. A series of cases argued before the Supreme Court was modifying (and would ultimately reverse) the doctrine of separate but equal, enunciated in *Plessy v. Ferguson*, a case that reached the Supreme Court in 1896, when a black traveler appealed a state law requiring racial segregation on passenger trains. In the field of education, a dozen years of Supreme Court decisions, beginning with *Missouri ex rel. Gaines v. Canada* in 1938, forced the states to provide within their borders equal professional training and undergraduate instruction for blacks and whites.[5]

Furthermore, the Court addressed the question of segregation in interstate travel, largely dormant since *Plessy v. Ferguson*, and the impact of racism on voting rights. Of far-reaching potential, in view of the recent efforts of presidential candidates to attract the votes of blacks, was *Smith v. Allwright*, heard in 1944. William H. Hastie, who had resigned during the previous year from the War Department because he felt he could do more as an outsider to advance the cause of civil rights, joined another black attorney, Thurgood Marshall, in arguing against a Texas law that barred blacks from participating in the Democratic primary election. Eight of the nine justices agreed that Texas could not, in effect, nullify a right guaranteed in the Constitution by imposing restrictions that prevented black citizens from helping choose candidates for federal elections. Turning to segregation in interstate travel, which had been a source of anger among black servicemen during the war, the Court in 1946 decided cases dealing with both railroads and bus lines. *Henderson v. the United States*, argued by Marshall, established the principle that segregated dining cars were unconstitutional. *Morgan v. Virginia* upheld the argument, advanced by Hastie and Marshall, that a state could not require racial segregation among the passengers on interstate buses.[6]

These decisions sounded a trumpet before the walls of racial segregation but did not bring the ramparts tumbling down. Change seemed possible, but it would not come immediately. Nonetheless, the series of legal victories signaled a reversal in judicial thinking that would have revolutionary consequences.

At the time, civil rights organizations heaped deserved plaudits upon the successful attorneys, especially upon Marshall, who in 1967 would become the first black ever to serve as a justice of the Supreme Court of the United States. These victories and future triumphs, as well, ultimately depended, however, on the courage of those otherwise anonymous blacks who dared challenge segregation, thus setting the legal machinery in motion. Irene Morgan, for one, was just another passenger on a bus bound from rural Gloucester County, Virginia, to Baltimore, Maryland, but she refused to give up her seat to a white passenger and move to the rear of the vehicle. She was arrested, found guilty, and fined, but as presented before the Supreme Court by Hastie and Marshall her act of defiance led ultimately to the striking down of the Virginia statute that required racial segregation in all forms of public transportation.

Overlooked at the time were two actions that foreshadowed the tactics used widely and successfully some twenty years later in a renewed fight against racial discrimination. An interracial "Journey of Reconciliation" sought to publicize the Morgan decision, visiting several southern cities but in the process merely demonstrating that Jim Crow still survived, regardless of the Supreme Court's declaration. More successful was a small group, led by James Farmer, which during World War II "sat in" at a restaurant in Chicago that refused to wait on black patrons. After the manager called police to eject the trespassers, Farmer and the others cited an all-but-forgotten Illinois law that forbade racial discrimination in public places. Ultimately, Farmer's tactics and those of the Journey of Reconciliation would be revived to compel federal agencies to enforce the Supreme Court decisions that outlawed Jim Crow.[7]

Within American society racial attitudes were showing signs of change, but Jim Crow still prevailed, especially in the South, and the armed forces reflected this division. The recent war had demonstrated the feasibility of racial integration, but that step seemed dangerously radical as a permanent measure, likely to alienate many white Americans, whether in uniform or civilians. The Army and Navy would have to accept blacks, that much the war had clearly demonstrated, but for the present the services also wanted to preserve the old order, racial segregation. The Army would offer blacks broader opportunities within a segregated service. Although retaining the racial policy announced during the war, in practice the Navy sought to reinstate firm segregation by occupational specialty, with blacks serving in the galley or waiting upon officers in the wardroom. The Marine Corps, on the other hand, still resisted the idea of accepting blacks. Indeed, to recall the metaphor used by General Holcomb in 1942, the corps now hoped to expel the black undesirables from the white man's club, though it would fall short of achieving this goal.

The Navy's first step was to gather the relevant facts. In November 1945, before the separation of practice from policy, Lester Granger was sent to conduct an informal survey of race relations in the Navy. Upon his return, he reported to Secretary Forrestal that prospects for blacks had greatly improved during the last years of World War II, even though conditions varied markedly from one ship or installation to another. The black sailors who profited most from the changes in racial policy were those men actually serving at sea, and they appeared to perform the best. Of three ships visited at Pearl Harbor, two were commanded by officers who had made a determined effort to integrate the races, evenhandedly assigning quarters and duties and looking solely at a man's accomplishments in making recommendations for promotion. Surprisingly, on the one vessel where some degree of racial prejudice did prevail, Granger found that black crewmen still accomplished more and were better satisfied than many members of their race serving ashore. The difference in performance and attitude resulted at least in part from the sense of being a part of the real Navy that was shared by those blacks on board the 200 ships with racially mixed crews. In short, better to be a messman afloat that a messman ashore; but best of all to be a seaman or the holder of some rating like machinist or yeoman in a racially integrated crew.

Not every installation ashore seethed with discontent or exhibited inefficiency, as Granger learned. The commanding officer of the Naval Air Station at Kaneohe in the Hawaiian Islands, for instance, tried to create the atmosphere of equality that prevailed in the best-run ships. In contrast, certain Seabee units got around Secretary Forrestal's directives requiring racial integration by concentrating the whites in the battalion headquarters and headquarters companies and assigning the blacks to the outfits that actually did the work. In organizations where segregation predominated, Granger found the nadir in morale and accomplishment.[8]

Visiting naval installations in the southern United States, Granger discovered that commanders sometimes absorbed, consciously or otherwise, the Jim Crow customs of the area. At a repair base in the Algiers section of New Orleans, Louisiana, the master at arms responsible for maintaining order enforced racially segregated seating in the mess hall and theater. Black sailors at the Naval Air Station, Corpus Christi, Texas, were supposed to work beside white civilians from the nearby town, but the plan went awry. With the cooperation of naval offices, these employees succeeded for the most part in converting the base into a replica of Corpus Christi, at least in terms of the relationship between the races. Jim Crow practices prevailed on the buses operating between the airfield and the town, at the air station's dining halls and recreational facilities, and in the off-base housing—trailers made available by the Navy—open to black servicemen. The Naval Mine Depot at Yorktown, Virginia, also enforced the separation of the races, but just 20 miles away at Camp Peary, the commanding officer defied attempts to apply the state's Jim Crow laws to Navy buses carrying black sailors on liberty. Despite the racial policies imposed at Algiers, Yorktown, and

Corpus Christi, Granger remained convinced that progress could be made toward integration, even in the south, "if leadership is sufficiently interested and courageous."[9]

Wartime experience and the results of Granger's tours of inspection should have propelled the Navy toward complete integration of the general service, but once again a dichotomy gradually appeared between policy and reality. At the outset, however, all seemed well. The Bureau of Naval Personnel, which had defended racial segregation during the early months of the recent conflict, now advocated the opposite course. Rear Admiral Louis E. Denfeld, currently the chief of the bureau, who had been an assistant to Admiral Jacobs when the wartime Navy began to integrate the races on a small scale, fashioned a policy reflecting Forrestal's belief that the Navy could not operate efficiently if burdened by racial segregation. To transfer blacks from certain units or stations ashore to specific ships, struggling throughout the process to match specific occupations without running afoul of a racial quota, offended Denfeld's sense of order. The solution lay, he believed, in ignoring race to assign men wherever their skills were needed.

Admiral Denfeld's arguments proved persuasive, and the Navy modified its racial policy, announcing in February 1946 that "all restrictions governing types of assignments for which Negro naval personnel are eligible are hereby lifted." There would be no special accommodations for blacks and no opportunity to use certain units, such as some components of Seabee battalions, to maintain segregation. Ostensibly to prevent this sort of subterfuge, the Navy Department decreed that no ship or shore station could have a complement that was more than 10 percent black. Questions as to the Navy's sincerity arose immediately, for there was one ominous exception, the absence of any limit on the percentage of blacks in the stewards' detachment at the Naval Academy.

Granger was proud of what the Navy had done and confident that the reforms would continue until black sailors were fully integrated into the service. He hoped to share this pride with twenty-three black newspaper publishers or editors, whom he invited to accompany him on a tour of the fleet and its supporting installations. Not one accepted. They feared quite simply that they would become window dressing for racial segregation. Despite the new policies and the obvious sincerity of Forrestal and Granger, they believed that the Navy would somehow avoid compliance, and they were right. The divergence of practice from policy was already under way.

The ceiling of no more than 10 percent blacks in any unit (except for the various messes at the academy), roughly the proportion of blacks in the populace, had the effect of imposing a racial quota on the entire Navy, for blacks could never exceed one-tenth of the overall enlisted force. In fact, the recent pattern of enlistments indicated that the number of blacks in the Navy would not exceed 5 percent, and the perceived needs of the service, as demonstrated by the exception for stewards at the Naval Academy, would dictate that many of the 5 percent would end up as servants. Forrestal could have made a difference by insisting upon recruiting up to the quota and closely monitoring the enforcement of the regulations, but that was not his style. He looked upon regulations as almost self-enforcing, assuming the good will of those at whom they were directed. More important, Forrestal faced other problems—the struggle to preserve the Navy's share of a shrinking defense budget and the often heated negotiations attendant upon creating a third service, the United States Air Force. Finally, in September 1947 he left the Navy Department to become the nation's first Secretary of Defense.[10]

The Marine Corps, although it never deviated from a wartime policy of segregation, had undergone comparatively little of the racial turbulence that had troubled the other services. Experience during World War II seemed, therefore, to justify the continued assignment of however many blacks might remain in the ranks to small, racially exclusive units, most of which would train to perform labor rather than to engage in combat. The number of blacks would be small, however, consisting mainly of wartime marines who had reenlisted. Such a policy contradicted the measures announced by the Navy, but the Marine Corps, though an element of the naval establishment, had staff agencies of its own that shaped personnel regulations for the corps. To weigh any possible benefits to be derived from the kind of policy that Forrestal had proposed for the Navy (but not enforced) against the apparently demonstrable success of wartime segregation became the task of the Division of Plans and Policies, a component of Marine Corps headquarters. In charge of the division was Brigadier General Gerald C. Thomas, a combat leader in both world wars.

The general and his staff officers seemed willing to meet the question head-on, for he acknowledged that "the Negro question is a national one which grows more controversial yet is more evaded as time goes by." He then described "a solution to the issue . . . to entirely eliminate any racial discriminations within the services, and to remove such practices as separate Negro units. . . ." General Thomas was unwilling, however, to subject his corps to so revolutionary a change. *A* solution, he pointed out, need not be *the* solution. The Navy, after all, while banning racial segregation, had in effect imposed a quota on black enlistments. Nor should the armed forces, the general argued, "go further than that which is already custom," and since American society still condoned racial segregation, the Marine Corps should not follow "such a radical trend as complete racial non-distinction." He recommended instead that the wartime practice of "supporting separate units for the assignment of Marines be continued into the peace-time Marine Corps, and that the total number of Negroes in the Marine Corps be based on an established quota." Such was the policy approved in September 1946 by General Alexander A. Vandegrift, who had succeeded General Holcomb as Commandant midway through the war, and immediately incorporated in Marine Corps personnel regulations.[11]

In the meantime, the War Department had been grappling with the question of how to employ black soldiers in the peacetime Army. Studies dealing with the subject began before the conflict had ended. The Adjutant General, J. A. Ulio, in May 1945 announced that the Army Service Forces, Ground Forces, and Air Forces were to evaluate the performance of black units, officers, noncommissioned officers, and enlisted soldiers. The study thus set in motion would also concern itself with the extent to which commanders were maintaining segregation, their views on that policy, and their interpretation of the causes of racial tension. Of special interest were the comparative scores of blacks and whites on the Army General Classification Test.[12]

The implications of General Ulio's circular troubled Truman Gibson, who urged that "the current study avoid an unquestioning acceptance of the premises on which past policy was based and recognize that the nature of the racial problem before the Army has materially changed since 1940." Not only did the new Army attract a different kind of man than the prewar regular establishment, the educational level among black Americans had risen markedly in the past decade. Gibson wanted the War Department to examine the Navy's racial policy, which on the surface seemed so enlightened, evaluating it against the Army's practices. He, like General Ulio, was interested in test scores, noting that 83 percent of the men in the lowest two categories had been blacks. By insisting upon maintaining large, segregated units, Gibson suggested, the War Department had brought together men drawn to a great extent from these two test groups. "Certainly, the effects of such a concentration should be carefully considered along with reports of performance."[13]

The studies conducted in response to General Ulio's directive justified Gibson's concerns, for their principal recommendations could be summarized as more of the same. The Army Service Forces, for example, did not take any position "on the wisdom of segregation in a social sense" but endorsed the practice as a means "to insure the most efficient training and utilization of Negro manpower in the postwar military establishment."[14] Similarly, the Army Air Forces bestowed approval on racial segregation in "recreation, messing, and social activities . . . in accordance with the customs prevailing within the surrounding civilian communities."[15] The Army Ground Forces also accepted segregation, though with one concession to recent experience—small units made up of blacks might serve as components of larger white combat organizations, as the black rifle platoons had served in white companies during the final months of the war in Europe.[16] Thus did the three major components of the Army propose to pursue in peacetime a policy of providing greater opportunity and better treatment without disrupting racial segregation.

The assertion that racial segregation promoted efficiency did not pass unchallenged. Colonel Noel Parrish, reviewing his experience at the Tuskegee Army Air Field, warned his superiors in the Air Forces of the inefficiency and demoralization that stemmed from the treatment accorded black servicemen. "Since there is no provision in the Constitution or in fundamental army regulation for the treatment of individuals other than as individuals, or for the maintenance of a kind of negro army within the white army," he pointed out, "this negro army within the white army must be maintained by unofficial means, by various underwritten understandings which change from day to day, or from individual to individual." Lumped together to form the policy of racial segregation, these understandings sought to group black enlisted airmen by unit, as in the aviation companies, and black officers according to base—Tuskegee, for example, or Freeman Field, Indiana. The objective of segregating blacks, said Parrish, was "to 'impose' them upon as few people as possible," an attitude based on "the assumption that it is far better for a hundred people in one place to worry with the problems surrounding a thousand Negroes than for a thousand people in several places to worry about the problems surrounding one hundred Negroes."

This grouping of black soldiers or airmen, though it eased the immediate burdens of the white Army or its predominantly white air arm, contained the potential for trouble. "People handled in groups rather than as individuals come to react as a group rather than as individuals," the colonel warned. "Pushed together in larger and larger groups, even against their own individual wills, they think and act as groups," inevitably developing "group feeling and group spirit, which is often contrary to National feeling and National spirit." Indeed, this group solidarity could frustrate discipline, since punishment for one, however guilty, would be interpreted and resented as punishment for all. "Criticism, even necessary and wholesome criticism," could as a result arouse such fierce resentment "that even the boldest commander will not dare criticize his troops or their performance if they happen to be colored."

Parrish offered an alternative to segregation that would ensure discipline and order. "It is recommended that future policy, instead of retreating defensibly further and further, with more and more group concessions, openly progress by slow and reasonable but definite steps toward the employment and treatment of Negroes as individuals which law requires and military efficiency demands." The Army—or at least the Air Forces, which in 1947 was to emerge as a separate service—would have to challenge the established wisdom, as General Lee had done in Europe with service and combat troops during a critical period of World War II.[17]

Nor was the War Department content merely to perpetuate the old racial policy, even though some recent studies favored just such a decision. Robert P. Patterson, who had succeeded Secretary of War Stimson in the fall of 1945, approved John R. McCloy's proposal that a group of senior officers make an objective assessment of the future use of black troops. The task of evaluation fell to Lieutenant General Alvan C. Gillem, Jr., a corps commander during World War II, Major General Lewis A. Pick, the engineer responsible for building the Ledo Road in Burma, and Brigadier General Winslow C. Morse of the Army Air Forces. Assisting them was Brigadier General Aln D. Warnock, a National Guardsman, who served as nonvoting recorder during their deliberations. The so-called Gillem Board questioned some sixty witnesses in just six weeks and plowed through a mountain of reports, as the members formulated a racial policy for the postwar Army.[18]

The findings of the Gillem Board, incorporated in War Department Circular 124 of April 27, 1946, represented a modification of segregationist tradition in the light of recent experience. The members, in short, were making an honest effort to profit from the lessons of World War II. The directive they produced acknowledged the right and duty of black citizens to participate in the defense of their country but insisted that the Army had an obligation to make the most efficient use of the nation's manpower, a task that required a modified form of racial segregation. In the interests of efficiency, as the board visualized it, there would no longer be any large units composed almost exclusively of blacks, like the ill-starred 92nd Infantry Division, but large numbers of small, equally exclusive units would remain. The War Department hoped to expand the practice, tried successfully during the European fighting, of assigning small

all-black units, like tank battalions, to larger white ones. Although aware of the need to provide equal opportunity regardless of race and to allow blacks to compete with whites as individuals, the Army nevertheless yielded to tradition, insisting upon segregation in mess halls and barracks, if not on the job or at recreational facilities. A further restriction on opportunity and assignment was a racial quota, based on the assumption that the percentage of blacks in the Army should reflect their share of the entire populace, roughly 10 percent, but no more.[19]

A number of officials commented upon the policy drafted by the Gillem Board. Among them were two persons who were leaving the government service, Assistant Secretary of War John McCloy and Truman Gibson, the civilian adviser to the Secretary of War on matters affecting blacks. McCloy complained that the board had failed to address "the basic issue of segregation," in general avoiding mention of the practice instead of condemning it. He also objected to the adoption of a quota on black enlistments, pointing out that a fixed percentage would arbitrarily exclude potential recruits regardless of their education or aptitude. He did not see "any place for a quota in a policy that looks to the utilization of Negroes on the basis of ability." Despite these misgivings, McCloy credited Gillem and his colleagues with "a fine achievement," a starting point on the path toward racial integration.[20]

Gibson shared McCloy's opposition to the racial quota and urged that the board's final report contain a statement establishing the abolition of segregation as an ultimate goal, a recommendation that was not adopted, even though the board itself believed that segregation would eventually disappear. Gillem and his colleagues maintained that the United States would never again fight a war with a racially segregated Army, but they did not expect another conflict to break out for generation or more.

Like McCloy, Gibson considered the work of the Gillem Board a watershed in race relations within the Army. The American military establishment had struggled up a steep slope, leaving total segregation behind, and was now starting down a gradual incline leading eventually to racial integration. Gibson took heart from the fact that the War Department seemed willing to modify its old policy instead of defending it as military necessity, for he was certain that any softening of segregation would reveal its folly and lead inevitably, though perhaps slowly, to its elimination.

In short, Gibson reasoned that the reforms proposed by Gillem Board, if carried out, would weaken racism in the military, much as the federal courts were undermining the barriers that denied blacks equal access to higher education, interstate buses and trains, and the ballot box in elections for federal office. In his opinion, the decisions of the judiciary and the policy set forth by the Gillem Board were lighting the way toward the objective of racial equality. The black press tended to share Gibson's optimism to some degree. Despite an occasional warning that the Army was trying to disguise racism rather than uproot it, the consensus of editorial opinion seemed to be that the military should have a chance to demonstrate its sincerity.[21]

Just as some officials in the South were ignoring the directives of the courts, officers within the military establishment were not unanimously enthusiastic about modifying racial segregation. The dissenters included Lieutenant General Ira C. Eaker, the deputy commander of the Army Air Forces, who objected strenuously to assigning black units to larger white organizations. Ignoring the effect of inexperience, unavoidable because almost all the black fliers began training at the same time, Eaker declared that the 99th Fighter Squadron had been a failure because of the poor quality of the assigned pilots. His judgment was not influenced by the successful fighter-bomber and escort missions flown during the last year and a half of the war in Europe. The general conceded, however, that the training of all wartime aviators had been flawed and agreed with the Gillem Board's insistence upon equal training for soldiers of both races assigned the same duties. In the future, Eaker promised, student pilots of both races would attend the same flight schools.

In commenting upon the work of the board, Eaker predicted that there would not be many black pilots in the postwar air arm. The racial quota would limit total recruiting, he reasoned, and few of those who did gain admittance would have the aptitude and education to qualify for flight training. As for the vast majority, they "should be assigned to AAF service units in which it has been found their war-time record was the best."

The deputy commanding general of the Army Air Forces zeroed in on a real problem when he spoke of aptitude and education. During the war, the air arm had taken the cream of the crop, draftees or volunteers with high scores on the standard intelligence test, who were likely to master such skills as radar operation or engine maintenance. Because of the inadequacy of their segregated schooling, blacks as a class did not do as well as whites on the general classification test. If the Air Forces succeeded in demanding higher test scores on the average than the Ground Forces or Service Forces, it would accept fewer blacks, thus easing the task of assimilation by shifting the burden elsewhere in the Army.

Eaker remained an advocate of racial segregation, although he would make exceptions, for instance in pilot training. Because black air cadets would be so few and flight proficiency was so important, he concluded that the expensive duplication of training facilities might well prove self-defeating. A new Tuskegee could dilute the overall level of skill among Army fliers; better that all pilots train together under equally well-qualified instructors.

Convinced that blacks could not function compatibly with whites, the general saw no need for equal access by members of both races to officer's clubs, post theaters, or even post exchanges at bases located near communities that enforced Jim Crow laws. In a social sense, the installation would become a reflection of the civilian milieu, absorbing local racial custom instead of challenging it. Indeed, he warned of the danger that the armed forces might move ahead of public opinion, which he believed approved of racial segregation, thus putting themselves "in a position of stimulating racial disorders rather than overcoming them."[22]

After reflecting upon wartime experience, the Navy chose to revive racial segregation, while the Marine Corps clung tenaciously to that policy. In both cases, few blacks flocked to the recruiting offices, although a number of wartime veterans did reenlist. There were too many for the Marine Corps to ignore but too few to force the Navy to carry out the racial policy that Forrestal, soon to become Secretary of Defense, had inspired. Could the Navy ever attract enough blacks with an adequate variety of backgrounds to assign them in the announced ratio throughout the service? And what of the messmen currently on active duty? Would they be retrained and reassigned to break up a group made up almost entirely of blacks?

Similar questions faced Army planners, although the racial quota affected that service differently. Recent experience indicated that blacks would volunteer in numbers reflecting their share of the populace. The problem lay in quality. Would the black 10 percent include the caliber of skilled recruits needed to establish the various kinds of small units envisaged by General Gillem and his colleagues? After all, failure to attract highly qualified enlistees might well force the Army to settle for ill-educated blacks with limited potential as soldiers and thus give rise to the temptation to banish them to large service or housekeeping detachments, as had happened so consistently in recent wars.

The Army Air Forces, soon to become the U.S. Air Force, stood at a crossroads. Would the viewpoint expressed by General Eaker prevail and racial segregation survive almost intact? Or would the air arm heed the advice of Colonel Parrish and abandon a practice that had failed?

14

Failed Policies

ON THE WHOLE, the status of the black serviceman grew worse when World War II ended; his opportunities for training and advancement were fewer in 1946 than they had been in the spring of 1945. Only the Marine Corps acknowledged this fact, making no pretense that it considered its few blacks anything but an inconvenience. In contrast, the Army had empowered the Gillem Board to study the lessons of World War II and revise the service's racial policies accordingly. The board issued a report calling for broader opportunities for blacks within a segregated service; racial integration remained a distant goal attainable over several decades and certain to be in effect when the nation next went to war. The Army's leadership, in carrying out the board's recommendations, stressed segregation today rather than integration tomorrow. For all its integrationist policies, the Navy offered blacks even fewer opportunities for useful service than did the Army; afloat or ashore, the black sailor usually ended up serving food or waiting upon officers.

The occasional gesture toward easing the separation of the races could arouse the ire of segregationists, even as the reaffirmation of segregation was drawing criticism from the foes of racism. Typical of the advocates of racial segregation was Representative Stephen Pace, a Democrat from Georgia, who reported receiving "a very distressing letter from a young friend of mine, now stationed on the U.S.S. Wyoming, advising that Negro seamen have been placed on this ship and the white boys are being forced to sleep with these Negroes." Congressman Pace went on to describe for the Secretary of the Navy "how displeasing it is to those of us who believe a sensible policy of segregation is the most practical method of handling the race problem." The representative from Georgia predicted that "forced social association will only lead to trouble and lots of it."[1]

Whereas Pace argued that the Navy had gone too far, Lester Granger, who had contributed to the service's postwar racial policy, warned that the Navy had not yet achieved the degree of integration that it had established for itself. Granger, having left the Navy Department to return to the Urban League, realized that naval policy had not achieved the results he had expected. The stewards' branch remained the exclusive province of blacks and Filipinos. Moreover, the highest-ranking stewards were treated more like valued retainers than full-fledged petty officers. The taint of being servants, not sailors, still clung to members of this branch regardless of their length of service or demonstrated competence. Granger concluded that the diminished status of chief stewards, all of whom were black, could be attributed to the lower educational standards required for enlistment in the branch and might well be corrected by establishing the same standards for stewards as for seamen. "Much of the criticism directed at the stewards' branch would be abated," he argued, "if it were made known that any sailor has the right to join the steward's branch regardless of race," a change in policy that "would wipe out the last vestige of 'jim-crow' rates, with correspondingly good reaction from the public."[2] In fact, the Navy did consider the person with the rate or specialty of steward to be something less than a sailor, a consideration that made the branch seem unattractive as a career and influenced the service to emphasize the difference in status between the mess attendant and the machinist or gunner.

Although the Navy refused to throw open the stewards' branch to anyone who might be interested, it did make an effort to incorporate stewards more fully into the naval service. Training became more demanding, and transfers from the branch to the general service easier to obtain. At the same time, those blacks not already stewards who might desire to enter the branch had to make formal application, a rule designed to prevent commanding officers from channeling members of racial minorities into that specialty.[3] Regardless of these reforms, however, the racial composition of the branch remained unchanged; as late as 1948, 60 percent of the blacks serving in the Navy were stewards.[4]

As had been the case during the recent conflict, the postwar Navy attracted few black women, either as members of the women's auxiliary or as nurses. In wartime, the service had accepted them only reluctantly, and as a result the response had been less than enthusiastic. Only a handful of black women served during the conflict, and fewer still competed for the small number of openings in the rapidly shrinking peacetime establishment. Roughly one-half of 1 percent of the WAVES who remained in the naval service were blacks. Moreover, only one of the four black nurses who had served during World War II remained on active duty.[5]

Following the cessation of hostilities, most of the black officers holding reserve commissions returned to civilian life. This was not the result of race, for most reservists considered themselves wartime officers and put aside the uniform once the fighting had ended. Demobilization reduced the opportunities for reservists, regardless of race, to remain in the Navy, although some blacks such as Dennis Nelson, continued on active duty. Others, such as Samuel Gravely, would leave the Navy but soon return. A few transferred to the regular Navy, including Edith DeVoe, the only wartime black nurse still on active duty, and Ensign John Lee. Jesse Brown completed training as a naval aviation cadet, the first of his race to wear the wings of gold. In June 1949, Wesley A. Brown became the first black to graduate from the U.S. Naval Academy; only five others were enrolled as midshipmen at the time. The racial composition of the Navy's officer corps was changing, but ever so slowly.[6]

Kept on active duty at the insistence of Secretary of the Navy John L. Sullivan, Dennis Nelson took over some of the duties that Christopher Sargent and Lester Granger had performed when James Forrestal headed the Navy Department. Nelson had experienced the frustrations of the black reservists commissioned during the war; although no formal quota existed, none of them could embark upon active duty unless a vacancy existed, and many commanding officers did not consider blacks to be suitable replacements for departing whites. Like Sargent, Nelson tried to broaden the scope of racial integration, zeroing in on the stewards' branch. Specifically he sought to put an end to the practice of addressing messmen as "boys" and to do away with the distinctive white jackets worn when waiting upon officers or serving food. A sailor, Nelson believed, should dress like a sailor and be treated like one.

In addition, Lieutenant Nelson replaced Granger as an inspector at large, visiting ships or units ashore and reporting on compliance with the Navy's announced racial policies. Among the problems he passed along to the Secretary of the Navy was a recurring one—haircuts. Typically, a black sailor reported that the shipboard barber had refused to cut his hair, and this form of racism was difficult to correct. In one case, when all else failed, a white officer designated a volunteer barber, using a specific chair, to take care of the only black sailor on board. All too frequently, Nelson had to alert his white superiors to similar instances of discrimination, which otherwise would have passed unnoticed except by the black victims. Besides conducting investigations and making recommendations, the lieutenant assisted another black reserve officer, Lieutenant Commander Edward Hope, in establishing contact between the Navy and black colleges and high schools, drumming up interest in reserve officer training programs.[7]

One reform sought first by Granger and then by Nelson became official policy in the summer of 1949. The Navy, responding to complaints of discrimination against chief cooks and chief stewards, decreed that they "were to be considered Chief Petty Officers in all respects." Besides carrying out the "military requirements" expected of a chief, they were to enjoy the "messing, berthing, club facilities, and other privileges" appropriate to the Navy's highest enlisted grade.[8] The reform had symbolic value, inspiring everyone in the the stewards' branch, even though it directly affected comparatively few individuals and did not challenge the overall policy of segregation.

During the immediate postwar years, the Navy's racial policy did not achieve the integrationist goal that Forrestal had sought during his tenure as Secretary of the Navy. Opportunities for blacks did not expand, nor could their horizons broaden without an intensive campaign of recruitment that sought ability as well as numbers. In the last year of the war, when blacks approached 10 percent of the enlisted force, the Navy had integrated the crews of no more than a few auxiliary ships and had admitted blacks to a number of schools and specialties formerly closed to them. The trend did not continue, however. In the absence of the necessary program of recruiting, the proportion of blacks declined after the war to just 4.3 percent of a much smaller Navy, with most of them concentrated in the stewards' branch.[9]

While the Navy was imposing a quota on black enlistments, a specific proportion that was never met, the Marine Corps proposed to recruit a fixed number, initially some 2,600 blacks, and to group them together, not trying for even a limited degree of integration. Roughly 10 percent would be stewards. Slightly more than a third would receive assignments to the Fleet Marine Force, the combat element of the corps, joining either a composite—exclusively black—antiaircraft artillery battalion or any of several combat service units. Most of the rest would become members of racially exclusive security detachments for the naval ammunition depots at Earle, New Jersey, and McAlester, Oklahoma, or the bases on Guam and

Saipan in the Marianas. The plan failed, due in part to an inability to recruit the necessary number of blacks but also as a result of changes in the deployment and total strength of the Marine Corps. Blacks were in no rush to join a Marine Corps that clung to racial segregation at a time when the Army and Navy were trying, although with little success, to expand opportunities for blacks within the pattern of racial separation. In addition, shrinking appropriations brought reductions in strength that relieved any pressure the corps might otherwise have felt to turn to blacks to swell its ranks.[10]

Resistance to the continued use of blacks as antiaircraft artillerymen developed immediately after the war. The commander of a defense battalion described this specialty as "one of, if not the most highly technical and complicated" in the entire corps and then cited the results of wartime aptitude tests to support the claim that an "average colored Marine can be expected to have lower intelligence and mechanical aptitude than . . . the average white Marine."[11] No wonder, therefore, that a reduction of antiaircraft strength within the Fleet Marine Force, a result of shrinking appropriations, caused the elimination of the black gun crews.

Within a year following the establishment of a quota for blacks, Congress reduced the authorized strength of the Marine Corps, a change that promised to increase the ratio of blacks to whites unless the numerical quota was lowered. Lowered it was, declining early in 1947 to a mere 1,500 men. Eliminated along with the antiaircraft artillery were the black security detachments at bases in the Marianas group. As these units disappeared, the authorized number of stewards increased to 350, or almost one-fourth of the planned number of black marines.[12]

Another change that occurred following the establishment of the original quota was the substitution of Port Chicago, California, for McAlester, Oklahoma, as the site of a black security detachment. Lieutenant Colonel Clarence J. O'Donnell, who commanded the detachment at the Oklahoma ammunition depot, reported that although "the black marines here on the depot are treated with equal privileges as those prevailing for white personnel," they became subject to Jim Crow laws "the moment they leave the depot." The black security guards had no suitable area outside the base for liberty or recreation. More important, Jim Crow tradition prevented them from questioning, let alone arresting, the racially conscious white civilians employed at the depot. Consequently, the detachment commander recommended assigning only white marines there.[13] Despite the Navy's own policy of racial integration, both the naval officer in command at McAlester and the Chief of Naval Operations, Admiral Nimitz, an advocate of integration, agreed that conditions unique to this remote installation provided an irrefutable argument against assigning black marines there.[14]

Although the 1,500-man quota remained in effect, time unavoidably lost in processing enlistments and discharges caused the actual number of blacks to lag somewhat behind the authorized figure. Soon the Marine Corps gave up trying to recruit blacks against specific vacancies and simply divided the total number among those units designated as black organizations. Inefficient though it was in the use of manpower, such a policy could be tolerated because the proportion of blacks to whites remained so small, between 1.3 and 2 percent during the four years ending in June 1950.[15]

In spite of lingering opposition to racial integration and the existence of a quota that imposed restrictions on first enlistments, the Marine Corps accepted some blacks not only in the regular forces but in the reserve, as well, and occasionally granted them regular or reserve commissions. Within the reserve, black enlisted men existed in a sort of limbo, subject to extended periods of active duty in a corps that had no plan for mobilizing them. Similarly, the few reserve officers could not exercise command over whites, an impediment to useful service in the unlikely event of mobilization. The same restriction upon his authority as an officer also applied to Second Lieutenant John E. Rudder, the first black to hold a regular commission in the Marine Corps.[16]

While the Marine Corps resisted change, though establishing precedents that might serve ultimately to undermine segregation, the Army struggled to carry out the self-contradictory mandate of the Gillem Board, trying to to provide greater opportunity for blacks within the restrictions imposed by racial segregation. The Army's new policy went into effect at a time of rapid demobilization, further complicating the already staggering task of creating an organization, about 10 percent black, in which the minority members served in small, racially segregated units that formed components of larger white organizations.

The findings of the Gillem Board had not yet been promulgated as official policy when the Assistant Chief of Staff for Personnel, Major General Willard S. Paul, concluded that the postwar Army, already contracting in size from 8 million to 1.8 million, would be 15 percent black, half again the proportion envisaged by the board. Many of these black soldiers, the general believed, possessed skills no longer needed by a smaller peacetime Army that had comparatively few service and housekeeping elements. Noncommissioned officers who had served in wartime truck, construction, and base maintenance units were reenlisting, even though their former billets no longer existed. To strike a balance between vacancies and skills,

General Paul launched a two-pronged offensive. He sought to get rid of those blacks who lacked the abilities needed by the postwar Army, replacing them with blacks able to make higher scores on the general classification test, and to assign members of that racial minority more equitably throughout the service.[17] As a result, each overseas theater would be required to accept blacks amounting to 15 percent of total strength, and the remainder would be divided among the commands in the United States.[18]

However appealing such a course of action might be, the Army found it could not at this time discourage blacks from enlisting. The Truman administration was campaigning to retain selective service—or, ideally, to institute some form of universal military training—despite the rapid demobilization of the wartime armed forces. Had the Army somehow succeeded in barring from its ranks the members of a particular segment of American society, such a policy would have alienated support for the peacetime draft. The Soviet Union had yet to emerge in the early months of 1947 as a clearly recognized threat to the nation's security, which would justify a revived Selective Service System.

The announcement that each overseas command would have to accept black soldiers approximately in proportion to the percentage of blacks in the entire Army ran afoul of understandings between the Department of State and foreign nations. The military sought to make the most efficient use of manpower, though without doing violence to racial segregation; the diplomats, however, gave no thought to military matters in deferring to the racial attitudes of the host countries. Informal arrangements of this sort, some of them dating from World War II, prevented the Army from sending black servicemen, even in segregated units, to the Azores, Panama, or Iceland. The exclusion of blacks from locations like these meant that more of them would have to serve elsewhere in the overseas theaters, causing large concentrations in a few places.

Concerned by the prospect of a glut of poorly educated black soldiers, the commanders in Europe and the Far East argued that they could accept only about half the quota the War Department had established. The reductions were granted, in part because of the limitations imposed by the Army's policy of racial segregation on what black soldiers could do. They could not, for instance, supervise white civilian employees or serve in the constabulary, the occupation force in the American zone of Germany. The fear of large numbers of ill-educated blacks was not unfounded, as the European Command discovered. The commanding general there, Lieutenant General Clarence R. Huebner, had to launch a special program to provide remedial military training and basic academic instruction through the high school level. Similarly, the Far East Command directed that blacks who had not completed the fifth grade or had scored badly on the aptitude tests should undergo special schooling.

Circumstances thus prevented General Paul from distributing members of this racial minority proportionately throughout the Army. Worse yet, he failed to prevent poorly qualified blacks, those individuals who required remedial instruction when assigned to Europe or Japan, from entering the Army. At a time when opportunities in civilian life seemed attractive, qualified volunteers, whether white or black, proved hard to find. Some recruiters therefore ignored standards to meet their quotas; any warm body would do. Nevertheless, the proportion of black soldiers in the Army fell short of the 15 percent that General Paul had anticipated, stabilizing during 1946 at about 184,000 men, or roughly one-tenth of the aggregate strength. The segregated Army simply was not attracting blacks in the numbers the general expected.

The War Department seemed blind to reality, intentionally or otherwise. The Army's leadership did not accept the fact that blacks were not responding to the promise of greater opportunity when it went hand in hand with the certainty of racial segregation. Even though the earlier prediction of an Army 15 percent black had not come to pass, the leaders of the service insisted that the percentage of black soldiers might double during 1947.

A cynic might conclude, although the evidence is incomplete, that the actual purpose of the projection of an Army one-fifth black was to provide an argument for limiting the intake of black recruits. At any rate, citing this projection as justification, the Army risked the loss of some political support for the peacetime draft by banning first enlistments on the part of blacks except for those with experience in needed skills. The influx of recruits with poor test scores slowed as a result. Marcus Ray, who had replaced Truman Gibson as the black aide to the Secretary of War, proposed taking advantage of the respite thus gained to eliminate all soldiers, regardless of race, whose scores on the general classification test were in the lowest category. He felt that the time had come to raise the level of intelligence throughout the enlisted force, disregarding race. The policy advocated by Ray, during the recent war a lieutenant colonel commanding an artillery battalion in the 92nd Infantry Division, cut too deeply into peacetime strength, for the Army could ill afford to discharge an estimated 92,000 men, half of them whites.

A segregated Army was able, in fact, to obtain a useful contribution from most of the whites among the 92,000 troops with the lowest test scores. In a service overwhelmingly white, the whites among the slow learners could be parceled out a few to a unit, with an eye to the kind of duties they could be taught to perform. On-the-job training, administered slowly and patiently, served the same purpose for these whites that remedial training classes—inefficiently large, by the way—did for their black counterparts. The classes did not solve the problem, however. The least capable of the blacks formed a larger share of their racial group, and because of segregation they had to be concentrated in a limited number of organizations and a narrow range of specialties. Successful completion of remedial training did not mean that the Army would find a useful assignment for the black soldier.

Although the medicine proposed by Marcus Ray seemed too strong, the War Department nevertheless adopted procedures that made it easier to discharge those soldiers, a disproportionate share of them blacks, judged incapable of making a useful contribution to the functioning of the peacetime Army. The ability to earn promotion within a reasonable time to the grade of private first class or corporal served to demonstrate adequate competence. In addition, recruiters continued to demand experience in certain career fields from blacks trying to enlist for the first time. Finally, the War Department imposed a ceiling on the number of blacks accepted and required that to win acceptance, black applicants attain a test score of 30 points higher than that demanded of whites. From the Army's point of view, this policy eased the assimilation of blacks by raising the level of aptitude within the segregated units while restricting the number accepted.

The new barriers to black enlistment had a double effect: they sharply reduced the percentage of blacks in the Army, and they aroused protests among civil rights organizations and prominent citizens. By the end of June 1947, the black share of the Army's enlisted force stood at 8.99 percent, down roughly 1 percent since the previous year. The apparition of an Army 20 percent black had not materialized. As this decline in the proportion of blacks was taking place, a variety of persons objected to the imposition of a racial quota and the other means of controlling the percentage of blacks in the ranks.

The critics included Senator Robert F. LaFollette, Jr., a Republican from Wisconsin, Walter P. Reuther, president of the United Automobile Workers, and John Haynes Holmes of the American Civil Liberties Union. To these men the Army replied that the measures were temporary and designed to bring about a proportion of blacks to whites that reflected the current racial composition of the nation's populace. Despite the assurances, the Department of the Army, as the War Department was redesignated in September 1947, decided that a racial quota was essential, though the related measures could be applied selectively, as circumstances warranted. Only on those occasions when an expected influx of black recruits seemed likely to upset the desired racial balance would the authorities suspend enlistments by blacks, demand higher test scores on their part, or invoke other restrictions.[19]

As it struggled with the problem of racial balance, the Army created a variety of black units that were to function as components of larger white organizations. The existing 24th Infantry became an organic part of the 25th Infantry Division, but most other black outfits were attached to white ones, an arrangement that emphasized the separation of the races. For instance, a battalion of black parachute infantry formed an adjunct to, but was not really an element of, the 82nd Airborne Division. The 25th Infantry disbanded, so that one of the regiment's three rifle battalions could be attached to each of the three different divisions. The 9th and 10th Cavalry, disbanded during the war, now surfaced as tank battalions rather than cavalry regiments, occupying separate cantonment areas from the division to which they were assigned. By 1950, however, a need to increase combat strength compelled the Army to flesh out two skeletal regiments, the 9th and 188th Infantry, by decreeing that each would have a battalion, organic rather than attached, composed of blacks.

Although willing to assign a battalion of blacks to a white infantry regiment, personnel planners balked at similar treatment for service units. A probable consideration was the large number of blacks still serving in these organizations and the anticipated difficulty in achieving a racial balance that staff officers considered manageable, a proportion that ensured the blacks would remain in a minority although numerous enough to have their own clubs, mess halls, exchanges, and theaters. Far from creating black service units parallel in structure and function to white units of the same type— black heavy construction and white heavy construction; white warehousemen and black—the Army tended to use any black element of a quartermaster or engineer battalion or similar outfit as a catch-all for men engaged in area beautification or other housekeeping chores. Whites, in short, did the real work and blacks cleaned up afterwards.[20]

In these circumstances, the opportunities for black soldiers did not expand as the Gillem Board had intended; their opportunities blossomed briefly but then withered. At the urging of General Paul, Edward F. Witsell, the Adjutant General, increased the quotas for blacks at a variety of schools and directed a black graduate of West Point, Major James D. Fowler, to determine whether a further broadening of opportunity was necessary. Fowler concluded that additional blacks should train for specialties within the Infantry,

Signal Corps, Medical Corps, and other supporting and combat arms. Blacks became eligible for almost half the schools operated by the Army and for a time made up almost 14 percent of the total enrollment. The number and types of black units anticipated by the Gillem Board did not materialize, however, and correspondingly fewer specialists were needed, so that instead of enjoying access to about half the available courses, blacks soon could qualify for less than one-fifth.[21]

Little change took place in the treatment blacks received. In Europe, for example, discriminatory practices reported in the summer of 1946 by a visiting black newspaper executive persisted throughout the year and beyond. Frank L. Stanley, president of the Negro Newspaper Publishers, advised the Secretary of War that white military police tended to pounce on any black soldier who happened to be in the company of a white woman. He urged that blacks be assigned as military policemen, a recommendation echoed at year's end by Marcus Ray after his visit to Europe. The War Department accepted but did not enforce the recommendation to open the ranks of the military police, and the issue of black men and white women remained unresolved. To avoid interracial dances or dating, some Red Cross clubs, as they had during the war, continued to close their doors to black soldiers. Stanley insisted, and Ray probably would have agreed, that competition for local women was the principal source of racial strife in Europe.

In other words, the same factors that had triggered the incident at Bamber Bridge in England in 1943 still persisted as the decade drew to a close. White soldiers resented the fact that European women would associate with blacks, and military police, whites almost to a man, continued to shoulder the self-imposed burden of protecting white womanhood. A simple, though admittedly incomplete, solution would have been to allow blacks to share in maintaining order, but the myth died hard that the black soldier had an innate respect for white authority and would not obey black military police.

Actually, the all-white composition brought out the worst racial prejudices among the military police and aroused hatred rather than respect in black troops. Resentment at discrimination by white military police caused some black American soldiers in the French zone of occupied Germany to throw rocks at a passing jeep carrying white American officers. The victims, one of whom was injured, summoned French military police, but the black detachment, consisting of some thirty armed men, prevented the arrest of anyone. French officials protested because the blacks had prevented the men from carrying out their duty, but the American commander, General

Joseph T. McNarney of the Air Forces, refused to honor a request to bar blacks from the French zone. Citing the policy established by the Gillem Board, he declared that to exclude them would be discriminatory and therefore illegal. American blacks continued to enter the zone on official business, but in deference to the French, McNarney saw to it that none remained there on long-term assignment.

Although the members of the Gillem Board saw their report as marking the beginning of a gradual transition from segregation to integration, the Army's leaders interpreted it as a means of prolonging indefinitely the separation of the races. Emphasis shifted from greater opportunity within segregation to segregation itself. As a result, the Army's concerns during 1946 and 1947 included finding replacements for musicians in all-black bands and obtaining an adequate number of black junior officers for segregated units. The officers would be reservists, useful in dealing with the large number of blacks currently in the Army, rather than career officers. The retraining program for blacks in Europe, instead of broadening opportunities for graduates, served mainly to increase the effectiveness of existing segregated units, many of them service organizations. The pattern of racial employment followed during World War II had survived, regardless of the Gillem Board; segregation remained the first consideration, if necessary at the expense of efficiency. Absent since the coming of peace was the great wartime impetus for racial integration even on a limited scale—the need for infantry replacements that had resulted in the integration of the battlefield.[22]

Racial turmoil, the product of segregation, was confined neither to Europe nor to the Ground or Service Forces. At MacDill Army Air Field, near Tampa, Florida, tensions between black airmen and whites erupted in violence. For almost a year racial amity had been deteriorating, with blacks alerting newspapers like the *Chicago Defender* to the emerging pattern of racial discrimination, but complaints to the black press had no effect upon the attitudes of the white officers in charge. As a result, quarters for the blacks remained second-rate, their assignments continued to require a minimum of skill, and Jim Crow ruled on both sides of the installation's perimeter fence.

On October 27, 1946, the youngest among the black enlisted men rioted. Ironically, the uprising stemmed from a fight among blacks. Private soldiers tried to muscle their way into a dance held by the noncommissioned officers. A brawl erupted but soon died away when the disgruntled troops decided that the sergeants were not the real enemy. The difference between black private and black sergeant seemed to amount to nothing compared with the gap in power and privilege between black soldiers and whites. As a result, the black rioters, most of them recent recruits, rebelled against white authority, took the weapons from the white guards at the main gate, and in effect made a prisoner of the white Army Air Forces officer commanding the black detachment. For a time, the mutineers threatened to invade and vandalize a housing area for the families of white servicemen. The white general officer who commanded the operational forces at the base at last persuaded the blacks to return to their quarters. Their anger spent, the rioters would listen to an officer of the "real" Air Forces, though not to the non-flying officers in command of the housekeeping units in which the blacks served.

When peace had returned, the Strategic Air Command, whose bombers operated from the Florida base, sent a black counterintelligence agent, Walter L. Harris, to pose as an airman and ferret out evidence of communist involvement. On the contrary, he discovered that the riot had represented a spontaneous protest against racial discrimination on the base and in the city of Tampa. Lacking useful work and receiving no encouragement in the performance of their routine duties, the blacks passed from boredom through resentment to violence, going on a rampage that resulted in prison sentences for nine of them.[23]

MacDill Army Air Field had one of the largest concentrations of blacks in the air arm, a result of the opposition, first voiced by General Spaatz in April 1946 when the report of the Gillem Board was being incorporated into Army regulations, to the assigning of small units made up of blacks to larger ones composed of whites. The commanding general of the Army Air Forces had taken issue with the board's assumption that the percentage of blacks in the Army should reflect their share of the general populace. "Never in history," he complained, "has an Army selected its manpower on the basis of a proportionate share of the population, be that selection on the basis of color or creed." Nor did he agree to the attachment of black squadrons to white groups. The formation of racially composite units at this organizational level was out of the question, he declared, "since personnel and equipment are often interchanged and common messes utilized by persons of more than one squadron." Instead, Spaatz recommended that "intelligency [sic] or professional ability" should be the criteria for accepting black volunteers, and those actually accepted would not serve in any racially mixed organization unless it was large enough to support messes and similar facilities. For all his talk of making intelligence and skill the sole criteria for recruitment, he was determined at this time to limit the contact between the races.[24]

The policy outlined by General Spaatz in the spring of 1946 resulted in the concentration of blacks at a few locations. One was

MacDill Army Air Field, where the pressures that would lead to violence in the autumn of that year already were building. At the Florida base, two black officers and almost 1,600 men performed routine housekeeping duty. No wonder that blacks in the lower enlisted grades believed in the existence of a hostile white command structure or that the Army was seeking more black junior officers in the hope of defusing the situation. Other similar sites were the various training facilities in the San Antonio area of Texas, where two officers and some 3,400 men were stationed, and Lockbourne Army Air Field, Columbus, Ohio, where 192 black officers (81 percent of the total number in the entire air arm) and 1,862 men were serving. Except for the 477th Composite Group at Lockborne, none of the blacks served in tactical units. If not undergoing training, those at San Antonio and MacDill or scattered among some fifty other bases (no more than 540 at any one place) performed housekeeping duties.[25]

At most locations, black airmen were treated as surplus manpower, excess to the true needs of the Army Air Forces and later the U.S. Air Force. Base commanders tended to group these men, regardless of their aptitudes, in general service squadrons that, in effect, formed a labor pool for an airfield or wing. Citing the fact that black enlisted men had a lower average score on the general classification tests than a cross section of white airmen (many of the blacks occupying the lowest two of five categories), the officers who shaped racial policy for the air service ignored the warning of Colonel Parrish—if, indeed, they were aware of it—and treated blacks as a class, rather than as individuals, thus inviting class solidarity and class action. No wonder the men stationed at MacDill came to thinking of themselves as an oppressed minority instead of uniformed members of the nation's armed forces.[26]

Officers of the 477th Composite Group, the only flying unit in the postwar Army Air Forces that was made up of blacks, had rebelled against Jim Crow clubs when the unit was stationed at Freeman Field, Indiana. As a result of this incident, the Army Air Forces substituted black officers for whites throughout the organization and transferred it to Godman Field, Kentucky. Benjamin O. Davis, Jr., now a colonel, assumed command and remained in charge after the move from Godman to Lockbourne. After the Air Force became independent of the Army in September 1947, with the Tuskegee airfield shut down, black aviators had to choose between joining the unit at Lockbourne, reconstituted as the 332nd Fighter Group in mid-1947, and leaving the service.[27]

The 332nd Fighter Group encountered some of the same problems that had bedeviled segregated organizations since World War

I. All too many of the enlisted men stationed at Lockbourne had fared poorly on the basic aptitude tests and could contribute little to the smooth functioning of an operational unit. Replacements for pilots, staff officers, and mechanics proved scarce. Before Davis took command, the difficulty in obtaining key individuals like these may have contributed to a series of crashes and thus undermined flying efficiency, but the safety record improved so rapidly that carelessness on the flight line and in the cockpit (or even a statistical anomaly) may have been the root cause.

Fortunately, Davis was one of the more skilled and experienced commanders in the Air Force. His capable leadership helped the unit overcome the obstacles imposed by racial segregation, participate successfully in maneuvers (during one of which the black officers were barred from the officers' club at Fort Campbell, Kentucky), and allay to some degree the fear and suspicion with which the the white citizens of Columbus viewed the black servicemen. Success in athletics, specifically the gold medal won in the 1948 Olympic Games by Sergeant Mal Whitfield, combined with discipline and obvious military efficiency and helped change the attitudes of local whites.[28]

Attitudes toward black airmen also were changing within the Air Force, though some senior officers saw no need to increase the proportion of blacks beyond the 6 percent serving early in 1948. The racial composition of the service, after all, seemed a minor element in the establishment of an independent Air Force equipped with expensive aircraft like the six-engine B-36, which could drop the atomic bomb almost anywhere in the world. Yet at least one of the generals helping to shape the new Air Force interpreted the question of racial composition in terms of the unique situation facing the United States.

Relations with the Soviet Union had grown worse, foreshadowing a period of sustained competition that, barring the outbreak of war, promised to continue far into the future. Would Congress, year after year, persist in voting the funds to buy the B-36s and other weapons if the Air Force excluded a segment of the populace from its ranks? Lieutenant General Idwal H. Edwards, the Deputy Chief of Staff for Personnel, believed that the Air Force would have to make efficient use of all airmen, black and white, or run afoul of Congress. Moreover, the Selective Service System, about to be reenacted in 1948, might bring into the Air Force additional blacks, who would have to be absorbed into a smoothly functioning military organization. Such were the practical considerations that reinforced his opposition to racial segregation.

Because of the efforts of General Edwards, by January 1948 the leaders of the independent Air Force had become aware that the current racial policy was failing. Early that month the Air Board, a panel that advised both the Secretary of the Air Force and the Air Force Chief of Staff, convened at Washington to discuss, among other things, the employment of black airmen. Mention of the possible benefits of assigning small numbers of blacks to larger white units, an action endorsed by the Gillem Board, caused Lieutenant General James H. Doolittle to suggest a more radical move, the abolition of racial segregation.

An executive with Shell Oil before World War II, the former racing pilot had reverted to reserve status and rejoined Shell after a wartime career during which he had led the first attack on Tokyo and commanded air forces in North Africa and Europe. He drew upon all this experience, military and civilian, in making his recommendation. "Hugh," he told Major General Hugh J. Knerr, secretary general of the Air Board, "I don't like to be naive about this but I am convinced that the solution of the situation is to forget they are colored." The eradication of segregation was "being forced on industry," he advised his colleagues, "and it is going to be forced on the military. You are merely postponing the inevitable and you might as well take it gracefully."

Follett Bradley, a retired major general and now a consultant to Sperry Gyroscope, endorsed Doolittle's views, pointing out that American industry was learning to get along without racial segregation. "Colored women," he reported, "are working right alongside white women—men alongside men and women, too—all mixed up together. What do they care?"

Additional support came from a civilian, Roy Alexander of the *Time–Life* journalistic empire. Sitting with the board as an adviser on public relations, he quickly pointed out that the first of the services to take the step that Doolittle advocated would reap a harvest of good will. Alexander clearly wanted the Air Force to lead the way.

General Edwards expected the Air Board to endorse what Doolittle and Bradley had recommended and he favored.[29] Indeed, he was already laying the groundwork for implementation of that very policy. The advisory body disappointed him, however. It merely urged that the Air Force carry out to the letter the recommendations of the Gillem Board, thus trying to give blacks the same opportunities as whites without embracing racial integration. Unfortunately, as the Army was demonstrating, equality of opportunity was impossible in a racially segregated service.[30]

In spite of the board's reluctance, the Air Force tottered at the brink of change. General Spaatz, who had once inveighed against accepting a fixed proportion of blacks in the air arm, now agreed that they should "approximate the 1 in 10 ratio of the Negro civilian population to the total population of the nation, provided the Negro personnel can qualify for Air Force standards." Besides giving this qualified endorsement to a key principle of the Gillem Board's report, the general declared that "it is the feeling of this headquarters that the ultimate Air Force objective must be to eliminate segregation among its personnel by the unrestricted use of Negro personnel in competition for any duty for which they may qualify."[31]

For the present, the announced racial policies of the armed services had failed within three years. The Navy, regardless of its wartime experience and its endorsement of integration, had not tried to attract a large number of blacks with varied potential skills, settling instead for cooks and waiters. The Marine Corps had been unable to purge its ranks of blacks and had failed to find suitable assignments for those who remained. The Army had not achieved even the limited aims of the Gillem Board; it had concerned itself more with the proportion of blacks in the service than the opportunities available to them. Within the Air Force, influential officers like Colonel Parrish and Generals Edwards, Doolittle, and Bradley were pushing for change, but institutional inertia yet prevailed.

15

Politics and Principle

As the nation emerged from World War II, the blinding of Isaac Woodard and other instances of racial violence revealed a strain of viciousness deeply ingrained in American life. But on the side of justice, the reaction to the assault on the former sergeant disclosed a growing sense of disgust with racism, at least in its most violent manifestations.

The federal courts had taken the lead in challenging racial discrimination, but the executive branch had moved slowly to enforce these recent legal intepretations and Congress reacted impassively to the plight of black citizens. The mood of executive diffidence, if not the congressional lethargy, was about to change, for President Truman, moved by the fate of Isaac Woodard, found himself in circumstances where he could obtain political advantage by attacking what he perceived as a monstrous injustice. Attack he did, launching his campaign in the armed forces, which were constitutionally subject to his authority as Commander in Chief, although the Constitution could not guarantee their enthusiastic obedience.

We have seen that opposing forces also were affecting racial policy within the service, especially in the Air Force. There, Generals Follett Bradley and Jimmy Doolittle, one retired and the other a reservist, had become prominent in the world of business and consequently could examine in the light of recent social change the Army's attempt to retain racial segregation. They concluded that racial integration was encompassing the workplace and inevitably would spread to the armed forces. These two officers and others who shared their views urged that the new Air Force embrace racial integration at once rather than wait to yield grudgingly to the gathering social forces. The most influential of the active-duty officers to endorse change was General Idwal H. Edwards, Deputy Chief of Staff for Personnel. But a number of his respected brother officers did not agree that the Air Force should be color-blind. The prevailing view was that expressed by Lieutenant General Elwood "Pete" Quesada, who insisted that "anyone who says the negro is up to the white man is just not telling the truth." For the moment at least, the old order would survive.[1]

The result of the internal debate within the Air Force, the Navy's failure to carry out the racial policies it had adopted, and the failure of the Gillem Board's reforms to ameliorate the effects of segregation meant that the services would not voluntarily make any change in the relationship between the races. The initiative lay with the Chief Executive. Reared in a segregated society, President Truman did not let the prejudices to which he had been exposed during his youth warp his sense of justice or, for that matter, deaden his political instincts. Even so, he retained some of the trappings of his background. For example, he habitually referred to "niggers" in casual conversation with other whites, offhandedly and apparently without malice using a term familiar from his past. Merle Miller, a writer whose attitude toward the former Chief Executive varied from the patronizing to the admiring, concluded after a series of long and far-ranging interviews with an elderly Mr. Truman that the ex-President's record on racial matters was all the more remarkable in view of his heritage.[2]

As President, Truman detected a change in the public mood, a growing sense of embarrassment that the nation which had called upon some 290,000 of its sons to sacrifice their lives in the fight to destroy the Axis could continue to tolerate racists within its own borders. Although concerned that he might be moving too quickly for the consensus that he sensed was forming, Mr. Truman appealed for public support to push President Roosevelt's New Deal to its logical conclusion by removing the remaining barriers to equal opportunity which were based on race or religion. A key element in this fulfillment of the New Deal was the replacement of the wartime Fair Employment Practices Commission, established by his predecessor to monitor defense contractors, with a permanent commission of broader scope and authority. As a symbol of his commitment to civil rights, Truman became the first Chief Executive to address, in person, a convention of the National Association for the Advancement of Colored People, something Mr. Roosevelt had avoided.

The President now had the opportunity to guide public sentiment and take advantage of a willingness, if not yet eagerness, on the part of a growing minority of whites to support action to protect the rights of black Americans. Wartime propaganda had tried to mobilize public opinion against the German racist, who systematically murdered Jews and Slavs, or the Japanese militarist, who routinely slaughtered supposedly subhuman peoples like the Chinese. This attempt to shape attitudes had an effect on some whites, as did reports of racist savagery in the South and contacts with individual blacks in the service or on the assembly line. White Americans were beginning to realize what their black fellow citizens knew all too well: separate but equal was a contradiction in terms; there could be no equality in a society that enforced racial segregation. The possibility therefore existed that a move against racial segregation need not be political suicide for the President. In fact, it might provide the key to electoral victory.[3]

As Truman calculated his prospects for election to a Presidential term of his own, Walter White's report of the attack on Isaac Woodard strengthened his resolve to fight racism. In explaining his attitude toward blacks, unusual for a man of his age and background, the Chief Executive wrote to a man with whom he had served in World War I, "When a Mayor and a City Marshal can take a Negro sergeant off a bus in South Carolina, beat him and put out one of his eyes, and nothing is done about it by State Authorities, then something is radically wrong with the system."[4] The President may have forgotten the exact details, but the horror of the attack on Woodard had moved him deeply.

Although unable in 1947 to persuade the Congress to create a Fair Employment Practices Commission, Truman exercised the authority of his office to appoint the President's Committee on Civil Rights, an investigatory body. Headed by Charles E. Wilson, the president of General Electric, the group included several prominent whites—business, religious, educational, and civic leaders—and two blacks, Sadie T. M. Alexander, an attorney, and Channing H. Tobias, the director of a philanthropic foundation. *To Secure These Rights*, the report submitted by the committee, examined most aspects of American life, including the armed forces. Besides endorsing the President's call for an agency to enforce fair employment practices, the members recommended such other measures as the creation of a permanent civil rights commission, home rule for the District of Columbia (where a large number of blacks resided), indemnification of the Japanese-Americans held in wartime internment camps, and a law making lynching a federal crime.[5]

Addressing the topic of military service, the President's committee accepted the truism that every citizen had a right and an obligation to bear arms in time of national emergency but at the same time pointed out that the nation owed certain things to its defenders. "When an individual enters the service of the country, he necessarily surrenders some of the rights and privileges which inhere in American citizenship," the report conceded, but it added that "the government in return undertakes to protect his integrity as an individual and the dignity of his profession." To protect the serviceman's individual integrity, the document recommended putting an end to "all discrimination and segregation based on race, color, creed, or national origin, in the organization and activities of all branches of the Armed Services." To ensure the dignity of the profession of arms, no member of the armed forces should be "subject to discrimination of any kind by any public authority or place of public accommodation, recreation, transportation, or other service or business."[6]

The report, entitled *To Secure These Rights*, appeared as the military establishment was undergoing a postwar reorganization. The new National Military Establishment (later the Department of Defense) comprised three coequal services, the Army, Navy, and Air Force, and was headed by the Secretary of Defense. The civilian advisers to James Forrestal, the first person to hold the office of Secretary, urged him to do precisely what the President's Committee on Civil Rights had recommended and issue a directive prohibiting racial discrimination on military bases or affecting men in uniform. Forrestal refused. Despite his commitment to racial integration, which he had revealed anew while Secretary of the Navy, Forrestal saw his new role as that of mediator, working to create a consensus among the three services rather than imposing his will upon them. He was convinced, moreover, that a directive could not by itself alter the relationship between the white and black races. Any such change, he maintained, had to begin with education and progress slowly on the basis of accumulated experience.

Whereas Forrestal trusted education to effect gradual change, A. Philip Randolph did not. In 1940 Randolph had used the threat of a march on Washington to wrest concessions from Franklin Roosevelt; he now proposed to use Mr. Truman's insistence upon an extension of the draft or some form of universal military service as leverage to force the Chief Executive into carrying out the recommendations of the committee on civil rights. Randolph declared that it was a crime to induct blacks into a racially segregated Army and vowed to organize resistance, calling upon all young men, black or white, who opposed racism to refuse to register for the draft.

Aware that Randolph was giving voice to the resentment felt by many blacks, Forrestal's aides persisted in advising him to take action against discrimination in the armed forces. James C. Evans, the highest-ranking black in the Department of Defense (for a short time he doubled as civilian aide to the Secretary of the Army and to Secretary of Defense Forrestal as well), joined Lester Granger and Forrestal's executive assistant, John H. Ohly, in recommending the creation of a departmental committee on racial matters patterned after the wartime body headed by John J. McCloy. Although Secretary Forrestal refused to endorse coercing the services, even by means of a committee, he did agree to an exchange of views among spokesmen for the black community and military policy makers, whether uniformed or civilian. Heeding the advice of Granger and Marx Leva, a special assistant to the Secretary of Defense, Forrestal invited fifteen black leaders to a meeting at the Pentagon during which the services would outline their racial policies.

The group that met on April 26, 1948, included the two blacks who had served on the President's Committee on Civil Rights, Sadie T. M. Alexander and Channing Tobias. Also in attendance were Mary McLeod Bethune, a confidante of Eleanor Roosevelt, and Walter White, a veteran of many a civil rights campaign. Conspicuous by his absence was A. Philip Randolph, who already had formed his own Committee against Jim Crow to wage war against a segregated Army.[7]

During the discussions, the Navy's representatives reaffirmed their commitment to racial integration, but they had no evidence of progress toward that goal except for slight increase in the number of black recruits. As the black leaders soon realized, the stewards' branch remained the dumping ground for all too many black sailors. Even though the Navy boasted that transfers out of the branch were receiving official encouragement, it had to concede that a large number of stewards with long service lacked any incentive to master another specialty late in their careers.

The Assistant Secretary of the Air Force dealing with manpower, Eugene Zuckert, began by sketching the current policy based on the report of the Gillem Board, which looked to an Air Force that was about 10 percent black, with this number divided among small, racially exclusive units that were attached to larger white ones. Zuckert, however, proposed going far beyond a policy of greater opportunity within a system of segregation. His blueprint was a plan for doing away with segregation recently drawn up by General Edwards in anticipation of approval by the Air Board. Though the board had disappointed him despite support by Doolittle and Bradley, a program was nonetheless ready to lend substance to Zuckert's declaration that "the ultimate Air Force objective must be to eliminate segregation among its personnel by the unrestricted use of Negro personnel in free competition for any duty within the Air Force for which they may qualify."[8]

In contrast, the Army committed itself to carrying out the basic policy of the Gillem Board, which thus far had preserved segregation without expanding opportunities for blacks. Nothing was said of pursuing the board's recommendations to the logical, if distant, conclusion of eventual racial integration. The Secretary of the Army, Kenneth C. Royall of North Carolina, insisted, however, that the policy of racial segregation remained the subject of continuing review. "The door," he said, "is not closed to the future." This promise had a hollow ring, for even as he spoke of change in the racial policy for the Army, he conceded that he would have insisted upon the separation of the races in the National Guard, insofar as permissible under the laws of the individual states, even if the Army General Staff had recommended otherwise.

The black leaders came away from the meeting disappointed, most of their questions unanswered, their concerns unresolved. They had heard encouraging words from Zuckert, more of the same old promises from the Navy, and a defense of its existing policy on the part of the Army. They did not understand why Forrestal hung back, refusing to call in the service secretaries and issue them orders to carry out a racial policy that he clearly favored. They saw Forrestal as a kind of civilian czar over the armed forces, whereas Forrestal saw himself as a negotiator, bargaining with the civilian leaders to achieve his goals. Because of this basic misunderstanding, the meeting could not generate good will among the black leadership and confidence in the intentions of the services.[9]

As had occurred in the two previous presidential elections, segregation in the armed forces became a campaign issue. The Republicans, who again nominated Thomas E. Dewey, resolved, "We are opposed to the idea of racial segregation in the armed services of the United States." At issue was the black vote, which might well be wrested from a Democratic Party torn by contending liberal, radical, and conservative factions. A split already was developing in Democratic ranks between those who believed, along with former Vice President Henry A. Wallace, that accommodation with the Soviet Union was not only possible but desirable and those who shared President Truman's wariness concerning Soviet motives. Before the summer ended, Wallace had formed his own party, a political organization that drew heavily upon the radical elements within the Democratic Party.

Following the custom in recent presidential elections, the Democrats, meeting in convention, sought to adopt a civil rights plant in their campaign platform that bridged the gap between liberals and conservatives, proponents of federal authority and advocates of states' rights, integrationists and segregationists. This time the usual strategy failed. Stirred by the impassioned oratory of Hubert H. Humphrey, the mayor of Minneapolis, Minnesota, the delegates incorporated in the party platform all the civil rights measures that Mr. Truman supported but had hoped to avoid raising as campaign issues. The platform committee lost control, and the delegates ignored the pattern of compromise, which Truman himself hoped to follow, and pledged their candidate to a series of far-reaching actions dealing with race relations. The nominee would have to promise to protect the voting rights of blacks, guarantee them equality of opportunity within the federal civil service, make lynching a federal crime, and end segregation within the armed forces. The southern delegations, infuriated by this action, walked out of the hall, promptly formed their own Dixiecrat Party, and nominated for the Presidency Governor J. Strom Thurmond of South Carolina, a segregationist.[10]

Suddenly the Democratic phalanx that had stood firm for almost two decades was shorn of its far left wing, which marched off behind Wallace, and its far right, which now followed Thurmond. A number of President Truman's closest advisers believed that he could turn these defections to his advantage. Clark Clifford, for one, had been insisting for the past year that black voters could hold the key to victory in the 1948 presidential election. Another adviser, Oscar Ewing, urged the Chief Executive to issue at once a series of directives based on the controversial civil rights plank. No longer able to compromise, Mr. Truman had to take a stand.

Assuredly the President had no choice, for he could not scrap the party platform without alienating what remained of his political following. Indeed, the platform and the defections it caused gave him a measure of independence. Relieved of the burden of placating the southern extremists, he could follow his own instincts and take executive action to secure the basic rights of black citizens. Far from jeopardizing his hopes for election, this marriage of politics and principle might represent his only chance to remain in office.

Clifford, Ewing, and Philleo Nash, another of the President's advisers, hurriedly prepared the draft of an executive order requiring equality of treatment and opportunity within the armed forces. They chose to begin here because the Constitution designated the President as Commander in Chief, with the authority to establish policy for the services. Another course of action might require legislative initiative, and Congress had already demonstrated a reluctance to act. Truman Gibson offered his advice on the wording of the directive, and both Walter White and A. Philip Randolph had an opportunity to read the proclamation. Secretary of Defense Forrestal, upon reviewing the document, expressed confidence that Secretary of the Air Force Stuart Symington and Secretary of the Navy John L. Sullivan would endorse the new policy but suggested that Ewing discuss it with Royall, who might be a hold-out. The Secretary of the Army, despite his Southern background and conservatism concerning racial matters declared that he personally and the Army as an institution would carry out the directive.[11]

"It is hereby declared," intoned the executive order of July 26, 1948, "that there shall be equality of treatment and opportunity for all persons in the armed services without regard to race, color, religion, or national origin." The new policy was to go into effect "as rapidly as possible, having due regard to the time required to effectuate any necessary changes without impairing efficiency or morale." The directive also established a seven-member President's Committee on Equality of Treatment and Opportunity in the Armed Forces to investigate compliance and make any necessary recommendations to the President and the service secretaries. By establishing this organization, which would serve at the discretion of the Chief Executive, Mr. Truman removed himself from the day-to-day enforcement of his policy, avoiding the hard bargaining and the exerting of pressure that was likely to occur. Nevertheless, the credit for adopting a policy of equal opportunity—or the blame, as opponents would have it—rested solely on the President.[12]

What did the order mean? Was it merely a broadening of the Army's failed policy of increasing opportunity without disturbing racial segregation? It definitely was not. When asked during a press conference if his "advocacy of equal treatment and opportunity in the Armed Forces" foretold the eventual end of segregation, the President's answer was an unequivocal "Yes."[13]

Words like these produced the effect that Truman, the politician, wanted. All but the most skeptical of black leaders rallied behind him. Among those who took the President at his word was A. Philip Randolph, for the black union leader abandoned his plan to organize resistance to the draft.[14]

The question remained whether Truman, the civil rights advocate, could impose his will upon the services, only one of which, the Air Force, had made any advance preparations for racial integration. The Navy had announced bold programs that were never carried out. The Marine Corps was grudgingly accepting a comparative handful of blacks. The Army pointed with pride to the policy shaped by the Gillem Board but was using it to maintain segregation rather than to ease the service toward eventual integration.

Even assuming the best of intentions, the armed forces faced problems that would require time to solve. The Navy, for instance, had to attract more blacks, especially as commissioned officers, and somehow integrate the stewards' branch. The Army had to convert its existing segregated units into vehicles for increasing opportunities for blacks. Should the military establishment choose to circumvent the policy, the President might yield in the face of the opposition, accept the temporary political advantage, and forgo genuine reform. If the services tried to cling to segregation and Truman insisted upon integration, he would face a test of political skill rivaling any election campaign in which he had ever participated.[15]

The foot-dragging began with the Navy, which responded to the Presidential directive with a salvo of self-congratulation, lauding past accomplishments and ignoring the future. Instead of making an effort to seek out the black recruits and officer candidates needed to make integration work, departmental officials pointed out that the proportion of its black sailors in the nominally integrated general service had increased since the war from 6 percent to 38 percent. Statements like this ignored the contrasting size of the peacetime and wartime navies. The actual number of black seamen assigned to the general service had declined from slightly under 10,000 to about 6,000. Furthermore, 62 percent of the black sailors in the peacetime Navy were cooks or stewards—almost 11,000 men, or not quite twice the number in the general service.[16]

The Marine Corps also looked to the past. As the Commandant, General Clifton B. Cates, made clear during the months following the Presidential directive, his organization had no intention of abandoning its existing racial restrictions. "The problem of segregation is not the responsibility of the Armed Forces," he declared, "but is a problem of the nation." Segregation should therefore prevail in the military establishment until "non-segregation . . . is accepted as a custom of the nation."[17]

The Army, although more amenable to change than the Marine Corps, remained committed to the kind of modified racial segregation that had resulted from the findings of the Gillem Board. General Omar N. Bradley, the Chief of Staff, had worried about the difficulty of absorbing poorly educated blacks, taught in second-rate segregated schools, into the modern Army. During an address to military instructors at Fort Knox, Kentucky, he gave voice to these doubts. Convinced that decades would pass before the educational level of blacks approached that of whites and unaware of the President's directive, which had just been issued, he suggested that the

Army would have to remain segregated as long as that practice prevailed in American society. The general was also unaware that reporters were present, and accounts of his views stirred a brief tempest that he calmed with an apology to the Chief Executive. President Truman accepted the apology, too easily satisfied that Bradley would carry out orders to the letter. Perhaps the Commander in Chief was especially sympathetic because the general came from a social background not unlike his own.[18]

Opposition to racial integration lingered within the Air Force. For example, General George C. Kenney, the wartime commander of Allied Air Forces in the Southwest Pacific, invoked one of the hoariest defenses of racial segregation, arguing that integration would be unfair to blacks, placing them at a disadvantage by forcing them to compete with whites. Similarly, Brigadier General Dean C. Strother, who had seen the wartime Tuskegee airmen in action and come away unimpressed, expressed concern that the service was moving too quickly toward racial integration.

These were influential officers—Strother was director of military personnel (a principal subordinate of General Edwards, the most effective advocate of integration), and Kenney had been the first commanding general of the Strategic Air Command. They were professionals, however, and as such would follow orders. Secretary of the Air Force Stuart Symington had been an advocate of racial integration since his days as an executive of Emerson Electric, and there was little doubt what the orders would say. Indeed, Symington would describe integration as the "right thing to do . . . morally, . . . legally, . . . militarily," adding, "The commander in chief said this should be done and so we did it."[19]

The architect of Air Force racial policy was Idwal Edwards. Even though the Air Board refused to endorse such a policy when the question first arose, he kept on making preparations for a change that he considered inevitable and desirable. His disgust with segregation stemmed from his association with Brigadier General Benjamin O. Davis, Sr., with whom he had served on the wartime McCloy committee. Edwards had come to understand the cruelty of racism when the older officer remarked that as a black man, even though he wore the uniform of a general officer in the Army of the United States, he could be served at only one restaurant in the national capital.[20]

Thus inspired, Edwards had done his work well. Colonel Jack Marr, an officer in Edward's staff section, had already begun drafting a plan for assimilating blacks into a racially integrated Air Force. Once President Truman made his decision, the Air Force swung into action, and the plan became reality. Both Marr and General Edwards realized that the task would grow progressively harder as the best-trained and most experienced blacks joined new units, for eventually there would remain a few comparatively large, racially exclusive outfits containing the blacks with the least competence and potential. Reassigning them would be the greatest challenge, but the two officers were confident it could be done. Thanks to Marr's planning, the success of Colonel Benjamin Davis, Jr., as a commander, and the persuasive power of General Edwards, the Air Force alone of the services was ready to carry out President Truman's directive.

The greatest accomplishment of General Edwards was to convert the new Air Force Chief of Staff, General Hoyt S. Vandenberg, to the cause of racial integration. A relative of Senator Arthur S. Vandenberg of Michigan, a Republican with presidential ambitions, the Chief of Staff put into effect the racial policy desired by President Truman. Immediately after World War II, General Vandenberg had declared that most blacks were so lacking in intelligence and capacity to lead that any attempt to train large numbers of them as officers, or even as enlisted technicians, was not economically sound.[21] As Chief of Staff, however, he changed his mind, influenced at least as much by the arguments advanced by Edwards as by the directives of President Truman and the Secretary of the Air Force. The service, Vandenberg believed, could not arbitrarily exclude blacks and expect to convince Congress that it faced an emergency that required continued and heavy expenditures.

Vandenberg's assistant, Major General William F. "Bozo" McKee, who usually saw no evil or failed to remember it, insisted that the Chief of Staff had never doubted for a moment the wisdom or success of racial integration.[22] A more likely explanation is that the racial composition of the Air Force ranked too low on Vandenberg's agenda to arouse either enthusiasm or violent opposition. The Chief of Staff was building a nuclear striking force, battling the other services for appropriations, and taking over tasks formerly performed for the air arm by the Army Service Forces. Racial matters assumed major importance only when they affected efficiency (like the recent riot at MacDill Army Air Field) or threatened to undermine congressional funding.

With the 1948 election fast approaching and the armed forces, except for the Air Force, moving slowly and reluctantly to eliminate segregation, Mr. Truman's aides hurriedly recruited seven members for the President's Committee on Equality of Treatment and Opportunity in the Armed Forces, the investigative body authorized by the Chief Executive's recent directive. The appointment of this group, the administration believed, would demonstrate to the Army and

Navy, to the black electorate, and to the American public at large that the President fully intended that racial integration prevail throughout the services. The committee members included Charles Luckman of Lever Brothers, a soap manufacturer. He was a veteran of the recent committee on civil rights that had approved the report *To Secure These Rights*, with its powerful call for federal action that included the abolition of segregation within the armed forces. Serving with Luckman were two blacks, John H. Sengstacke, a journalist, and Lester Granger, and three other whites—William Stevenson, the president of Oberlin College in Ohio, Adolphus J. Donohue, an industrialist, and Dwight Palmer, an executive of the General Cable Corporation. Appointed chairman was Charles "Whisper" Fahy, a soft-spoken native of Georgia, described by David Niles, a special assistant to Mr. Truman, as a "reconstructed southerner, liberal on race." Of the seven members, two did not play an active role, Luckman because of the press of business and Donohue because of illness.[23]

In the bureaucratic hierarchy, the Fahy Committee remained an advisory body to the Secretary of Defense. Both James Forrestal, during whose tenure the group began its deliberations, and Louis A. Johnson, who took office after Forrestal left the cabinet, believed that the Army, Navy, and Air Force should each adopt a racial policy based on the findings and recommendations of Fahy and his colleagues. The established procedures called for the services to draw up programs of compliance with the recent Presidential directive. The committee would then review these drafts, making sure that the same standards, accurately reflecting the President's wishes, applied throughout the armed forces. Forrestal did not want his National Military Establishment to force the services to adopt regulations that they found objectionable. Fahy's group filled the resulting void, negotiating with the armed forces, although it was unable to enforce the resulting understandings. Compliance depended upon the willingness of President Truman, acting through his Secretary of Defense or intervening directly as Commander in Chief, to throw his constitutional weight behind the committee. Whatever its bureaucratic status, the Fahy Committee was a tool that the Chief Executive could use to impose his will upon the reluctant Army and Navy.[24]

When the committee met for the first time on January 12, 1949, the President's influence approached its zenith, for he had gained a startling victory over Thomas E. Dewey in the November election. The coalition of "workers, veterans, and Negroes" had returned Mr. Truman to the White House, as Clark Clifford had predicted.[25] The contribution of blacks to Truman's electoral triumph strengthened his resolve to fight for his civil rights program, which included enforcement of his directive on equality of treatment and opportunity in the armed forces.

In each of three states won by the President—Illinois, Ohio, and California—the black minority numbered at least a half million, including enough potential voters to account for his narrow margins of victory. The three states netted him 78 electoral votes out of the 303 that he received. Had they ended up in the Republican column, Governor Dewey would have been President. Other factors besides the black vote influenced the outcome, though, for all three states had large numbers of union members, whose leaders had endorsed Truman. Also, the 78 electoral votes would have meant nothing had the President failed to carry agricultural states like Iowa. Nor did the black voters of New York, New Jersey, and Pennsylvania prove decisive, for all three cast their votes for Dewey.[26] The upshot of the election was that President Truman could ill afford to alienate any element of the triad that had elected him—neither labor nor farmers nor blacks.

As the President sensed, the times were changing, to some extent at least. Along with the recent Supreme Court decisions dealing with the rights of blacks to travel, vote, and obtain an education—which admittedly were being enforced only sporadically—wartime experience had penetrated the national consciousness and to a degree eroded the foundations of institutionalized racism. Wartime youth, like the children who had paid with contributions to the scrap-metal drive for admission to the Saturday matinee at the movie house, were growing up and perhaps proving more susceptible than their elders to the idealized version of America that they had seen on the screen. Films with a high content of propaganda—like *Sahara*, in which a brutal Nazi insulted an intelligent and desert-wise black African—not only aroused contempt for Hitler's vaunted Aryan master race but also bred a gnawing discomfort with discriminatory practices in the United States. (Of course, the thought-provoking scenes might be excised from films shown in the South.)[27] Also, a good many wartime workers had shared the experience of Inez Sauer, who discovered at Boeing Aircraft that "because a girl is a Negro she's not necessarily a maid, and because a man is a Negro doesn't mean all he can do is dig."[28] Abroad in the land was a feeling, not yet a conviction, inarticulate and far from pervasive, that the black man or woman should have a chance to demonstrate whatever abilities he or she might have. This attitude contributed to the appearance of the first blacks in major-league baseball, exclusively white since the emergence of baseball as the national sport at about the turn of the century.[29]

Besides court decisions and changing public sentiment, another consideration helped strengthen the Fahy Committee's hand. This was the growing perception that a foreign threat menaced the United States. The weak showing in the 1948 presidential election of Henry Wallace, who had argued that Soviet domination of eastern Europe was an excusable reaction to American policy, indicated a widespread public recognition of a grim rivalry between the United States and the Soviet Union, a fact of international life that promised to endure far into the future, unless it erupted in armed conflict. America's past wars, which had as an objective the destruction of the armed forces of a particular enemy and the occupation of his territory, were finite in duration. In those circumstances, military leaders had argued successfully against social experimentation, a term of condemnation for any challenge to racial segregation, which might reduce efficiency and delay victory. Against the backdrop of the new and persistent danger, Fahy and his colleagues could point out that the armed forces could not ignore one-tenth of the populace in maintaining the long-term armed might required to deal with a menace that might last, not for a few years, but for decades or even generations.

World War I, in which the United States took part for perhaps a year and a half, remained confined to Europe and did not last long enough to require the integration of blacks into the armed forces. World War II lasted roughly three times as long, covered the entire globe, and forced some degree of racial integration upon the military and naval establishments. The postwar crisis seemed of such gravity, likely duration, and geographic scope that the nation no longer could afford the luxury of racism. In short, the efficient use of manpower and racial segregation were incompatible.[30]

The attitude of the Air Force also worked to the advantage of the Fahy Committee, for on the second day that the group was in session, the newest of the armed forces had presented the draft of a directive designed to achieve racial integration. The proposed circular reflected a year or more of work by Colonel Marr, whom General Edwards had put to work on an integration plan even before Doolittle, Follett Bradley, and the other members of the Air Board began discussing racial policy. As a result of the general's success in persuading the Chief of Staff that integration would promote the efficient use of manpower and thus assure the continued flow of congressional appropriations, the Air Force was able to move rapidly once the President issued his order requiring equality of treatment and opportunity.[31]

On May 11, 1949, the Air Force announced a new policy requiring "that there shall be equality of treatment and opportunity for all persons in the Air Force without regard to race, color, religion, or national origin." The directive, which was to go into effect on November 11, banned racial or ethnic quotas, specified that enlistment, promotion, and assignment be based on "individual merit and ability," and pledged that blacks would be eligible for any assignment for which they were qualified.[32]

Although the Air Force directive acknowledged that some units composed exclusively of blacks would survive for the time being,[33] the task of breaking up the largest concentrations began at once. In mid-May, days after the announcement of the new policy, evaluation teams began interviewing the officers and men of the segregated 332nd Fighter Group, administering tests to determine proficiency and aptitude. The overwhelming majority of those tested retained their occupational specialties, and some qualified for additional training. More important, one member in five was reassigned from Lockbourne to bases overseas.

By year's end, slightly more than 25,000 blacks wore the uniform of the U.S. Air Force, an increase of 4,000 since May. Some 7,000 continued to serve in racially exclusive squadrons, another 7,000 were in the process of being assigned or reassigned to racially mixed units, and the remaining 11,000 had already joined integrated organizations. The screening process that contributed to the readjustment from totally segregated to less than 30 percent segregated resulted in the elimination of the least qualified blacks, as many as 23 percent at Lockbourne, usually by rejecting applications for reenlistment. Regardless of this culling out, the Air Force was attracting a greater proportion of blacks, in excess of one in ten of all recruits, at the end of the year than at the beginning.[34]

The actions of this service during 1949 demonstrated that the Fahy Committee and Secretary Johnson had not erred in accepting the plan first submitted in January. The prompt submission and rapid implementation on the part of the Air Force contrasted with the positions of the other services, whose initial programs had shown no intention of expanding opportunities for or altering the treatment of black soldiers and sailors. Indeed, the first plans offered by the Army and Navy adhered so closely to the status quo that Secretary Johnson may well have sought to use their obstinacy to advance his own political ambitions.

The new Secretary of Defense had taken over in March 1949, the second person to hold the office. Forrestal resigned, his departure caused at least in part by the administration's dissatisfaction with his lack of participation in President Truman's successful election campaign, although he also was displaying symptoms of the mental illness that resulted in his suicide a few months later. By exerting pressure on the Army and Navy, influencing service policies as Forrestal had been reluctant to do, Johnson hoped to rally black leaders behind him, upstage the Fahy Committee, and consolidate his own position within the administration. For this reason, early in April he had established a deadline of May 1, 1949, by which the Army and Navy would have to explain precisely how they intended to carry out the President's directive.[35]

The example of the Air Force and the demands pressed by the new Secretary of Defense, who seemed less patient than Forrestal had been, propelled the Navy into action. Late in May, Acting Secretary of the Navy Dan A. Kimball adopted the various reforms that the Fahy Committee had been urging upon him. Specifically, the Navy promised to make a greater effort to attract enough black recruits and officer candidates to make integration work. Black petty officers, working with black reserve officers recalled to active duty for the purpose, would launch a recruiting campaign that incorporated posters, brochures, and other forms of advertising that emphasized equality of treatment and opportunity. In addition, the stewards' branch was to undergo a thorough overhaul. The status of chief stewards as full-fledged petty officers was reaffirmed, active recruitment of white stewards would begin, and black members of the branch would receive new opportunities to transfer elsewhere. The new policy announced by Acting Secretary Kimball also specified that the Marine Corps was to inaugurate racially integrated recruit training.[36]

On June 23, 1949, a new Secretary of the Navy, Francis P. Matthews, issued a statement of policy applicable to the Navy and Marine Corps. Secretary Matthews, who had served on the President's Committee on Civil Rights, ratified the agreement that Kimball had made with the Fahy Committee. In content and spirit, the directive governing the naval establishment closely resembled the regulations adopted during the previous month by the Air Force. It remained to be seen whether the policy would be carried out.

When the directive came out, the Commandant of the Marine Corps, General Cates, issued instructions that called for the assignment of individual blacks solely by matching specialities with existing vacancies. Although black units would survive for a time, as was true even in the Air Force, the racial integration of the corps was at last getting under way. By this time blacks were playing on base or unit athletic teams, and it already had become too costly to operate separate schools for black cooks, stewards, and bakers. The Montford Point camp shut down, the separate black platoons at the Parris Island, South Carolina, training depot soon disbanded, and race no longer determined the assignment of recruits. By year's end, moreover, the first blacks had joined the Women Marines. But revolutionary as these changes were in the context of the history of the Corps, not until the influx of draftees during the Korean War did the number of black marines increase sufficiently to bring about genuine integration. A need for replacements in combat would make the difference, as the dictates of military necessity forced compliance with the declarations of policy.[37]

Although the Air Force had complied promptly and the Navy soon fell into line, the Army stood firm, acknowledging that its wartime racial policy had been wasteful and inefficient but insisting, in effect, that the Gillem Board had solved the problem. The Fahy Committee urged reforms upon the service, and Secretary Johnson exerted the same pressure that he had applied to the Navy. Eventually the Army responded, but with a glacial slowness.

When Johnson imposed his deadline, the Army reacted by expressing confidence that its existing racial policies "are sound in the light of actual experience, and are in accord with the policies of the National Military Establishment," as set forth by the Secretary of Defense, "and with Executive Order 9981," the President's directive calling for equality of treatment and opportunity. In support of this sweeping conclusion, Secretary of the Army Royall cited a commitment to uniform standards, impartially applied, in making promotions and assignments. He also directed Johnson's attention to the dozen units of the Reserve Officer Training Corps at black colleges, the fifty-odd regular officers who were blacks, and the 2,500 reserve officers, more than a thousand of them on tours of extended active duty.[38]

The Army's reply and the evidence presented in its support might well have persuaded Fahy, who was at home with legal jargon but at a loss to interpret the soldier's patois, which like the language of the law sought to conceal as much as to reveal, with its arcane references to capabilities, military efficiency, enlistment standards, assignments, and missions. But at this point, one of the whites on the committee staff, Edwin W. "Ned" Kenworthy, arranged for a number of blacks, all of them familiar with Army personnel practices, to scatter the verbal smokescreen that concealed what the service actually was doing. Men like Roy K. Davenport, a civilian employee specializing in the application of the Army's personnel policies, and Major James Fowler, the black graduate of the Military Academy who had worked to broaden opportunities at service schools, explained that all was not as Secretary Royall claimed. They pointed out that the number and nature of black units, rather than impartial standards and individual skills, determined the assignments for which black soldiers were eligible. As a result, the Army excluded non-whites from 198 of 490 military occupational specialities; regardless of his aptitude or experience, no black could enter or train for any of these fields. The efficient use of manpower yielded to considerations of race in the training and assignment of black soldiers.[39]

All of this having become clear, the Fahy Committee concentrated upon certain basic reforms designed to introduce efficiency into the Army's use of manpower. In brief, the group's proposal called for access to jobs and schools for all qualified soldiers, regardless of race; an end to the practice of shunting blacks into segregated units, with reliance instead upon individual ability and the needs of the service in making assignments; and the abolition of racial quotas. Gordon Gray, who succeeded Royall as Secretary of the Army in June 1949 after serving for several months as acting secretary, received this proposal and parried the thrust with yet another defense of the work of the Gillem Board.[40]

To prod the Army into action, the committee suggested a substitute for the racial quota, the Army General Classification Test. Once the quota had been discarded, test scores would supersede race as the principal factor in determining eligibility to enlist or reenlist. Demanding higher test scores would achieve one of the objectives of the Gillem Board, the elimination of the "professional privates," many of them blacks, who soldiered on with little hope of promotion. The poor education and limited skills that kept them from advancing in the service also prevented them from finding work in civilian life. Furthermore, reliance on evidence of aptitude seemed unlikely to alter radically the racial composition of the Army; blacks would not be excluded, although somewhat reduced in numbers, and those who remained would enjoy better prospects for training and promotion.[41]

Secretary Gray agreed to make an individual's qualifications the only condition for promotion, attendance at service schools, and the award of military occupational specialities. He balked, however, at breaking up all-black units and reassigning the members without regard to race. He believed, moreover, that "no practicable substitute had been developed for the Army's present policy of regulating original negro enlistments on the basis of population ratio." The racial quota, he argued, was essential to ensure that the Army accepted only the highest quality of black recruit.[42]

The Army thus rejected two points upon which the Fahy Committee insisted—termination of the racial quota and the reassignment of blacks throughout the service without regard to race. Nevertheless, Secretary of Defense Johnson promptly approved the plan. In doing so, the cabinet officer contradicted both his own record on civil rights and the expressed wishes of the President.[43]

Why had the Secretary of Defense ignored the President's wishes? Why did Johnson cease supporting the cause of black Americans? Perhaps he sensed that the Army would stand firm, frustrating his attempt (and that of Mr. Truman) to obtain political advantage by seeking to integrate the military service. He may have thought he was putting the best possible face on a certain defeat, in the process avoiding embarrassment to the Chief Executive and keeping alive his own hopes for the Presidency. If Secretary Johnson had any such political ambitions, as his earlier conduct indicated, the outbreak of the Korean War ended them, for by then he had become the administration's spokesman for reductions in defense spending, a policy discredited by the outbreak of hostilities.[44]

Instead of accepting Gray's proposal and Johnson's endorsement of it, Judge Fahy went directly to President Truman, demonstrating for the Chief Executive the contradictions inherent in the policy that the Army intended to follow. The Commander in Chief quickly realized the impossibility of enforcing a racial quota, maintaining segregated units, and at the same time proclaiming equality of treatment and opportunity. Continued segregation made a mockery of any pledge to eliminate race as a consideration in promotion and assignment. With Truman's backing, Fahy continued to negotiate with Secretary Gray, at last reaching an agreement that the Army, the President, and the committee could endorse, with varying degrees of enthusiasm.[45]

The first step toward carrying out that agreement was taken in mid-January 1950 when the Department of the Army issued a new regulation governing the utilization of black soldiers. This document contained a concession on one of the points at issue between the military and the Fahy Committee. Secretary Gray established as "the objective of the Department of the Army that Negro manpower possessing appropriate skills and qualifications will be utilized in accordance with such skills and qualifications." In attaining this goal, the Army would assign soldiers to units that needed them without regard to race.[46]

Fahy and his colleagues now turned to the remaining issue, the racial quota, demonstrating mathematically that a mandatory score of 90 points on the classification test would leave 16.5 percent of the black populace and 62.4 percent of the whites eligible to enlist. Such a standard, the committee again insisted, would improve the overall competence of the enlisted force without excluding qualified blacks.[47]

This time the Army yielded. In March 1950, Secretary Gray advised the President that the Army was eliminating the racial quota to rely instead on a "single set of mental, physical, psychiatric, and moral enlistment standards." Even as he yielded on this point, the Secretary of the Army reserved the right, after a "fair trial of this new system," to return "to a system which will, in effect, control enlistments by race."[48] But Truman, in expressing his appreciation for Gray's efforts, added, "I am sure that everything will work out as it should," words that politely but firmly foreclosed any attempt to return openly to the old racial policy.[49]

The racial quota ended on the last day of March 1950, and the Army moved haltingly toward fulfillment of the pledges it had made to admit blacks to schools and occupations formerly closed to them.[50] Because of these delays, the committee's final report confessed that it was "too early to appraise the effect of the Army's new policy." Fahy and the other members were confident, however, that "within a relatively short time Negro soldiers will enjoy complete equality of treatment and opportunity."[51]

Truman had won a political victory by merely announcing his determination to integrate the armed forces and then appointing a committee to oversee the task. With the final report of Judge Fahy's group, he seemed to have scored a real triumph over the reluctant Army, thus redeeming his pledge to bring integration to the defense establishment. Within three years, the reforms did come to pass, but they were more the product of the demand for manpower created by a war in the Far East than a result of Fahy's reasoned arguments. Indeed, the confidence expressed by the Fahy Committee might have foundered upon the Army's obstinacy had fighting not broken out in Korea and forced the military to make efficient use of its manpower.

16

The Korean War: Racial Integration Affirmed

ON JUNE 25, 1950, the North Korean People's Army swarmed across the 38th parallel, north latitude, the boundary with South Korea, as the communist regime headed by Premier Kim Il Sung tried to overwhelm the neighboring republic. American politicians and military planners had been focusing their attention on Europe, where the Soviet Union was creating a postwar empire. The United States had withdrawn its occupation forces from the Korean peninsula after disarming the Japanese forces in the south and providing light weapons and military training to the constabulary of the new Republic of Korea. The invaders, armed with tanks and artillery, drove rapidly southward, until President Truman, carrying out a resolution of the United Nations Security Council, adopted in the absence of the Soviet delegation, intervened first with air forces and then with ground troops.

Fresh from a sedentary life in Japan, the first American infantry to enter combat proved to be in poor physical condition, overconfident, and handicapped by the lack of armor and other heavy weapons needed for battle but not required by an occupation force. The invading North Koreans used their greater numbers, firepower, and mobility to drive the defenders to the southern tip of the Korean peninsula. The American forces that initially came to grips with the enemy fared badly, lacking discipline, stamina, and training, although several officers and enlisted men displayed conspicuous gallantry.

Among the troops who performed badly were the black soldiers of the 24th Infantry, organized as a combat team and assigned with two white regiments to the 25th Infantry Division. In one skirmish, for example, almost an entire company melted away, leaving the commander, most of his noncommissioned officers, and a few riflemen to man the unit's foxholes. In another instance an entire battalion drifted off, exposing the artillery batteries in the rear and forcing the gunners to fire some 3,000 rounds directly into the advancing enemy.

Although exclusively white units also performed feebly, the 24th Infantry posed a special problem. Officers and men could be rotated among white units, weeding out the incompetents and replacing them with skilled troops and stronger leaders. Such was not the case with the 24th Infantry, for racial segregation required that black soldiers replace blacks, and initially, few trained noncommissioned officers, weapons specialists, or even riflemen were available in the Far East or the United States, for that matter.[1]

If the black regiment was to succeed, something would have to be done to raise the self-esteem of the black soldier, to ensure the timely arrival of trained replacements, and to weed out the unfit. These reforms, however, were impossible in a racially segregated Army. Unfortunately, segregation was still ingrained in the service despite the work of the Fahy Committee. The Army had demonstrated before the Korean War—indeed, while it was negotiating with Judge Fahy and his colleagues—that racial integration would be slow in coming to its ranks. In the autumn of 1949, a board headed by Lieutenant General Stephen J. Chamberlain began a routine reexamination of racial policies. Shortly after the turn of the year, the Chamberlain group advised Secretary of the Army Gray to retain the racial quota of 10 percent and, insofar as possible, the other practices set forth in the report of the Gillem Board. The quota, Chamberlain and his fellow officers argued, was essential in a peacetime Army that would form "a cadre to provide leadership and skills which an emergency may require," for, in their opinion, American blacks, although comprising 10 percent of the populace, possessed "well below 10% of the leadership and skills of the nation as a whole." It was incumbent upon "the white man" to "supply the deficiency."[2]

The Army, reflecting the attitude toward racial integration expressed in the Chamberlain report rather than its concessions to the Fahy Committee, went into combat in Korea as a segregated force. There had been little time or inclination to carry out the agreement made in January 1950 to begin integrating the service. As in recent wars, the largest exclusively black unit performed poorly. By the end of August, roughly two months after American forces had intervened to check the North Korean advance, the 24th Infantry had shown a tendency to "bug out," to break under fire, that earned it a reputation as the weakest element of its parent division. So unreliable was this regiment that Major General William B. Kean, who commanded the 25th Infantry Division, insisted that its presence jeopardized not only his unit but the entire United Nations effort to hurl back the invaders of South Korea.

General Kean acknowledged that individuals in the 24th Infantry had demonstrated competence, even heroism. Private First Class William Thompson had been the first American soldier to earn the Medal of Honor in Korea. During the dark days of August, when a company of riflemen bolted in panic, he set up his machine gun and kept firing on the advancing North Koreans until he was killed. Another member of the regiment, Sergeant Cornelius H. Charlton, would earn the same award for heroism in June 1951, when, despite wounds that proved fatal, he led three assaults on an enemy-held ridge line, finally driving off the defenders. Kean did not believe, however, that a few courageous men like these could redeem the entire organization. His solution was to do what had been done experimentally in Europe during the final months of World War II, to disband the regiment and assign all black soldiers to currently white units at the ratio of one to ten.[3]

The inspector general of the Eighth Army, the U.S. Army's major command in Korea, agreed that racial integration was the answer. Brigadier General Edwin A. Zundel recommended using the normal system of rotation, the replacement of troops after a tour that came to be fixed at one year, to distribute blacks so that they would make up roughly 15 percent of the complement in the various elements of the Eighth Army. This racial breakdown would, he believed, bring about integration while preventing the concentration of men with low test scores, many of them blacks, in a few units. General Zundel's investigation of the 24th Infantry, which led him to this conclusion, revealed that the regiment exhibited some of the same failings that had undermined the effectiveness of the segregated 92nd Infantry Division during World War II. Principally, too many individuals with low scores on the aptitude tests had been gathered together in the same organization. Although the Gillem Board had foreseen this possibility and recommended that extra officers be assigned to those units where the average test score was well below normal, this had not been done in the case of the 24th Infantry. Once again the positive aspects of the board's work had been ignored; indeed, conservative officers tended to interpret the circular incorporating the recommendations of General Gillem and his associates as a defense of segregation rather than as a program for improving the the treatment of black soldiers and broadening their opportunities.

Whereas the combat record of the 24th Infantry disturbed the senior American commanders in Korea, the National Association for the Advancement of Colored People had become troubled by the frequency of courts-martial involving members of the unit and the severity of the punishment meted out. This resulted in an investigation of military justice in Korea by Thurgood Marshall, undertaken on behalf of the civil rights organization. General of the Army Douglas MacArthur, the commander in chief of the far eastern theater, extended complete cooperation to Marshall's investigation.

Marshall made his journey in response to a plea from thirty-nine soldiers of the 24th Infantry who had been convicted of serious breaches of discipline, including running away from the enemy. Interviews and reviews of court-martial records convinced the attorney that a pattern of inconsistency existed; twice as many blacks as whites faced military tribunals in the the Far East Command even though fewer than one soldier in six was a black. Furthermore, black officers rarely sat as members of courts-martial, and black defendants tended to receive harsher punishment than whites convicted of the same kind of crime. Marshall pointed out that one black enlisted man had been tried, convicted, and sentenced to life imprisonment in just forty-two minutes. Said the disgusted attorney, "even in Mississippi a Negro will get a trial longer than 42 minutes, if he is fortunate enough to be brought to trial."

Marshall attributed the inconsistencies in the treatment of blacks and whites to racial discrimination that, he believed, permeated the Far East Command from the bunkers in Korea to the theater headquarters in Tokyo. He pointed out to General MacArthur that no blacks at all seemed to be on duty at the general's headquarters, but the only response he received was assurance from a staff officer that the topic of race relations was under study. Although cooperative in the conduct of the investigation, MacArthur's headquarters was less than enthusiastic about acknowledging its faults. Whether in Tokyo or South Korea, the visiting attorney found that segregation sapped the morale of the black soldier, numbed his sense of purpose, and thus encouraged him to defy or ignore the rules incorporated by his white superiors into the Uniform Code of Military Justice.

In emphasizing the baneful effects of segregation, Marshall trod on firm ground. His investigation and the work of other representatives of the National Association for the Advancement of Colored

People resulted in reversed convictions or reduced sentences for most of the thirty-nine individuals who had sought the organization's help. Moreover, his inquiry called attention to a perception that had endured since before the Houston riot of 1917 and would persist long after the guns fell silent in Korea—many a black soldier believed that he was being oppressed by rules made by white men for their own benefit.

By the time Thurgood Marshall made his findings public, President Truman had relieved MacArthur of his command in the Far East. The general had publicly advanced a plan for carrying the war into China, an ally of North Korea, although he knew full well that the Commander in Chief intended to confine the hostilities to the Korean peninsula. To replace MacArthur, the President turned to General Matthew B. Ridgway, who moved from command of the Eighth Army to take over the Far East Command. A few years earlier politics and principle had coincided for Truman, enabling him to attack segregation during his campaign for the Presidency; now Ridgway found that by following his personal convictions about racial integration, he could improve the efficiency of his command.[4]

Convinced that segregation was "both un-American and un-Christian," Ridgway opposed the separation of the races on moral grounds.[5] Moreover, the efficiency of his command depended upon the prompt arrival of trained replacements, but badly needed black infantrymen idled away their time in Japan because white units could not accept them. As a result, the general in the spring of 1951 formally asked permission of the Department of the Army to integrate racially the Army forces within his theater of operations. He considered this request necessary because his command contained two federalized National Guard units, the 40th Infantry Division from California and Oklahoma's 45th Infantry Division. At issue was the delicate question of federal-state relationships. Although under federal control, the two organizations had ties to the states where they were formed, and the general wanted to be absolutely sure he had the authority to deal with them as he intended.[6]

General Ridgway proposed to return the colors of the 24th Infantry to the United States, create a biracial component of the 25th Infantry Division to replace it, and bestow upon the new regiment the lineage (or traditions) and colors of the 37th Infantry, which had served on the Mexican border during World War I and in the Aleutians during World War II. In addition, he planned to assign replacements and effect transfers in order to integrate the races in all combat units, whether components of Regular Army or National Guard divisions, establishing a proportion of 10 percent black to 90 percent white. Racial integration would also come to the service units of the Far East Command, although Ridgway did not set a specific ratio of blacks to whites.

Since Congress in 1950 had repealed the law, on the books since 1869, that compelled the Army to maintain four black regiments, one obstacle to Ridgway's plan had already been eliminated. Having absorbed the great lesson of the Korean War thus far, that segregation resulted in poor performance on the part of the all-black units, the Department of the Army raised no objection, based on law or custom of the service, to the racial integration of the mobilized National Guard divisions or the other elements of the Far East Command.[7]

Meanwhile, pressures were increasing within the Department of the Army to extend racial integration from the Far East throughout the entire service. Project Clear, a study of the efficient utilization of black manpower prepared by a civilian "think tank" under contract to the Army, provided some of the impetus for the change. The project's report concluded that racial integration enhanced the effectiveness of the Army (and conversely that segregation undermined it), that integration should be extended throughout the Army, with blacks comprising not more than 15 to 20 percent of any unit, and finally that no racial quota was necessary, since the percentage of blacks in the populace would stabilize their proportion of the Army's manpower at the desired share. Even as pressure for integration mounted in Korea, social scientists under contract to the military were advocating the same course of action as a result of their scholarly research.[8]

Although reluctant to abandon the racial quota, despite the arguments of the Fahy Committee and the recent experience in Korea, Lieutenant General Anthony C. McAuliffe, the Army's chief of personnel, endorsed the major findings of Project Clear. It was McAuliffe, at Bastogne, Belgium, in December 1944, who had replied to a German demand for surrender with a single word, "Nuts!" Then he had captured the headlines; now he proposed to proceed toward integration "with a minimum of press publicity."[9]

During the Korean fighting, the strength of the American forces in Europe increased markedly, for the belief persisted that the aggression in Korea was designed to divert attention from a Soviet move toward the English Channel. American strength in the European theater more than tripled during 1951 to reach a total of 234,000 officers and men. This headlong reinforcement raised the total of black troops in Europe from 9,000 to more than 27,000, or from less than 9 percent to almost more than 11 percent. This influx overwhelmed the instructional center at Kitzingen, West Germany, where blacks received remedial training, forcing General Thomas T. Handy, the Commanding General, European Command, to shut down the segregated facility and integrate training throughout the theater. Nevertheless, segregation among American troops in Europe died slowly. By the end of December 1951, although all blacks assigned to elements of the Women's Army Corps in Europe were serving in racially mixed units, 93 percent of the male enlisted men and 83 percent of the officers served in segregated organizations. The need for efficiency imposed by the Korean War did not make itself felt in Europe.

Unlike Ridgway in the Far East, the senior Army officers in Europe demonstrated a reluctance to go beyond the limits established by the Gillem Board but by this time abolished in Korea as a result of the pressures of war and theoretically ended elsewhere by the Fahy Committee. Eli Ginzberg, an emissary from the Department of the Army, failed to overcome the opposition; he returned to Washington convinced that the generals he spoke with simply did not believe his account of successful racial integration in Korea. Actually the process had paid off in greater skill and aggressiveness on the battlefield, simpler administration procedures, and a more efficient use of manpower. Discussing the impact of racial integration on fighting units, the famed military analyst, S. L. A. Marshall, paid a special tribute to the courage of a recently integrated rifle company of the 9th Infantry, a company temporarily commanded at the time by a black officer and one in which 10 percent of the enlisted men were blacks. However, enthusiastic reports from Korea went unread or encountered disbelief in Europe. As a result, the Army Chief of Staff, General J. Lawton Collins, decided to take a hand. He conferred with General Handy during a visit to Europe and followed up with personal messages prodding the theater commander into action.

Genuine racial integration began in Europe in the spring of 1952, about one year after the process commenced in Korea, and proceeded slowly. A larger than anticipated percentage of black soldiers frustrated Handy's initial plan to integrate units at the one-to-ten ratio that prevailed in the general populace. Before he could react to the crisis, however, he turned the command over to General Alfred M. Gruenther. The proportion of blacks in the European Command reached 16 percent by July 1953, forcing General Gruenther to ignore Handy's goal of 10 percent in assigning blacks to combat and service units—indeed, some transportation battalions became almost 50 percent black—while at the same time raising standards for reenlistment to discourage marginally qualified blacks. In spite of these obstacles, the last segregated element in the entire command, an engineer battalion, became racially integrated in April 1954.[10]

When the North Korean army invaded South Korea in June 1950, setting in motion the chain of events that assured the racial integration of the Army, some 74,000 marines were serving on active duty. Of these, just 1,075 were blacks, and 427 of them were assigned as stewards.[11] Despite the mobilization of the Marine Corps Reserve and an increase in recruiting (supplemented by draft calls before the fighting ended), the recently announced commitment to equality of treatment and opportunity took effect slowly. As late as May 1951, a black reporter for the *Pittsburgh Courier* could visit Camp Lejeune, North Carolina, receiving there the complete cooperation of the Marine Corps, and come away skeptical of the results of the new policy. He discovered that the corps was undergoing change—the exclusively black units had disappeared—but the distribution of blacks among the various service specialties was not as broad as it should have been.

The journalist complained, for instance, that blacks assigned to the 2nd Marine Division, which was based there, seemed to be overly represented at the cookstove or behind the food-serving counter. In reply, his hosts pointed out that regulations had eliminated race as a consideration in making assignments. All too often to suit the reporter, officers at the base cited policy rather than specific accomplishments.

Whatever the rules might say about race as a factor, he doubted that a black master sergeant whom the Commandant of the Marine Corps was supposed to have personally recommended for officer candidate school could not gain admission because 500 men were better qualified. He also suspected, but could not really prove, that the practice of entering racial designations on routine paperwork had an effect on assignments and selection for schools. On the other hand, despite persisting evidence of racism, the reporter had to concede that a black could now enlist in the Marine Corps with a more realistic expectation of becoming a rifleman or machine gunner instead of a steward than had been the case a few years earlier.[12]

Gradually the pressures of the Korean War eased those problems that resulted from racial imbalance, for the corps needed men to fight in Korea and could not waste time sorting them out by race and assigning them accordingly. By June 1953, as the armistice drew near, almost 15,000 blacks were serving in a Marine Corps numbering about a quarter million, about 6 percent of the total or almost six times the proportion on active duty when the fighting began. More important, the number of black stewards increased by only 111, while the members of this minority wearing the uniform of the corps rose during the war by more than 13,000. These figures indicated that the Marine Corps was trying to make assignments without regard to race; indeed, it could not be otherwise, for riflemen and artillerymen were needed in Korea, not massive numbers of food servers or security guards. A wartime military organization could not waste manpower in jobs not directly related to combat or tie up clerk administrators in the operation of separate systems of classification and assignment for the white and black races.

Major General O. P. Smith, whose roots extended deep into the old corps, an exclusively white organization, reported that in Korea he had commanded a division with "a thousand Negroes" (about 6 percent of the complement). These men, he related, "did whatever they were qualified to do," serving as "communicators . . . , cooks, truck drivers, . . . [or] plain infantry." Whatever their assignments, the general "had no complaint on their performance of duty."[13] Clearly the needs of the service took precedence over the question of race in training and assignment.

Platoon leader Herbert M. Hart, a white like General Smith, declared that "it didn't make any difference if you are white, red, black, green, or turquoise to the men over there." Overly dramatic perhaps, but testimony, nevertheless, to the fact that in wartime skill now counted for more than race. Indeed, by the end of the war there was no way of discovering a marine's race by looking at travel orders or rosters, although racial designations continued to appear in the person's records jacket—the file that followed him wherever he was assigned. "When we receive a draft of men," Hart explained, "they are assigned by name and experience only."[14]

As General Smith would insist, the black marines sent to Korea performed as well as the whites who served alongside them, successfully carrying out responsible assignments. For example, Hashmark Johnson, who had trained at the segregated Montford Point camp during World War II, was now a senior noncommissioned officer, able to take over as company first sergeant and later battalion sergeant major. Edgar Huff, formerly a sergeant in a segregated guard detachment at the Naval Ammunition Depot, Earle, New Jersey, saw service in Korea as a gunnery sergeant, first sergeant, and sergeant major of racially integrated units.

In addition, a handful of black officers fought in this conflict, some of them embarking on long and successful careers in the Marine Corps. Second Lieutenant Frank E. Peterson, for instance, became the first black aviator in the corps, flying sixty-four combat missions in the spring and summer of 1953; he would become a general officer. Two other young, black officers, Hurdle L. Maxwell and Kenneth H. Berthoud, obtained regular commissions and served for more than twenty years. All in all, considering that the Marine Corps had remained exclusively white for almost 140 of its 170-odd years, the organization had moved with surprising speed toward racial integration. The change occurred in response to President Truman's directive, the manpower demands of the Korean War, and changing attitudes toward racial segregation among an increasing number of white Americans. Acceptable to most whites, North and South, as recently as 1940, racial segregation was beginning to come under sharply critical public scrutiny. The decisive factor, however, was the realization that segregation resulted in a waste of valuable manpower, as potential machine gunners ladled out food.[15]

The Navy's practices in the training and assignment of blacks still had not caught up with announced policy, a fact that the service chose to ignore. During the summer of 1953 a committee of three naval officers investigated the progress that had been made toward racial integration since the President's directive of 1948. They found that their service had fashioned "a sound and practical policy" and was making "excellent progress in continuing its efforts to more efficiently utilize Negro personnel."[16] Despite this enthusiastic assessment, progress actually was sluggish. One problem that the Navy refused to address was numbers. While the Fahy Committee was yet meeting, Lieutenant Dennis Nelson, a black former reservist who had earned a regular commission, had called attention to the need to recruit more blacks and to persuade the best of them to become officer candidates, tasks of recruiting and persuading that could best be done by black officers and petty officers. Despite assurance to make such an effort, this kind of large-scale recruiting effort did not come to pass.[17]

Another stumbling block besides the small number of blacks was the racial composition of the stewards' branch. Although four years had elapsed since the Truman directive, Secretary of the Navy Dan A. Kimball reported in 1952 that 133 black stewards had transferred out of the branch but conceded that the organization remained 64 percent black. In 1948, when Truman ordered the services to integrate the races, blacks had made up some 5 percent of the Navy's enlisted force, with 65 percent of them in the stewards' branch. Although aware from the outset of the small proportion of blacks and their overrepresentation in the stewards' branch, the Navy had done nothing.[18]

The proportion of blacks in the service declined below 4 percent in 1950, remaining at that level through 1955, but the actual number of black sailors increased, reflecting the growth of the Navy during the Korean War. From 18,000 in 1948, the total number of blacks in the naval service dipped below 15,000 in 1950, then expanded 24,000 once the fighting began. The influx resulted not from the kind of aggressive recruiting that Lieutenant Nelson had proposed, but from the pressures of the Korean War, which compelled the Navy to lower its standards and accept a share of those men, many of them blacks, who had scored poorly on the general classification test. More important, the service had to make use of these men, for they were too numerous to be hidden away in meaningless jobs. Despite their projected lack of aptitude, recruits in this category rendered useful service in a variety of specialties during their enlistments, serving as clerks and even becoming medical or dental aides. This broadening of opportunities for low-scoring recruits was true of blacks as well as whites, for the stewards' branch could no longer absorb 60 or 65 percent of the larger number of black sailors.

This condition persisted after the war, since the Navy of the late 1950s numbered more than a half-million men, at least 200,000 more than when the Korean conflict began. Not until the decade ended did the number of black seamen decline to 26,000, not quite twice the number on duty in the early months of the Korean fighting. In 1955, some 18 months after hostilities ended, the Navy was assigning one black in two as a steward, but the proportion dropped to one in four during the following year. In 1956, with the last of the wartime three-year enlistments expiring, three-fourths of the 37,000 blacks in a 591,000-man force received assignments to the general service.[19]

The Navy's expansion for the Korean War attracted more black recruits than could be absorbed in the stewards' branch, thus forcing the service to broadening opportunities for training in other specialties. The conflict also provided evidence that heroism ignored racial barriers. Ensign Jesse L. Brown, the first black to become a naval aviator, crash-landed his plane not far from the ice-covered Chosin Reservoir in December 1950. Other pilots circling overhead saw that Brown was alive, though trapped in the smoldering wreckage. Lieutenant (Junior Grade) Thomas J. Hudner, a white, immediately made a belly landing beside the downed plane, tried unsuccessfully to free the injured pilot, and stood by helplessly as a helicopter, already summoned by the other airmen, brought cutting tools to the crash site. The rescue craft touched safely down in the snow, but Jesse Brown died before he could be freed. The helicopter then carried off Hudner, who received the Medal of Honor for his attempted rescue. The incident reversed the scene, so popular in fiction, of the loyal black willing to risk his life for the white whom he admired.[20]

The racial integration of the Air Force had begun before the North Korean invasion of South Korea and continued during the conflict. When he visited Tokyo, Thurgood Marshall was pleased to see black security police on guard in front of the headquarters of the

Far East Air Forces, the major U.S. Air Force Command in Asia. With the largest concentrations of black airmen already broken up when the fighting started, redistribution proceeded apace, assisted by an increase in the proportion of blacks from less than 5 percent to almost 8. An increase in black recruits during 1949 and early 1950 accounted for the change. Immediately after the outbreak of hostilities, the mobilization of reservists and members of the Air National Guard, most of them whites, caused a decline in the percentage of blacks on active duty, but this proved to be a statistical aberration.

Racial integration consisted of more than numbers or percentages, however. Colonel Jack Marr, author of the Air Force integration plan, continued to function as a project officer, charting the progress that was being made. Except at Maxwell Air Force Base, Montgomery, Alabama, blacks and whites soon came to enjoy equal access to training courses, recreational facilities, and the various amenities of service life. Occasional racial incidents did erupt: white civilians at Brookley Air Force Base, Alabama, scuffled with blacks who dared to drink from a water fountain formerly reserved for whites; barbers sometimes refused service to black airmen at base exchanges; and on occasion, blacks were barred from dances at service clubs. Gradually these irritations were resolved, for the Air Force insisted that those who wished to remain in the service had to accept racial integration. Indeed, during 1951 Maxwell Air Force Base ceased concentrating blacks in the so-called shanty town, a rundown part of the base used to house custodial units. So widespread was the new policy throughout the Air Force that Senator Strom Thurmond, unsuccessful Dixiecrat candidate for President in 1948, felt compelled to protest that black and white cadets were sharing the same barracks at summer encampments of the Air Force Reserve Officer Training Corps.

The Korean War contributed little to the racial integration of the Air Force except to provide examples of success—and occasionally of failure. Reporters fastened their attention upon the successful exploits of pilots like Captain Daniel James, Jr., nicknamed "Chappie," who had trained at Tuskegee during World War II and now flew reconnaissance craft, and First Lieutenant Dayton Ragland, the first black to shoot down a North Korean jet. Later Ragland was shot down, but he survived imprisonment to return after the war ended with a truce and exchange of prisoners in July 1953.

The acceptance of blacks in the air arm was not complete, however. Lieutenant General Earle E. Partridge, commanding general of the Far East Air Forces, apparently clung to the belief that the black man was inherently inferior to the white. Such an inference could be drawn from his reaction to two instances in which black aviators serving as airborne controllers had mistakenly directed strikes against friendly troops. Instead of focusing on the individuals responsible for these tragic errors, he declared all blacks ineligible for this assignment. At most, a mere handful of pilots could have been affected, for the number of black officers in the wartime Air Force never exceeded 1,400, no more than 1 percent of the total, and most of these were nonaviators.[21]

By 1955, a year and a half after the Korean armistice, the racial policies insisted upon by President Truman and shaped by the Fahy Committee and the services governed treatment and opportunity on military and naval installations. What happened outside the gate depended upon the attitudes in nearby communities. For example, a reporter for the *Pittsburgh Courier*, who had visited Camp Lejeune in the summer of 1951, found "the ugliest and most shocking type of both segregation and discrimination" in off-base housing developments, even those that were subsidized by the federal government.

Officials at the North Carolina base maintained that they could do nothing. The citizens of nearby Jacksonville and several communities near other Marine Corps posts had "very strong feelings relating to race, religion, and military service personnel in general," presenting local commanders with "continuous problems that are seemingly insurmountable and unending." Solutions, when they at last appeared, would be the result of "time, understanding, patience, and work."[22]

Individual servicemen occasionally tested local attitudes. Sometimes it happened accidentally, when a white serviceman and a black from his outfit happened to enter a bar, restaurant, or theater that catered exclusively to whites. At other times it was deliberate, as at San Antonio, Texas, where whites ordered food or drinks for a friend who would join them and the friend turned out to be black. In the Texas cases and similar instances, local commanders discouraged efforts to transplant to alien soil the racial practices that flourished on base.[23]

Despite the policy of not interfering with local custom, a commander could improve the lot of black servicemen in nearby communities without toppling Jim Crow from his increasingly shaky throne. At Big Spring, Texas, for instance, Colonel Fred M. Dean realized that married blacks assigned to Webb Air Force Base could not find housing for their families. So few blacks lived in the area that no segregated neighborhood existed; all the white leaders knew for sure was that they wanted no influx of black servicemen into their town. After pointing out that a half-dozen years of drought had left the town economically dependent upon the air base, Dean convinced the community's leadership to set aside a parcel of land, ill-suited to private development, where the federal government could finance housing for airmen and their families. Although the project was not segregated by law, it was understood that only blacks would move in. Colonel Dean had not advanced the cause of racial integration, but he did improve living conditions for the married blacks in his command.[24]

In effect, the Department of Defense was operating a racially integrated society sealed off from nearby civilian communities, with its own stores, its own sources of recreation, and in many instances its own family housing. Racial integration in the armed services came to embrace even the schools operated on military or naval bases for dependent children. During the final years of the Truman Presidency, Hubert Humphrey, now a senator from Minnesota, had urged the armed forces to do away with racially segregated schools on federal property, but nothing happened until a new Chief Executive, Dwight D. Eisenhower, decided to look into the matter. Shortly after taking office early in 1953, President Eisenhower declared that "all must share, regardless of such inconsequential factors as race and religion," in any federal assistance to education.

Taking his cue from the President, Secretary of Defense Charles E. Wilson, formerly an executive at General Motors and not the person who had served on President Truman's committee on civil rights, launched a campaign to bring racial integration to all schools operated on federal property for the dependents of servicemen. One-third of the sixty-three schools in this category were located within the borders of states that maintained segregated educational systems. Wilson plunged ahead despite words of caution from Oveta Culp Hobby, wartime head of the Women's Army Corps and now the Secretary of Health, Education, and Welfare, who proposed waiting for the Supreme Court to rule on the constitutionality of school segregation. As a result, the racial integration of these schools was already under way when the Supreme Court delivered the judgment for which Mrs. Hobby had proposed to wait, ruling that segregated schools were unconstitutional. Wilson's efforts lost momentum, however. Despite the high court's action, some local boards of education were resisting Wilson's pressure. Those districts which had used local tax revenue to build schools on land donated by the federal government held out until 1963 before yielding to the court's decision and to the threat that the government would build new schools on the bases and terminate all aid to the local systems.[25]

What Generals Edwards, Doolittle, and Follett Bradley had proposed for the Air Force thus came to pass in the Army, the Marine Corps, and to a lesser extent the Navy. The armed forces had adopted a policy of racial integration that was beginning to take hold in industry and were pushing it further and faster than civil society as a whole. For the time being at least, the services seemed a model of racial amity for the rest of American life. By carrying out the policy announced by President Truman, the Department of Defense could for the moment claim the lead in bringing racial integration to the United States. Leadership, however, was passing to the federal courts, the Department of Justice, and ultimately the citizens of both races and various religions joining forces to cause change.

17

Black Americans Force the Issue

AT TIMES IN AMERICAN HISTORY the armed forces have been powerful agents in effecting change in racial relations, as have the churches, the civil rights organizations, political organizations, and in the distant past the abolitionist movement. Such was the case at the end of the Korean conflict, when racial integration was under way in all the services. Whites and blacks shared barracks and clubs, stood in the same lines, and slogged through the mud and rain as members of the same rifle or weapons squads. A white drafted from a large middle western city might find himself waiting in line at the post exchange while the barber trimmed the hair of a black soldier—something that could not have happened in a hometown where blacks lived, shopped, and had their hair cut in a specific neighborhood. For the moment, the armed services pointed the way for the rest of society.

But soon even more powerful agents of change would assert themselves. Led by an old guard of civil rights activists and a new breed that included the Rev. Martin Luther King, Jr., a mass movement began to take shape in the early 1950s. Borrowing the tactics of nonviolent resistance used by Mohandas K. Gandhi against the British rulers of India, this rapidly expanding civil rights movement sought to compel federal authorities to enforce the recent Supreme Court decisions guaranteeing blacks an equal opportunity to obtain an education, to travel without hindrance, and to vote. The movement began in the law courts, often with cases argued by black attorneys, gathered strength in the black churches, and spilled onto the streets of southern cities where blacks and whites, including persons of several religions, submitted to arrest and violence to dramatize injustice and cry out for change.

The arena in which the struggle for equal rights was taking place thus shifted away from the armed forces, where President Truman had used his authority to set in motion the chain of events that resulted in racial integration on military and naval installations. For years segregationists had warned that the military would forfeit the support of white Americans if it embraced racial integration. It did so, thanks to Truman's prodding and the pressures of the Korean War, and nonetheless survived as a respected institution. Indeed, within a decade American society as a whole promised to surpass the armed forces in accepting equality of treatment and opportunity. The change proved swift and far-reaching. During the late 1950s and early 1960s, black leaders like Dr. King and James Farmer and their white allies, working through a variety of civil rights and religious organizations, had effected a revolution in race relations.

The armed forces made an important if indirect contribution to this revolution, for in the racially integrated military large numbers of whites and blacks learned, although sometimes reluctantly, not only to get along but to work together toward a common goal. From 1953, the year in which the Korean fighting ended, until the close of the decade, almost 1.5 million men were inducted into the armed services and exposed to this experience.[1] In basic training, some of these men associated for the first time as equals with members of another race, sharing fatigue and harassment during their introduction to an alien world. The association of blacks and whites continued beyond basic training or boot camp, but the early months were critical. This was the time when old habits were being exorcised and new ones substituted, a process that applied to race relations as well as to dress, grooming, and obedience.

For a brief time early in the Eisenhower administration, the Department of Defense had taken tentative first steps toward integrating the races in schools operated on military bases to educate the children of servicemen. On May 17, 1954, however, the Supreme Court's unanimous decision in *Oliver Brown et al. v. Board of Education of Topeka* signaled the end of racial segregation in public schools throughout the United States. A single court decision and its subsequent enforcement by federal authorities eclipsed the effort of the armed forces to integrate schools for military dependents. This and other court decisions, demonstrations, and the resulting federal law enforcement actions propelled civil society ahead of the military in the field of race relations. After a decade, the victories won by the civil rights movement had so altered race relations in the United States that the black serviceman, who in 1955 had belonged to one of the few racially integrated institutions in the nation, found that pressures to extend this racial policy to such areas as off-duty activity, promotion, and military justice were rapidly easing. The greatest and most dramatic progress toward fuller integration was occurring outside the armed forces.

The most important changes stemmed from the Supreme Court's decision in *Brown v. Board of Education*, which struck at the very legal foundations of racial segregation in the United States. A struggling chapter of the National Association for the Advancement of Colored People in the Kansas town had brought suit to force the school system to carry out the racial integration of all classrooms. After the case wound its way through the judicial system, the Supreme Court addressed the issue, in the process examining *Plessy v. Ferguson*, the decision that in 1896 had established separate but equal as the guiding principle governing race relations in the United States. *Plessy v. Ferguson*, the justices decided, was not a logical interpretation of the nation's basic law. The Constitution demanded equality of treatment and opportunity, and the Supreme Court accepted the argument of Thurgood Marshall and a team of attorneys assembled by the National Association for the Advancement of Colored People that segregated schools imposed a lesser status on minority students and placed restrictions on their opportunities to develop their abilities. Any belief on the part of segregationists that the doctrine of separate but equal might somehow survive vanished on May 31 of the following year, when the Supreme Court directed that the principles enunciated in the *Brown v. Board of Education* decision be implemented by the states "with all deliberate speed."[2]

After the Civil War, generations of white racists insisted that American blacks, alone of all free men, had received their freedom without fighting and therefore did not deserve it. This lie ignored the contributions of blacks in earlier wars and of the U.S. Colored Troops on battlefields from Virginia to Mississippi during the War of the Rebellion, not to mention the work of black sailors against Confederate forces on the high seas and inland waterways. A century after Appomattox, the old libel surfaced again, with a new twist. Now it was laws and court decisions that conferred full citizenship on somehow undeserving blacks. Like those who had overlooked the black soldier and sailor in the Civil War, the persons who repeated this story ignored the risks that individual blacks took in challenging unjust laws to prod the government into acting; they closed their eyes, for instance, to the heroism of Rosa Parks.

On December 1, 1955, Rosa Parks, a seamstress at a Montgomery, Alabama, department store, boarded a bus and took a seat behind the line that separated the races. After all the seats forward of the line had been taken, white passengers continued to board, so the driver ordered her to give up her seat and stand at the rear of the Jim Crow section. She refused, and her arrest triggered a bus boycott that brought to the fore as a civil rights leader the young black minister Martin Luther King, Jr., recently arrived from Atlanta, Georgia. Despite bombings and the arrest of Dr. King for violating a state law against boycotts, the black citizens of Montgomery persisted for more than a year in their nonviolent campaign. The first bus without a Jim Crow section traveled the streets of Montgomery on December 21, 1956, a change abetted by federal court decisions that racial segregation in local transportation infringed upon the fundamental rights of citizenship. A flurry of bombings and beatings greeted the integration of the buses, but the old order could not be revived.[3]

Ironically, some two years before Rosa Parks defied Jim Crow, an Air Force pilot stationed in Alabama had refused to move to the rear of a public bus. Far from rallying behind him as Montgomery's black citizens would mass behind her, his military superiors issued a reprimand that helped terminate his career. "Your open violation of the segregation policy," the statement declared, is "indicative of poor judgment on your part and reflects unfavorably on your qualifications as a commissioned officer." The armed forces might enforce integration on military bases, but civilian society was not their concern. Patterns of racially integrated behavior required on a military base might be the cause for arrest in some nearby city or town, but military authorities would not intervene. Fighting segregation within the services was battle enough for the time being.[4]

As supreme commander in Europe, Dwight D. Eisenhower had approved Court House Lee's plan to introduce black riflemen into white infantry units, though he phrased his endorsement in cautious terms. During his campaign for the Presidency in 1952, he had ignored the issue of racial discrimination. Upon being elected, Eisenhower carried out the existing policy of bringing racial integration to military and naval bases. He also followed the practice, by this time almost a custom, of appointing a few qualified blacks to subcabinet positions. Personally, the new President abhorred the injustices inflicted upon blacks and believed the federal government should intervene on their behalf in certain circumstances. However, he lacked the sense of outrage and moral passion displayed by his predecessor, Mr. Truman, and was reluctant to make frontal assaults on the status quo.[5]

Illustrative of the ambivalent attitude of the Eisenhower administration toward racial matters was its reaction to the refusal by a white employee of a Howard Johnson restaurant at Dover, Delaware, to wait on a black customer, K. A. Gbedemah, Finance Minister for the African nation of Ghana. Humiliation of the sort experienced by the foreign dignitary in October 1957 was inflicted on American blacks as a matter of course in many parts of the nation, but in this case President Eisenhower and Vice president Richard M. Nixon moved swiftly to make amends to the foreign official. Besides inviting him to the White House, they revived a plan to help finance a dam and smelter on the Volta River, a plan that came to fruition during the Presidency of John F. Kennedy.[6] The nation's elected leaders were becoming aware that racism, as practiced here, had a baneful effect among the Asian and African states that formed the ideological battleground between the United States and the Soviet Union.

The war of ideas being waged against communism inspired the Southern Christian Leadership Conference, an outgrowth of the Montgomery bus boycott, to make a direct appeal to President Eisenhower to become personally involved in the civil rights movement. Specifically, spokesmen for the organization asked in January 1957 that the administration show as much concern for black Americans as it had for the recently arrived Hungarian refugees who had fled Soviet repression in their homeland. The Chief Executive held back, however, continuing to support civil rights legislation but refusing to involve himself as directly as Truman had.[7]

Then in 1957, the Eisenhower administration succeeded where Truman had hung back, obtaining the passage of the first civil rights legislation since Reconstruction. With the assistance of Democrats like Senators Lyndon B. Johnson of Texas and Albert Gore and Estes Kefauver of Tennessee, a Republican administration had persuaded Congress to approve a law that set up a bipartisan Civil Rights Commission to conduct a two-year study of discriminatory practices, empowered the Attorney General to file suit on behalf of anyone denied the right to vote—which President Eisenhower considered the critical element in any program of civil rights—and established within the Justice Department a Civil Rights Division headed by an assistant attorney general.

Despite the adoption of this first civil rights legislation since 1875, the President could be seen as lacking interest in the cause of civil rights. He had, for example, done nothing early in 1956 when pressure from White Citizen's Councils and from segregationists in the student body prevented Autherine Lucy from exercising her right, affirmed by *Brown v. Board of Education*, to enter the University of Alabama. Yet the President professed a deep commitment to constitutional government. He described his beliefs in a letter to a friend from his youth at Abilene, Kansas. He told Edward Everett "Swede" Hazlett, who left Abilene for the Naval Academy when Eisenhower entered West Point, "There must be respect for the Constitution—which means the Supreme Court's interpretation of the Constitution—or we shall have chaos." At the heart of this contradiction were his respect for some white southerners who believed in segregation, his conviction that the Brown decision was a mistake because it sought to do too much too soon, and possibly an interpretation of the harassment of Autherine Lucy as an act against an individual rather than defiance of the Constitution.[8]

Immediately after the passage of the Civil Rights Act of 1957, the President found himself in circumstances in which he did act. Eisenhower faced a direct challenge to the Constitution and the federal courts when Orval Faubus, the governor of Arkansas and hardly the kind of wealthy southerner that the President might and sometimes did befriend, used state forces to prevent the racial integration of the public schools in Little Rock. In this instance, the administration reacted by federalizing the Arkansas National Guard, removing it from the governor's control so that he could not use it to enforce segregation, and sending U.S. Army troops and federal marshals to restore order and enforce the decision of the Supreme Court. When challenged directly, the President would act, though in doing so here, he permitted Faubus to save face by avoiding compliance until the fall of 1959.[9]

While the governor was fighting this rear-guard action against the court-ordered racial integration of the public schools in Little Rock, President Eisenhower approved challenging another school system within the state of Arkansas, an unusual step by a Chief Executive who felt, as Eisenhower did, that equal access to schools was less important to blacks than the right to vote. Pulaski County was operating a school for the children of servicemen stationed at Little Rock Air Force Base. Although located on land outside the reservation itself, the buildings had been constructed with federal funds. When the county board of education refused to allow racial integration, the Chief Executive proposed seizing the site by right of eminent domain, a clear indication that he identified segregation as an affront to the public good. Unfortunately, the problem encountered in Pulaski County was more widespread than he had realized. Upon learning that as many as fifteen schools throughout the South fell into the same category, he abandoned this time-consuming and costly idea. The courts seemed a better, if slower, alternative. Once Governor Faubus had yielded to federal authority, however, the position of Pulaski County became untenable and the first blacks entered the school. The other southern schools built with federal funds on land outside military posts gradually fell into line, a process that lasted until the mid-1960s.[10]

The year 1960 saw the first of the sit-ins, a form of nonviolent civil disobedience designed to test local laws requiring racial segregation at restaurants and other public accommodations. When Dr.

King was jailed for participating in this form of civil rights activity, Robert Kennedy, brother of the Democratic Presidential candidate, sent a message of support to King's wife and helped arrange his release. John F. Kennedy then won the Presidential election, although by a razor-thin margin. Since he had run extremely well in districts with large concentrations of black voters, the new Chief Executive felt he owed a debt to black Americans, for whom Dr. King was rapidly becoming the embodiment of their hopes and ambition.[11]

Upon taking office in 1961, President Kennedy thought mostly in terms of example, apparently confident that his leadership could effect highly visible reforms that would inspire further change and contribute to the widespread acceptance of racial integration. Typical of this attitude was his reaction to the fact that the Coast Guard contingent in his inaugural parade consisted exclusively of whites. He called Douglas Dillon, his designated Secretary of the Treasury, the department then responsible for the Coast Guard, and beginning with the next class the first blacks entered the academy at New London, Connecticut. Similarly he promptly issued an executive order reaffirming the nation's commitment to equality of opportunity and pledging the executive branch to strive toward that goal. He appointed a special assistant for civil rights and designated Vice President Lyndon B. Johnson as the head of an ad hoc Committee on Equal Opportunity to supervise federal employment policy and the hiring practices of federal contractors.[12] A few months later, when President Kwame Nkrumah of Ghana visited Washington, Kennedy complained to officials of the Department of Defense because so few blacks appeared in the guard of honor turned out for the African leader. Although the Air Force ceremonial detachment was 14 percent black, blacks made up 9 percent of the Army unit and just 2.2 percent of the Marine Corps unit. The Navy ceremonial unit was exclusively white.[13]

President Kennedy's concern about the composition of military organizations brought about change, but symbolic action was not enough. Like the blacks in civilian life who were conducting sit-ins or trying to integrate interstate buses by means of Freedom Rides, their counterparts in the armed forces were losing patience with the persisting manifestations of racial discrimination. Black servicemen were finding racism galling both in communities near military and naval bases and on the installations themselves. For example, Charles C. Diggs, a member of the House of Representatives from Michigan, had amassed a catalogue of complaints sent him by servicemen. "Major complaints," he reported, "include: Double standards for promotion as between white and Negro servicemen, lack of communication between command[ers] and personnel, discrimination and segregation of on and off base recreational facilities and off base housing, participation of . . . [officer] personnel in local community discriminatory practices, inequality of treatment of dependent[s] . . ., use of symbols of racial intolerance on bases, intimidation of complainants concerning racial discrimination, and severe comparative penalities for offenses committed by Negro service personnel." Since 1960, his own tours of bases in the United States and overseas and the letters he had received from black servicemen revealed hundreds of instances of racial discrimination. These varied from an article in a base newspaper bemoaning the effects of racial integration on the quality of the armed forces to the illegal use of military police to enforce discriminatory laws in towns near military reservations. What Diggs and other blacks found especially infuriating were the tendencies of commanders to ally themselves with local authorities in communities that enforced Jim Crow practices and to refuse to investigate complaints by blacks that their rights were being denied.

The servicemen continued to work within the system, protesting to a sympathetic congressman like Diggs but avoiding the confrontations that had come to characterize the civil rights movement. The black noncommissioned officer had seen firsthand the changes that had taken place since the Korean War. He appreciated the greater acceptance and opportunity that he enjoyed in comparison to the black serviceman of the 1940s, and he refused to jeopardize this improved status by defying established procedures. Although conservative in this sense, he nevertheless was a realist. He knew that the drive for racial integration in the military had largely spent itself, having begun to lose momentum after the Korean emergency ended. The armed forces could not turn the clock back to the 1940s, nor did they want to, for they had learned that racial integration improved morale and administrative efficiency. They were, however, content with what they had done, satisfied with the progress made since 1948, and reluctant to undertake the difficult job of pushing racial integration to its logical conclusion, overhauling promotion policies, eliminating race as a consideration in the administration of justice, and extending the racial policies that prevailed on military bases into nearby communities.[14]

While the American public, indeed much of the world, riveted its attention on the bus-riding Freedom Riders and their struggle to integrate segregated facilities in the South, the Kennedy administration addressed with varying determination and mixed success two of the injustices that servicemen had reported to Congressman Diggs. The President sought to ensure that they—as well as other blacks—enjoyed equal access to federally sponsored housing, an important consideration for married enlisted men in the lower pay grades, and to sever the ties between the command structure at various bases and the leaders of local communities or organizations that enforced racial segregation. Kennedy also decided to try to eliminate race as a consideration in hiring or promotion in the federal civil service, which included, of course, the Department of Defense.[15]

Throughout the civil service, hiring and promotion practices for civilians resisted change. Within the Department of Defense, Adam Yarmolinsky, a special assistant to Secretary Robert S. McNamara, began investigating the opportunities available to blacks for jobs or advancement only to discover that little documentation existed. Much of the advice that supervisors received on hiring or promotion came from ad hoc screening committees that kept no records. All Secretary McNamara could do at this time was to remind supervisors and workers throughout the department of the President's commitment to equal opportunity.[16]

The attempt to deal with racial discrimination in housing also accomplished little. During the campaign, Kennedy declared that he could end segregation in federally subsidized housing with a stroke of the pen; when he failed to do, thousands of blacks sent pens to the White House. Although Secretary McNamara's advisers in the defense establishment urged him to move boldly against discrimination in the sale or rental of housing to servicemen and their families, he declined to do so. He had other tasks that enjoyed a higher priority, such as restructuring the budget process for the armed forces, but he also may have realized how intractable the problem was. As late as 1966, a poll revealed that 46 percent of white Americans objected to having a black family live next door. He came to regret it later, but he narrowed the scope of his action, finally banning discriminatory practices only in the housing units leased by the armed forces—not in those bought or rented by individual servicemen. He also decreed that base commanders should become the cutting edge (blunt though it was) in this limited offensive against segregation, culling from housing referral lists any owners who invoked racial restrictions in leasing or selling property. Not until 1967 did Secretary McNamara take more vigorous action in this area.[17]

The administration, moreover, found it difficult to prevent base commanders from endorsing, inadvertently or otherwise, the practice of segregation in nearby communities. Secretary McNamara issued orders prohibiting elements of the Department of Defense from sponsoring any organizations practicing racial discrimination. A commander at Maxwell Air Force Base, Alabama, logically enough interpreted the directive as a denial of federal facilities to all groups, whether boys' club baseball teams or service clubs in the city of Montgomery, that barred blacks from membership. Upon learning how the directive was being applied, Senator Lister Hill, a Democrat from Alabama, protested, and the Department of Defense backed down. A veteran senator could not easily be defied by an administration that might need his help.[18]

Across the state at Mobile, another Air Force commander barred the local minor-league baseball team from selling discount tickets through a recreation council operated by civilian employees of the Brookley Air Force Base. He issued the ban because the team's management restricted blacks to a specific section of the grandstand. In this instance, when there was no senatorial reaction, the department followed Yarmolinksy's advice and supported the officer. Faced with a loss of ticket sales, the team agreed to set aside a racially integrated section for Brookley employees and in return received permission to renew its arrangement with the recreation council.

In matters affecting relations between servicemen and citizens of communities located near bases, the Department of Defense tried to uphold the rights of the man in uniform without arousing hostility among the townspeople. This usually resulted in offering empty assurances to the soldier or sailor while bowing to the wishes of the local government. Responsibility for negotiating with community leaders again fell to the base commander, who, since he rarely could look to the Pentagon for support, had little in the way of bargaining strength. Far from imposing sanctions, such as declaring establishments off limits, the Department of Defense reflected the current attitude of the Kennedy administration, which was to avoid rocking the boat.

The defense establishment also adopted a policy of avoiding contact with the civil rights movement and the nonviolent activity in which it engaged. A ban on participating in demonstrations or marches in support of racial equality, however peaceful these might be, persisted until the summer of 1963, when Secretary McNamara agreed that servicemen might take part provided they wore civilian clothes. On the other hand, the action of a commander at Fort Hood, Texas, who used military police to break up a civil rights rally shocked the Department of Defense into forbidding intervention of this sort.[19]

In brief, Secretary McNamara's action on the domestic front during 1961 and 1962 reflected the administration's concern with civil rights, its awareness that in winning the recent election it had incurred a debt to the black community, and a realization that southern intransigents in Congress could cause trouble. The Department of Defense was trying to ensure equal opportunity and fair treatment without challenging the southern senators and representatives who might carry out reprisals against President Kennedy's legislative initiatives. Yet something controversial might have to be done in view of the kaleidoscopic changes in race relations throughout the nation and the volume of complaints from within the armed forces.

President Kennedy found himself facing racial problems in the armed forces and mounting pressure for civil rights legislation in political circumstances not unlike those that Mr. Truman had faced some fifteen years earlier. During the Truman administration, racial prejudice in the services had been widespread and blatant; now it tended to be hidden, ingrained in such matters as promotion, and therefore difficult to root out and destroy. The Congress had grown more tolerant of racial integration since Truman's day, but Kennedy believed that in the spring of 1962 the southern Democrats could still prevent the passage of a strong, far-reaching civil rights law. Because the political climate was so similar, Adam Yarmolinsky proposed that the new President try what the old one had done: avoid making an issue of the civil rights law, concentrate on the armed forces, and revive the Fahy Committee, though with some basic changes.

Once again the investigating group would be nominally independent but certain to reach conclusions that the President could accept. Moreover, Kennedy, like Truman before him, would be able to disassociate himself from the give-and-take of the committee's deliberations, which would produce nonpolitical reforms not attributable to the administration or even the Democratic Party. The armed forces remained subject to the authority of the Commander in Chief, so that the committee's recommendations, like those of the Fahy group, could be carried out by executive rather than legislative action.

Despite the similarities between the Truman and Kennedy eras that inspired the resurrection of the Fahy Committee, times had changed. President Truman and his committee had taken the bold but obvious first steps; they had addressed the basic injustices. The remaining manifestations of racial discrimination would be hard to isolate and harder to eliminate. The surviving examples of racism touched upon the basic fabric of military life such as the power of the commander to promote and assign his men or affected the traditional racial practices in communities near military bases. For example, the question arose whether a commanding officer had the authority or duty to enforce the racial policy of the armed forces beyond the limits of his installation.

As Yarmolinsky pointed out, President Truman's Executive Order 9981 remained in force. The current Chief Executive could therefore invoke it to convene another group to examine the progress toward racial integration made by the armed forces since 1949. This Mr. Kennedy did, announcing on June 24, 1962, that he had selected Gerhard A. Gesell, an attorney in Washington, D.C., who later became a federal judge, as the chairman of a President's Committee on Equal Opportunity in the Armed Forces. The membership included three blacks—John H. Sengstacke, a Chicago publisher and a veteran of the Fahy Committee, Nathaniel S. Colley, an attorney from California involved in the civil rights activity of the National Association for the Advancement of Colored People, and Whitney Young, Jr., of the Urban League. The balance of the group were whites—Benjamin Muse, a civil rights advocate, Abe Fortas, an attorney in Washington, and another lawyer, Louis Hector, who joined the committee when Joseph O'Meara, dean of the University of Notre Dame law school, fell ill. Laurence I. Hewes III, a recent graduate of the Yale law school now an attorney in the Department of Commerce, served as committee counsel.[20]

As its resemblance to the Fahy Committee and the presence among its members of someone from the earlier group might indicate, the new group reflected its predecessor in status and authority. Theoretically, the Gesell Committee was to advise the President how to "improve the effectiveness of current policies and procedures . . . with regard to equality of treatment and opportunity for persons in the Armed Forces and their dependents in the civilian community.[21] In fact, as Secretary McNamara pointed out, "Calling it a President's Committee was just window dressing." Like the Fahy group, the Gesell Committee did not function as the direct proxy of the Chief Executive in working out racial policies for the services. The old committee had bargained with the services, the resulting agreements subject to the approval of the Secretary of Defense. The new organization was to gather information upon which Secretary McNamara, rather than President Kennedy himself, could base a directive governing the entire defense establishment.[22]

In essence, President Kennedy envisioned himself as a mediator, appealing to rational men both black and white to join together for the common good. He resisted being swept along on the tide of civil rights activism, but he could not muster any sympathy for the southern racists, whom he detested. He realized that the civil rights movement was a just cause and deserved to prevail, but he felt that his administration needed the help of representatives and senators from the South in carrying out its domestic and foreign policies. To avoid alienating either the pro-civil rights forces or the segregationists until he had created a personal following and felt more confident of reelection, he appointed the carefully picked committee to improve the lot of blacks in the armed services and left its management to Secretary McNamara, who had a nonpolitical image and a Republican past.

Gesell was impressed with what the services had done since 1948. No longer did industry, in his opinion, lead the way toward racial integration, as it had when Idwal Edwards, Jimmy Doolittle, and Follett Bradley were urging such a policy of leadership on the recently established U.S. Air Force. The committee chairman believed that the Department of Defense had become the "pace setter . . . way ahead of General Motors and the other great corporations."[23]

All was not perfect, however, as the Gesell Committee conceded in an initial report issued in June 1963. Problems existed in both the regular and reserve components, on bases and in nearby communities. Moreover, despite some two decades of complaints, racial integration had not yet affected the composition of the teams of military police or shore patrolmen sent to keep order in towns near service installations. Whites kept order in a supposedly integrated military establishment, and when operating in civilian communities they tended to pick up and magnify any existing prejudice against blacks. Also, communication between the largely white officer corps and black enlisted men could be so tenuous that a commander might remain blissfully unaware of patterns of racial discrimination that black servicemen found infuriating. To improve communication, the committee believed that every organization needed an officer to serve as a point of contact for black complainants, someone empowered to investigate charges and, assuming the problem arose on the base, to eliminate the cause.[24]

Meanwhile, the U.S. Commission on Civil Rights, a product of the 1957 Civil Rights Act, also examined the plight of blacks in the armed forces. This agency agreed with Gesell that progress had occurred, although racism persisted to some degree in military life and flourished outside the gates of defense installations. The Civil Rights Commission concluded that "all but a few aspects of racial discrimination" had been "abolished from the military installation," even though "in neighboring communities the Negro serviceman and his family still encounter the traditional patterns of discrimination and segregation." These "galling reminders that second class citizenship has not been eradicated," the commission declared, had "a detrimental effect on morale and efficiency." As a result, the Department of Defense owed it to the nation as a whole and to America's black servicemen to encourage open housing and equal access to schools and public accommodations in towns where these men or their families lived, shopped, or sought recreation. If necessary, businesses that refused to abandon racial segregation could be declared off limits to military personnel.

In addition, said the Civil Rights Commission, the armed forces should eliminate the last traces of segregation from within the services. The Navy might require special attention, for it seemed to have "shown little or no improvement" since World War II. Every component of the Department of Defense, however, would have to take action to ensure that race was not a factor in promotion, retention, or assignment, if necessary removing all racial identification from the files reviewed for these purposes.[25] The Gesell Committee would not have disagreed with these overall findings, though it was more concerned with obtaining compliance than with merely identifying the needed reforms.

By the end of July 1963, less than two weeks after the initial report of the Gesell Committee but before the Civil Rights Commission had released its findings, Secretary McNamara set up within his department a hierarchy of bureaucratic institutions designed to eliminate the last vestiges of racism from the armed forces. At the apex of this hierarchy was the Assistant Secretary of Defense (Manpower), who was to serve as the representative of the Secretary in all "civil rights matters," directing the programs designed to bring about equality of treatment and opportunity, establishing general policy, and charting progress.[26] To help him carry out these duties, Norman S. Paul, the incumbent Assistant Secretary of Defense (Manpower), was to rely upon a Deputy Assistant Secretary of Defense (Civil Rights). Chosen for this important job was Alfred B. Fitt, who as an official of the Department of the Army had been responsible for preparing the basic directive turning the initial report of the Gesell Committee into service policy. Fitt now became the key agent in the field of civil rights within the Department of Defense. In executing the racial policy based on the findings of the Gesell Committee and set forth by Norman Paul, Fitt had three assistants. One was the Deputy Assistant Secretary of Defense (Civilian Personnel and Industrial Relations), Stephen N. Shulman, who shaped policies relating to federal employees and the employees of government contractors. Fitt's second aide, Ralph Horton, Jr., converted Shulman's personnel policies into action. The third was Adam Yarmolinsky, still a special assistant to Secretary McNamara; Yarmolinsky continued to maintain liaison between the Department of Defense and the Gesell Committee, which had resumed its investigation.[27] This was a bureaucrat's solution, an attempt to devise a mechanism that would automatically ensure compliance, but it nonetheless did reveal the keen interest of the Secretary of Defense in eliminating the sources of racial friction.

Outside Mr. McNamara's departmental bureaucracy, the key individual was the base commander, who had "the responsibility to oppose discriminatory practices affecting his men and their dependents." Besides ensuring equal treatment and opportunity in "areas under his immediate control," he was to intervene "in nearby communities" where servicemen and their families "may live or gather in off-duty hours." In discharging this weighty obligation, a commanding officer would have to rely mainly upon persuasion in his dealings with civilians, for he could not declare any business or housing development off limits except with permission from the appropriate service secretary.[28]

Although the Kennedy administration tended to move gingerly in matters affecting the civil rights of servicemen and women, passing the buck to local commanders, it could act decisively when state authorities challenged the power of the federal government. In 1962, when James Meredith, a black, attempted to enter the University of Mississippi, violence rocked the campus, despite the presence of some 300 U.S. marshals and a supposed understanding that Governor Ross Barnett would maintain order. For fifteen hours a mob raged through the town of Oxford, laying siege to the building where the marshals were posted and killing two persons, one of them a French journalist. As a precaution, President Kennedy had already called the Mississippi National Guard to active duty, and he now dispatched federal troops to the scene. These forces, some 5,000 strong, finally quelled the rioting. Similarly, the President had gathered overwhelming federal force, including 3,000 soldiers, when Governor George C. Wallace vowed to "stand in the schoolhouse door" to prevent the racial integration of the University of Alabama. The governor's words of defiance proved to be an empty gesture, however; the state did not resist, and the troops were not needed when Vivian Malone and James A. Hood appeared on campus to register.[29]

By mid-1963, President Kennedy had upheld federal authority in the field of civil rights, staring down such arch-segregationists as Governors Barnett, Wallace, and Jimmie Davis of Louisiana. Moreover, the administration had dealt successfully with the threat of Russian missiles based in Cuba and was attempting to negotiate with the Soviet Union an agreement to ban nuclear testing in the atmosphere. Growing increasingly confident of his ability to lead, President Kennedy now lent his endorsement to some of the reforms called for in the Gesell Committee's initial report. In short, he endorsed Secretary McNamara's bureaucratic solution, called for unimpeded access to public accommodations, but remained silent on the subject of access by blacks to housing.

Self-confidence no doubt emboldened the Chief Executive to accept the advice of the Gesell Committee, but another factor in his decision was the momentum gathering behind the civil rights movement. Gallant individuals of both races, men and women, Christians and Jews, had risked injury or death to catch the conscience of the nation's leaders and of a fair proportion of the populace as a whole. Indeed, after moving cautiously for two years, carefully cultivating popular and congressional support, the Chief Executive himself at last had gone on the offensive on civil rights. In February 1963 he had started calling upon Congress for action to support the civil rights of all Americans. As the weeks passed, he reminded the citizenry of the inherent injustice of racial discrimination. By midsummer, the legislators were debating an administration civil rights bill that, among other things, gave the executive branch the authority to cut off funds for federally supported programs that discriminated against minorities, imposed a ban on segregation in public accommodations, and authorized the Attorney General to file suit seeking to force public school systems to abandon racial segregation. The great March on Washington of August 28, 1963, became the inspirational symbol of progress toward equal rights. Organized by a coalition of civil rights, labor, and religious groups, the meeting attracted as many as a quarter-million people, who heard Dr. King describe his dream of an America in which all persons were truly equal, regardless of race or religion.[30]

President Kennedy seemed confident that he could obtain passage of the civil rights bill and nevertheless prevent the southern wing of the Democratic Party from deserting him as it had Harry Truman. Still, obtaining approval of so ambitious a piece of legislation would prove difficult indeed. As one sign of this, some southern Democrats on Capitol Hill had denounced even the modest reforms adopted by the services upon the recommendation of the Gesell Committee, although these applied to men in uniform, their dependents, and the residents of comparatively few communities. One member of the opposition, Senator John Stennis of Mississippi, decried the "new and unheard of mission . . . designed to shape our military force as an instrument for social reform" and predicted that involvement of the armed services "in the misguided . . . so-called civil rights drive" could only be "detrimental to military tradition, discipline, and morale."[31]

The drive for equal rights aimed at the reform of American society, of which the armed forces formed a minor part. Despite the efforts of Representative Diggs and the continuing work of the Gesell Committee, equal treatment and opportunity for blacks in uniform remained a secondary consideration. The immediate task that Dr. King, his colleagues, and his supporters saw before them was to sustain the enthusiasm generated by the great rally at Washington and to follow up the nonviolent victories in the South, such as the integration of buses in Montgomery and of colleges and public accommodations elsewhere in the South.

Such was the status of the movement for equal rights on November 22, 1963, when an assassin's bullet killed John F. Kennedy. His successor, Lyndon B. Johnson, inherited the Gesell Committee, the machinery now functioning in the Department of Defense to ensure equality of treatment and opportunity, and the civil rights legislation sought by the murdered President. The new Chief Executive found himself adrift in the same stream, now a raging torrent, that had propelled three of his successors—Truman, Eisenhower, and Kennedy—in directions and at speeds that they might not have voluntarily chosen. Would the momentum of the equal rights movement similarly capture the new President?

18

From Nonviolence to Violence

THE NEW PRESIDENT OF THE UNITED STATES, Lyndon B. Johnson, was determined not to be propelled by the civil rights movement into taking the kind of political risks that his predecessor had in dispatching troops and federal marshals to protect those challenging Jim Crow, but he had a broad vision of an America free of racism. Although the new Chief Executive had inherited the Gesell Committee, he did not feel that he needed it as a symbol of his commitment to equality for blacks. Instead, he was determined to bring to fruition the civil rights legislation introduced by John F. Kennedy.

Of his three most recent predecessors, President Johnson most resembled Harry Truman in the emotional depth of his commitment to equal rights. Unlike Eisenhower, drawn deeper into the struggle against racism by a challenge to the Constitution, or Kennedy, whose dedication to the cause of civil rights seemed coolly rational, Johnson felt a genuine sympathy toward the black victims of racism. Robert C. Weaver, a one-time member of Eleanor Roosevelt's "black cabinet" and Johnson's Secretary of Housing and Urban Development, thus compared Kennedy with his successor: "I think Kennedy had an intellectual commitment for civil rights and a broad view of social legislation. Johnson had a gut commitment for changing the entire social fabric of this country . . ."[1]

The kind of person that Weaver described in his sketch of President Johnson could not be satisfied with a symbolic and carefully controlled gesture like the Gesell Committee. The integration of the armed forces, after all, formed but a small element in his grand design for the Great Society. Confident of his political skills, Mr. Johnson was certain he could bring about passage of the Kennedy civil rights legislation and incorporate it into his Great Society. Should President Johnson's vision become reality, it would affect almost every aspect of American life, including the armed services.

President Johnson did manage to secure the passage of the Kennedy civil rights bill, under debate since the summer of 1963. The shock of the assassination, the fraternal afterglow of the March on Washington, and active lobbying by various civil rights organizations, labor unions, and interdenominational religious groups eased the task of the Chief Executive. But also, the President's skill at manipulating legislators was formidable, and he used it now to pry the bill out of committee and win support for it in Congress. On July 2, 1964, he signed the new law. The Civil Rights Act of 1964, among other things prohibited discrimination in public accommodations, permitted the suspension of funds for locally administered federal programs that practiced racial discrimination, and created a series of committees and agencies to ease the work of racial integration.[2]

At last, the civil rights bureaucracy in the Department of Defense and the various commanding officers largely responsible for carrying out departmental policy had a legal basis for challenging racial discrimination as practiced in civilian communities against servicemen and their families. In this respect, the new law overlooked only one type of grievance—racial restrictions limiting access to off-base housing. Clearly the question of racial integration of the armed services had become part of a greater movement, a movement more daring than the deliberations of a hand-picked committee like that headed by Judge Gesell and for those actively involved sometimes infinitely more dangerous.

For instance, while Congress was taking action on this legislation, a coalition of civil rights organizations embarked upon a campaign of voter education among the disenfranchised blacks of Mississippi. The volunteers, many of them white students at northeastern universities, began their work in June and encountered violence almost immediately. When the burning of black churches supporting voter registration failed to stop the crusade, white terrorists resorted to murder. Among the victims were three volunteers who disappeared near Philadelphia in Neoshoba County on June 21, some two weeks before the signing of the 1964 Civil Rights Act. Following a tip from an informant, federal authorities investigated an earthen dam; buried within it they discovered the bodies of Michael Schwerner and Andrew Goodman, Jewish students from New York City, and James Chaney, a black from Meridian, Mississippi.[3]

As the struggle for voting rights continued in the South, the racial integration of the armed forces slogged forward. The bureaucratic machinery that Secretary McNamara set up in response to the initial report of the Gesell Committee had begun functioning even as the group worked on toward its final report. Now, however, the Civil Rights Act rather than the bureaucracy of the Department of Defense provided the most powerful impetus for change. The Office of the Secretary of Defense, instead of exerting pressure of its own, chose to defer to the new law and to federal enforcement agencies.

This attitude of diffidence on the part of defense officials reflected the reality of the moment. Blacks in uniform, especially those who were making the service a career, enjoyed opportunities denied to them a few years earlier. For a noncommissioned officer who had enlisted in the 1950s, the ensuing years had brought dramatic change in terms of eligibility for service schools, opportunity for promotion, and even the treatment received in communities near military bases. Clearly the greatest dissatisfaction and the strongest efforts for change existed among blacks in civil society and not among black servicemen. Except for a comparatively few draftees or recent recruits, blacks in uniform were more content than ever before. Unfortunately this feeling of satisfaction enabled the armed forces to avoid taking a critical look at the effects of their own racial policies. Granted that the status of blacks had improved, had all the inequities in treatment and opportunity actually been corrected?

Statistics on the number of blacks on active duty contributed to the satisfaction felt by most black servicemen and the complacency of the defense establishment. By 1967 the proportion of blacks in the armed forces stood at 9.9 percent. Overall the ratio of blacks to whites closely approached the racial composition of society as a whole. A total of 295,000 blacks were serving in the Army, Navy, Marine Corps, and Air Force.

If marches, demonstrations, and confrontation characterized the civil rights movement in civilian life, offices and agencies were the hallmark of the campaign mounted by the Department of Defense against racism in the military. A vast bureaucracy tried a bureaucratic solution, creating a mechanism staffed, cynics would say, by do-gooders who had never risked the blows of an enraged white southern sheriff. The reforms adopted as a result of the first report of the Gesell committee could not eliminate the remaining vestiges of racism unless this civil rights machinery responded swiftly to complaints by blacks, challenging the offending policies and making sure they were changed. Vigor of this sort, unfortunately, would run counter to the natural tendencies of any bureaucracy, military or civilian, increasing the risk that the services would announce a policy, create an enforcement agency, and then step back to engage in self-congratulation. Hypnotized by routine, the leadership might well lose contact with the blacks who were supposed to benefit from the reforms. The result could be demoralization, as injustices unnoticed by white authority infuriated the black victims.

The Defense Department's machinery for ensuring equal treatment and opportunity became complete when James C. Evans, a black who had formerly served as a special assistant to Secretary McNamara on racial matters, in the summer of 1963 joined the new office of the Deputy Assistant Secretary of Defense for Civil Rights. By the end of the year, however, the mechanism for policy enforcement ground to a temporary halt, not because of a departmental decision, but because the administration had grown fearful that vigorous action might imperil the passage of what became the Civil Rights Act of 1964. The White House therefore reined in Alfred Fitt and the other members of the department's office of civil rights, who felt a deep commitment to the goals of the Gesell Committee. Actually, this degree of caution proved excessive, for as the year 1964 wore on, it became clear that the racial integration of the armed forces aroused little opposition—or approval, for that matter—in the context of the shocking murders of voter education volunteers in Mississippi.[4]

While the Gesell Committee began conducting the investigations that produced its final report and the Office of the Secretary of Defense tried to avoid the limelight, the three services quietly drew up programs of their own to ensure equality of treatment and opportunity, especially in communities near military or naval bases. The Department of Defense had made commanders responsible for compliance by local officials, but only the Army was willing to make an officer's success in eliminating segregation in civilian communities a specific consideration affecting promotion or retention. The Navy, in contrast, remained content merely to observe how the commander dealt with this matter and suggest possible improvement, without rating him on his degree of success. The Air Force gave commanding officers broad latitude in dealing with local government, enabling them to tailor their actions to a specific situation, but did not address the topic on fitness reports. In general, the armed forces accepted the spirit of the Gesell Committee's initial report but did not commit themselves fully to carrying out the detailed recommendations.

The services agreed, at least in principle, with the report's emphasis on communication between the races and between officers and those they led. Commanding officers therefore received instructions to confer with interracial councils made up of servicemen and their dependents, as well as with civilian organizations, whether governmental, civic, or fraternal. Also as a consequence of the initial report, the military departments and the Office of the Secretary of

Defense began insisting upon systematic reports of actions in the field of race relations, thus obtaining some means, not necessarily adequate, of charting the progress of commanders. The services, moreover, pledged themselves to eliminate racial segregation in promotion and assignment, but little thought was given to the means of making good on the promise.[5] At the heart of the measures was a belief that a bureaucracy that monitored interracial communication and the actions of commanders could influence race relations.

Little concrete action was under way within the Army, Navy, and Air Force when the Gesell Committee in November 1964 presented its final report. Judge Gesell and his colleagues concentrated on two topics: equality of treatment and opportunity for black servicemen stationed overseas, and the participation of members of racial minorities in the National Guard. Both presented special problems. Men serving overseas were subject to agreements made with host governments, and the Guard remained subject in varying degree to both state and federal authority.

Concerning the armed forces overseas, the committee found that officers in command of installations, "with some notable exceptions, have . . . allowed discriminatory conditions to become more and more rigid, and the resulting disorders to become widely publicized." The recurring incidents not only damaged morale among American troops but also presented "a false image of our country to the nationals of the host countries." Gesell and his associates therefore recommended that the armed forces adopt overseas the same policies advocated in the initial report for bases and the adjacent communities in the United States. As at domestic installations, a commanding officer would have to allay the fears and prejudices of the local citizens and gain their cooperation. To help accomplish these ends, he might patrol a town or village with military police, preferably in racially mixed teams. Should persuasion fail or a lapse occur in military discipline, he might as a last resort declare a particularly troublesome civilian establishment off limits. Unlike the committee, the Department of Defense discouraged this kind of initiative on the part of a commanding officer. Even in the United States, authorities were reluctant to allow a commander to take this action, which could have harmful consequences not only on the business involved but possibly on an entire community. Overseas, where American servicemen, technically at least, were guests of a foreign power, an aggressive commander could undo the work of diplomacy by controlling the spending by his troops, to the detriment of the host country.

The committee's examination of the National Guard revealed "a complete or almost complete absence of Negroes in officer ranks" within some states, and instances where "the participation of blacks in the enlisted ranks . . . is still only on a token basis. . . ." Yet despite the current status of the Guard, the committee saw signs of progress, specifically, voluntary efforts at integration, though these efforts needed to be "closely and frequently monitored" with a view toward encouraging them. Specifically, Gesell and the other committee members wanted the President himself to insist upon the acceptance of blacks, the National Guard Bureau to maintain better records on the racial composition of the various state units, and the Guard as a whole to make a special effort to recruit qualified blacks. The committee pointed out that the National Guard, since it received federal funds, was subject to the provisions of the Civil Rights Act of 1964 that empowered the government to suspend support for programs that practiced racial discrimination.[6]

The Gesell Committee had produced solid results, isolating the manifestations of racism that had survived President Truman's directive, the Fahy Committee, and the Korean War. Especially important was its emphasis on the demoralizing effect of the segregationist practices encountered by servicemen and their families in civilian communities. The committee's deliberations also contributed to the creation of a civil rights bureaucracy within the Department of Defense—an entity that, however much annoying paperwork it might generate, served as a reminder of the commitment within the upper reaches of government to the principle of racial equality.

Nonetheless, because of the progress toward racial integration in civil life, the committee and its accomplishments tended to fade from sight. After Mississippi, public attention became riveted upon Alabama where Martin Luther King was employing the tactics of nonviolent confrontation to open the voters' rolls to black citizens. The focus of Dr. King's concern was Selma, the seat of government for Dallas County, a jurisdiction in which just 333 of 15,000 potential black voters were able to exercise their right to vote. Opposing the voter registration drive was Sheriff Jim Clark, who summarized his response to racial integration in a single word: "Never!" To suppress the peaceful protests organized by King, the sheriff turned to clubs, dogs, and even gunfire. Again there were fatalities among the marchers, and the victims included whites like James Reeb, a Unitarian minister from Boston, as well as blacks like Jimmie Lee Jackson, a woodcutter from rural Alabama.

The most dramatic part of the campaign was the march from Selma to the state capitol at Montgomery, led by King and approved by order of a federal court. This demonstration attracted some 25,000 participants—and 800 federal troops for their protection—to the birthplace of the Confederacy. Equally important, however, were hurried trips by King to Washington to confer with President Johnson about federal action to protect voting rights, as well as fact-finding visits to Alabama by various congressmen or their aides. These behind-the-scenes activities, along with the courage of the demonstrators in the face of violence, contributed to the passage of the Voting Rights Act of 1965, another element in President Johnson's plan for the creation of his Great Society.[7]

Upon succeeding the murdered John F. Kennedy, President Johnson had worried that the civil rights movement might plunge ahead out of control, alienating support for the Great Society. His dream, however, was being challenged by a different reality. Events overseas were generating a momentum that could not help but affect that vision of an America from which poverty had been eliminated. The challenge was military in nature, testing the racially integrated armed forces and the willingness of the American people to finance both war and socioeconomic reforms. One test was easy enough, requiring no real combat and not jeopardizing his domestic program. During the spring of 1965, the President intervened in the Dominican Republic, sending troops to sustain a military junta against rebel forces that he believed had been infiltrated by communists. The other test, anything but easy, was the long and bitterly divisive war that was being fought in Southeast Asia.

When the French were struggling to retain their possessions in Indochina, the United States had provided equipment and technicians. Despite this limited aid, the communist Viet Minh had triumphed in 1954, consolidating their control over North Vietnam, while South Vietnam emerged from the conflict as an independent state. Under President Eisenhower, the United States undertook a program of military and economic assistance to the noncommunist South, and as the pressure from the North and from domestic insurgents intensified, the volume of aid increased. During the Kennedy administration, the dangers facing South Vietnam became so great that American military advisers began participating in combat under the guise of training South Vietnamese forces.

Overt American involvement began during the summer of 1964, when Navy airmen attacked targets in North Vietnam to avenge two attacks, one real and one imagined, by North Vietnamese patrol craft against American warships in the Tonkin Gulf. At this time, President Johnson obtained from Congress a resolution empowering him to take whatever action he considered necessary to punish North Vietnamese aggression. In the spring of 1965, he approved the systematic aerial bombardment of the North, at first in response to guerrilla attacks upon American troops in South Vietnam and afterward to force North Vietnam to give up its plans to conquer the South. As the months passed, the American armed forces, racially integrated for more than a decade in the interest of greater efficiency and effectiveness, took over full responsibility for military operations against the communist forces in South Vietnam. Within three years, the conflict in Southeast Asia would disrupt the civil rights movement and alienate a vast segment of American society.[8]

The influence of the civil rights movement, with its insistence on nonviolent resistance to unjust laws, had reached its peak at Selma. When the march from that town to Montgomery ended, George Wallace peeped through drawn venetian blinds from his darkened office as thousands of blacks and their white allies gathered outside the state capitol.[9] Even as the wary governor concealed himself from the peaceful demonstrators—in later years he would make common cause with them—the Department of Defense was growing complacent about the progress being made by the armed forces toward racial integration. A larger proportion of blacks than whites were reenlisting, an encouraging sign. For the most part, commanders seemed to be carrying out their responsibilities under the policies emanating from the Gesell Committee, and the cooperation on the part of civil authorities appeared surprisingly good, although some trailer parks and housing developments persisted in barring black servicemen and their families, despite requests from local commanders. The Civil Rights Act of 1964, however, rather than the initiatives of the Department of Defense, turned the key to gaining access to schools, public accommodations, and other facilities in various communities. The civil rights bureaucracy of the armed forces had acknowledged as much when it proposed to assist those servicemen interested in bringing suit under the 1964 law, an offer that had comparatively few takers. Blacks in the military, especially the veteran noncommissioned officers, preferred to work within the framework of the armed forces, relying upon the bargaining power of their commanders and responding enthusiastically when a commanding officer succeeded in persuading a business to accept black patrons or a housing development to admit black renters.[10]

Meanwhile, the war in Southeast Asia was beginning to affect the civil rights movement. The transition from adviser to principal combatant brought long lists of casualties and aroused protest in the nation, alienating many of the very individuals, inside the government or out, who had supported the President's efforts to gain the passage of the civil rights and voting rights legislation.

Among those who broke with President Johnson was Martin Luther King, Jr. As the American involvement in Vietnam deepened, the Nobel laureate came to question the wisdom and morality of the war. He found no reassurance in conversations with Arthur Goldberg, who had left the Supreme Court to become ambassador to the United Nations and, as he understood his assignment, the President's agent in the quest for peace. Before the year 1965 ended, Dr. King publicly endorsed a negotiated settlement of a conflict that he considered a tragedy in terms of domestic policy as well as international relations. He had become convinced that the resources needed to improve the lot of the poor in the United States were being diverted to Vietnam, where American forces were the allies of a repressive government. The Chief Executive took note of King's opposition and excluded the organizer of the Selma victory from a meeting of civil rights leaders, a session designed to demonstrate that blacks did not oppose the war but considered housing, jobs, and health care more important issues than the peace movement.[11]

Dr. King persevered in his opposition to the war. On the other hand, some persons long active in advancing the cause of civil rights, such as Carl Rowan, Whitney Young, and Roy Wilkins, became concerned that what they interpreted as an attempt to merge the campaign against racism with a burgeoning antiwar movement would endanger further progress toward equal rights. Opposition to the war, spearheaded at the time by white, middle-class youths, might well swallow up the civil rights movement. Moreover, as Dr. King's exile from the President's inner circle of advisers demonstrated, no one could challenge Mr. Johnson on the war and hope to exert influence on any other subject. For the President, the war had become the test that separated friend from enemy; no one could publicly oppose his conduct of the war without being seen as a traitor to the administration, if not to the nation. Even the *New York Times*, which had supported King since the days of the bus boycott in Montgomery, felt compelled in April 1967 to publish an editorial, "Dr. King's Error," warning him that to offend President Johnson could only hurt the cause of civil rights and the "War on Poverty," which along with the expansion of civil rights formed a key element in the campaign for a Great Society.

As all this suggests, the coalition that made up the civil rights movement was showing signs of cracking because of the war. The board that shaped policy for the National Association for the Advancement of Colored People could not agree with Dr. King that waging war against Orientals was a manifestation of racism. Elements of organized labor, hardly a monolith, had joined the auto workers in supporting the March on Washington in 1963, and the cause of civil rights in general. The skilled crafts, however, had tended to react defensively to charges of segregation within their ranks. Much of the labor movement, notably the crafts but other groups as well, gave uncritical endorsement to the war; the unions that rallied behind the President joined in the chorus denouncing King for his antiwar statements.[12]

Other influences besides Dr. King's preoccupation with the Vietnam War imposed a strain on the civil rights movement. Out of Mississippi came a new slogan, "Black Power." Uttered by militants like Stokely Carmichael, this phrase drowned out King's eloquent plea for brotherhood, giving rise to reactions among whites that varied from the patronizing to the terror-stricken.[13]

Rioting broke out in the black ghettos. The new urban rioters were venting their rage against whites, an alien race whose representatives were the police that patrolled the streets, the store owner who seemed habitually to overcharge, and the landlord's agent to whom an exorbitant rent was paid.

Harlem erupted in the summer of 1964, and 144 persons were injured. The worst of the riots occurred, however, in the Watts district of Los Angeles, a city where blacks seemed to enjoy opportunities not found elsewhere. The trouble began on the night of August 11, 1965, and ended after six days with 34 killed, some 900 injured, almost 4,000 arrested, and entire blocks gutted by fire. When the ashes of Watts finally cooled—the rioting never spilled over into nearby neighborhoods—an occupation force of 1,600 police and 14,000 National Guardsmen was maintaining order. From Watts came another slogan, "Burn, Baby, Burn." Originally part of a disc jockey's patter, adopted as the catch phrase of a campaign to remove trash from the streets of Watts, the words seemed to foretell the future of urban America, as a succession of riots followed in San Francisco, Newark, Atlanta, and Detroit. This latest slogan took its place beside the call for "Black Power" and inspired fear among white Americans.[14] The poor, ill-educated black living in the ghetto of a town like Newark or Detroit tended to think in terms of slogans, oversimplifying the social and economic forces that pressed him down. He did, however, have a convenient symbol of oppression, for he dealt frequently with slum landlords or shopkeepers, most of them whites and many of them Jews. Out of these contacts arose not only a hatred of whites but a "Negro anti-Semitism" that was "substantially a Northern ghetto phenomenon," unknown among rural blacks in the South. To Martin Luther King, this form of racial prejudice, now being expressed in the streets, was a "tragic . . . mistake . . . immoral and self-destructive."[15]

At first, the armed services seemed immune to the violence that was sweeping urban America, but the immunity could not last. Selective service was calling up young blacks, and others were enlisting. Many of them were city dwellers exposed to the same forces that had caused the rioting. The civil rights machinery within the Department of Defense—not to mention unit commanders and non-commissioned officers—would find these men less tractable than the career serviceman who understood and appreciated the reforms that had taken place over the past decade. The kind of communication involving blacks and whites, officers and enlisted men, that the Gesell Committee had advocated became impossible as increasing numbers of angry young blacks entered the services in these circumstances.

The urban riots dramatically revealed that at least one major recommendation of the Gesell Committee remained to be carried out. The National Guard units that helped restore order at Watts, in Detroit, and elsewhere were almost exclusively white, a characteristic guaranteed to feed the alienation felt by urban blacks. Two members of the National Advisory Commission on Civil Disorders, Chairman Otto Kerner, the governor of Illinois, and Mayor John V. Lindsay of New York City, told the President that blacks comprised only 1.15 percent of the Army National Guard and 0.6 percent of the air units. On behalf of the commission, they called for a special recruiting effort.[16]

Actually blacks had shown little interest in either the reserve or the National Guard since the decline of the black militia units early in the century. Marion Barry, a black civil rights activist who later became mayor of Washington, D.C., pointed out that the Guard and reserve afforded none of the benefits of regular enlistment—neither a decent living nor travel nor social status—but did prevent the part-time soldier or airman from holding a weekend or evening job. Other observers added that many Air National Guard units had been overstrength for years, that the organizations tended to reflect the racial composition of the area where they were recruited, and that young blacks would have nothing to do with a military force that might be called upon to invade the ghetto and take action against members of their race.[17]

To increase the number of blacks in both National Guard and reserve units, the Department of Defense, at the direction of Secretary McNamara, authorized recruiters to exceed assigned strength by 10 percent provided the additional men were blacks.[18] The state of New Jersey, after riots at Newark and New Brunswick, launched such a program and demonstrated that aggressive selling could attract black recruits. Elsewhere a feeling of indifference persisted among potential black recruits, but the Department of Defense, perhaps encouraged by the results in New Jersey, tried nonetheless to alter the racial composition of the reserve components to mirror the populace as a whole. Progress remained disappointing, however, with the increasing number of black ex-servicemen offering the likeliest means of approaching this goal, provided they could be induced to join.[19]

A source of growing concern at this time of domestic turmoil was the disproportionate share of casualties being suffered by black soldiers in South Vietnam. Although blacks made up about 10.5 percent of the Army, they accounted for some 13 percent of the killed and wounded, a phenomenon the Department of Defense could explain but not remedy. The statistical difference reflected the fact that blacks tended to serve in the units that did most of the fighting. Assignment to the infantry awaited many draftees, who would serve for just two years, not long enough to master a complex technical speciality. Especially vulnerable were those men with poor test scores and no skills useful to the military, not even typing, and black draftees often fell into this category. Moreover, black career soldiers often volunteered for airborne or airmobile units, usually because of the prestige, but also because parachute infantrymen qualified for additional pay. Whatever the reasons, black soldiers made up 60 percent of the complement of some rifle platoons in airborne units, which greatly increased their chance of seeing combat and becoming casualties.[20]

As recently as World War II, spokesmen for the black community had campaigned vigorously so that black soldiers could fight for their country rather than serve as military laborers. By 1962, however, the chances of a black recruit's joining a combat unit were three times greater than in 1945. In 1967, just two years after the Americanization of the Vietnam conflict, some blacks had begun complaining that too many of their race were receiving combat assignments.[21]

Unquestionably, certain elements of society made greater sacrifices than others during the war. A Harvard graduating class sent two of its members to Vietnam out of some 1,500 draft-age males, while a working-class part of Boston with a total population of 35,000 of all ages and both sexes, lost twenty-five of its sons killed in action. Deferments were available to those able to enroll in colleges or professional schools, join the National Guard or reserve, or take advantage of courses in dodging the draft offered by groups opposed to the war. Furthermore, draft boards applied standards of their own, reflecting the views of those who exercised political or economic power within a community. In the year 1967, ominously for blacks, 98.5 percent of the 17,123 persons serving on local draft boards were white, and not a single black served on any of these groups in Alabama, Arkansas, Louisiana, or Mississippi. In the next three years, selective service officials made an effort to improve the racial balance of the local boards, but despite the attempt the proportion of blacks fell short of 7 percent.

Undeterred by such obvious injustices, Secretary McNamara sincerely believed that the war could produce social benefits. To that end, he launched Project 100,000, begun during 1966 to assist at least that number of the unemployed and poorly educated by lowering standards, admitting them to the armed forces, and teaching them skills they could not otherwise acquire. However noble Secretary McNamara's purposes, those who took advantage of this dubious opportunity for self-improvement—41 percent of them young blacks—usually ended up as riflemen. Few men recruited under Project 100,000 qualified for training that could pay off in better jobs upon their return to civilian status. Moreover, the men who took advantage of the program tended to be those most affected by notions of black power or its equally violent opposite, white power—sensitive to insults, quarrelsome, and lacking self-discipline. Besides adding to the increasingly volatile nature of the armed services, Project 100,000 resulted in an infusion of manpower that helped forestall the mobilization of the National Guard and reserve, which provided a haven for draft-age men, the majority of them whites.[22]

Although Project 100,000 failed utterly, Secretary McNamara did make progress toward a long-delayed social reform. He demonstrated that he could achieve at least limited success in putting an end to racial discrimination in the sale or rental of housing to the families of servicemen, an undertaking that he had previously avoided. During 1967, with President Johnson again urging Congress to enact an open housing law, the Secretary of Defense began exerting pressure to obtain equal access to housing for all men in uniform and their dependents. He delegated Thomas D. Morris, his Assistant Secretary for Manpower, to establish a program to integrate housing in the vicinity of Washington, D.C. What was done in the capital and its environs would serve as a model for installations throughout the nation. By making speeches and negotiating with realtors, Morris hoped to establish a pattern for base commanders to follow.

Taking the defense establishment at its word, the legislature of Maryland called upon Mr. McNamara to put an end to the discrimination in housing encountered by blacks stationed at Andrews Air Force Base, just outside the national capital, and at other military and naval installations throughout the state. In response to this invitation, the Secretary of Defense issued a directive forbidding servicemen from renting in any segregated development or trailer park located within a three-and-one-half-mile radius of the air base.

Secretary McNamara applied similar restrictions at other installations in Maryland and threatened to take action elsewhere. Instead of proceeding on a state-by-state basis, however, he again turned to the local base commanders, directing them to establish, at all installations with 500 servicemen or more, housing referral offices to direct potential renters to landlords who did not practice racial discrimination. Once again he failed to press the campaign to completion, possibly because he was distracted by his growing disillusionment with the Vietnam conflict, which he had once acknowledged as "McNamara's war." Not until the passage of a federal open housing law, the Civil Rights Act of 1968, did the Department of Defense, by that time under the direction of Clark Clifford, obtain a suitable weapon against racial restriction in the sale or rental of housing to servicemen and their dependents.[23]

The armed forces were confident that their response to President Truman's integration order and to the subsequent recommendations of the Fahy and Gesell committees had largely eliminated racial discrimination within the services and was on the way to doing so in communities near military and naval bases. The civil rights bureaucracy in the Department of Defense set in motion a program designed to ensure compliance with the recommendations of the Gesell Committee and then stepped back. Civil rights laws, backed by the authority of federal enforcement agencies, protected blacks in the services from acts of discrimination beyond the gates of military reservations and naval bases. If anything, the Department of Defense relied too heavily on the laws passed in 1964 and after. In cases of discrimination, commanding officers and departmental authorities preferred to seek voluntary compliance; if rebuffed, however, they avoided exerting pressure of their own and considered the matter a subject for action by the aggrieved party under the appropriate law. The armed forces thus avoided alienating community leaders, although at the cost of delayed enforcement of the announced policy of the Department of Defense. The department's civil rights specialists could point to the changes that had taken place since 1944, when Court House Lee had broached his plan for limited racial integration. What these authorities tended to overlook was persisting, often subtle discrimination in assignment, promotion, and the administration of justice—aspects of military life that President Johnson's civil rights laws left untouched. Progress, in short, bred a certain smugness that concealed less visible but insidious forms of discrimination.[24]

Because of this smugness, military leaders ignored nagging questions, such as the comparison of court-martial rates and casualty rates among black and white soldiers, and took heart from evidence of racial harmony on the battlefields of Vietnam. As *Time* magazine phrased it, "More than anything, the performance of the Negro G.I. under fire reaffirms the success—and diversity—of the American experiment." The conflict had produced numerous black heroes like Lawrence Joel, a medical aid man. Although shot in the legs when his unit was ambushed, he risked death to minister to the other wounded, refusing to ease his own pain with morphine, which he feared might impair his ability to care for his comrades. Joel survived to receive the Medal of Honor. For Milton Olive, the award was posthumous; he sacrificed his life by throwing himself on a grenade to save the men, both blacks and whites, in his rifle squad.

Time described an isolated society, untouched by racism or the riots in the cities, where blacks and whites willingly laid down their lives for one another. Black soldiers in this idealistic world rejected the Black Muslim message of separatism and black supremacy, equating the leader of that sect with the Grand Dragon of the Ku Klux Klan. Furthermore, *Time* continued, "What burns . . . most Negro fighting men is the charge—first proclaimed by Stokely Carmichael and echoed by the likes of Martin Luther King—that Vietnam is a race war in which the white U.S. Establishment is using colored mercenaries to murder brown-skinned freedom fighters." In short, neither urban riots nor the disaffection of Dr. King had any effect upon black troops in Vietnam, or so the magazine reported.[25]

The accounts of interracial cooperation on the battlefield were accurate enough, but they ignored ominous developments such as the appearance in rear areas of Confederate flags and whites trying to recruit for the Ku Klux Klan, along with a growing perception among blacks that whites tended to be assigned to administrative jobs, whereas blacks could expect to serve in the units that actually did the fighting. For a black infantryman to return from an outpost in the highlands of South Vietnam to find a group of whites living in comparative comfort, displaying a rebel flag that was a reminder of slavery, and playing the hated "red-neck" country music was reason enough for a brawl.

Said one black soldier, "The racial incidents didn't happen in the field. Just when we went to the back. It wasn't so much that they were against us. It was just that we felt we were being taken advantage of, 'cause it seemed like more blacks in the field than in the rear."[26] Precisely because racial incidents occurred in the rear areas after periods of fighting, military authorities turned a blind eye to racial friction, tending to excuse it as the action of battle-weary troops letting off steam. Racial violence seemed to be the exclusive problem of civilians back in the United States.

Certainly urban violence was having an impact on domestic society, heightening resentment among blacks, fear among whites, and hatred on the part of both. Among the more obvious victims were a number of liberal politicians. Some observers concluded, for example, that the burning of Watts delayed until 1973 the election of Tom Bradley as the first black mayor of Los Angeles and helped Ronald Reagan defeat the incumbent governor, Edmund "Pat" Brown.[27]

The riots, moreover, along with calls for black separatism and the emergence of anti-Semitism among urban blacks, had an effect upon Dr. King. Although he did not abandon his dream of a racially integrated America, he came to believe that the improvement of the economic status of urban blacks was essential to achieving this goal. He concluded that better-paying jobs would give them pride and a stake in the improvement of their communities, while at the same time reducing tensions with store owners and landlords. Relations between blacks and Jews would thus improve and an interracial society take form. Dr. King's new priorities brought him to Memphis, Tennessee, where he lent his prestige and talent for organization to an attempt by black sanitation workers to establish a union and bargain for better wages and working conditions. At Memphis, on April 4, 1968, a white escaped convict named James Earl Ray murdered the black leader. The assassination triggered a wave of violence throughout the black quarters of 110 American cities, claiming thirty-nine lives and requiring the presence of 75,000 troops and federalized National Guardsmen. Ironically, as the fires died away, President Johnson signed the recently passed legislation banning racial discrimination in the sale or rental of some 80 percent of the nation's housing.[28] Unfortunately, the flames that spread through the nation following Dr. King's death also erupted overseas and consumed *Time's* vision of racial amity in South Vietnam.

19

Turbulence in the Armed Forces

JUST FOUR AND ONE-HALF YEARS after discovering in South Vietnam an island of racial amity unaffected by the turmoil in the United States, *Time* acknowledged that "it has become increasingly clear that the military, too, has its share of racism."[1] The murder of Dr. King brought to the surface racial animosity that had been seething for months, especially among noncombat troops. For the thoughtful black soldier, the irony of King's death was truly bitter: while black riflemen risked their lives in Vietnam to prevent the assassination of district chiefs and village leaders, no one was looking out for the safety of a black leader in the United States, a Nobel laureate, a man of God.

Many white servicemen did not understand why the black soldier should feel a strong kinship with a man who had described the Vietnamese communists as victims of white oppression. They simply could not accept the fact that black troops saw this man as an embodiment of everything black Americans were striving for—power, respect, and honors at home and abroad. This lack of awareness among white soldiers reinforced the growing belief on the part of black servicemen that they were being taken advantage of, manipulated for the benefit of white authorities, given the most dangerous assignments to spare the lives of whites.

Signs of racial polarization surfaced almost immediately after the assassination in Memphis, which seemed to signal the death of the dream of equality that Dr. King had revealed in his speech dur-

ing the march on Washington almost five years before. The first reaction of a black staff sergeant at an Air Force base in Southeast
Asia was to want "to run out and punch the first white guy I saw."[2]
In contrast, many whites serving at comparatively safe locations in
Vietnam, where interracial cooperation was not a matter of life or
death, grew weary of hearing about what seemed like endless trib-
utes to a black antiwar leader. The racists among them staged demonstrations against King, even parading around in makeshift robes
modeled after those of the Ku Klux Klan and burning crosses in imi-
tation of Klan ritual. At Cam Ranh Bay, South Vietnam, the site of a
vast naval installation, hooded sailors burned a cross and hoisted a
Confederate banner on the flagstaff in front of the headquarters.[3]

The riots that erupted in American cities following the murder
of Dr. King had reverberations in Southeast Asia, where some white
commanders saw the burning ghettos in the United States as con-
firming their belief that blacks were born troublemakers. Black soldiers in South Vietnam became convinced that commanders were
retaliating against them for the riots back home, transferring the
more vocal or sullen among them from the comparative safety of
support units at the rear, where they might find time for agitation
and a receptive audience, to combat outfits, where protest had to be
muted in the interest of survival. Evidence to prove the charge did
not exist, but the belief persisted.[4]

Earlier indications of dangerous racial friction had for the most
part escaped the notice of both visiting journalists and commanding
officers. Although the Gesell Committee had tried to alert commanders to the need for communication with servicemen belonging
to racial or ethnic minorities, the advice had gone unheeded in
Southeast Asia, in part because of the rapid turnover of officers assigned there. The fixed tour, usually one year, and the possibility of
rotation among several assignments meant that commanders of
combat units might change after a few months, although the same
officer might command an air base or logistics complex for a longer
period.

The continuing turnover of men and officers in Southeast Asia
prevented the seriousness of racial problems there from surfacing,
and communication between leaders and led was little better in the
United States. At domestic installations, commanders seized upon
positive indications and ignored (or were not told of) the others. On
the positive side, as late as 1967 blacks were reenlisting at twice the
rate of whites, even though fewer soldiers of both races were remaining in the Army than did before the war. On the negative side,
white troops occasionally objected to taking orders from blacks,
and a black soldier might sometimes show resentment of the white

officers or black noncommissioned officers who enforced Army regulations. Nevertheless, the only obvious source of disharmony that
had persisted over the years was the sight of interracial couples at
dances or other social events, something that a good many white soldiers still could not abide.[5]

Any hope that the cross burnings and other incidents triggered
by Dr. King's death were isolated exceptions to an apparent racial
calm vanished a few months afterward. A savage riot broke out in
the U.S. Army stockade at Long Binh, South Vietnam, a facility nicknamed LBJ, which stood for Long Binh Jail as well as for Lyndon
Baines Johnson. The understrength contingent of military police,
most of them whites, was trying to maintain order in a prison, pop-
ulated mainly by blacks, so overcrowded that shipping containers
from cargo vessels served as cells. The most dangerous of the black
prisoners, those convicted of assault and other violent crimes, ignited the riot, in which one white soldier was killed and several
other white soldiers injured. The embers of violence continued to
glow for several weeks.

White authorities tried to wait until the mob had spent its fury,
for they were reluctant to intervene with force for fear of touching
off widespread racial rioting beyond the confines of the jail. Hundreds of defiant prisoners refused to respond to their names or se-
rial numbers. Some of them shed much of their clothing and danced
about in the compound, while others pounded rhythmically on oil
drums. A hurriedly reinforced prison staff threw canned rations
over the fence to feed the mutineers (euphemistically called "nonco-
operatives"), and teams of Army psychologists tried to question
them through the barbed wire. Despite hearing accusations that
white guards had mistreated blacks, claims that the whole system of
military justice was corrupt and biased against blacks, and charges
of favoritism toward white prisoners, the interrogators rejected
race as an issue, insisting that most of the rebels wanted "out of the
Army and out of Vietnam." Similarly, spokesmen for the American
headquarters in South Vietnam described the riot as "a fight among
prisoners," a description that did not hold up under scrutiny.

Regardless of official pronouncements to the contrary and the
findings of the psychologists, race clearly lay at the root of the problem. Such was the judgment of Robert Stokes, the *Newsweek* correspondent who investigated the outburst. At the Long Binh Jail the
bonds of mutual respect and shared responsibility, strongest in
combat units where blacks and whites faced a common danger, had
dissolved as the two races lashed out at each other. The white
guards, partly in self-defense because 700 men were crowded into a
space that could decently accommodate no more than 400, treated

the inmates like caged beasts, and the black prisoners responded with animal-like hatred. According to Stokes, "black soldiers, rightly or wrongly, felt they faced the same kind of prejudice that they had encountered in the ghettos of the U.S. and quickly discovered their built-in resentment of authority." The Army's attempts to provide equality of treatment and opportunity were flawed in the best of circumstances, he wrote, and could not "erase the ingrained tensions that unfortunately exist between white and black Americans." As Stokes observed, tensions existed at the normal duty station; they could only be intensified at a place like the Long Binh Jail.[6]

Like the Army, the Marine Corps had been experiencing occasional racial clashes since 1965, the year of the Watts riot and the Americanization of the Vietnam War. Like their counterparts in the Army, senior Marine Corps officers saw no emerging pattern and treated the incidents as unrelated lapses in discipline. There are no black marines and no white marines, only green marines (a reference to the color of the uniform), ran the slogan of the mid-1960s. In the spring of 1969, violence exploded at Camp Lejeune, claiming one life. The victim was Corporal Edward G. Bankston, who had returned from Vietnam, where he had been wounded three times, only to be beaten to death by a marauding group of black marines.

Camp Lejeune had become a powder keg. The explosive combination included short-timers of both races, men back from Vietnam who would be leaving the Marine Corps within a few months. Because these marines were about to receive their discharge papers, they did not take part in training programs, but ended up performing housekeeping duties like painting buildings, moving furniture, or collecting trash. The blacks in particular resented being assigned to menial jobs like these, which served only to fill their remaining days of military service, and complained that they always had to do the dirtiest and most boring work. Although a general at the base discovered that the detail sent to clean up the area around his residence consisted entirely of blacks, except for the noncommissioned officer in charge, the racial composition of such a group could be explained away by the fact that so many blacks were awaiting discharge. The black marines complained, but only among themselves, for they were sure that the white senior officers were not listening.

In these circumstances, the sight of a rebel flag, the use of words like "nigger" or "boy," or the telling of racial jokes brought retaliation, at first against the individuals responsible and later against any white who happened to be at hand. Black civilians in the major American cities had rioted in the despair after the murder of Dr. King; convinced of the hollowness of the promises of equal treatment and opportunity, the black marines also fought back when they felt threatened or abused, reacting in a manner as destructive to the Marine Corps as the urban violence had been to civil society.

The anger continued after Bankston's death, with more than 160 violent incidents taking place at Camp Lejeune during the first eight months of 1969. At times the interracial warfare spilled over beyond the limits of the reservation. White marines, out to settle racial scores, drove to the home of a recently retired black sergeant major, hurled white phosphorus grenades into his house and station wagon, and also set fire to a neighbor's Cadillac—which they assumed belonged to the sergeant—before roaring off into the dusk. Ironically, the same noncommissioned officer had braved enemy fire while in Vietnam to save the life of another marine, who happened to be white.

Corporal Bankston's murder and the continuing violence jolted the Marine Corps into action. Major General Michael Ryan, a decorated veteran of some of the most savage amphibious fighting of World War II, tried to discover the cause of the violence and eliminate it. Not only did he encourage young marines of both races to speak out, he listened to what they were saying.

General Ryan's investigation revealed that racial relations on the base, and indeed within the entire corps, had deteriorated over the past four years and a pattern of mutual hostility had gradually emerged. Blacks and whites had grown suspicious of the other. Whites saw blacks congregating and feared violence, whereas blacks saw gatherings of whites and believed they were being excluded, made fun of, conspired against, shunned. Members of both races became convinced that the other group was receiving preferential treatment, although blacks were especially resentful at having to perform menial labor. The mutual loathing, made worse by a lack of interracial communication, was not unique to the military; the attitude had its root in quarrels over the racial integration of the public schools and over the attempt to redress old wrongs by hiring or promoting blacks in occupations formerly closed to them. The services had once provided an introduction to racial integration; now tensions in society tore at the fabric of the armed forces. In this explosive situation, perceptions of prejudice against blacks or of what whites were calling "reverse discrimination" proved as dangerous as actual incidents. Symbols therefore played a part in the growing hostility, whether the Confederate flag with its connotation of slavery, the leather wristbands worn by blacks as a badge of solidarity, or the nonregulation Afro haircut, which white authorities found particularly objectionable. In these circumstances, barracks humor easily gave way to insult, and insult to violence.

General Ryan took steps to end the turmoil at Camp Lejeune. Openness became the watchword, as he established discussion groups for the airing of racial grievances. He approved a new haircut for blacks, a compromise with the Afro, and insisted that all barbers employed on the base learn this hair style. Magazines, books, clothing, and grooming aids for blacks appeared in exchanges and other facilities, and he managed to allay the concerns of veteran white noncommissioned officers that because of these reforms the Marine Corps was going to hell. Taken individually, none of the changes amounted to much; taken together, they signaled an attitude that both races found more congenial.[7]

There also was violence on Army posts in the United States. At Fort Benning, Georgia, for example, groups of black soldiers roamed throughout portions of the base terrorizing white soldiers. Conditions were similar to those at Camp Lejeune, with short-timers, many of them blacks, enduring such unpopular jobs as collecting garbage or firing off blanks during interminable series of night "problems" conducted at the Infantry School. Here too resentment mounted, communication between the races became an exchange of taunts, and violence flared. Secretary of the Army Stanley Resor acknowledged that the black soldier of the late 1960s "is far different from his counterpart of ten years ago. Today he is more likely to make his resentment known. Today, in the young black soldier there is more personal and racial pride, more bitterness at real or imagined injustice. Like white persons entering the Army, he seeks to retain his personal identity, and in that identity his race is a part. The Negro in uniform does not cease to be a Negro and become a soldier instead. He becomes a Negro solider."

In dealing with the black soldier described by Secretary Resor, officers at Fort Benning and other Army posts did essentially what General Ryan had done at Camp Lejeune. Listening was the first and most important step. Often the mere opportunity for blacks to speak out with an expectation of being heard was enough to defuse a potentially explosive situation.[8]

The recurring racial outbursts, particularly in South Vietnam, coincided with another even more serious problem, the widespread use of illegal drugs. This was especially acute in Southeast Asia, where locally grown marijuana was readily available, as was heroin refined from opium obtained in Laos. Drug addiction was a more dramatic problem than racial turbulence; taking drugs was likelier to have an immediate effect upon behavior in combat.

Initially, drug abuse seemed amenable to disciplinary measures. Heroin or marijuana could be found and confiscated; urinalysis or the observation of bizarre actions provided adequate evidence of the misuse of drugs, and the offender could then be punished. Such was the belief until the 1970s, when commanders realized that the problem was widespread. Some officers believed that drug abuse had reached epidemic proportion among the younger enlisted men in all the services, blacks and whites. Youth, loneliness, and alienation determined who would become involved with drugs. At first whites seemed to favor marijuana and blacks heroin, but as heroin became more easily available it tended to supplant marijuana, which was bulkier and harder to conceal, among both whites and blacks. As more and more of the troops became involved with drugs, education programs and the granting of amnesty from prosecution in return for voluntary rehabilitation came to take the place of immediate punishment.

By 1970 the outbreaks of racial violence and the frequency of instances of drug abuse could be seen as manifestations of a general collapse of morale and failure of purpose that permeated the armed forces, especially the units in South Vietnam. At root of the problem was a loss of confidence in the military as an institution, its officers, and its values. Mistrust gave way to contempt, and contempt to disobedience and revenge. Troops in combat in South Vietnam refused to obey orders they considered foolish, and assaults upon unpopular officers and noncommissioned officers were taking place in the Army and Marine Corps. Almost a hundred such incidents occurred in the Army alone during 1969 and more than two hundred the following year; the Army's death toll for the two years was seventy-one. These attacks came to be grouped under the category of "fragging," because the fragmentation grenade was a favorite tool of assassination. The dissident soldier or marine could easily obtain these weapons and could remain concealed as he hurled one into the intended victim's quarters.[9]

Some officers attributed racial strife, drug abuse, and the overall failure of discipline to poor leadership, to the manifestation by commanders of a spirit of "permissiveness," reflected in the abandonment of the old standards for "haircuts, moustaches, and dress. . . ." An Air Force colonel in South Vietnam complained that "we are tumbling all over ourselves to avoid confrontation in racial matters, in drug abuse, and in just plain discipline." Indeed, the natural desire to succeed induced many a commanding officer to try to avoid taking up the challenge of those who defied official policy or the customs of the service. Confrontation, after all, could result in protest, violent or otherwise, and lead to a poor efficiency report and a diminished chance for promotion or retention. Maintaining the appearance of harmony—between blacks and whites, between "lifers," or career men, and draftees or those who enlisted to avoid the infantry, between the beer drinkers and the marijuana smokers—became more important than addressing the problems that caused friction within the command.[10]

The line between destabilizing permissiveness and genuine sensitivity proved hard to determine, as demonstrated by the following events at the Great Lakes Naval Base, Illinois. At 2 A.M. on July 10, 1970, four black WAVES attacked a fifth woman, also a black and a sailor, who screamed for help. Security police responded, taking the assailants into custody. A distorted account of the incident began circulating almost immediately, attracting a crowd of some fifty black seamen, who demanded the release of the four women. A group of whites then arrived, eager for a fight, but an officer succeeded in preventing a riot. Instead of pursuing a collision course, he conferred with representatives of the black men, explaining the details of the fight and the fact that the four WAVES had been placed on report—the equivalent of being booked by civilian police—and would be released to return to their quarters. Deprived of a cause, the group of blacks broke up, and the whites also scattered.

The base commander, Captain Draper L. Kauffman, then engaged in what some might have called permissiveness. Acting upon the findings of investigation teams sent out to Great Lakes by the Bureau of Naval Personnel and the Office of the Secretary of the Navy, he identified the sources of racial tension and moved swiftly to remove them. The major changes resulted in the inauguration of seminars in race relations to promote understanding. In pursuit of the same goal, he converted an existing committee on equal treatment and opportunity into a channel of interracial communication. Other reforms brought additional black barbers and beauticians into the post exchange, increased the availability of books, magazines, and exchange items intended for blacks, and streamlined reassignment procedures so that large numbers of sailors, whether black or white, no longer spent a great deal of idle time at the base while awaiting transfer. Thanks to these actions, tensions eased at Great Lakes.[11]

The Air Force, too, was having problems. Violence erupted in March 1970 at Goose Bay, Labrador, where 1,000 whites and 300 blacks were serving. The trouble arose because white airmen resented the fact that white women, who attended dances at the base, danced with blacks assigned there. An argument about the kind of music being played resulted in a fight during which a white serviceman, believed to be organizing a unit of the Ku Klux Klan at Goose Bay, stabbed a black, inflicting superficial injuries. Friends of the victim began searching for the assailant, assaulting some thirteen whites before they found and beat up the person they sought.

Incredibly, authorities at Goose Bay brought charges against five blacks but not against the white who had done the stabbing. When advised by the National Association for the Advancement of Colored People of the manner in which justice was being administered at the base in Labrador, Secretary of the Air Force Robert C. Seamans, Jr., maintained official silence, but charges against the five were dropped; the knife-wielding airman still escaped prosecution. The commanding officer, who was so insensitive to the feelings of blacks that he believed he was being complimentary when he compared blacks with Afro hair styles to well-kept sheep or poodles, received an assignment elsewhere. The departure of this officer, who had been responsible for the original charges against the black airmen, eased racial tensions. Once the crisis had passed, James P. Goode, the Acting Assistant Secretary of the Air Force for Manpower and Reserve Affairs, thanked the National Association for the Advancement of Colored People for its "first hand account of conditions" at Goose Bay and also for "keeping the situation in proper perspective."[12]

Racial conflict surfaced in all the armed forces, everywhere that American servicemen were stationed, from South Vietnam to Labrador to West Germany. Some of the complaints voiced by blacks serving in Germany in the late 1960s were the same as those heard elsewhere, charges of racial discrimination in promotion, for instance, and in the administration of justice. An anonymous black soldier summed up his feelings by declaring, "If I fail to blouse my boots, or [if I] wear an Afro, I get socked. Yet the Company Commander can thumb his nose at any order from General [James H.] Polk [Commanding General, U.S. Army, Europe] he doesn't like if it deals with blacks, and nothing is done."[13] This black soldier believed, with justification, that two standards applied in military justice, one for whites and another for blacks. Such a belief had surfaced during the Civil War because of the harsh punishment visited upon black dissenters during the controversy whether the U.S. Colored Troops should receive the same pay as white volunteers. It had intensified due to the punishment for the Brownsville rioters, who were discharged dishonorably, and the Houston rioters, who were hanged, and by the 1970s it had become almost an article of faith among black servicemen.

The racial discrimination directed against blacks in the rental of housing in Germany proved especially galling. In March 1971, Willy Brandt, then the mayor of Berlin, criticized his fellow citizens for their treatment of blacks, which reflected an attitude that had arisen after World War II. In part, the West Germans had absorbed the racism that had infected the American Army in the years immediately after the war, but by 1971 they were reacting to a different kind of black soldier. The courteous black of the immediate postwar years, often a native of the rural South, seemed but a memory, his place taken by a louder, more aggressive product of some urban ghetto, the representative of a culture that seemed utterly alien even to many American whites. If the white resident of a small American town or distant suburb was fearful of the inner city and the loud-talking blacks who congregated on street corners, portable radios blaring, how else could the Germans react to the black invaders of their towns and villages?[14]

Whether in the United States, Asia, or Europe, military discipline remained essential, but, as Captain Kauffman had shown, some flexibility was needed. The armed forces gradually discovered that the campaign against drug abuse required education and treatment, along with detection and punishment. A similarly judicious approach had to be followed in dealing with racial tensions. During 1969, as violent outbursts were occurring more frequently, Melvin R. Laird, Secretary of Defense in the cabinet of President Richard M. Nixon, created an interservice task force to coordinate efforts to improve understanding between commanders and their men and between servicemen of the black and white races.[15]

Out of this project came a statement of human goals, promulgated in August 1969. The document, largely a collection of platitudes, acknowledged that the nation "was founded on the principle that the individual has infinite dignity and worth," then promised that the Department of Defense would be guided by that belief. The goals announced in the declaration included a pledge to "make military and civilian service in the Department of Defense a model of equal opportunity for all, regardless of race, sex, creed, or national origin. . . .[16] At best, the pronouncement served to remind commanders of the need to understand the ambitions and concerns of their men, whether whites, blacks, or members of some other identifiable group. At worst, it repeated what had been said time and again over the past twenty-five years and had yet to prevail in practice.

The principal means of ensuring the kind of communication called for by Secretary Laird's task force were interracial panels, discussion groups, and councils, and sometimes the informal awareness groups made up exclusively of blacks to promote an understanding of their racial heritage. As a result of this emphasis on the exchange of ideas, the service began doing on a broad scale what Captain Kauffman had done at Great Lakes. Besides encouraging discussion, commanders found room at clubs and exchanges for magazines and newspapers of interest to blacks, the music they liked, their favorite food, and even cosmetics used by black service-women. Furthermore, the Afro, albeit in a modified form, became an acceptable hair style for men in uniform. Of less interest, perhaps, to the average black in the armed forces, attempts were renewed to obtain more black officers, through either reserve officer training programs or the service academies.[17] Results were disappointing, however, for in 1971 only 2.3 percent of the officers in the services were black. This represented a distinct improvement over the 1.6 percent of commissioned officers in 1962, but much remained to be done.

At the same time—the late 1960s and early 1970s—the first of a group of black officers who were veterans of the segregated armed forces were receiving promotion to flag rank, joining such pioneers as Benjamin O. Davis, Jr., who retired in 1970, and Daniel James, Jr., both of the Air Force. By the end of 1973, there were twelve black generals in the Army, three in the Air Force, and one flag officer in the Navy. What did this mean for the average black serviceman? In 1971 the black journalist Carl Rowan, an officer in the naval reserve during World War II, answered by recalling the time that President Kennedy had selected him to be Deputy Assistant Secretary of State for Public Affairs, the highest position in the Department of State held by a person of his race.

"I'll never forget," Rowan said, "the day that a black employee came to tell me that he had tried for years to get a raise, but a white southerner . . . always blocked him. That is until the newspapers announced my appointment—meaning that I was now the southerner's boss.

"The prejudiced State Department officer quickly called the black employee in and said, 'John, I've got good news for you. I just arranged for you to get a double promotion.'"[18]

Rowan expected the presence of a number of black admirals and generals to have a similar effect on those officers still ignoring the directives that called for equal opportunity and treatment, regardless of race. Life in the armed forces was not that simple. Because of the hierarchical structure and corporate nature of the defense establishment, the comparatively junior black flag officers had to have the cooperation of their white seniors to effect change.

Of all the services the Navy, with just one black admiral, reacted the most vigorously to the racial problems that surfaced during the Vietnam conflict. Although described by Rowan as "always a bit backward, racially speaking,"[19] the naval service had changed since he earned his commission in 1944 and now moved quickly forward. Samuel L. Gravely, Jr., who in 1971 became the first black to attain flag rank, lacked the seniority to alter naval policy. The leader in the campaign against racism was a white officer, Admiral Elmo R. Zumwalt, sworn in as Chief of Naval Operations in June 1970.

The new Chief of Naval Operations fired a broadside of directives, called Z-grams, designed to banish "Mickey Mouse"—a term that embraced every form of petty harassment and excessive regulation that made life in the Navy unattractive. Included in the category were prohibitions against growing beards and senseless restrictions on the kind of clothing that could be worn off duty by sailors or members of their families. Zumwalt realized, however, that racial discrimination had an impact far more devastating than the annoyance caused by pointless rules. The admiral had become aware of this while assigned to the Bureau of Personnel; there he discovered that black officers, of whom there were very few, routinely received assignments that afforded little or no opportunity for promotion. No wonder that by mid-1970 the proportion of black officers in the Navy stood at just 0.7 percent. Nor were blacks suitably represented in the enlisted forces, totaling just 5.5 percent, about half the percentage of blacks in the general populace.[20]

Addressing the question of race relations, Admiral Zumwalt saw to it that the Navy did what the other services were doing—and more. He broadened the variety of articles stocked by exchanges, and he sought to open communication between the races and between an overwhelmingly white officer corps and the Navy's black enlisted men. But he went further, at long last redeeming the Navy's pledge, frequently repeated since World War II, to increase the number of blacks in the service. Taking advantage of lower educational standards for enlistment (which would have unfortunate consequences later because remedial instruction was not available), recruiters tried to convince young men that "you can be black and Navy, too." Zumwalt's efforts also increased to 150 the number of black midshipmen at the Naval Academy and resulted in the establishment of new reserve officer training programs at predominately black high schools and colleges.[21]

Circumstances, however, prevented Zumwalt from recruiting a large number of blacks with the potential to fashion careers in a Navy that relied heavily on aptitude tests in making assignments for enlisted men. Since the summer of 1969, American participation in the Vietnam War had been declining, albeit spasmodically, with a corresponding decline in the size of the American contingent in South Vietnam and in the monthly draft calls. Since the possibility of being conscripted into the Army and sent to Vietnam no longer served as an incentive to join the Navy, recruiting lagged, forcing the naval service to take full advantage of the lower standards. The Navy had to accept an increasing number of men who had fared poorly on the classification tests and in previous years would have been rejected. Many of the persons in this category were members of racial minorities. As a consequence, the service during the year ending in June 1972 accepted 12,000 blacks out of about 133,000 recruits, or roughly 9 percent. All too many of the new sailors, perhaps two-thirds of them, could not qualify for technical training. Assuming the validity of the tests that thus branded them, such men were condemned to the least desirable jobs in the Navy. Zumwalt himself did not concede this validity, but he acknowledged that the system of testing was able to measure what a man had done, how well he had mastered such basic skills as reading and arithmetic, even though it could not predict his future contribution to the Navy.

The admiral found himself caught between the Navy's traditional insistence upon high scores and his own doubts about using the test scores to place a man or woman in a particular career field. Because the system had its uses, he could not discard it. He could, however, tinker with the minimum test scores, running the risk of accepting individuals who had lacked the self-discipline to apply themselves in high school. The need for manpower forced him to lower standards and accept the risk. To minimize the danger, he also tried to overhaul the recruiting service, using the tests for screening more than placement and eliminating insofar as he could any conscious or institutional bias that denied blacks the technical training for which they might have a natural aptitude.[22]

Whereas the Navy tried a systematic approach to the problem of racial discrimination, the Department of Defense in the summer of 1970 embarked upon yet another study of race relations, this one headed by a black officer, Air Force Colonel Lucius Theus. The department, however, responded only with unfulfilled plans, dragging its feet on the group's principal recommendation, the establishment of a program of education in race relations for all the armed forces.[23] This tardiness could have resulted from the belief, unfortunately not founded in fact, that friction between the races was fast abating or, more likely, from preoccupation with the problem of drug abuse.

The Theus plan did not take concrete shape until a violent outburst finally shook the Department of Defense from its lethargy. At Travis Air Force Base, California, a number of grievances, some real but others imagined, triggered an especially destructive riot. There were two major complaints that fueled the violence there. Black airmen resented the base commander's failure to declare off limits an apartment development that practiced racial discrimination. Meanwhile, an investigation of one of the clubs on the base turned up evidence of kickbacks to wholesalers and outright theft that resulted in the firing of a number of black employees. To blacks already upset by the housing issue, this seemed like another example of racial discrimination.

A comparatively trifling matter, loud music from a record player, served as the catalyst. The songs being played, rather than the volume, caused the fighting, for two kinds of music had emerged. There was black music by "soul" singers like James Brown, and there was white music, usually "red-neck" country and western tunes. The songs favored by one group infuriated the other, and in this instance widespread violence was the result. The race riot, which began on May 21, 1971, lasted four days, brought injury to at least thirty persons, and claimed one life, that of a civilian fireman who suffered a heart attack while helping put out a blaze started by arsonists in the transient officers' quarters. At one time, some 200 airmen were battling each other with fists, rocks, and a variety of improvised weapons. Seventy policemen from nearby communities helped Air Force security police restore order, in the process arresting 135 airmen, only 25 of them whites. Since a head count of the rioters was obviously impossible and estimates often reflect a person's prejudice, it cannot be said whether the numbers reflected the proportion of blacks among the rioters or greater zeal in apprehending blacks.[24]

Barely a month after the rioting at Travis Air Force Base, the educational program recommended by Colonel Theus and his colleagues had taken shape. On June 24, 1971, Deputy Secretary of Defense David Packard announced an effort designed to "eliminate and prevent racial tensions, unrest, and violence." In charge of the undertaking was the Assistant Secretary of Defense (Manpower and Reserve Affairs), who would be assisted by an advisory body, the Race Relations Education Board, made up of the assistant secretaries for manpower and reserve affairs in each of the services and representatives of the Deputy Assistant Secretaries of Defense (Equal Opportunity), (Education), and (Reserve Affairs). A Department of Defense Race Relations Institute at Patrick Air Force Base, Florida, got the mission of "training . . . Armed Forces personnel designated as instructors in race relations," developing "doctrine and curricula in education for race relations," conducting research, evaluating the effectiveness of the program, and disseminating instructional materials. The classes conducted throughout the armed services by the trained instructors would be supplemented by whatever "additional educational activities" local commanders might consider "necessary to maintain racial harmony."[25]

Before the riot at Travis Air Force Base, the educational effort recommended by Colonel Theus had impressed one Air Force officer involved in the planning as being "in a holding pattern,"[26] a term describing a plane's circling while waiting its turn to land. The plans for racial education were circulating among staff agencies without coming to rest on the desk of a decision maker. That no longer was the case. The Air Force in particular moved rapidly to educate its men and women in the importance of racial amity to the successful accomplishment of its assigned mission to fly and fight.

Within fewer than forty months since the assassination of Dr. Martin Luther King, Jr., great changes had taken place in the military. When he died in April 1968, the armed forces were confident that the bureaucratic machinery established as a result of the Gesell Committee, reinforced by the recent civil rights legislation, was automatically ensuring that all servicemen, regardless of race, enjoyed equal treatment and opportunity. Events rapidly revealed the meaninglessness of the carefully drawn diagrams with individual boxes and lines of responsibility running upward to the Office of the Secretary of Defense. The civil rights bureaucracy within the department had turned inward upon itself, engaging in self-congratulation while ignoring the men and women in uniform whose rights it was supposed to safeguard. Violence and even death proved necessary to drive home the realization that the various assistant secretaries, special assistants, and even commanding officers had only the faintest idea what the black man and woman in the service were thinking. Could the new program reopen communication, ease the racial tension that had been building, and restore unity of purpose to the armed forces?

20

Emphasis on Education

SINCE THE ACCEPTANCE of the Gesell Committee reports of 1963 and 1964, the Department of Defense had looked upon communication—whether between the races or between leaders and those they led—as the key to racial amity. Now the emphasis shifted to education, with the Air Force, in reaction to the Travis riot, suddenly displaying the kind of initiative it had shown in responding to President Truman's integration order of 1948. Although all the services undertook similar programs, the Air Force showed the greatest zeal; besides the violence at Travis Air Force Base, another factor contributing to this enthusiasm may have been the fact that the Defense Race Relations Institute, which served the needs of the entire defense establishment, was located at an Air Force installation, Patrick Air Force Base, Florida. Within the Air Force, a program of indoctrination, mandatory for officers, enlisted men, and civilian employees, got under way even as instructors were being trained and instructional materials prepared at the institute. The educational center at Patrick Air Force Base was to develop a uniformed "faculty" to train specialists in race relations and to write the manuals that these men and women would use in spreading the message of racial cooperation.

The Air Force was trying, said an officer involved in the effort, "to improve the understanding of people for each other," thus bringing about a keener appreciation of "the different cultural and ethnic backgrounds that make up our society and, as a practical matter, improving motivation. . . . and productivity on the job." The program would unfold in three phases, the first a hurriedly organized response to the brawling and arson at Travis Air Force Base. The two subsequent phases, which together were to reach the entire Air Force over a period of four years or more, would take fuller advantage of the instructors and techniques produced by the race relations institute.

"Phase I was rather disorganized," Lieutenant Colonel Thomas J. Sizemore recalled in an interview in 1977, "with individuals who were grabbed wherever we could get them to perform the duties of instructors." The instruction, he continued, "was a confrontation type of course, using trigger words to get reactions and the hostilities of individuals to come out." The staged confrontations sought to promote understanding by anticipating and neutralizing potentially dangerous situations that might otherwise occur in the barracks or office. Unfortunately, an overly aggressive instructor, demanding that his audience abandon attitudes that they found comforting but he considered foolish, could inspire resistance to his message of harmony rather than acceptance. Largely because of the self-righteousness of many instructors, this first phase generated more resistance than the subsequent efforts.

For example, at Wright Patterson Air Force Base, a large installation on the outskirts of Dayton, Ohio, the first sessions stirred up a loud clamor from blacks as well as whites. All too often, because of the inexperience of the instructors, discussion became heated argument and attitudes hardened. The principal qualification for teaching in the course was a desire to change racial attitudes; tact and teaching skill were desirable rather than essential. The subsequent phases benefited from a better-trained staff that could dramatize prejudice without creating emotional resistance.

As a more proficient instructional staff became available, the Air Force entered the second phase. Once again the objective was to heighten sensitivity toward racism, this time using subtler techniques developed at the Defense Race Relations Institute, which had been functioning at Patrick Air Force Base since the summer of 1971. The confrontations of the first phase, sometimes as much a vent for pent-up emotion as a serious educational experience, gave way to a quieter, less direct approach in which individuals assumed various roles in loosely scripted plays. Improvisation was encouraged, however, with a black airman, for instance, donning the attitudes, as he saw them, of a white officer. A typical session began with introductions, as class members formed small groups and exchanged information about themselves, their hopes, their attitudes. The script, such as it was, typically called for some white volunteer to play the part of a bigot—sometimes called Mr. Arbunk after the television character Archie Bunker, whose lifestyle was threatened in each episode by the encroachment of some minority or other—while a black volunteer played the part of an airman, cool in his approach and casual about such matters as wearing the uniform or interracial dating. The two became the catalysts as a skilled moderator steered the class members to a more sympathetic understanding of each other.

The third phase of the educational program dealt with supervisors, whether officers, noncommissioned officers, or civilians, and used the same techniques employed in the second segment. Besides seeking to improve understanding among groups and individuals, this course stressed the need for discipline, equitably applied. "Here," reported a veteran of the program, "our goal is to acquaint the supervisor with the importance of having standards, the importance of applying those standards equally across the board . . . , and the necessity in the military environment for discipline."

The first phase differed from the second largely in that the latter had more skillful instructors who used more imaginative instructional techniques to keep the discussion on track toward a useful goal. The third phase differed from the other two because the participants were officers, noncommissioned officers, or civilian supervisors, and the exchange of ideas was skewed toward the topics of management and discipline. In every phase, the sessions presupposed a certain receptiveness on the part of the class; there were no failures and no remedial instruction. Of course, evidence of interest on the part of the Air Force leadership was enough to ensure responsiveness on the part of those interested in their careers.[1]

The Air Force embarked on other programs which dealt with race and were educational in the broadest sense, including an attempt to attract more black cadets to the Air Force Academy at Colorado Springs, Colorado. Toward this end, the service inaugurated a special remedial course, preliminary to the normal Air Force Academy Prep School, at which black high school graduates could make up for any academic deficiencies. Education, along with experience, also played a part in a new promotion system for enlisted airmen, in which objective examinations replaced subjective evaluations by supervisors as the principal measure of suitability for promotion or retention.

The new emphasis on education did not result in abandonment of efforts to improve communication between the races, especially between white officers and black enlisted men. "Perhaps," said Secretary of the Air Force Robert C. Seamans, Jr., "we need to recall that 'the Open Door policy works best when it is the commander who walks though the door.'" Visits with the enlisted force seemed essential if the commanding officer was really to understand their concerns. In gaining this insight, he could rely for advice upon his noncommissioned officers and upon trained equal opportunity officers, who sought to stimulate informal exchanges between the commander and his men.[2]

The prompt response of the Air Force to the Travis riot did not prevent other racial incidents, though they became increasingly infrequent, tended to deal with problems beyond the main gate, and lacked the fury of the rampage at the California base. In September 1972, for example, at Laredo Air Force Base, Texas, black demonstrators gave vent to their resentment over racial discrimination by seizing a mess hall. They presented the base commander, Colonel L. W. Svendson, with "grievances ranging from lack of 'black-oriented clothes at the post exchange' to what many of them called 'racism among Mexican-Americans on the base and in the town.'" The Air Force Chief of Staff, General John D. Ryan, reacted by advising all commanders and supervisors to "support the USAF Equal Opportunity and Race Relations Education Programs with the same vigor that is given to the flying mission." The incident at Laredo resulted, moveover, in the replacement of the commanding officer, not because of any discriminatory action on his part, but because he was unaware of the tensions that were building among his black enlisted men.[3]

Racial violence shook the Navy in 1972 with a suddenness and severity completely unexpected in the light of the policies that Admiral Zumwalt was pursuing. In fact, the first of three racial incidents occurred on a ship with a strong program designed to ensure equal treatment and opportunity. The violence broke out on the aircraft carrier *Kitty Hawk*, en route from Subic Bay in the Philippines to the waters of the Tonkin Gulf, off North Vietnam.

The spark that ignited the conflict was the questioning of a black apprentice seaman, accused of refusing to obey an order and assault upon a petty officer during a brawl in the town of Olongapao before *Kitty Hawk* sailed. The sailor, who had brought some fellow blacks with him, stormed out of the interrogation, and the group then attacked a white mess attendant, the first of some sixty persons, almost all of them white, injured during sporadic fighting on October 12 and 13, 1972. Once the ship reached its assigned station, the violence subsided, and the executive officer, a black, restored order, for discipline was his responsibility. No more than 4 percent of the 5,000-men crew took part in the incident or became its victims; the authorities charged twenty-six sailors, all of them blacks, with various offenses against good order and discipline.

On October 16, when *Kitty Hawk* was back in action against the North Vietnamese, a similar uprising occurred on board the fleet oiler *Hassayampa*. Unlike the aircraft carrier, the oiler had no program at all for addressing the problems of racial minorities. A dozen black crew members complained to the executive officer that a white sailor had stolen money from one of them. Unless the cash was returned, the blacks declared, they would not sail from Subic Bay and would take revenge on any whites whom they happened to encounter. They lost no time carrying out the threat to avenge the theft. Brandishing walking sticks with a carved clenched fist—a symbol of black power—for a handle, they attacked seven white seamen, inflicting superficial injuries. A detachment of marines went on board *Hassayampa* and restored order, arresting eleven blacks, who received a choice of sailing with the oiler and facing a subsequent hearing or awaiting trial in the brig at Subic Bay. All but one sailed with the ship; six of the group received some form of punishment.[4]

Violence next erupted on board the carrier *Constellation* during a training exercise off the coast of California. Although few members of *Constellation*'s crew suffered physical injury, Admiral Zumwalt considered this breach of discipline, which occurred on November 3, 1972, "more troubling" than the other two. The incidents on board *Hassayampa* and *Kitty Hawk*, the Chief of Naval Operations believed, represented "spontaneous outbursts of anger, nasty evidence of past racial injustice and of present institutional inability to cope with it"; yet both had been "tactically simple to bring under control." In contrast, the multiple problems that led to trouble on the *Constellation* arose from several complex and interrelated sources.[5]

The *Constellation* was preparing for a seventh combat tour off North Vietnam (prospects for a cease fire, which actually went in to effect in January 1973, seemed dim in November), even though some 900 new men had recently reported on board and were not yet assimilated into the ship's complement of 4,500 officers and men. Many of the newcomers had scored poorly on the aptitude tests, had no prospects for technical training because of the emphasis that continued to be placed on test scores, and could look forward to serving out their time in some assignment that required little in the way of skill. Admiral Zumwalt in response to the need for manpower had lowered standards to admit them to the Navy, but despite his lack of confidence in the value of aptitude tests, he had found no real substitute for testing in shaping a sailor's career. The blacks in this group tended to think of themselves as victims of racial discrimination, hemmed in by regulations devised by white officers, declared ineligible for training that might prove valuable later in life, and subject to punishment at the whim of the executive officer.

At the heart of the problem was a perception of injustice. A subsequent investigation by a congressional panel made up of representatives conservative on questions of race relations and hostile to Admiral Zumwalt declared that it found "no substantial evidence of racial discrimination" that could be cited as provoking the troubles that disrupted the ship. There were, however, "many perceptions of discrimination by young blacks, who, because of their sensitivity to real or fancied oppression, enlist with a 'chip on their shoulder.'" Angry young blacks, suddenly transported from an urban ghetto into a world afloat that was tightly controlled by white officers and petty officers, interpreted some normal forms of discipline as racism and banded together against the supposed oppressor.[6]

On November 2, 1972, a half-dozen men, individuals with low test scores and histories of indifferent performance in boring and repetitive jobs, got word that they would receive general discharges under honorable conditions. This administrative procedure was the Navy's way of eliminating men or women who were troublemakers or did not quite measure up to the standards of the service. In this instance, the six men were believed to be the instigators of a series of meetings at which black sailors had demanded access to the records of nonjudicial actions in order to determine if blacks were receiving a disproportionate share of the punishment meted out on the authority of the ship's captain at the so-called "captain's mast." The notification of these sailors lent credence to rumors, which had been circulating for about two weeks, that 250 first-term crewmen would be separated from the Navy in the same fashion to make room for airmen and technicians, who were needed for combat operations in Southeast Asia. The prospect of being thrown out of the Navy provoked new protest meetings and ultimately the refusal by more than a hundred black sailors to perform their assigned duties.

The ship's commanding officer, Captain J. D. Ward, invited the disaffected crewmen to take advantage of the machinery for resolving racial grievances, utilizing the *Constellation*'s Human Resources Council. When the group did not respond, he carried out a show of force, assembling a detachment of marines fitted out with riot gear. He then offered the dissidents an opportunity to present their complaints to officers ashore, and 130 seamen, only 8 of them whites, accepted. They were constituted as a so-called beach detachment and sent to the air station at North Island in San Diego Bay. Ten of the men, including all the whites, then changed their minds and returned to the ship.

Those who remained at North Island faced judicial proceedings convened by the commandant of that station, Captain Robert Mc Kenzie. In administering justice, naval authorities seemed content to break up the group involved in the incident on board the *Constellation*, scattering 69 of the 120 sailors among other ships, though not one of them reported to another aircraft carrier, probably because of a lack of the skills needed on these ships. Of the others, 34 received honorable discharges and 10 the less desirable discharge under honorable conditions. The remaining 7 faced the possibility of discharge, either at their own request or because of medical problems that had come to light since their transfer from the carrier.[7]

Although Zumwalt himself was especially concerned about events on board the *Constellation* because the outburst had occurred despite a strong program to improve race relations, the *Kitty Hawk* uprising represented a violent and therefore more serious breach of discipline. Despite the violence, evidence proved scarce, so that most of the men involved were convicted of lesser crimes, like assault or insubordination, instead of mutiny. A court-martial did, however, convict one black sailor, Cleveland Mallory, of riot and assault, basing the verdict on the word of an eyewitness and sentencing the prisoner to a bad-conduct discharge. An investigator from the National Association for the Advancement of Colored People then intervened, demonstrating that the eyewitness had not been as certain in his identification as the court chose to believe and thus demolishing the case upon which the verdict was based. Clearly the authorities had been as interested in making an example of someone as in meting out justice.[8]

To Admiral Zumwalt, the three instances of racial violence indicated that his directives on race relations were not being carried out. He therefore called upon his senior officers for "even-handed leadership of men" and the resolution of racial tension "within the framework of disciplined, efficient, orderly, and ethical military operations"—in short, for actions to make "equal opportunity a reality and discrimination for any reason an unacceptable practice." He was determined that his reforms would prevail despite opposition within the service and on Capitol Hill—a hostility that intensified with the departure of Secretary of the Navy John Chafee, a strong supporter of Zumwalt's efforts.

Within the Navy the opposition to Zumwalt came from a number of sources. Especially effective were the many senior officers who feared the destruction of tradition in dress, courtesy, discipline, and appearance. They had a definite picture of the American sailor, how he should look, act, and be treated. He might be black, but he had to have discipline according to a white definition of the word and conform to white notions of neatness and grooming. For these captains and admirals, discipline was essential to the success of the Navy; racial amity was important, to be sure, but it could best be ensured by establishing rules and punishing those who broke them. If sailors behaved as the blacks had on *Hassayampa, Kitty Hawk,* or *Constellation,* they should be court-martialed and punished; it was as simple as that. Zumwalt's talk of eliminating what was purposeless in naval discipline and instituting what he called "programs for people" won no converts among those who saw the Navy as an institution imposing its will upon its members and not as a group of persons unified for a common purpose. Assessing the opposition to Zumwalt, the *Atlanta World,* a black newspaper, wondered if the Navy would enter the twentieth century before the twenty-first century began.[9]

The loudest denunciations of Zumwalt emanated from Congress. Although the Chief of Naval Operations specifically denied that his program resulted in the substitution of permissiveness for traditional discipline, a subcommittee of the House Armed Services Committee found otherwise. In condemning Zumwalt for fostering permissiveness, the group reflected the views of F. Edward Hebert, the Democrat from Louisiana who headed the parent committee. An indication of Hebert's attitude on race was the fact that he had described the 1964 Civil Rights Act as "Big Brotherism"—a reference to the dictator in George Orwell's *1984*—and insisted that every American, black or white, had all the protection he needed in the Bill of Rights, the first ten amendments to the Constitution. Actually, Zumwalt in reaching an accommodation with blacks, was doing little more than the other service chiefs, but he was doing it in a highly visible style, which caught the attention of the congressman and aroused his wrath.

To conduct an investigation of the incidents on board *Constellation* and *Kitty Hawk,* the chairman chose three committee members who shared his opinion of Zumwalt. Dan Daniel, a Democrat from Virginia, had served in the Navy and became the national commander of the American Legion, an organization for veterans. Alexander Pirnie, a Republican from New York, had risen to the rank of colonel in the Army during World War II. Floyd Hicks of Washington, a Democrat, had served in the wartime Army Air Forces. All three were white men. When a caucus of black congressmen asked to be represented on a group investigating incidents in which race was a factor, the request was denied.

After taking testimony concerning events on the two aircraft carriers, the subcommittee declared that "those in authority turn to negotiation and then to appeasement rather than immediately to firm and fair enforcement of existing regulations." Unfortunately, what appeared "firm and fair" to a member of Congress might seem an act of flagrant injustice to a poorly educated black sailor, already dismayed by his inability to qualify for technical training or challenging assignments. Acknowledging that perceived injustice could prove as demoralizing as documented instances of racial discrimination, the group nevertheless charged that Zumwalt's attempts to eliminate real and imagined friction were creating "an environment of leniency, appeasement and permissiveness." The Navy, said the subcommittee, "is now confronted with pressures, both from within and without, which, if not controlled, will surely destroy its enviable tradition of discipline."[10]

In 1974, as he prepared to retire, Zumwalt did rescind the Z-grams, which had aroused ire in Congress. By that time, however, the content of the key messages had been incorporated into the body of Navy regulations. The main elements of his "programs for people" thus survived, although future Chiefs of Naval Operations would prove less enthusiastic about implementing them. In fact, by the beginning of 1985 that most innocuous of changes, permission for sailors to wear neatly trimmed beards, had been countermanded, to the delight of barbers near naval bases everywhere. Mickey Mouse thus survived, as Zumwalt might have said, or, in the view of his opponents, tradition reasserted itself.[11]

Although most aspects of Zumwalt's racial policy were useful in the long run, his decision to lower standards to attract additional black recruits proved self-defeating, for no systematic effort was made to help them overcome their educational shortcomings. The admiral had encouraged the recruitment of blacks, but as he did so, American participation in the Vietnam fighting diminished, draft calls declined, the selective service machinery was modified, and pressures to enlist in the Navy and avoid the infantry rapidly eased. Circumstances thus forced Zumwalt to accept blacks with poor records of past achievement as well as low scores on the aptitude tests. Unfortunately, test scores remained the key to training and assignment despite the admiral's lack of confidence in their validity. Those blacks with poor scores and native ability could not benefit from enlisting because the remedial training was not available that might have enabled them to compensate for their lack of formal schooling. Although farsighted in trying to broaden the racial composition of the service, the Chief of Naval Operations had failed to take into account the need of many black recruits for some form of remedial education. Why Zumwalt neglected this is not clear; perhaps the Navy simply was not equipped to provide the necessary instruction on so large a scale. Whatever the circumstances, the lack of potential for promotion or specialized training contributed to the alienation of those blacks who had rebelled against authority on the *Kitty Hawk*, *Hassayampa*, and *Constellation*. The circumstances surrounding the uprisings on board the three ships—sailors marginally qualified for the naval service, the ready use of racial slurs by both blacks and whites, and the pressures of war—resulted in light sentences or transfers to other duties, but Zumwalt approved a quiet effort to cull out those recently enlisted blacks whose test scores indicated that they lacked the aptitude for advancement. The practice of issuing administrative discharges under honorable conditions, which had contributed to the trouble on the *Constellation*, continued afterward, although administered with greater discretion.[12]

The Army, too, had been seeking to educate its troops to the need for racial harmony in the ranks. The Commanding General, U.S. Army, Europe, General Michael E. Davison, attempted to restore discipline and amity between the races to a command where morale and efficiency had declined. By the summer of 1971, racial relations had so deteriorated that a civilian attorney from New York City, Stanley Faulkner, could employ a unique defense to obtain the freedom of two black soldiers, Sergeant Ronald Bolden and Specialist Fourth Class Samuel Robertson, accused of absence without official leave. Faulkner proved that the treatment they had received from white soldiers forced them to flee. Whereas the prosecution hammered away at the fact of the offense, the defense attorney emphasized mitigating circumstances, such as the knowledge by the defendants of instances of suicide or mental breakdown by blacks subjected to racial harassment while serving in Europe. A special court-martial, of which only one member was a black, decided that the occurrence of suicide or breakdown was frequent enough to explain the decision to escape and found Robertson not guilty. Charges against Bolden were dropped.

In November 1971, General Davison launched his program of education, an effort in which he was assisted by Major General F. E. Davison, the second highest-ranking black in the Army, who was now a staff officer in West Germany. First on the agenda was an interracial meeting at Berchtesgaden, once Hitler's lair, during which representatives of the National Association for the Advancement of Colored People and the Urban League called attention to the flawed administration of justice in the European Command. A human relations program promptly got under way, with emphasis on formal instruction, seminars, human relations councils, and the exchange of views among members of different races.[13]

The American forces in Europe kept close watch over the results of these efforts and by the spring of 1973 could report some encouraging results. Surveys of the attitudes of servicemen stationed in Europe revealed that they were becoming increasingly aware of the Army's commitment to equality of treatment and opportunity. Furthermore, the affirmative or negative responses of the soldiers to specific questions showed a tendency to trust, or at least not distrust, members of a different race. Two or more blacks no longer constituted a potential riot in the view of whites, and blacks realized that groups of whites did not laugh exclusively at racial jokes. On the other hand, the instructor seemed to be supplanting the commanding officer in the field of race relations, so that some soldiers came to believe that their leaders were less actively concerned than before with equal treatment and opportunity. Also, blacks and whites for the most part continued to congregate off duty in groups that were racially exclusive, though no longer as overtly antagonistic toward each other as before.[14]

The Marine Corps did not lag behind the other services in trying to eliminate the remaining vestiges of racism. During 1972, the Commandant, General Robert E. Cushman, Jr., declared that racial discrimination had no place in the corps and demonstrated that he meant what he said. In short, he did what the Gesell Committee had recommended almost a decade before; he banned race as a consideration in the assignment of quarters, the selection of individuals for work details, or the administration of justice. General Cushman also directed commanding officers to demand equal treatment regardless of race in bars, restaurants, and other businesses frequented by off-duty marines. Given the obvious fact that the recommendations of the Gesell Committee had never really been carried out, compliance with General Cushman's directive was going to require careful and persistent monitoring.[15]

Race relations within the armed forces were improving as the military and naval authorities, through educational efforts and other programs, tried to convince servicemen of the adverse effect of racism on efficient operation. The senior officials now realized that the individual who could not accept as equals, or at the very least tolerate, members of other races had no place in the ranks, as General Cushman had declared with regard to the Marine Corps. In encouraging cooperation between the races, the military emphasized upon the actions of individual servicemen or civilians, whether seeking to adjust racial attitudes through education, to punish uniformed offenders, or to exert pressure for nondiscrimination on civilian businessmen. The question now arose whether there existed another form of racism, not attributable to any person or persons, but endemic to the armed forces as an institution.

Institutional racism seemed to have an especially pronounced effect upon the administration of military justice. Such, at least, was the judgment of the majority of the members of a task force charged by Secretary of Defense Laird with investigating the administration of justice in the armed services. This majority included of all the panel's blacks: Adolph Holmes of the Urban League, Nathaniel R. Jones of the National Association for the Advancement of Colored People, attorneys W. Haywood Burns and Joseph C. Howard, and Patricia Ann King, the deputy director of the Office of Civil Rights, Department of Health, Education, and Welfare. They joined forces with three whites to argue that there existed two kinds of racial discrimination, which they called *"intentional* and *systemic."* The intentional type they defined as "the policy of a military authority or action of an individual or group of individuals which is intended to have a negative effect on minority individuals or groups without having such an effect on others." In contrast, systemic discrimination consisted of "neutral practices or policies which disproportionately impact harmfully or negatively on minorities." The majority report was pointing out that discrimination need not originate from prejudiced individuals or avowedly racist policies; the impersonal workings of the system could produce the same effect.[16]

Systemic discrimination, the report of the majority of the members of task force concluded, seemed especially prevalent in the administration of justice. Statistics indicated that blacks were more likely than whites to run afoul of regulations. Furthermore, black servicemen had the greater probability of undergoing trial by court-martial, being confined before the trial, being convicted, and receiving long sentences. Blacks also were more likely to receive the sort of administrative discharge that had figured in the *Constellation* incident and to come before a captain's mast where they faced nonjudicial punishment, administered on the authority of the commanding officer for comparatively minor offenses. The statistical disparity, a minority's being involved in far more than its share of disciplinary proceedings, existed despite what the task force agreed was a genuine effort on the part of the armed forces to ensure equal treatment.[17]

The malfunctioning of the justice system, a majority of the task force believed, resulted from the systemic racial discrimination that pervaded American society. The instinctive responses of many teachers, policemen, school administrators, and employers created and nourished this form of racism, not the deliberate actions of prejudiced individuals. Indeed, some of those whites who unthinkingly discriminated against blacks could actually believe that they were being helpful, much as key military leaders had sought to help blacks during the 1920s and 1930s by shielding them from competition with whites. In a recent study of urban violence, Otto Kerner, a former Governor of Illinois, had declared that two societies were emerging in the United States, "one black, one white; separate and unequal." The differences in education, economic opportunity, and identification with society as a whole resulted in a self-conscious-ness among blacks that heightened racial tensions. Blacks clung to symbols—the Afro haircut, ritual handshakes, and the use of street talk—that reinforced their own identity but tended to infuriate whites, many of whom had absorbed before entering the service a growing resentment of programs designed specifically to expand the economic or educational horizons of blacks. A decade after *Brown vs. Board of Education*, the racial integration of the public schools, especially if it involved mass transfers of white students, divided en-tire cities, and cries of reverse discrimination greeted attempts to compensate for years of injustice by training blacks for skilled or supervisory jobs. At some posts, white soldiers followed the exam-ple of their civilian counterparts and adopted their own rituals, call-ing for the exercise of "white power."

In the armed forces, the difference in average education be-tween blacks and whites proved decisive. Since assignments and ac-cess to technical training depended so heavily upon test scores, the black graduate of a second-rate school remained at a disadvantage from the moment he donned the uniform. Lack of opportunity, moreover, served to feed his sense of alienation and encourage him to band together with others of his race, who also had scant prospects for advancement, and to defy predominantly white au-thority.[18]

Although aware that the armed services could not be entirely free of racism as long as society in general remained infected, the majority of the panel suggested a means of addressing the phenome-non as it appeared among men and women in uniform. First off, said the report of the task force, the Department of Defense should do more of what it had been doing. The current campaign of education, for example, had demonstrated its value, but the administrative ma-chinery behind it seemed in need of overhaul. Specifically, the Dep-uty Assistant Secretary of Defense (Equal Opportunity) should be-come a full-fledged assistant secretary, and the Defense Race Relations Institute should improve the quality of the instructors it was producing and expand its curriculum to include, among other things, the subject of military justice. Furthermore, in choosing among candidates for technical training, the services should take into account experience and interest, as well as test scores; such a change could help blacks overcome the educational disadvantage that embittered so many of them.

Addressing the subject of military justice per se, the report called for some general reforms to include better training for members of the judge advocate organizations, uniformity of punishment in the various kinds of proceedings, and greater emphasis on the rights of the accused. For example, before receiving nonjudicial punishment, the defendant would have access to counsel, and all administrative or punitive discharges would undergo review for evidence of racial discrimination.[19]

The report of the task force also pointed out that minorities other than blacks could be victims of discrimination. Hispanic-Americans, for instance, formed the second largest minority in the United States, and prejudice toward them clearly existed. Nevertheless, the Department of Defense had failed to devise a program designed to meet their needs. In many aspects of life in the armed services, language was proving the same barrier for Hispanic-Americans that education did for blacks; individuals whose principal language was not English fared poorly on aptitude tests and could not obtain the sort of career counseling they obviously needed.[20]

As if to demonstrate the divisiveness of the racial issue, five members of the task force, all whites, took sharp exception to the findings of the majority, which consisted of all five of the groups's blacks and three whites. The dissenters were Stanley C. Blair, a federal judge, James V. Bennett, the retired director of the federal prison system, Rear Admiral Merlin H. Staring, Judge Advocate General of the Navy, Major General George S. Prugh, the Army's Judge Advocate General, and Brigadier General Clyde R. Marin, the principal legal officer of the Marine Corps. They objected to the idea that an institution could be tainted by racism. For them systemic racism simply did not exist; every instance of discrimination had to be the fault of an individual. Racism, all five agreed, had to be eliminated from the armed forces but this could be done only by holding individuals responsible for carrying out official directives.[21]

For the present, the Department of Defense could not accept the view that it could be guilty of institutional racism, as became apparent when the principal recommendations of the majority were ignored. By the end of the decade, the Defense Race Relations Institute would be offering instruction on how to overcome systemic discrimination, but for the present the minority view tended to prevail. Far from becoming an assistant secretary, the official in charge of equal opportunity within the Office of the Secretary of Defense found himself demoted to the status of a division chief and grouped with the person responsible for safety policy in the Office of the Deputy Assistant Secretary of Defense for Equal Opportunity and Safety Policy, itself a component of the Office of the Assistant Secretary (Manpower, Reserve Affairs, and Logistics). Nor did the authorities see any need to modify the review process for discharges or the procedures for nonjudicial punishment.[22]

Racial discrimination persisted, although in a diminished form. The efforts of Martin Luther King, Jr., President Johnson, and others had not exorcised the demon from civil life, nor had President Truman, Judges Fahy and Gesell, or Admiral Zumwalt imposed a thoroughgoing racial integration on the armed forces. The solutions tried by the Department of Defense had worked to a great extent, but racial discrimination still affected to varying degrees the administration of justice, promotions, and assignments. The military had reacted to a succession of crises, usually by creating some bureaucratic mechanism to monitor progress or to change attitudes through directives and education. Unfortunately, the programs generated more self-satisfaction than enduring change; certainly a mood of overconfidence contributed to the tendency to place the civil rights function at progressively lower levels within the Office of the Secretary of Defense.

Nevertheless, racial friction abated within the armed forces, more as the result of the quality of recruits than because of any program. During the 1970s, the very nature of the military changed. Not only did the Vietnam War end in a cease-fire and an American withdrawal, the Selective Service System gave way to all-volunteer armed forces (although registration for the draft was revived). Would the Department of Defense in this new atmosphere retain an interest in equality of treatment and opportunity? If not, protecting the civil rights of black men and women in uniform could easily succumb to other concerns.

21

Volunteers, Racial Representation, and the Tipping Point

THE RIOT at Travis Air Force Base in 1971 lent new urgency to a program of education designed to promote interracial understanding and, along with other reforms, prevent future outbursts of this sort. As the program gathered momentum, racial violence became less and less frequent. It appeared on the surface, especially to those within the defense establishment who were administering the program, that men and women in uniform were learning to substitute cooperation for instinctive hatred and getting along for the good of themselves and their service. Following up on an effort that began in earnest with President Truman and the Fahy Committee and continued under Presidents Kennedy and Johnson with the Gesell Committee, the Defense Race Relations Institute clearly helped to eliminate the most blatant forms of racial discrimination from the military.

Despite obvious progress, a certain cynicism persisted among blacks regarding the impartiality of military justice, an indication that the succession of directives, committees, and programs had not done all that was expected of them. But however imperfect the system of justice might be, racial calm gradually descended upon the armed forces. This harmony resulted not only from the education program and other official efforts but also from the shift from draftees to volunteers.

When a serious attempt to replace selective service began shortly after the inauguration of President Nixon in 1969, race relations were at best a minor consideration. The new Chief Executive was preoccupied with ending the Vietnam War, which he viewed as the greatest single source of turmoil within American society. When his initial efforts to negotiate a settlement were rebuffed by the North Vietnamese, he decided to do something about the draft, an especially irritating aspect of the conflict, since it demanded unequal sacrifice from the different social and economic classes. Many white college students employed a variety of tricks to avoid a potentially fatal interruption to their planned careers—faking homosexuality or drug addiction, continuing their studies abroad, or enrolling in a school of theology with no intention of ever completing the course of study. The poor and less educated could not escape in this fashion, and they resented serving while others avoided the petty harassment and mortal danger.

Although draft-age youth were more or less united in their contempt for the draft, many veterans of previous wars, especially the members of labor unions and veterans' organizations, whose support the President had courted, focused their wrath on those who dodged the draft, in particular those who fled to Canada. As a result, Mr. Nixon had to move carefully to avoid giving the appearance of slighting those who had entered the armed forces through selective service in other wars. His cautious first step toward abolishing the draft was to appoint a commission, headed by Thomas S. Gates, Jr., a Secretary of Defense when Nixon was Eisenhower's Vice President, that was charged with developing "a comprehensive plan for eliminating conscription and moving toward an all-volunteer armed force."[1]

Commissions move slowly, however, and on May 13, 1969, some six weeks after the Gates Commission began its deliberations, Nixon decided that circumstances compelled him to take a stronger stand. He therefore asked the Congress to amend the existing draft law to "limit the disruption caused by the system and to make it as fair as possible." Specifically, the President wanted random selection, beginning with the youngest eligibles during a clearly defined period of "vulnerability," in which a person could be inducted, and consistent rules for granting deferments. He sought to retain the student deferment for both graduate students and undergraduates and to postpone the period of greatest vulnerability until the deferment had expired. He thus made it clear to veterans of other wars that his quarrel was with the administration of the law and not the process itself.[2]

Scarcely had the Chief Executive issued this call when events in South Vietnam intensified opposition to the war and to the draft. During a series of assaults on Dong Ap Bia, a fortified mountaintop overlooking the A Shau Valley, thirty-seven American soliders were killed and a hundred wounded. The survivors of what they considered a meat grinder of an operation took to calling the height Hamburger Hill, a name that reporters picked up and repeated in their accounts of the action. Since this latest thrust into the A Shau Valley had been designed to disrupt the flow of supplies and destroy cargo stored there, the assault troops withdrew immediately after the battle.[3]

Reports of the action in which Dong Ap Bia had been gained at great cost and then abandoned rekindled opposition to the war in Congress. Edward M. Kennedy, brother of the murdered President and now a senator from Massachusetts, urged Mr. Nixon to put an end to operations like these, branding the assault on Hamburger Hill "senseless and irresponsible." Assuming that the United States was seeking a negotiated settlement rather than victory, the Democrat from Massachusetts asked, "How then can we justify sending our boys against a hill a dozen times or more until soldiers themselves question the madness of the action?"[4]

Spokesmen for the administration criticized Kennedy for second-guessing the commander in the field.[5] The President, however, took pains to clarify the rules under which General Creighton Abrams was fighting the war. During a visit to South Vietnam in July 1969, Mr. Nixon, as he later told the American people, advised his commander in that country that "the primary mission of our troops is to enable the South Vietnamese forces to assume full responsibility for the security of South Vietnam."[6]

The modified instructions reflected the President's determination to Vietnamize the war by turning over progressively more of the fighting to South Vietnamese troops. The policy of Vietnamization required the substitution of air power for American ground forces as a means of protecting the South Vietnamese as they acquired additional weapons and learned to use them. The adoption of a policy that might be described as fighting without looking for a fight helped reduce American casualties as Vietnamization took hold, enabling the Chief Executive to begin withdrawing ground units to the United States. Since the Air Force had not resorted to the Selective Service System, the use of air power to safeguard Vietnamization meant that the American share of the fighting would be done mainly by professional officers and enlisted volunteers rather than by draftees, and casualties among draftees tended to have greater repercussions, political and emotional, than losses among volunteers or career servicemen.

Thanks to Vietnamization, the increasing use of American air power, and the diminishing involvement of American ground forces, the military no longer needed large numbers of inductees. By the time Congress, in November 1969, got around to replacing the Selective Service System with the kind of lottery that Mr. Nixon had proposed some six months earlier, the President had reduced the authorized American strength in South Vietnam by more than 65,000. From 549,000 in the spring of the year, the maximum number assigned there during the course of the conflict, the total declined to 484,000, establishing a trend that continued for the remainder of the war. Casualties, too, declined in number over the coming months, except during the American invasion of Cambodia in the spring of 1970, an action that President Nixon described as being necessary to prevent still greater loss of American lives in the future. The advance into Cambodia and the resultant casualties triggered antiwar demonstrations in the streets and in the legislative branch another flurry of opposition to the war.[7]

In January 1970, during the lull in the fighting in Southeast Asia that continued until the incursion into Cambodia, the Gates Commission submitted its report. "We unanimously believe," the members declared, "that the nation's interests will be better served by an all-volunteer force, supported by an effective stand-by draft, than a mixed force of volunteers and conscripts." At this point, eighteen months before the riot at Travis Air Force Base, the question of race surfaced only to be dismissed out of hand. The report suggested that aside from costs the most controversial aspect of the proposed force would be its probable racial composition. The commission flatly denied that armed forces made up exclusively of volunteers would attract a disproportionate share of blacks. "Our best projections," the members concluded, "indicate that the composition of the armed forces will not be fundamentally changed by ending conscription." Instead of the current 10.6 percent, the proportion of blacks in the enlisted grades would not exceed 15 percent. The greatest concentration would continue to serve in the Army, with the percentage among enlisted men increasing from 12.8 to 19.

Applying the principle of a free market to service in the uniform of the United States, President Nixon's appointees found "service by free choice" inherently better than compulsory service. "With conscription," their report declared, "some blacks are compelled to serve at earnings below what they would earn in the civilian economy," whereas the volunteer freely struck a bargain, exchanging his services for remuneration in terms of pay, training, and travel. Under the new system, therefore, the black volunteer should see military service as an opportunity rather than a burden. "Denial of this opportunity," Gates and his associates warned, "would reflect either bias or a paternalistic belief that blacks are not capable of making the 'right' decisions concerning their lives." In short, blacks deserved the right to take advantage of military service if they so desired, but it seemed unlikely that they would exercise this right in sufficient numbers to have a marked effect on the present racial balance.[8]

Although the right of blacks to serve was linked to the assumption that they would not do so in disconcertingly large numbers, the obvious belief that the armed forces should be predominately white passed largely unchallenged by civil rights organizations. Far from questioning this premise, students of the American military merely asked whether the current racial balance, which they considered satisfactory, would prevail when volunteers replaced inductees. A "think tank," the Institute for Defense Analyses, suggested that black high school graduates could earn more in uniform than in the civilian jobs normally available to them and that anyone without a high school diploma would also be better off in the armed forces. Since young blacks had proved more likely than whites to leave school without graduating, these drop-outs would find military service especially attractive; they would join black high school graduates in the ranks, and the racial composition of the armed services would be affected accordingly. Assuming as the Gates Commission had that individuals would act in their own monetary interest, the Institute for Defense Analyses predicted that the all-volunteer military would attract a large number of blacks, members of other minorities with poor prospects for civilian employment, and the least educated of whites.[9]

Although the Selective Service System had never drawn upon a real cross-section of American youth, tending to ignore the wealthiest and best educated and focus upon working-class high school graduates, it had paid direct or indirect dividends to all the armed forces, even those components, like the Air Force during the Vietnam conflict, that did not happen to be accepting draftees. Not only did the draftees swell the ranks of the combat arms, the threat of becoming an infantryman or a marine inspired qualified individuals to enlist in the other services or for technical specialties within the Army. Now the armed forces had to find a way to attract volunteers and, because the investment in them would be greater, to retain them beyond the first enlistment, relying upon bonuses in those specialties that were considered essential or difficult to fill. The programs may have varied somewhat, but all the services panicked at first and tinkered at least briefly with disciplinary measures and standards for enlistment, softening the former and lowering the latter. This process began in 1971, when Vietnamization and the withdrawal of American ground forces from Southeast Asia resulted in smaller draft calls and eased the pressure to enlist for duty less dangerous than infantry combat. Concessions made by the Air Force may have contributed to the outburst of violence at Travis Air Force Base. Speaking for the Navy, Admiral Zumwalt acknowledged his error in lowering admission standards without adopting some form of training to compensate for the educational deficiencies among the new recruits, a mistake that contributed to the incidents on the *Hassayampa, Constellation,* and *Kitty Hawk* during 1972. The Army embarked on a slick advertising campaign that declared, "Today's Army wants to join you," and, as the slogan implied, lowered recruiting standards and relaxed discipline. (The Marine Corps persisted, however, in its search for "a few good men.") By the time the draft ended, reverting in 1973 to standby status, the services had realized that discipline had to be maintained and that councils and committees, although helpful in easing racial tensions and otherwise promoting harmony within a unit, could not shoulder the responsibilities that rightly devolved upon the commander.[10]

The declining reliance on the draft and the decision early in 1973 to shelve the Selective Service System, except as an emergency source of manpower in the future, had a greater impact on the racial composition of the armed forces than the Gates Commission had anticipated. By June 1974, even though the services were becoming more demanding in terms of recruitment and discipline, the black share of the enlisted force already approximated the 15 percent for the armed forces and 19 percent for the Army that the group had predicted; the figures were 14.9 percent for the defense establishment as a whole and 19.9 percent in the Army. The percentage of black enlisted men in the Air Force had increased from 12.3 in 1971 to 13.8, the Navy from 5.4 to 8.1, and the Marine Corps from 11.4 to 17.7.

A racial breakdown of enlistees indicated that the trend would continue. In April 1974, for instance, only the Navy, in which blacks made up 11 percent of the first-term volunteers, was attracting members of that race in proportion to their share of the populace. In the Army 27 percent of the new recruits enlisting that month were blacks, in the Marine Corps 20 percent, and in the Air Force 16. The statistics on reenlistment offered further evidence of the changing racial composition of the armed forces. During the year ending on June 30, 1973, for example, 52 percent of the soldiers signing on for a second enlistment were blacks.

In the face of this influx of blacks, the armed forces continued the programs of education and communication that had been adopted before the draft ended, and these efforts seemed to be paying off. Their success, however, resulted at least in part from the type of volunteers that the services were attracting. Compared with the draftees inducted during the latter stages of the Vietnam War, the black volunteers were less likely to be streetwise advocates of black power who would take offense at injustices, real or imagined, and lash out violently. Similarly, the white volunteer tended to be more interested in making a success of his time in the service than the draftees of a few years before and therefore more willing to make accommodations with blacks instead of engaging in harassment and even violence. Despite the calm, though, not every source of friction had been removed, especially in promotions and the administration of justice.

Although problems like these lingered, the reaction among black civilians remained muted. This lack of response stemmed in part from President Nixon's efforts to use race as a wedge to sunder the Democratic Party. Seizing upon an issue that divided whites from blacks, he proposed restrictions on the busing of students to achieve racial balance in the schools and on racial quotas in hiring. He enjoyed some success in setting the various components of the Democratic coalition—principally blacks and blue-collar workers—against each other. Since the political power of black Americans was being threatened, eliminating the vestiges of racial discrimination from the armed forces seemed a peripheral issue.

In a period of interracial quiet, with little pressure being exerted by the black community, the armed forces tended to worry about abstractions instead of moving decisively against the remaining sources of racial friction among men and women in uniform. A topic that received disproportionate study was "the tipping point." Some students of human behavior, examining the question of racial integration in housing, had concluded that when the proportion of blacks in a development or neighborhood reached a certain percentage, the remaining whites would flee. Obviously, the preference of whites to live among their own, provided no unacceptable sacrifices were necessary, played a part in the "white flight" from racially mixed cities to racially exclusive suburbs. Other factors—some the result of intentional discrimination, others due to systemic forces—proved influential, however. These included manipulation by real estate speculators, the general noise level, the upkeep of houses, and the tendency of some local governments to scrimp on public education and other services in areas into which large numbers of blacks were moving. Simplistic though it was as an explanation of changing patterns in housing, personnel planners tried to apply the concept to military service, raising the possibility that an Army 30 or 35 percent black might fail to attract white volunteers and forfeit the support of a predominately white society. The prophets of doom foretold a black Army that, racially speaking, was a foreign legion defending white America.[11]

If a tipping point did exist and was applicable to the armed forces, it was rapidly coming within reach. By 1976, the proportion of blacks in the different services had increased still further. Blacks now made up 16.6 percent of all enlisted men and 3.4 percent of the entire officer corps. Again the Army had the greatest concentration, 23.7 percent of its enlisted strength and 5.2 percent of its officers. The proportion of blacks in the Marine Corps reached 3.5 percent of the officers, and 17 percent of the enlisted men were black. The Air Force's percentages were 14.7 for enlisted men and 2.8 for officers; the Navy's blacks comprised just 8 percent of the enlisted force and 1.6 percent of the officers.

The apparently inexorable advance continued. In 1978 blacks made up 18.4 percent of the aggregate enlisted strength of the military establishment. In the Army, 27.5 percent of the enlisted men were blacks, in the Marine Corps 17.9 percent, in the Air Force 14.7 percent, and in the Navy 9 percent. (Incredibly, the Navy was just now approaching the goal of an enlisted force 10 percent black that it had established for itself in 1945.) The proportion of black officers had increased slightly since 1976, from 3.4 percent to 4 percent for the entire Department of Defense. Once again the greatest share was in the Army, where blacks formed 6.4 percent of the commissioned strength.[12]

By 1981, signs appeared that the tipping point had been reached in the Army, if not in the other services. The Army's enlisted strength was now 33.2 percent black, the Navy's 12 percent, that of the Marine Corps 22 percent, and the Air Force's 14.4 percent, for an overall percentage of 19.8. Evidence of renewed Ku Klux Klan activity was surfacing at military posts, and Secretary of the Army Martin R. Hoffman reported that in recent months his service had been forced to reconstitute its cadre of noncommissioned officers, presumably because of retirements or refusals to reenlist by whites who objected to the influx of blacks.

Many of those whites who left the Army in 1979 or 1980 had served during the late 1960s when racial clashes were frequent and violent, and their attitudes had hardened at that time. They viewed change in racial policies as surrender to black militants and could not believe that the latest black recruits did not exchange clenched-fist salutes and preach black power. The Army's reaching the tipping point, far from undermining the institution as some critics had feared, served mainly to purge the service of many whites whose prejudices kept them from tolerating blacks, let alone working with them in the new all-volunteer force.[13]

Unlike the enlisted component, the officer corps of all the armed forces remained overwhelmingly white. Any tipping point for officers lay far in the distant future. When the 1970s came to an end, blacks made up just 5.3 percent of the aggregate commissioned strength—7.8 percent in the Army, 2.7 percent in the Navy, 4 percent in the Marine Corps, and 4.8 percent in the Air Force. In short, although black recruits were enlisting with greater enthusiasm than the Gates Commission had predicted, the programs for attracting black officers were by comparison moving only fitfully toward objectives generally stated in vague terms such as greater representation on the part of blacks. Only the Air Force had announced a definite proportion as a goal; that service was just 0.8 percent short of its self-imposed objective of an officer corps 5.6 percent black. The proportion of black officers in the Navy had increased ninefold since 1964 but nevertheless fell short of 3 percent. Even the Army, although it had more than doubled its percentage of black officers since 1964, had an officer corps that was more than 90 percent white.[14]

Instead of brooding about tipping points, the services should have addressed the actual problems that remained. The Army should have made a systematic effort to educate its white noncommissioned officers to accept the racial composition of the volunteer force, and the Navy, Marine Corps, and Air Force should have tried harder to attract black officers. Unfortunately, programs dealing with racial matters no longer seemed as important as before because of the prevailing racial calm, and the machinery designed to ensure equal treatment and opportunity for black servicemen was losing momentum.

When applied to the armed services, the concept of a tipping point proved to be a myth. Economic self-interest and not race caused whites to avoid the recruiting office for much of the 1970s. As long as the American economy was functioning smoothly, the young white was likely to find a civilian job that seemed more attractive than anything the services could offer. Not so his black counterpart, who was therefore more willing to subject himself to the demands of life in the armed forces in return for the combination of pay, allowances, and the promise of training and travel.[15]

In its projections of the racial composition of the all-volunteer armed services, the Institute for Defense Analyses had proved more accurate than the Gates Commission. The Institute was wrong, however, in predicting that the military would become a magnet attracting ill-educated youth unable to succeed in civilian life. Once the draft ended, the number of black high school graduates to enlist steadily increased between 1974 and 1977, the proportion of black recruits with diplomas rising from 47 to 65 percent. Despite the large proportion of young blacks who dropped out of high school, the military was getting black high school graduates, the best of their group, well-motivated men and women who, as the Gates Commission had suggested, looked upon military service as an opportunity. Similarly, the whites enlisting for the first time included a slightly greater proportion of high school graduates, in part the result of a policy that demanded higher test scores from drop-outs than from graduates, regardless of race. While the proportion of black high school graduates entering the service increased by some 18 percentage points during the three years ending in 1977, the proportion of white recruits with the same educational attainments rose from 47 to 53 percent, a smaller increase but an increase nonetheless. At the same time, service in the armed forces had become the only occupation that was attracting blacks with more education than their white counterparts.[16]

Although the proportion of blacks in the military was increasing, they remained a minority, and they encountered many of the same difficulties they had experienced before the coming of the all-volunteer force. The system of military justice remained the source of frequent complaints. Blacks, for example, made up half the prisoners locked up in Army jails, a percentage drastically out of proportion to their representation in the service. Furthermore, black enlisted men, regardless of the uniform they wore, were more likely than whites to be convicted of unauthorized absence, an offense less serious than desertion. Whereas the blacks tended to stay away for a short time, going absent without leave and returning to duty or overstaying a leave, an unusually large number of whites remained away long enough to be classified as deserters. The Navy, with comparatively few black sailors, had a desertion rate during 1977 of 3.16 per hundred that harkened back to the days of sail, salt pork, and wormy biscuit. Indeed, the desertion rate among all the services was high in comparison to the most recent period of extended peace. Male volunteers proved more likely than women to become fed up with military life and desert or go over the hill for a short time. Among women, blacks proved less willing to commit these offenses. This jumble of statistics raised more questions than it answered; race clearly was a factor, but the numbers could not reveal the extent of its influence.[17]

Besides being less likely to desert than the white serviceman, the black man or woman in uniform proved statistically more certain of successfully completing the term of enlistment. This trait was probably a function of education. In general, the person who had failed to persevere through high school stood a greater chance of rebelling against discipline and failing to honor his commitment to the service. Since a greater proportion of blacks held high school diplomas, they were a better bet than white enlistees to fulfill their voluntary obligation.[18]

While the defense establishment had fretted about the tipping point, circumstances had presented the military with an enlisted force stable in comparison to the draftees of the Vietnam War era, largely unaffected by notions of black power or white power, and possessing the aptitude for complex and highly technical jobs. Then, instead of making that force even better by finally addressing the surviving inequities in the administration of justice or in selection for promotion, the defense analysts went chasing after yet another phantom. This one, first noticed by 1980, was called "overrepresentation."

According to its discoverers, most of them whites, the overrepresentation of blacks in the armed forces seemed likely to have damaging effects upon black recruits. Traditionally members of this minority had viewed military service as a vehicle for economic betterment, and for individuals, though not always for the race as a whole, it tended to be one. Yet to perform the function of economic advancement (or so the argument ran), military society had to reflect, insofar as possible given the necessary regimentation and discipline, the widely shared values and customs of American society. As the percentage of blacks increased, however, military society came to reflect one specific component of American life, instead of mirroring society as a whole, thus tending to reinforce rather than broaden the outlook that black recruits brought with them into the armed forces.[19]

A corollary to this argument held that in the event the all-volunteer armed forces had to fight a war, black Americans would suffer a disproportionate share of the casualties. This was another consequence of overrepresentation, especially in the Army. Some observers believed that the imbalance would be far more pronounced than during the Vietnam conflict, when blacks made up 13 percent of the casualty list for the entire war. Indeed, the losses among black troops at the outset of a similar war might be half again as great as the 21 percent during the bloodiest fighting in 1968 and 1969 that marked the worst toll suffered by blacks during any phase of the fighting in Southeast Asia.[20]

The whole issue of overrepresentation struck few responsive chords among prominent blacks. Shirley Chisholm, at the time a member of Congress from New York City, voiced her suspicion that crocodile tears over unequal sacrifice on the part of blacks were being shed by those who preferred an Army that was comfortably white.[21] Addressing the topic of casualties, former Secretary of the Army Clifford L. Alexander, Jr., suggested that given the current racial composition of the United States Navy, a naval campaign like the recent struggle between Britain and Argentina in the waters off the Falkland Islands could produce a casualty list that was overwhelmingly white. In Alexander's opinion, fear that black civilians might react violently to losses in some future war or that black troops might refuse certain kinds of duty—whether restoring order in the cities or going to the aid of a repressive white government in South Africa—reflected racism on the part of those whites who shared this concern.[22]

What did concern blacks was the persistent racism blacks in the armed forces had to put up with. As late as 1983, for example, a reporter from the *Chicago Tribune* found that nightclubs in West Germany turned away black American soldiers but admitted whites, this despite the fact that commanders were supposed to be using their influence with civil authorities to prevent racial discrimination. The number of complaints of racial discrimination had declined from the previous year, possibly because they were not followed up aggressively. On the other hand, an occasional club owner insisted that he preferred blacks as patrons, having concluded that they tended to behave better than whites. In this area of race relations, jealousy played a role too, in that German men resented having to compete for local women with well-paid American soldiers, especially the blacks, for over the years Germans had been infected with a bias against blacks. Another source of the resentment felt by Germans was the refusal of most American soldiers, regardless of race, to learn the language or the customs of the country.[23]

Nor had unqualified success crowned the efforts over the years to ensure equal treatment and opportunity for civilian employees of the Department of Defense. In November 1983, for instance, the Virginia chapter of the Southern Christian Leadership Conference—a civil rights organization that could trace its history to Martin Luther King, Jr., and the Montgomery bus boycott—protested that supervisors at the Quantico Marine Base, the largest employer in Prince William County, habitually discriminated against blacks and women who were eligible for promotion. Admittedly, the overwhelming proportion of blacks worked as custodians, laborers, or drivers, and white men held a near monopoly on professional and administrative jobs. Race may not, however, have been the only con-

sideration, for professional jobs usually required a college education, possibly an advanced degree, and white males were the likeliest to fulfill this requirement.[24]

The greatest source of complaints by civil rights advocates continued to be the administration of justice. The belief that the armed
forces unjustly imposed the white man's rules on black servicemen,
which could trace its origins at least as far as the executions following the Houston riot and the mass discharges after the Brownsville
incident, still seemed valid. The task force that investigated the administration of military justice for Secretary Laird in the early
1970s had dramatized, by its lack of unanimity, a sharp division between blacks and whites on the question of responsibility for racial
discrimination. Those who opposed reforms based on the concept of
systemic discrimination had all been whites, whereas all the blacks
had favored such changes. The issue of injustice persisted, however,
into the era of the all-volunteer force.

For example, the same civil rights organization that had protested racial discrimination in the work force at Quantico, the Virginia chapter of the Southern Christian Leadership Conference, also
complained about the severity of the punishment meted out to a
black marine on the basis of shaky evidence.[25] The marine, Corporal
Lindsey Scott, had been convicted in October 1983 of raping the wife
of a white fellow marine, even though he did not fit the description
initially given by the victim. His counsel, a white civilian with scant
experience as a trial lawyer, staked his client's freedom on a motion
to dismiss the charges for lack of evidence and lost. Scott received a
sentence of thirty years' imprisonment. The corporal appealed the
verdict on two counts—the question of his lawyer's competence and
the appearance of a security guard willing to testify that Scott had
been at a shopping center when the crime was committed. The
court, however, challenged the credibility of the witness and concluded that the defendant had received adequate representation by
counsel. The commanding general of the Quantico Marine Base
thereupon refused to exercise his authority to call for a new trial.
The appeal then began making its way through the military appeals
system, while Scott remained in prison.[26]

Although an incident like the Scott case might capture the headlines briefly and engage the attention of a civil rights organization, it
did not send shock waves through the military. The kind of heavy-
handed racism that stirred violent protest no longer existed; it was
subtle forms of discrimination that survived. Rioting had once
shaken the Department of Defense into launching programs to improve race relations; racial harmony now lulled the armed forces

into inaction. The undertakings that were designed to improve relations through education and interracial communication gradually withered away.[27]

The disappearance of programs intended expressly to aid blacks reflected the fact that the Army and Marine Corps, and to a lesser extent the other services, had become an amalgam of whites, blacks, and Hispanic Americans, male and female.[28] The new minorities had not emerged overnight. As early as 1972, Secretary of the Air Force Seamans, though he emphasized the need for harmony between the black and white races, acknowledged, almost as an afterthought, that women deserved the same opportunities as men.[29] The following year, Secretary of Defense Laird's task force for investigating military justice took note of the existence of discrimination against Hispanic Americans.[30]

Hispanic Americans and women of every race soon became so important to the armed forces that the program of education in race relations had to be modified to address their needs. Signs of change first appeared in 1972, and the course of instruction at the Defense Race Relations Institute rapidly expanded to include study of the customs and problems not only of blacks but also of Hispanic Americans, American Indians, Asian Americans, Jews, and two categories of whites—urban, blue-collar workers and the rural residents of Appalachia. Although the course did not yet treat women as a distinct minority within the armed forces, students and instructors soon found that they had to deal with categories of women's problems that cut across racial or ethnic boundaries.

The armed services, moreover, came to accept the concept, resisted for a half-dozen years, that systemic, or institutional, racism could exist. As a result, beginning about 1978, officers responsible for the educational effort began to assume an advisory role. Graduates of the course at Patrick Air Force Base continued for a time to teach servicemen and civilian employees of the military to understand one another and also counseled drug users, alcoholics, and the like, but they devoted more and more time to advising commanders. When functioning as a special staff officer, the graduate of the training course advised the commanding officer how to recognize and correct institutional racism. Yet, even as he helped deal with the abiding problems of racial discrimination, the specialist in race relations also tended more to serve as spokesmen for the drug and alcohol rehabilitation programs.[31]

In late July 1979, the Defense Race Relations Institute became the Defense Equal Opportunity Management Institute, but the change had less to do with the shift of emphasis than with the professionalization of the program.[32] Race relations (now in the process of being broadened to human relations) had become the specialty of trained professionals, some 6,000 of whom had graduated from the institute at the Florida base during the years following the inception of the course in 1971. Gone forever was the kind of volunteer who had launched the ambitious program in which the Air Force had given formal instruction in race relations to an estimated 300,000 servicemen and 30,000 civilians. Some of these pioneers had chips on their shoulders and may have done as much harm as good, but their trained successors had subordinated personal feelings to the good of the program and done what they set out to do. They did improve race relations, although their very success led to a deemphasis of the efforts designed specifically to promote interracial understanding.

Improving race relations came to be subordinated to counseling on alcoholism and drug abuse and attempts to discourage sexual harassment, admittedly vital objectives in themselves. These various subjects formed a program of "social actions." Interests unique to Hispanic Americans or women—as well as problems like alcoholism, drug addiction, and other behavior that cut across divisions of race or sex—had supplanted the exclusive concerns of blacks as the armed forces sought to attract and retain volunteers. As the decade of the 1980s wore on, the continuing racial calm within the military, a result of reforms begun by President Truman in 1948 and enhanced in the 1980s by economic factors that enabled the services to attract stable recruits of both races, seemed to confirm the wisdom of allowing the social actions specialists to broaden their interests beyond racial discrimination.[33]

As if to dramatize the new importance of economic forces, the percentage of whites enlisting in the services began to rise. Once again the alarmists were confounded as overrepresentation went the way of the tipping point. As late as 1980, the only solution to black overrepresentation seemed to be a variant of the G.I. Bill that would attract white recruits by enabling them to exchange military service for a college education at least partially subsidized by the federal government. This bait for white recruits did not appear until 1984, due largely to congressional inaction, but educational benefits or none, the white race did not shun the Army. The change in racial composition that occurred in the first six months of 1983, when a revival of the G.I. Bill seemed unlikely, consisted in a decline of almost 2 percent in the proportion of blacks in the enlisted ranks of the armed forces.[34]

The resurgence of interest on the part of whites in military service resulted from an economic downturn that affected all youth regardless of race. Rising unemployment made military service seem more attractive, not only to young civilians but also to those men and women already in uniform. By the beginning of 1983, the reenlistment rates reached 79 percent for the Air Force, and 68 percent for the Navy. The Army, on contrast, showed a decline of 8 percentage points from 72 percent in 1982, the result of an effort to replace poorly educated soldiers with recruits who had graduated from high school.

Thanks to a faltering economy, the recruitment of men and women with high school diplomas proved even easier in the early 1980s than in the last years of the previous decade. Many graduates, both black and white, could find no civilian job that offered the combination of pay and benefits available in the armed forces. Consequently, all the services became more selective, tending to ignore the drop-out, whether white or black.

The increase in educational standards, a product of the sluggish economy, persisted into 1983. For the twelve months ending in September of that year, the Air Force could boast that 98 percent of its new recruits held high school diplomas, and the Navy 91 percent. The Marine Corps reported that 92 percent of those enlisting for the first time were high school graduates, and the Army 88 percent.

No longer dependent upon high school drop-outs, who during the late 1970s had provided so many of its white recruits, the Army raised its standards for enlistment. As the threshold rose, fewer blacks from inadequate rural or inner-city schools could attain the necessary test scores. As a result, the proportion of blacks among first-time enlistees declined from 36.7 percent in 1979 to 29.7 percent in 1980, 27.4 percent in 1981, and 24.6 percent in 1982. The same phenomenon affected all the armed forces, with the percentage of blacks among all new recruits falling from 26 percent in 1979 to 19 percent in 1982.[35]

Besides changing the racial make-up of the armed forces, the nation's economic difficulties closed this avenue of advancement for the poor and ill-educated black. As Alfonzo Blount, Jr., a young black who had dropped out of the District of Columbia school system, told a reporter for the *Washington Post*, "I think the Army should let these black kids in there. . . . When they get turned down, they got nowhere to turn to." Blount had attained a score on the standardized test that would have enabled him to enlist in 1981, but not in 1983, when economic conditions had made the Army more selective.[36]

Department of Defense officials proved reluctant to entertain the possibility that the economic recovery, which began gathering momentum in 1983 but soon showed signs of slackening, could make the services—especially the Army and the Marine Corps—the province of the least educated members of ethnic and racial minorities. In denying the connection between the economy and the quality of recruits, officials of the Reagan administration substituted flag-waving for logic. As late as November of that year, Lawrence Korb, the Assistant Secretary of Defense responsible for manpower, attributed the recent increase in the percentage of new recruits with high school diplomas to "a renewed sense of patriotism, pay and benefits . . . , and the quality of life in the service. . . ." At the time he disputed predictions that the by-then improving economy and the declining pool of potential recruits (the waning of the "baby boom" of the 1960s) might force the armed services to resort to the draft to maintain the existing educational standards.[37] Within six months, however, Korb conceded that "the Department of Defense will face an increased challenge . . . as the economy improves."[38]

Regardless of fluctuations in the economy and worries about overrepresentation and the tipping point, the proportion of black volunteers now formed a sizable minority within the military, and the recent recruits had more education and were more stable than the black draftees of the 1960s. Despite the decline in the early 1980s, since the end of conscription the proportion of black volunteers had increased in the active-duty forces, with the Navy slightly exceeding the proportion of blacks in the general populace and the other services exceeding the percentage by a factor of from 1.5 to as much as 3. The administration believed that quality could be maintained in the future as it had in the first part of the decade, regardless of the status of the economy.

In the meantime, the reserve components had undergone a racial transformation of their own. In the decade since the abolition of the draft, the long-standing apathy displayed by blacks toward serving in the reserve or National Guard had become less pronounced. By December 1982, 4.4 percent of the officers and 19.4 percent of the enlisted men in the various reserve components were blacks, for an overall proportion, including warrant officers, of 16.4 percent. As in the active-duty establishment, the Army led the way; blacks formed 23.1 percent of its organized reserve, including 6.4 percent of the officers, and 16.6 percent (5.2 percent among officers) of the National Guard. The Marine Corps Reserve also had a sizable proportion of blacks, 18.6 percent overall, though only 2.6 percent of the commissioned strength. The Air Force reported that blacks made up 14.4 percent of the reserve and 7.2 percent of the Air National Guard, including 2.6 percent of the reserve officers and 2.3 percent of those commissioned in the Guard. The Naval Reserve, like the active-duty Navy, had the smallest proportion of blacks, 8.3 percent, and just 1.4 percent of the reserve officers.

In general, the proportion of blacks in the reserve components reflected trends in the racial composition of the Army, Navy, Marine Corps, and Air Force. More blacks were enlisting in the armed forces, and a number of those who accepted discharges when their enlistments ended retained an interest in the service whose uniform they had worn. Serving alongside these veterans in the reserve were young blacks attracted by recruiting programs directed at them, especially by the Army and Marine Corps. Since the active-duty officer corps, even in the Army, included comparatively few blacks, the percentage in the reserve components also was small. Despite the lack of black officers, a decade earlier this degree of participation by blacks in the reserve and particularly in the National Guard would have triggered official rejoicing. Ten years of domestic tranquility had intervened, however, and having black National Guardsmen available to suppress black urban rioters no longer seemed so important.[39]

During the early 1980s, economic forces enhanced the attractiveness of military service and brought closer to completion a process of racial integration that had begun in colonial times, when blacks both free and slave had built stockades and cleared the muster grounds for white militiamen. Military necessity had forced blacks into the armed forces, where they performed competently, especially in the frontier Army and sailing Navy. Despite these and other examples of success, blacks were regarded as a manpower pool to be tapped only in a dire emergency. When the particular crisis passed, the contributions of blacks were forgotten and they reverted to their subsidiary role. After Jim Crow had imposed his hold on the nation, the status and effectiveness of black servicemen declined, but segregation did not survive. Blacks exerted pressure through the courts, through political organization, and through nonviolent confrontation to obtain their constitutional rights. Integration also came to the armed forces, preceding by a few years the decline of legally enforced racism in civil society. Presidential initiatives and a persisting need for manpower speeded the transition from segregation to racial integration in the military. Once a token number, often used as auxiliaries, black Americans now formed a large and reliable segment of the armed forces.

In the services and in civilian life, victories remained to be won, but in the mid-1980s the vestiges of racial discrimination in the armed forces formed a minor issue. Now manned solely by volunteers, the military tended to assume a social insularity. Gone was the interchange of attitudes between the armed forces and society at large, the exposure to new experiences and different races and social classes, that the draft had provided. The career soldier and his family could live and shop, except for making large purchases like refrigerators or automobiles, without ever leaving a military reservation, with the wife perhaps holding a job on the base. Even the children would find day-care centers, libraries, recreational programs, and entertainment within the confines of the installation; they need venture beyond the gates only to attend school. Like their counterparts in the peacetime Army of the 1920s and 1930s, the modern black volunteers became largely insulated from American society as a whole, although they were a source of interest and even pride for black civilians. The civil rights organizations retained their interest in the treatment received by black servicemen, rallying support for victims of injustice, but other issues seemed more important—among them jobs, education, and waning political power on the national, if not local, level.

Afterword

MIDWAY THROUGH THE 1980's, what were the prospects of the black serviceman? His future was largely intertwined with the fate of the all-volunteer force. Analysts of that institution no longer worried about the tipping point; white youths had not turned their backs upon the military, and the proportion of blacks among first-time enlistees was stabilizing at about 19 percent, with the Army receiving the largest share, about 25 percent. Concern persisted about the overrepresentation of blacks, who numbered about 14 percent of the total pool of young men and women eligible to enlist. Because of their large proportion, blacks in the armed forces seemed likely to reinforce their own values and experiences, wrapping themselves in a cultural blanket instead of being exposed to the usages of society as a whole. Yet even those who were troubled by this possibility had to concede that the military had never represented the overall racial, educational, and economic composition of the American people. This issue, now called "representativeness," seemed likely to go the way of the tipping point.

Regardless of the degree of representation, black Americans formed a vital element in the all-volunteer force. The greatest problem facing recruiters in the future seemed likely to be rooted in prosperity rather than race. Should the economic recovery take hold and well-paying jobs become readily available, the services would be hard pressed to maintain the current levels of aptitude and education among their enlisted men and women, whether black or white.[1]

An inevitable consequence of a military composed of volunteers was a certain isolation from civilian society. This did not mean, however, that the black populace ignored the accomplishments of servicemen like Guion S. Bluford, a lieutenant colonel in the Air Force, who became the first black astronaut. Earlier Major Robert H. Lawrence, a black officer selected to become the first of his race to train as an astronaut, had died in an airplane crash. Guy Bluford, a veteran of 144 combat missions during the war in Southeast Asia, had amassed some 3,400 hours at the controls of jet aircraft and earned advanced degrees in aeronautical engineering before entering the space program. On August 20, 1983, he thundered aloft as a member of the crew of the hundred-ton space shuttle *Challenger.* Although thoroughly detached and professional in his attitude, he nevertheless realized that he had become a model for young blacks, whom he advised to "get an education and be as prepared as you can for any opportunities that may come your way."[2]

Whereas Bluford served as an example to inspire black youth, the experiences of another black serviceman helped enhance the reputation of a leader in the civil rights movement, Rev. Jesse Jackson. On December 4, 1983, a Syrian antiaircraft-missile battery in Lebanon downed a Grumman A-6E, a Navy attack plane that was part of a mission sent to retaliate for firings at American reconnaissance craft. Although the pilot died of injuries sustained in ejecting from the burning aircraft, the electronic warfare officer, Robert O. Goodman, Jr., a black, survived and was taken prisoner by the Syrians. Concerned that Goodman might become a pawn in the confrontation between a Lebanese faction backed by the United States and the faction's rivals, supported by Syria and the Soviet Union, President Ronald Reagan (forty years earlier the narrator of the documentary about the Tuskegee airmen) avoided making the naval officer's freedom a major issue lest he thus put the captured officer in greater peril. Consequently, Donald Rumsfeld, a special envoy seeking to arrange a settlement in the region, did not mention Goodman during discussions with the Syrian leaders.

At year's end Rev. Jackson, the first black to make a bid to obtain the presidential nomination of the Democratic party, visited Syria as a private citizen and did what Rumsfeld had not tried— obtained Goodman's release. Why the Syrians yielded remains a matter of conjecture. They could have been responding to a humanitarian request or simply trying to embarrass an American President who faced a race for reelection in the near future. Although Good-

man returned to the anonymity of the Navy, the incident helped
Jackson become a political force, a symbol among blacks that for
the moment rivaled the memory of Dr. King.[3]

Lieutenant Goodman resumed his duties in a military establishment characterized by racial calm. Beginning in the late 1970s, the
functioning of the civil rights bureaucracy within the armed forces
and the programs of education designed to improve relations between blacks and whites seemed progressively less important because of this tranquility. Endeavors designed to ease tensions
involving blacks now embraced different subjects and minorities,
giving rise to the question whether the programs of communication
and the educational efforts that had once proved helpful in improving relations between blacks and whites would be diluted to the
point where they helped no one.

The eradication of the last vestiges of racial discrimination
from the armed services yielded during this period of quiet to such
objectives as improving relationships within military families and
rehabilitating drug users and alcoholics. Years of progress in race
relations had removed the worst manifestations of racism, the quality of recruits had improved, and the result was the pervasive calm
that encouraged the military to adjust its priorities. Unfortunately,
the history of race relations in the military since President Truman's integration order of 1948 teaches one inescapable lesson:
progress requires pressure, whether from elected officials, from the
demands of war, or from black American themselves. Left to its own
devices, the bureaucracy charged with ensuring equal treatment
and opportunity in the armed forces will avoid innovation, generating paperwork instead of taking decisive action. Evidence of this
tendency is the lack of response to the report of Secretary Laird's
Task Force on the Administration of Justice in the Armed Forces.
Except for the tacit admission that systemic discrimination does exist, the majority report could have gone unwritten for all it accomplished. On the other hand, policies governing promotion and
assignment, especially for enlisted men and women, placed less emphasis on race than ever before. The reform of the promotion and assignment systems did not come easy, however; it required pressure
from the Fahy and Gesell committees and a realization within each
of the services that racial bias in these matters undermined morale
and efficiency. During the late 1970s and early 1980s, this sort of
pressure eased. Energies that could have directed toward overhauling the administration of military justice focused upon theory
rather than reality. Planners worried for much of the period about
the representation of blacks in the enlisted force, the tipping point,
and casualties among blacks in some future war.

Given the preoccupation with theory and the lack of new initiatives, especially in the field of military justice, why had racial amity prevailed throughout the military? Two factors were responsible. First and more important, the really blatant forms of discrimination against blacks had ended, although certain serious problems remained, especially in the administration of military justice. Second, the caliber of recruits had changed, with the services attracting volunteers, both blacks and whites, who were better educated than the draftees of an earlier period and, unlike the servicemen of the 1940s and 1950s, had been exposed to some degree of interracial contact before taking the oath of enlistment. The contact had usually been amicable, for the slogans of the 1960s, whether calls for black power or white power, no longer echoed through the streets, and racial violence had become increasingly less common in civilian life. Instead of accepting the poor and poorly educated, the armed forces could insist on high school graduates, even seeking out the higher-ranking members of a class with some expectation of success. Given a choice between shelving their prejudices or leaving the service, recruits were electing to stay.

The principal incentives for making this choice were economic. A high rate of unemployment among young people, especially among blacks, made the armed forces seem especially attractive during the early 1980s. Should circumstances change and a soaring economy make military service less attractive (or should an emergency arise and the draft be revived), the programs for promoting racial harmony, which now seemed almost superfluous, might again assume a real urgency. Once again poorly educated blacks and whites from the bottom of the socio-economic ladder would enter the services in large numbers. Isolated as civilians from normal interracial contact, hostile toward authority and toward each other, lacking the education necessary for advancement, they would require the same combination of discipline, education, and counseling adopted to improve race relations as the Vietnam conflict was ending.

However uncertain the future in terms of programs and the acquisition of manpower, the black serviceman can look back upon more than 350 years of accomplishment. Taking advantage of limited opportunities for military service, black Americans have expanded their role, demonstrating courage afloat and ashore in defeating racism and institutionalized hostility as well as prevailing over the nation's enemies. Jim Crow, the personification of racial segregation in the United States and the most implacable of domestic foes, has been unable to withstand the bravery and dedication of black servicemen and civilians. No longer is the black sailor a seagoing servant as he was a half century ago, and thanks to the exploits of Spanky Roberts and Lucky Lester in World War II and Chappie James in Korea, no one doubts that blacks can fly military aircraft. Even the Marine Corps has reversed a policy of exclusion that lasted from its revival after the Revolutionary War until World War II, and now welcomes blacks as officers, noncommissioned officers, and enlisted men.

The armed forces of the United States cannot now reverse the process that has made blacks full partners in the racially integrated military establishment. Nor is there any incentive to do so. Racial integration, considered a dangerous social experiment as recently as the 1940s, has worked, improving the morale and efficiency of all the services.

Notes _____

Chapter 1. TOWARD A BLACK IDENTITY

1. Gary B. Nash, *Red, White, and Black: The Peoples of Early America* (Englewood Cliffs, New Jersey, paperback edition, 1974), pp. 292–293.
2. An Act of the General Assembly of the Province of South Carolina, December 22, 1703, in Morris J. MacGregor and Bernard C. Nalty, eds., *Blacks in the United States Armed Forces: Basic Documents* (Wilmington, Delaware, 1977), vol. I, item 2. All documents cited by item number in the chapter are reproduced in this volume.
3. Nash, *Red, White, and Black*, pp. 149–150.
4. Letter, Agent for Carolina and Merchants Trading Thither to the Right Honorable Lords Commissioners for Trade, July 18, 1715, item 9.
5. Nash, *Red, White, and Black*, pp. 150–151.
6. *Ibid.*, pp. 196, 293; Act of the Assembly of the Province of South Carolina for Enlisting Such Slaves as Shall Be Thought Serviceable to This Settlement in Time of Alarm, March 11, 1719, item 10; An Act of the Assembly of the Province of South Carolina for the Better Regulation of the Militia . . . , June 13, 1747, item 11; Harvey Wish, "American Slave Insurrections before 1861," in William M. Chace and Peter Collier, eds., *Justice Denied: The Black Man in White America* (New York, paperback edition, 1970), p. 84.
7. Nash, *Red, White, and Black*, p. 180; Acts of the General Assembly of Virginia, January 6, 1639, and May 9, 1723, items 1 and 12.
8. Lorenzo Johnston Greene, *The Negro in Colonial New England* (New York, paperback edition, 1974), pp. 98, 126–128, 187–190, 303; Act of the

General Court of Massachusetts, June 12, 1707; Pension Statement of George Gire, December 14, 1780, items 5 and 18; Leon F. Litwack, *North of Slavery: The Negro in the Free States, 1790–1860* (Chicago, paperback edition, 1961), p. 3.

9. Benjamin Quarles, *The Negro in the American Revolution* (Chapel Hill, North Carolina, 1961), pp. 3–8.

10. *Ibid.*, pp 9–11.

11. Letter, General John Thomas to John Adams, October 24, 1775, item 33.

12. Resolution of the Massachusetts Committee of Safety, May 20, 1775, item 20.

13. Instructions for the officers of the several Regiments of Massachusetts Bay forces . . . on recruiting duty, July 10, 1775, in Peter Force, ed., *American Archives*, series IV, vol. II (Washington, 1839), p. 1630.

14. Note of Debate in the Continental Congress, September 26, 1775, item 30.

15. Minutes of a Council of War held at Headquarters, October 8, 1775, and Minutes of a Conference with the General by a Committee of Conference, October 23, 1775, both in Force, *American Archives*, series IV, vol. III, pp. 1040, 1061.

16. Proclamation by the Governor of Virginia, November 7, 1775, in Force, *American Archives*, series IV, vol. III (Washington, 1840), p. 1385.

17. Proclamation of the people of the Colony and Dominion of Virginia, assembled in General Convention, in Force, *American Archives*, series IV, vol. IV (Washington, 1843), pp. 84–85.

18. Quarles, *The Negro in the American Revolution*, pp. 22–32; Willard M. Wallace, *Appeal to Arms: A Military History of the American Revolution* (New York, paperback edition, 1975), p. 90; *Purdie's Virginia Gazette*, July 19, 1776, in William James Morgan, ed., *Naval Documents of the American Revolution*, vol. V (Washington, 1970), pp. 1147–1151.

19. General Orders, December 30, 1775, in James C. Fitzpatrick, ed., *The Writings of George Washington from the Original Manuscript Sources* (Washington, 1931–1944), vol. IV, p. 194.

20. General Washington to the President of Congress, December 31, 1775, item 37; Quarles, *The Negro in the American Revolution*, pp. 11, 16.

21. Excerpt from the Act of the General Court of Massachusetts, January 22, 1776; Act of the Legislature of New Hampshire, September 19, 1776, items 39 and 50.

22. Letter, Lord Stirling to the President of Congress, March 14, 1776, in Force, *American Archives*, series IV, vol. V, pp. 217–218.

23. Minutes of the South Carolina Council of Safety, January 22, 1776, in William Bell Clark, ed., *Naval Documents of the American Revolution*, vol. III (Washington, 1968), p. 929.

24. Letter, Richard Hutson to Thomas Hutson, June 7, 1776, in Morgan, *Naval Documents of the American Revolution*, vol. V, p. 417.

25. A List of People on Board the *Andrew Doria*, May 10, 1776, in Morgan, *Naval Documents of the American Revolution*, vol. V, pp. 29–30; Muster

Roll of the Continental Sloop *Fly*, August 10, 1776; Letter, with enclosure, George Ross and James Hodges to Philip Stephens, July 31, 1776, and Extract of a Letter from Dover, July 31, 1776, in Morgan, *Naval Documents of the American Revolution*, vol. VI (Washington, 1972), pp. 138, 516–518.

26. Letter, Bureau of Pensions, Veterans Administration, to the Adjutant General, January 29, 1931, item 91.

27. George Livermore, *An Historical Research Respecting the Opinions of the Founders of the Republic on Negroes as Slaves, as Citizens, as Soldiers* (Boston, 1862), pp. 113–116.

28. Lorenzo Johnston Greene, "Some Observations on the Black Regiment of Rhode Island in the American Revolution," *Journal of Negro History*, vol. XXVII (1952), pp. 147–151, 155–156, 161–163, 169–171.

29. Letter, James Madison to James Jones, November 28, 1780, item 59.

30. Quarles, *The Negro in the American Revolution*, p. 183.

31. Letter, Bureau of Pensions, Veterans Administration to the Adjutant General, October 16, 1930, item 90.

32. Letters, John Cadwallader to George Washington, June 5, 1781, and Maryland Council to Marquis de Lafayette, July 3, 1781, in William H. Browne et al., eds., *Archives of Maryland* (Baltimore, 1883–1952), vol. XLV, p. 494.

33. Letter, Stephen Steward to Maryland Council, February 11, 1777, in Browne et al., *Archives of Maryland*, vol. XVI, p. 130.

34. Extract from the Proceedings of the Continental Congress, March 29, 1779, item 70.

35. Letters, John Rutledge to the South Carolina delegation of the Continental Congress, April 24, 1779, and Nathaniel Greene to George Washington, January 24, 1782, items 71 and 72.

36. Letter, John Laurens to George Washington, May 19, 1782, item 74.

37. Quarles, *The Negro in the American Revolution*, p. 82; Wallace, *Appeal to Arms*, pp. 206–209.

38. Roland C. McConnell, *Negro Troops of Antebellum Louisiana* (Baton Rouge, 1968), pp. 17–20.

39. Jack D. Foner, *Blacks and the Military in American History* (New York, paperback edition, 1974), p. 15; Robert Middlekauff, *The Glorious Cause: The American Revolution, 1763–1789*, vol. II of *The Oxford History of the United States* (New York, 1982), pp. 28, 32, 547.

40. Quarles, *The Negro in the American Revolution*, pp. 172–181.

Chapter 2. SERVICE IN TIME OF SLAVERY

1. Militia Act of 1792, *U.S. Statutes at Large*.

2. Foner, *Blacks and the Military*, p. 21.

3. Letter, Secretary of the Navy Benjamin Stoddert to Lieutenant Henry Kenyon, August 8, 1798, in Office of Naval Records and Library, *Naval*

Documents Related to the Quasi War between the United States and France, vol. I (Washington, 1935), p. 281.

4. Letter, Colonel William Ward Burrows to Lieutenant John Hall, September 8, 1798, Commandant's Letter Books, RG 127, National Archives.

5. Quarles, *The Negro in the American Revolution*, pp. 10–11; Edwin H. Simmons, *The United States Marines, 1775–1975* (New York, 1976), pp. 14–15; Richard H. Kohn, *Eagle and Sword: The Federalists and the Creation of the Military Establishment in America, 1783–1802* (New York, 1975), pp. 60–64, 176, 290.

6. Foner, *Blacks and the Military*, p. 21; Rayford W. Logan, "The Negro in the Quasi War, 1798–1800," *Negro History Bulletin*, vol. XIV (March 1951), pp. 131–132.

7. An Act for the Regulation of Seamen on Board Public and Private Vessels of the United States, March 3, 1813, *U.S. Statutes at Large*.

8. Extract from letter, Nathaniel Shaler, Commander, Private Armed Schooner *Governor Tompkins*, January 1, 1813, *Niles Weekly Register*, February 26, 1814.

9. Lorenzo Johnston Green, "The Negro in the War of 1812 and the Civil War," *Negro History Bulletin*, vol. XIV (March 1951), p. 133.

10. Frank Cassell, "Slaves of the Chesapeake and the War of 1812," *Journal of Negro History*, vol. LVII (April 1972), pp. 144–148, 150–151.

11. *Ibid.*, p. 152; Walter Lord, *The Dawn's Early Light* (New York, 1972), pp. 116–123.

12. Cassell, "Slaves of the Chesapeake," pp. 152–154.

13. Act of the Legislature of New York to Authorize the Raising of Two Regiments of Men of Color, October 24, 1814, in *The Negro in the Military Service of the United States*, National Archives Microfilm 858.

14. McConnell, *Negro Troops of Antebellum Louisiana*, pp. 22–23, 30–32.

15. Address from the Free People of Color to His Excellency William C. C. Claiborne, Governor General and Intendant of Louisiana, January 1804, in Clarence Edwin Carter, ed., *The Territorial Papers of the United States*, vol. IX, *Territory of Orleans, 1803–1812* (Washington, 1940), pp. 174–175.

16. Letter, James Brown to John Breckinridge, September 17, 1805, Carter, *Territorial Papers*, vol. IX, pp. 510–511.

17. McConnell, *Negro Troops of Antebellum Louisiana*, pp. 41–44.

18. *Ibid.*, p. 54; Act of the Legislature of Louisiana to Organize a Corps of Militia, September 6, 1812, and Commission of Second Lieutenant Isidore Honoré, Louisiana Militia, October 12, 1812, in MacGregor and Nalty, *Blacks in the Armed Forces*, vol. I, items 103 and 104.

19. Proclamation to the Free Colored Inhabitants of Louisiana, *Niles Weekly Register*, December 3, 1814.

20. McConnell, *Negro Troops of Antebellum Louisiana*, pp. 67, 70–71, 73–90.

21. General Orders, 7th Military District, January 21, 1815, *Niles Weekly Register*, February 25, 1815.

22. McConnell, *Negro Troops of Antebellum Louisiana*, p. 104.

23. War Department General Order, Feb. 18, 1820, and Colored Persons in the Army, a Letter from the Secretary of War, August 5, 1842, in *The Negro in the Military Service of the United States*.

24. William Cooper Nell, *The Colored Patriots of the American Revolution* (Boston, 1855), pp. 378–381.

25. Fifteenth Congress, 1st Session, *Rules, Regulations, and Instructions for the Naval Service*, April 20, 1818, in *American State Papers: Naval Affairs* (Washington, 1834), vol. I, p. 511.

26. Harold D. Langley, *Social Reform in the United States Navy, 1798–1862* (Urbana, Illinois, 1967), pp. 92–93.

27. Harold D. Langley, "The Negro in the Navy and the Merchant Service, 1798–1860," *Journal of Negro History*, vol. LII (October 1967), p. 218.

28. Navy Department Circular, September 13, 1839, in *Regulations, Circulars, Orders, and Decisions for the Guide of Officers of the Navy of the United States, Issued Since the Publication Authorized by the Navy in March 1832* (Washington, 1851).

29. Litwack, *North of Slavery*, p. 33.

30. Colored Persons in the Navy of the U.S., A Letter from the Secretary of the Navy, August 5, 1842, in *The Negro in the Military Service of the United States*.

31. Litwack, *North of Slavery*, pp. 225, 241, 244; Kenneth M. Stampp, *The Peculiar Institution: Slavery in the Ante-Bellum South* (New York, paperback edition, 1956), pp. 132–137; J. C. Furnas, *Goodbye to Uncle Tom* (New York, 1956), pp. 56, 201–202.

Chapter 3. Civil War and Emancipation

1. Allan Nevins, *The Emergence of Lincoln*, vol. II, *Prologue to the Civil War* (New York, 1950), pp. 5–11, 79–80, 328–335; Nevins, *The War for the Union*, vol. I, *The Improvised War, 1861–1862* (New York, 1959), pp. 12–19, 30–32.

2. Dudley Taylor Cornish, *The Sable Arm: Negro Troops in the Union Army*, 1861–1865 (New York, 1966), pp. 3–5, 10–11; Allan Nevins, *The War for the Union*, vol. II, *War Becomes a Revolution, 1862–1863* (New York, 1960), pp. 4–8.

3. Nevins, *The Improvised War*, pp. 331–339; Proclamation, Headquarters, Western Department, September 12, 1861, in MacGregor and Nalty, *Blacks in the Armed Forces*, vol. II, item 1. All documents cited by item number in the chapter are reproduced in this volume.

4. Brig. Gen. Thomas W. Sherman, Proclamation to the People of South Carolina, November 8, 1861, item 2; Nevins, *The Improvised War*, p. 398.

5. Foner, *Blacks and the Military*, p. 33; Headquarters, Department of Virginia, General Orders no. 34, November 1, 1861, *War of Rebellion Rec-*

ords: A Compilation of the Official Records of the Union and Confeder-
ate Armies (Washington, 1880–1891), series II, vol. I, pp. 774–775.

6. Headquarters, Expeditionary Corps, Hilton Head, South Carolina, General Orders no. 9, February 6, 1862, *The Negro in the Military Service of the United States.*

7. Headquarters, District of West Tennessee, General Orders no. 14, February 26, 1862, item 11.

8. Enclosure to Report of Flag Officer Silas H. Stringham, USN, commanding Atlantic Blockading Squadron, July 18, 1861, *Official Records of the Union and Confederate Navies in the War of Rebellion* (Washington, 1894–1921), series I, vol. VI, pp. 8–9.

9. Report of Commander E. G. Parrott, USN, commanding USS *Augusta,* May 13, 1862; Report of Volunteer Lieutenant Nickels, USN, commanding USS *Onward,* May 13, 1862; Letter, Secretary of the Navy to Flag Officer S. F. Dupont, transmitting a copy of an act of Congress in the Case of Robert Smalls and others, July 15, 1862; Report of Flag Officer DuPont, USN, regarding the apportionment of prize money to Robert Smalls and others, August 19, 1862; all in *War of Rebellion Records, Navies,* series I, vol. XII, pp. 820–826.

10. Herbert Aptheker, "The Negro in the Union Navy," *Journal of Negro History,* vol. XXXII (April 1947), p. 198.

11. Order of the Secretary of the Navy to Flag Officer Goldsborough, commanding Atlantic Blockading Squadron, regarding enlistment of contrabands, September 25, 1861, in *War of Rebellion Records, Navies,* series I, vol. VI, p. 252.

12. Report of Acting Rear Admiral David Dixon Porter, USN, regarding the need of men for the squadron, October 26, 1862, in *War of Rebellion Records, Navies,* series I, vol. XXIII, pp. 449–450.

13. General Order of Rear Admiral Porter, USN, regarding the employment of Negroes on naval vessels, July 26, 1863, in *War of Rebellion Records, Navies,* series I, vol. XXV, pp. 327–328.

14. Letter, Secretary of the Navy John D. Long to Representative C. E. Littlefield, April 2, 1902, item 61.

15. Foner, *Blacks and the Military,* pp. 33–34; Public Laws 160 and 161, July 17, 1862, *U.S. Statutes at Large.*

16. Nevins, *War Becomes a Revolution,* pp. 513–514; Cornish, *The Sable Arm,* pp. 37–41, 44–45, 52–55.

17. Letter, Colonel J. M. Williams to General T. J. Anderson, Adjutant General of Kansas, January 1, 1866, item 28.

18. Cornish, *The Sable Arm,* pp. 88–92; Nevins, *War Becomes a Revolution,* p. 515.

19. Report of Colonel T. W. Higginson, 1st South Carolina Infantry, February 1, 1863, in *War of Rebellion Records, Armies,* series I, vol. XIV, pp. 195–198.

20. Nevins, *War Becomes a Revolution,* pp. 148–149, 218–219, 233–237, 307.

21. *Ibid.,* p. 514; Donald E. Everett, "Ben Butler and the Louisiana Native

Guards, 1861–1862," *Journal of Southern History*, vol. XXIV (May 1958), pp. 201–205, 213.

22. Letter, Brevet Major General Daniel Ullman to General Richard C. Drum, the Adjutant General, April 16, 1887, item 23.

23. William Cullen Bryant, II, "A Yankee Soldier Looks at the Negro," *Civil War History*, vol. VII (June 1961), p. 141.

24. Letter, Ullmann to Drum.

25. Foner, *Blacks and the Military*, p. 38.

26. Testimony of Nathaniel Paige, Special Correspondent, New York *Tribune*, in Testimony Accompanying the Final Report of the American Freedman's Inquiry Commission, May 15, 1864, item 36.

27. Office of the Deputy Assistant Secretary of Defense for Equal Opportunity and Safety Policy, *Black Americans in Defense* of Our Nation (Washington, 1982), p. 54.

28. Testimony of Nathaniel Paige accompanying the Final Report of the American Freedman's Inquiry Commission, item 36.

29. Nevins, *War Becomes a Revolution*, pp. 526–527.

30. Ira Berlin, ed., with Joseph P. Reidy and Leslie S. Rowland, *Freedom: A Documentary History of Emancipation, 1861–1867*, series II, *The Black Military Experience* (Cambridge, England, 1982), pp. 362–366, 385–386, 401–402.

31. Wilbert H. Luck, *Journey to Honey Hill: The Fighting 55th Massachusetts Colored Infantry during the Civil War (1863–1865)* (Washington, 1976), pp. 54–55, 67–69; Foner, *Blacks and the Military*, p. 43.

32. Foner, *Blacks and the Military*, pp. 261–262.

33. Berlin, ed., with Reidy and Rowland, *The Black Military Experience*, pp. 367–368.

34. Nevins, *The War for Union: The Organized War, 1863–1864* (New York, 1971), pp. 122–130.

35. Testimony of Colonel T. W. Higginson accompanying the Final Report of the American Freedman's Inquiry Commission, item 36.

36. Testimony of General B. F. Butler accompanying the Final Report of the American Freedman's Inquiry Commission, item 36.

37. Letter, Gen. Daniel C. Ullmann to Sen. Henry Wilson, December 4, 1863, in *War of Rebellion Records, Armies*, series III, vol. III, pp. 1126–1128.

38. Cornish, *The Sable Arm*, pp. 229–231, 273–278.

39. *Ibid.*, p. 215; Report of the Provost-Marshal General's Bureau, March 17, 1866, part IV, in *War of Rebellion Records, Armies*, series III, vol. V, pp. 651–662; Testimony of Colonel T. W. Higginson and General B. F. Butler accompanying the Final Report of the American Freedman's Inquiry Commission, item 36.

40. Letter, Maj. Gen. O. M. Mitchel to Secretary of War Edwin M. Stanton, May 4, 1862, *War of Rebellion Records, Armies*, series I, vol. X, part 2, pp. 162–163.

41. Testimony of Vincent Colyer, Superintendent of the Poor, Department

of North Carolina, accompanying the Final Report of the American Freedman's Inquiry Commission, item 36.

42. Foner, *Blacks and the Military*, p. 46.

43. Joint Resolution adopted by the Confederate Congress on the subject of retaliation, April 30–May 1, 1863, in *War of Rebellion Records, Armies*, series II, vol. V, pp. 940–941; Nevins, *War Becomes a Revolution*, p. 521.

44. Thirty-eighth Congress, 1st Session, House of Representatives, Report no. 65, *Fort Pillow Massacre*, approved April 24, 1864; Cornish, *The Sable Arm*, pp. 173–174.

45. Foner, *Blacks and the Military*, p. 44.

46. Memorial, Maj. Gen. P.R. Cleburne, Brig. Gen. D. C. Govan, et al., to the Commanding General, the Corps, Division, Brigade, Regimental Commanders of the Army of Tennessee, January 2, 1864, in *War of Rebellion Records, Armies*, series I, vol. LII, part 2, pp. 586–592.

47. Letter [expressing the views of Davis], Secretary of War James H. Seddon to Gen. Joseph E. Johnston, January 24, 1864, in *War of Rebellion Records, Armies*, series I, vol. LII, part 2, pp. 606–607.

48. Message by President Jefferson Davis to the Senate and House of Representatives of the Confederate States of America, November 7, 1864, in *War of Rebellion Records, Armies*, series IV, vol. III, pp. 797–799.

49. Letter, Gen. Robert E. Lee to Andrew Hunter, January 11, 1865, in *War of Rebellion Records, Armies*, series IV, vol. III, pp. 1012–1013.

50. Directive to the Honorable the Courts of the Counties, Cities, etc., March 14, 1865, *War of Rebellion Records, Armies*, series IV, vol. III, pp. 1138–1139.

51. Foner, *Blacks and the Military*, p. 33.

52. *Ibid.*, p. 36.

Chapter 4. REACTION IN THE SOUTH, ACTION IN THE WEST

1. Okon Edet Uya, *From Slavery to Public Service: Robert Smalls, 1839–1915* (New York, 1971), pp. 37, 45–46; E. L. Thornbrough, ed., *Black Reconstructionists* (Englewood Cliffs, New Jersey, 1972), pp. 173–177; Berlin, ed., with Reidy and Rowland, *The Black Military Experience*, pp. 767–770.

2. Foner, *Blacks and the Military*, p. 68; Office of Deputy Assistant Secretary of Defense for Equal Opportunity and Safety Policy, *Black Americans in Defense of Our Nation* (Washington, 1982), p. 105.

3. Otis A. Singletary, *Negro Militia and Reconstruction* (Austin, Texas, 1971), pp. 118–127, 139–140.

4. Okon Edet Uya, *Robert Smalls*, pp. 82–87, 129–130; C. Vann Woodward, *The Strange Career of Jim Crow* (New York, paperback edition, 1968), pp. 52–53, 69–70.

5. Letter, General U. S. Grant to Senator Henry Wilson, January 12, 1866, MacGregor and Nalty, *Blacks in the Armed Forces*, vol. III, item 6. All

documents cited by item number in the chapter are reproduced in this volume.

6. "The Reorganization of the Army, Mr. Wilson's Bill," item 7.

7. Further Debate on the Wilson Bill, item 9.

8. War Department, Adjutant General's Office, General Order no. 56, August 1, 1866; Letter, Adjutant General E. D. Townsend to Secretary of War E. M. Stanton, November 24, 1866; Headquarters of the Army, Adjutant General's Office, General Order no. 17, March 15, 1869; items 10, 11, and 12.

9. Robert M. Utley, *Frontier Regulars: The United States Army and the Indian, 1866–1890* (New York, 1973), pp. 22–28.

10. Major John Bigelow, *A Historical Sketch of the Tenth Cavalry, 1866–1891*, item 13.

11. William H. Leckie, *The Buffalo Soldiers: A Narrative of the Negro Cavalry in the West* (Norman, Oklahoma, 1967), pp. 7–8, 12–15.

12. Bigelow, *A Historical Sketch of the Tenth Cavalry*.

13. Leckie, *The Buffalo Soldiers*, pp. 156–164.

14. Bigelow, *A Historical Sketch of the Tenth Cavalry*.

15. Leckie, *The Buffalo Soldiers*, pp. 7, 25–26; Letters, Major J. F. Wade to Assistant Adjutant General, Department of Texas, April 28, 1875, and May 12, 1875, and Stephen Powers to Major J. G. Boyle, U.S. District Attorney, Galveston, Texas, November 27, 1875; items 18, 19, and 22.

16. Letter, Colonel Edward Hatch to Assistant Adjutant General, Department of Texas, May 17, 1875, item 20.

17. John M. Carrol ed., *The Black Military Experience in the American West* (New York, 1973), pp. 53–60.

18. Foner, *Blacks and the Military*, p. 69.

19. Bigelow, *A Historical Sketch of the Tenth Cavalry*.

20. Endorsements, General William Tecumseh Sherman and Secretary of War George W. McCrary to letter, General C. C. Augur to Assistant Adjutant General, Division of the Atlantic, March 17, 1879, item 26.

21. Endorsement by M. C. Meigs, Quartermaster General, to letter, General C. C. Auger to Assistant Adjutant General, Division of the Atlantic, March 17, 1879, item 26.

22. Foner, *Blacks and the Military*, p. 53.

23. Endorsement by Meigs to letter, Auger to Assistant Adjutant General, Division of the Atlantic, March 17, 1879.

24. Marvin E. Fletcher, *The Negro Soldier and the United States Army, 1891–1917* (University of Wisconsin Ph.D. dissertation, 1968), p. 28.

25. Arlen Fowler, *The Black Infantry in the West, 1869–1901* (Westport, Connecticut, 1971), pp. 80–87, 100–101, 105–107; *Black Americans in Defense of Our Nation*, pp. 57–58; Foner, *Blacks and the Military*, p. 65.

26. Foner, *Blacks and the Military*, p. 70.

27. Frank N. Schubert, "Black Soldiers on the White Frontier: Some Fac-

tors Influencing Race Relations," *Phylon*, vol. XXXII (Winter 1971), p. 412.

28. Fowler, *The Black Infantry in the West*, pp. 58, 61–62.

29. Fletcher, *The Negro Soldier and the United States Army*, pp. 64–67.

30. Endorsement by General William Tecumseh Sherman to letter, Secretary of War J. D. Cameron to Benjamin F. Butler, January 20, 1877, item 25.

31. Foner, *Blacks and the Military*, pp. 66–67.

32. "Colored Troops," in Thomas M. Exley, Chief Examiner, Paymaster General's Office, *Compendium of Pay of the Army, 1785–1888* (Washington, 1888), p. 52.

33. Letter, Secretary of War Robert Todd Lincoln to the Chief Signal Officer, Brevet Major General W. B. Hazen, July 23, 1884, with endorsements, *Army-Navy Register*, October 4, 1884, p. 7.

34. Foner, *Blacks and the Military*, p. 69.

35. *Ibid.*, pp. 63–65.

36. *Annual Report of the Secretary of War*, 1880, part 2, pp. 223–230.

37. John E. Marszalek, Jr., *Court Martial: The Army vs Johnson Whittaker, an Account of the Ordeal of a Black Cadet at West Point* (New York, 1972), pp. 44–57, 238–239, 248–249, 269–270.

38. Leckie, *Buffalo Soldiers*, p. 238; Barry C. Johnson, *Flipper's Dismissal: The Ruin of Lt. Henry O. Flipper, USA, First Coloured Graduate of West Point* (London, 1980), pp. 63–65, 126–133.

39. Brevet Major General George W. Cullum, *Biographical Register of the Officers and Graduates of the U.S. Military Academy at West Point, New York, from Its Establishment in 1802*, vol. III, cases 3205, 3330, pp. 411, 430–431.

40. Schubert, "Black Soldiers on the White Frontier," p. 414; "The Suggs Affray: Black Cavalry in the Johnson County War," *Western History Quarterly*, vol. IV (January 1973), pp. 63–67; Leckie, *Buffalo Soldiers*, pp. 192–205, 252–258; Report of Brigadier General T. H. Ruger, Headquarters, Department of the Columbia, September 5, 1892, item 33.

41. Woodward, *The Strange Career of Jim Crow*, pp. 60–65.

42. Statement of the Condition of the National Guard of North Carolina, April 20, 1898; Consolidated Strength Return, Report of the Alabama Adjutant General, 1898; Report of the Adjutant General, Commonwealth of Virginia, 1898; items 40, 45, and 47.

43. Woodward, *The Strange Career of Jim Crow*, pp. 6–7, 35–37, 67–72, 78–79.

Chapter 5. To HELL WITH SPAIN

1. John Edward Weems, *The Fate of the Maine* (New York, 1958), pp. 79–81; Edward Wakin, *Black Fighting Men in U.S. History* (New York, 1971), p. 86.

2. Hyman G. Rickover, *How the Maine Was Destroyed* (Washington, 1976), pp. 1, 27–33, 125–128.

3. Willard B. Gatewood, Jr., "Black Americans and the Quest for Empire, 1898–1903," *Journal of Southern History*, vol. XXXVII (1972), pp. 548–550.

4. Fletcher, *The Negro Soldier and the United States Army*, pp. 185–188.

5. *Ibid.*, pp. 227–233.

6. Report of Tour of Duty by Major General J. C. Breckinridge, U.S. Volunteers, as Commander of the Separate Army in the Field, with Headquarters at Camp George H. Thomas, and as Commander of the First Army Corps within the United States, with Headquarters at Lexington, Kentucky, in MacGregor and Nalty, *Blacks in the Armed Forces*, vol. III, item 54. All documents cited by item number in the chapter are reproduced in this volume.

7. Fletcher, *The Negro Soldier and the United States Army*, pp. 237–238.

8. *Ibid.*, pp. 239–241.

9. Schubert, "Black Soldiers on the White Frontier," p. 414.

10. Willard B. Gatewood, Jr., "Negro Troops in Florida, 1898," *Florida Historical Quarterly*, vol. XLIX. (July 1970), pp. 4–5, 7–9.

11. Allen R. Millett, *The General: Robert L. Bullard and Officership in the United States Army, 1881–1925* (Westport, Connecticut, 1975), pp. 102–103.

12. William B. Gatewood, Jr., "Alabama's Negro Soldier Experiment, 1898–1899," *Journal of Negro History*, vol. LVII (October 1972), p. 346.

13. Millett, *The General*, p. 103.

14. Fletcher, *The Negro Soldier and the United States Army*, pp. 196–197.

15. Francis E. Lewis, *Negro Army Regulars in the Spanish-American War: Smoked Yankees at Santiago de Cuba* (University of Texas, Austin, M.A. report, 1969), pp. 18–19.

16. Message of Congratulations, Major General Joseph Wheeler to the Officers and Men of the Cavalry Division, September 20, 1898, item 53.

17. Lewis, *Smoked Yankees*, pp. 23–27.

18. Quoted in Herschel V. Cashin, Charles Alexander et al., *Under Fire with the Tenth Cavalry* (New York, reprinted 1969), p. 202.

19. Fletcher, *The Negro in the United States Army*, pp. 205–207; Myles V. Lynk, *The Black Troopers or the Daring Heroism of the Negro Soldiers in the Spanish-American War* (New York, reprinted 1971), pp. 43–44, 51; David F. Trask, *The War with Spain in 1898* (New York, 1981), pp. 238–240.

20. Donald Smyth, *Guerrilla Warrior: The Early Life of John J. Pershing* (New York, 1973), pp. 170–171.

21. Charles Johnson Post, *The Little War of Private Post* (Boston, 1960), pp. 170–171.

22. Report, Second Lieutenant Arthur Kerwin, Commanding Company D, to the Adjutant, 24th Infantry, July 3, 1898, *Annual Report of the Secre-*

tary of War, 1898, Report of the Major General Commanding the Army, pp. 436–437.

23. Reports, Captain Ben W. Leavell, Commanding Company A, and Captain Charles Dodge, Commanding Company C, to the Adjutant, 24th Infantry, July 13, 1898, *Annual Report of the Secretary of War*, 1898, Report of the Major General Commanding the Army, pp. 437–438.

24. Trask, *The War with Spain*, pp. 261–266.

25. Office of Deputy Assistant Secretary of Defense for Equal Opportunity and Safety Policy, *Black Americans in Defense of Our Nation* (Washington, 1982), pp. 60–61.

26. Trask, *The War with Spain*, pp. 311, 326.

27. Fletcher, *The Negro Soldier and the United States Army*, p. 425.

28. "The Second Call," Report of the Adjutant General, Illinois, 1897–1898, item 41; Willard B. Gatewood, Jr., "Kansas Negroes and the Spanish American War," *Kansas Historical Quarterly*, vol. XXXVII (Autumn 1971), p. 307.

29. Trask, *The War with Spain*, pp. 357–358, 366; Narrative by Colonel Rice, Report of the Adjutant General, Commonwealth of Massachusetts, 1898, item 44.

30. Foner, *Blacks and the Military*, p. 83.

31. Leon Wolff, *Little Brown Brother: How the United States Purchased and Pacified the Philippine Islands at the Century's Turn* (Garden City, New York, 1961), pp. 55–59, 75–76, 170–177, 218–221.

32. Gatewood, "Black Americans and the Quest for Empire," pp. 557–560.

33. Willard B. Gatewood, Jr., "North Carolina's Negro Regiment in the Spanish-American War," *North Carolina Historical Review*, vol. XLVIII (October 1971), pp. 384–386.

34. Fletcher, *The Negro Soldier and the United States Army*, pp. 289–290, 293–294, 297.

35. Report of Captain H. A. Leonhaeuser, November 21, 1899, *Annual Report of the Secretary of War*, 1900, Report of the Lieutenant General Commanding the Army, pp. 352–353.

36. Report of Colonel Charles Keller, January 1900, *Annual Report of the Secretary of War*, 1900, Report of the Lieutenant General Commanding the Army, pp. 448–449.

37. Fletcher, *The Negro Soldier and the United States Army*, p. 271; Michael C. Robinson and Frank N. Schubert, "David Fagen: An Afro-American Rebel in the Philippines, 1899–1901," *Pacific Historical Review*, vol. XLIV (February 1975), p. 72.

38. Robinson and Schubert, "David Fagen," pp. 74–75, 78, 81.

39. Wolff, *Little Brown Brother*, pp. 345, 363; Fletcher, *The Negro Soldier and the United States Army*, pp. 300–301.

40. Foner, *Blacks and the Military*, pp. 93–94.

41. Fletcher, *The Negro Soldier and the United States Army*, p. 301; Gatewood, "Black Americans and the Quest for Empire," pp. 564–565.

42. Cashin, *Under Fire with the Tenth Cavalry*, p. 147.

43. Fletcher, *The Negro Soldier and the United States Army*, p. 212.

44. Gatewood, "Black Americans and the Quest for Empire," p. 582.

Chapter 6. A GREAT WHITE FLEET

1. Robert A. Hart, *The Great White Fleet: Its Voyage Around the World, 1907–1909* (Boston, 1965), pp. 29–33, 50–51.

2. Daniel A. Nelson, "*Hamilton* and *Scourge*: Ghost Ships of the War of 1812," *National Geographic*, vol. CLXIII (March 1983), pp. 298–305; James Fenimore Cooper, *History of the Navy of the United States* (New York, 1864), three volumes in one, p. 172.

3. Frederick S. Harrod, *Manning the New Navy: The Development of a Modern Naval Enlisted Force, 1899–1940* (Westport, Connecticut, 1978), pp. 10–11.

4. Letter, Lieutenant George Steunenberg to the Editor, January 5, 1907, *Army and Navy Journal*, vol. XLIV (1907), p. 563.

5. Harrod, *Manning the New Navy*, pp. 10, 58.

6. Okon Edet Uya, *Robert Smalls*, p. 20.

7. Peter Karsten, *The Naval Aristocracy: The Golden Age of Annapolis and the Emergence of Modern American Navalism* (New York, 1972), p. 38; Lieutenant Commander R. L. Field, "The Black Midshipman at the U.S. Naval Academy," *U.S. Naval Institute Proceedings*, vol. XCIX (April 1973), pp. 28–30.

8. Letter, Captain P. H. Cooper to Secretary of the Navy John D. Long, May 11, 1897, in MacGregor and Nalty, *Blacks in the Armed Forces*, vol. III, item 35. Unless otherwise indicated, all documents cited by item numbers in the chapter are reproduced in this volume.

9. Field, "The Black Midshipman at the U.S. Naval Academy," pp. 30–31.

10. Karsten, *The Naval Aristocracy*, p. 217; *Annual Report of the Secretary of War*, 1880, part 2, pp. 229–230.

11. Hart, *The Great White Fleet*, pp. 56–57, 308.

12. Harrod, *Manning the New Navy*, pp. 54–55.

13. Navy Department, *Dictionary of American Naval Fighting Ships*, vol. I (Washington, 1970), p. 45; vol. II (Washington, 1969), p. 166; vol. VIII (Washington, 1981), p. 495.

14. Harrod, *Manning the New Navy*, pp. 57–58.

15. Lieutenant Commander T. P. Magruder, "The Enlisted Personnel," *U.S. Naval Institute Proceedings*, vol. XXXVI (1910), pp. 385–386.

16. *Army and Navy Journal*, vol. L (1913), p. 1140; *New York Times*, May 26, 1916, in MacGregor and Nalty, *Blacks in the Armed Forces*, item 78.

17. Harrod, *Manning the New Navy*, p. 60.

18. *Ibid.*, table 5.

19. Foner, *Blacks and the Military*, p. 124; Letter, Captain Chester W. Nimitz, USN, Acting Chief, Bureau of Navigation, to Representative Hamilton Fish, January 17, 1937, vol. IV, item 167.

20. Harrod, *Manning the New Navy*, p. 164.

21. *Ibid.*, p. 60; Historical Section, Bureau of Naval Personnel, "The Negro in the Navy in World War II," pp. 1–2, vol. VI, item 101.

22. Harrod, *Manning the New Navy*, p. 60.

23. *Ibid.*, p. 61.

24. Memorandum, Capt. H. A. Badt, USN, for the Officer in Charge, Public Relations, July 24, 1940, subject: Negroes in the U.S. Navy, vol. IV, item 187.

Chapter 7. A RACIAL BATTLEGROUND IN TEXAS

1. Letter, Booker T. Washington to William Howard Taft, March 3, 1906, in MacGregor and Nalty, *Blacks in the Armed Forces*, vol. III, item 65. All documents cited by item number in the chapter are reproduced in this volume.

2. Letter, Adjutant General George B. Davis to Secretary of War William Howard Taft, March 10, 1906, item 66.

3. Foner, *Blacks and the Military*, p. 106.

4. Letter, Emmett J. Scott to President Theodore Roosevelt, March 8, 1907, item 67.

5. Memorandum, Lieutenant Colonel T. W. Jones, Chief, Second Division [Military Intelligence], for the Secretary, General Staff, April 22, 1907, subject: (a) The probable qualifications of negroes for service in the artillery; (b) and recommendations as to what portion of the new artillery force should be composed of negroes, in case it be finally determined to organize a part of the artillery from colored men, item 69.

6. Memorandum, Major C. DeWitt Willcox for the Chief of Staff, April 16, 1907, subject: Negroes for the Artillery Service, item 70.

7. Foner, *Blacks and the Military*, pp. 95–96.

8. *Annual Report of the Secretary of War*, 1906, pp. 26–35.

9. Memorandum, Maj. C. DeW. Willcox for the Chief of Staff, April 16, 1907, item 70.

10. Sixtieth Congress, 1st Session, Senate, *The Brownsville Affray: Report of the Inspector General of the Army; Order of the President Discharging Men of Companies B, C, and D, 25th Infantry; Messages of the President to the Senate; and Majority and Minority Reports of the Senate Committee on Military Affairs* (Washington, 1908), Report of the Senate Committee on Military Affairs, part 3, item 62.

11. *Ibid.*, The Report of the Inspector General of the Army; John D. Weaver, *The Brownsville Raid* (New York, 1970), pp. 96–98.

12. *The Brownsville Affray*, The President's Message, December 19, 1906, item 62.

13. Letter, Booker T. Washington to Secretary of War William Howard Taft, November 20, 1906, item 61.

14. Weaver *Brownsville*, p. 110; Foner, *Blacks and the Military*, pp. 99, 102.

15. Weaver, *Brownsville*, pp. 140–141.

16. Henry F. Pringle, *Theodore Roosevelt: A Biography* (New York, 1931), pp. 461–462.

17. *The Brownsville Affray*, Report of the Senate Committee on Military Affairs, part 1, item 62.

18. *Ibid.*, part 2, item 62.

19. *Ibid.*

20. *Ibid.*, The President's Message of March 11, 1908.

21. Weaver, *Brownsville*, pp. 218–219.

22. Pringle, *Roosevelt*, pp. 504–505; Foner, *Blacks and the Military*, pp. 101–102; Theodore Roosevelt, *Theodore Roosevelt: An Autobiography* (New York, 1914)—see chapter X.

23. Pringle, *Roosevelt*, pp. 248–250; Leslie Fishel, Jr., and Benjamin Quarles, eds., *The Black American* (Glenview, Illinois, 1970), pp. 387–389.

24. Foner, *Blacks and the Military*, pp. 102–103; Department of the Army, The Brownsville Incident: Analysis of Essential Elements of the Case, item 63.

25. Clarence C. Clendenon, *Blood on the Border: The United States Army and Mexican Irregulars* (New York, 1969), pp. 127–128, 177–178, 181–184.

26. *Ibid.*, pp. 198–209; Harold E. Davis, "Mexico (1916–1917)," in Doris Condit and Bert Cooper, eds., *Challenge and Response in Internal Conflict*, vol. III, *The Experience in Africa and Latin America* (Washington, 1968), pp. 136–137.

27. Davis, "Mexico," p. 139; Robert S. Thomas and Inez V. Allen, *The Mexican Punitive Expedition under Brigadier General John J. Pershing, USA, 1916–1917* (Office of Chief of Military History, unpublished monograph, n.d.), pp. II:5–II:7.

28. Clendenon, *Blood on the Border*, pp. 257–259.,

29. Davis, "Mexico," p. 142; Col. Harry A. Toulmin, *With Pershing in Mexico* (Harrisburg, Pennsylvania, 1935), pp. 62–65.

30. Clendenon, *Blood on the Border*, pp. 288–289.

31. *Ibid.*, pp. 308–310.

32. *Ibid.*, p. 312; Thomas and Allen, *The Mexican Punitive Expedition*, pp. IV:21–IV:28.

33. Thomas and Allen, *The Mexican Punitive Expedition*, pp. IV:30–IV:33.

34. Clendenon, *Blood on the Border*, pp. 352–356.

35. Harvey A. DeWeerd, *President Wilson Fights His War: World War I and the American Intervention* (New York, 1968), pp. 20–21.

36. *Ibid.*, pp. 21–22.
37. Robert V. Haynes, *A Night of Violence: The Houston Riot of 1917* (Baton Rouge, Louisiana, 1976), pp. 25–32, 35–40, 64–65, 87–89.
38. Report of Colonel G. C. Cress to Commanding General, Southern Department, September 13, 1917, item 82.
39. *Ibid.*, Haynes, *A Night of Violence*, pp. 91–92.
40. Report of Colonel G. C. Cress, item 82.
41. Haynes, *A Night of Violence*, pp. 38, 110–111.
42. *Ibid.*, pp. 140–170.
43. *Ibid.*, pp. 2–7, 211–213, 254, 263–266, 271–276.
44. Letter, Secretary of War Newton D. Baker to President Woodrow Wilson, August 22, 1918, item 88.
45. Haynes, *A Night of Violence*, pp. 302–304, 309–314.
46. Report of Colonel G. C. Cress, item 82.
47. Haynes, *A Night of Violence*, pp. 203–207.

Chapter 8. WORLD WAR I: THE RESULTS OF CLOSING RANKS

1. *The Crisis*, July 1918, p. 111.
2. Foner, *Blacks and the Military*, pp. 109–110, 124; Allan R. Millett, *Semper Fidelis: The History of the United States Marine Corps* (New York, 1980), p. 293.
3. Letter, Major General Tasker H. Bliss, Assistant to the Chief of Staff, to General Robert K. Evans, April 4, 1917, MacGregor and Nalty, *Blacks in the Armed Forces*, vol. IV, item 1. All documents cited by item number in the chapter are reproduced in this volume.
4. Foner, *Blacks and the Military*, pp. 110–111.
5. Memorandum, Brigadier General Joseph E. Kuhn, Chief, War College Division, for the Chief of Staff, July 31, 1917, subject: Utilization of colored men drafted for the National Army, and Memorandum, Major General Tasker H. Bliss, Acting Chief of Staff for the Adjutant General, August 1, 1917, subject: same, items 3 and 4.
6. Memorandum, Major General Tasker Bliss for the Secretary of War, August 24, 1917, item 5.
7. Memorandum, Acting Chief of Staff for the Secretary of War, September 3, 1917, and War Department General Orders no. 109, August 16, 1917, items 6 and 8.
8. Memorandum, Secretary of War Newton D. Baker for General Scott, May 6, 1917, item 48.
9. Memorandum, Brigadier General Joseph E. Kuhn, Chief, War College Division, for the Chief of Staff, May 8, 1917, item 49.
10. Foner, *Blacks and the Military*, p. 110.
11. *Atlanta Independent*, May 1917, item 57.

12. Night letter, the Adjutant General to the Commanding General, Western Department, May 22, 1917, item 56.

13. Letter, President Woodrow Wilson to Secretary of War Newton D. Baker, June 25, 1917, item 60.

14. Note, Secretary Baker to General Bliss, n.d. [June 1917], item 62.

15. Letters, Secretary of War Baker to President Wilson, June 26, 1917, and July 7, 1917, items 61 and 65.

16. Foner, *Blacks and the Military*, p. 113.

17. Arthur E. Barbeau and Florette Henri, *The Unknown Soldiers: Black American Troops in World War I* (Philadelphia, 1974), pp. 74, 146–147.

18. American Battle Monuments Commission, *92nd Division: Summary of Operations in the World War* (Washington, 1944), p. 1; *93rd Division: Summary of Operations in the World War* (Washington, 1944), p. 1; Inclosure A to memorandum, Colonel D. W. Ketchum, Acting Chief, War College Division, for the Chief of Staff, December 27, 1917, subject: Training cadres for colored units, item 9; Haynes, *A Night of Violence*, p. 305.

19. Foner, *Blacks and the Military*, p. 119.

20. Memorandum, Brigadier General Henry Jervey, Director of Operations, for the Adjutant General, May 18, 1918, subject: Organization of 8 regiments of colored infantry, item 11.

21. Foner, *Blacks and the Military*, p. 121.

22. Memoranda: Brigadier General Lytle Brown, Director, War Plans Division, for the Chief of Staff, May 31, 1918, subject: White noncommissioned officers for labor battalions, item 30; Brigadier General William S. Graves, Assistant to the Chief of Staff, for the Adjutant General, May 31, 1918, subject: same, item 31; Brigadier General Brown for the Chief of Staff, June 14, 1918, subject: Organization of two labor battalions for service at the Port of Embarkation, Newport News, Va., item 32; Major General Frank McIntyre, Assistant to the Chief of Staff, for the Chief of Staff, July 15, 1918, subject: Colored Officers for Labor Battalions, item 34; Major General McIntyre for the Adjutant General, July 19, 1918, subject: same, item 35.

23. Report on 370th Infantry (Colored) brigaded in 73 Division (French), June 14, 1918; Letter, Colonel T. A. Roberts to Colonel Fox Conner, August 12, 1918, both in appendix 16 to Army War College History of Negro Troops in the World War, 1917–1918, item 118.

24. Appendix 14 to Army War College History of Negro Troops in the World War, 1917–1918, item 118.

25. Headquarters, 92nd Division, Bulletin no. 35, March 28, 1918, item 108.

26. *Brooklyn Eagle*, April 23, 1918, and *New York Journal* April 23, 1918, items 109 and 110.

27. "Help Us to Help," *The Crisis*, August 1918.

28. *The Crisis*, July 1918, p. 111.

29. William B. White, *The Military and the Melting Pot: The American Army*

and Minority Groups (University of Wisconsin, Ph.D. dissertation, 1968), p. 291.

30. "Secret Information Concerning Black American Troops," *The Crisis,* May 1919, pp. 16–17.

31. Cables, War Department to Pershing, A 726, February 2, 1918, and A 800, February 16, 1918, item 81.

32. Letter, Colonel C. C. Ballou to Assistant Commandant, General Staff College, March 14, 1920, subject: Use to be made of Negroes in the U.S. Military Service, appendix 26 to Army War College History of Negro Troops in the World War, 1917–1918, item 118.

33. Millett, *The General,* pp. 425–429; Barbeau and Henri, *The Unknown Soldiers,* pp. 159–160.

34. Letter, Colonel C. C. Ballou to Assistant Commandant, General Staff College, March 14, 1920, item 118.

35. Captain R. L. Bullard, "The Negro Volunteer: Some Characteristics," *Journal of the Military Service Institution of the United States,* vol. XXIX (1901), p. 39.

36. Major General Robert Lee Bullard, USA Retired, *Personalities and Reminiscences of the Great War* (Garden City, New York, 1925), p. 298.

37. Cable, Pershing to War Department, no. 626, February 21, 1918, item 81.

38. Arthur W. Little, *From Harlem to the Rhine: The Story of New York's Colored Volunteers* (New York, 1936), p. 146.

39. *Ibid.,* pp. ix–x, 3, 12, 108, 117, 120–124.

40. Letter, Commanding Officer, 369th Infantry, USA, to Commander in Chief, GHQ, AEF, October 9, 1918, subject: Condition of regiment and request for advice and instructions, item 95.

41. *Ibid.;* Little, *From Harlem to the Rhine,* pp. 192–200, 369; Barbeau and Henri, *The Unknown Soldiers,* p. 116.

42. Little, *From Harlem to the Rhine,* pp. 359–361; Brooke Hayward, *Haywire* (New York, 1977), p. 106.

43. Memorandum, Colonel T. A. Roberts for the Chief of Staff, May 8, 1918, item 89; American Battle Monuments Commission, *93rd Division Summary of Operations,* pp. 9–10, 25–26, 36.

44. Memorandum, Lieutenant Colonel Walter S. Grant for Assistant Chief of Staff, G-3, July 9, 1918, subject: Discipline of the 369th Infantry, item 91.

45. Barbeau and Henri, *The Unknown Soldiers,* pp. 122–124, 128–129, 131–132.

46. Memorandum, Brigadier General H. B. Fiske, Assistant Chief of Staff, G-5, for the Chief of Staff AEF, October 17, 1918, subject: Regiments of the 93rd Division, item 96.

47. Chester D. Heywood, *Negro Combat Troops in the World War: The Story of the 371st Infantry* (Worcester, Massachusetts, 1928), pp. 1, 9.

48. Memorandum, Colonel V. A. Caldwell, Infantry Retired, to Assistant Commandant, General Staff College, March 14, 1920, subject: Use to be made of negroes in the U. S. military service, item 120.

49. Extracts from memorandum for the Commandant, Army War College, August 30, 1924, item 124.

50. *The Crisis*, July 1919, pp. 20–21; Foner, *Blacks and the Military*, p. 124–125; Barbeau and Henri, *The Unknown Soldiers*, pp. 165–166.

51. *The Crisis*, July 1919, pp. 19–20.

52. Memorandum, Colonel Herschel Tupes to Colonel Allen J. Greer, War Plans Division, Office of Chief of Staff, War Department, March 26, 1919, subject: Employment of negroes in our military establishment, appendix 40 to Army War College History of Negro Troops in the World War, 1917–1918, item 118.

53. Statement of Dr. Charles H. Houston, Special Counsel for the NAACP and also representing the *Pittsburgh Courier*, Hearings before the Subcommittee of the Senate Committee on Military Affairs, 76th Congress, 3rd Session, *Selective Compulsory Military Training*, item 194.

54. Barbeau and Henri, *The Unknown Soldiers*, pp. 71–72, 74; Little, *From Harlem to the Rhine*, pp. 68–69.

55. P. J. Carisella and James W. Ryan, *The Black Swallow of Death: The Incredible Story of Eugene Jacques Bullard, the World's First Black Combat Aviator* (Boston, 1972), pp. 6, 113–114, 127–128, 188, 194–199.

56. *The Crisis*, August 1919, p. 179.

Chapter 9. OPPRESSION, INDIFFERENCE, AND A SURGE OF ACTIVISM

1. The Chicago Commission on Race Relations, "Race Riot, Chicago, in 1919," in Chace and Collier, *Justice Denied*, pp. 225–233.

2. Barbeau and Henri, *The Unknown Soldiers*, pp. 175–179; Roy Wilkins and Tom Mathews, *Standing Fast: The Autobiography of Roy Wilkins* (New York, 1982), pp. 41–44.

3. Robert K. Murray, *Red Scare: A Study of National Hysteria*, 1919–1920 (New York, paperback edition, 1964), pp. 177–180; Constance McLaughlin Green, *The Secret City: A History of Race Relations in the Nation's Capital* (Princeton, New Jersey, 1967), pp. 173–175, 191–192.

4. William E. Gibbs, "James Weldon Johnson: A Black Perspective on 'Big Stick' Diplomacy," *Diplomatic History*, vol. VIII (Fall 1984), pp. 331–332, 334, 336–346; Millett, *Semper Fidelis*, pp. 199, 202–204, 209.

5. War Department Circulars no. 271, May 23, 1919, Discontinuance of Enlistments for Colored Cavalry in the Philippine Islands; no. 355, July 16, 1919, Discontinuance of Enlistments for Colored Cavalry; no. 365, July 22, 1919, Colored Applicants for Enlistment; no. 392, August 8, 1919, Discontinuance of Enlistments of Colored Men—Amendment to Circular no. 355, War Department, 1919; no. 436, September 24, 1919, Discontinuance of Enlistments of Colored Men—Amendment to Circular no. 394 [sic], War Department, 1919; in MacGregor and Nalty, *Blacks in the Armed Forces*, vol. IV, items 128–132. Unless otherwise noted, all documents cited by item number in the chapter are reproduced in this volume.

6. Memoranda, Major General J. G. Harbord, Deputy Chief of Staff, for the Judge Advocate General, March 1, 1922; Lieutenant Colonel L. D. Gasser, Secretary, General Staff, for Mr. Gray, March 3, 1922, subject: Transfers between the 9th and 10th Cavalry; Major General Harbord for the Judge Advocate General, March 4, 1922, items 133–135.

7. Ulysses Lee, *The United States Army in World War II, Special Studies: The Employment of Negro Troops* (Washington, 1966), pp. 24–25.

8. Letter, Walter White to President Herbert Hoover, July 29, 1931, item 148; Letter, Walter White to General Douglas MacArthur, Chief of Staff, September 10, 1931, item 150; Letter, Robert R. Moton, Principal, Tuskegee Normal and Industrial Institute, to President Hoover, October 21, 1931, item 154.

9. Letter, General Douglas MacArthur to Robert R. Moton, November 18, 1931, item 156.

10. Letter, Brigadier General E. T. Conley, Acting Adjutant General, to Walter White, November 25, 1935, item 165.

11. Letter, Major General George Van Horn Moseley, Acting Chief of Staff, to Walter White, September 21, 1931, item 152.

12. Charles Johnson, "The Army, the Negro, and the Civilian Conservation Corps," *Military Affairs*, vol. XXXVI (October 1972), pp. 82–87.

13. Lee, *The Employment of Negro Troops*, pp. 56–57.

14. Major Everett C. Williams, Report of Special Investigation of Alleged Discrimination against Members of the 10th Cavalry, Fort Leavenworth, Kansas, October 28, 1938, item 177.

15. Letter, Robert L. Vann, editor, *The Pittsburgh Courier*, to Mr. James Roosevelt, Secretary to the President, March 5, 1938, item 172.

16. Memorandum, Brigadier General R. M. Beck, Jr., Assistant Chief of Staff, for the Chief of Staff, March 16, 1938, subject: Letter from Congressman Hamilton Fish, reference colored soldiers, and Letter, Louis Johnson, Acting Secretary of War, to Representative Hamilton Fish, March 24, 1938, items 173 and 174.

17. Lee, *The Employment of Negro Troops*, pp. 29–33, 39–44, 46–47.

18. Letter, Charles Houston to President Franklin D. Roosevelt, October 8, 1937, item 169.

19. Lee, *The Employment of Negro Troops*, pp. 52–54.

20. *Ibid.*, pp. 55–56; Senate Debate on the Schwartz Amendment to Public Law 18, To Expand the National Defense Program, *Congressional Record*, Senate, March 7, 1939, item 191; Establishment of a School for Training Negro Pilots, Statement of the Honorable H. H. Schwartz, a United States Senator from the State of Wyoming, Hearings before the Subcommittee of the House Committee on Appropriations, 76th Congress, 1st Session, *Supplemental Appropriations Bill for 1940*, item 189.

21. Letter, Walter White to President Roosevelt, September 15, 1939, item 182.

22. Letter, Chauncey E. Spencer to Lee Nichols, June 19, 1953, item 186.

23. Henry H. Adams, *Years of Deadly Peril: The Coming of the War, 1939–1941* (New York, 1969), pp. 292–294.

24. Statement of Rayford W. Logan, Chairman, Committee on the Participation of Negroes in the National Defense Program, Hearing before the House Committee on Military Affairs, 76th Congress, 3rd Session, *Selective Compulsory Military Training*, item 193.

25. Statement of Dr. Charles Houston, Special Counsel for the NAACP and also representing the *Pittsburgh Courier*, Hearings before the House Committee on Military Affairs, 76th Congress, 3rd Session, *Selective Compulsory Military Training*, item 194.

26. Logan Statement.

27. Senate Debate on Senator Robert H. Wagner's Antidiscrimination Amendment to the Selective Training and Service Act, *Congressional Record*, Senate, August 26, 1940, item 195.

28. Lee, *The Employment of Negro Troops*, pp. 73–74.

29. Joseph Lash, *Eleanor and Franklin: The Story of Their Relationship, Based on Eleanor Roosevelt's Private Papers* (New York, 1971), pp. 512–514, 518–519, 528–529.

30. *Ibid.*, p. 530; Lee, *The Employment of Negro Troops*, pp. 74–75; Report on Conference at the White House, September 27, 1940, subject: Discrimination against Negroes in the Armed Forces of the United States, vol. V, item 8; Richard M. Dalfiume, *Desegregation of the U.S. Armed Forces: Fighting on Two Fronts, 1939–1953* (Columbia, Missouri, 1969), pp. 34–46.

31. Memorandum, Assistant Secretary of War Robert P. Patterson to the President, October 8, 1940, with enclosure; Letter, Stephen Early, Secretary to the President, to Assistant Secretary of War Patterson, October 9, 1940; vol. V, items 10 and 11.

32. Lee, *The Employment of Negro Troops*, pp. 76–79.

33. Lash, *Eleanor and Franklin*, pp. 532–535; Dalfiume, *Desegregation of the U.S. Armed Forces*, pp. 57, 119n.

34. Lee, *The Employment of Negro Troops*, pp. 90–91, 98–100, 107–108.

35. Alan M. Osur, *Blacks in the Army Air Forces during World War II* (Washington, 1977), pp. 24–28.

36. *Ibid.*, pp. 11–12.

Chapter 10. THE ARMY'S BLACK EAGLES

1. Lawrence J. Paszek, "Separate but Equal? The Story of the 99th Fighter Squadron," *Aerospace Historian*, vol. XXIV (Fall/September 1977), p. 137; Robert A. Rose, "Lonely Eagles," part 1, *Journal of the American Aviation Historical Society*, vol. XX (Summer 1975), pp. 119–120; American Aviation Historical Society, *Newsletter* no. 74 (3rd quarter 1985), p. 6.

2. Rose, "Lonely Eagles," part 1, p. 124.

3. James C. Hasdorff, "Reflections on the Tuskegee Experiment: An Interview with Brig. Gen. Noel F. Parrish, USAF (Ret)," *Aerospace Historian*, vol. XXIV (Fall/September 1977), pp. 175–176.

4. Rose, "Lonely Eagles," part 1, p. 124.

5. *Ibid.*, p. 122; Paszek, "Separate but Equal?" p. 137

6. Summary and Recommendations Concerning the Integration of the Negro Soldier into the Army, Submitted to the Secretary of War, September 22, 1941, in MacGregor and Nalty, *Blacks in the Armed Forces*, vol. V, item 33. All documents cited by item number in the chapter are reproduced in this volume.

7. Memorandum with attachment, George C. Marshall, Chief of Staff, for the Secretary of War, December 1, 1941, subject: Report of Judge William H. Hastie, Civilian Aide to the Secretary of War, dated September 22, 1941, item 36.

8. Memorandum, William H. Hastie, Civilian Aide to the Secretary of War, through the Under Secretary of War, January 5, 1943, item 64; *Blacks in the Army Air Forces during World War II*, p. 36.

9. Memorandum, Hastie to the Secretary of War, January 5, 1943.

10. Memorandum, Major General George E. Stratemeyer, Chief of the Air Staff, for the Assistant Secretary of War, January 12, 1943, subject: Analysis of the Memorandum of Judge William H. Hastie to the Secretary of War, item 65.

11. Hasdorff, "An Interview with Brig. Gen. Noel F. Parrish," p. 175; Lee, *The Employment of Negro Troops*, p. 436.

12. Robert Rose, "Lonely Eagles," part 2, *Journal of the American Aviation Historical Society*, vol. XX (Winter 1975), p. 242; unpublished interview, James C. Hasdorff with Colonel Philip G. Cochran, October 20–21, and November 11, 1975, Office of Air Force History, pp. 121–126.

13. Paszek, "Separate but Equal?" p. 138.

14. Osur, *Blacks in the Army Air Forces during World War II*, pp. 48–50.

15. *Ibid.*, p. 50; Lee, *The Employment of Negro Troops*, pp. 157–158.

16. Osur, *Blacks in the Army Air Forces during World War II*, p. 51; Rose, "Lonely Eagles," part 2, p. 244; Lee, *The Employment of Negro Troops*, pp. 466–467.

17. Rose, "Lonely Eagles," part 2, pp. 250–251; Paszek, "Separate but Equal?" pp. 140–141; Maurer H. Maurer, ed., *Combat Squadrons of the Air Force, World War II* (Maxwell Air Force Base, 1982), pp. 329, 332, 365–366; U.S. Air Force Historical Study No. 85: *Victory Credits for the Destruction of Enemy Aircraft, World War II* (Washington, 1978), pp. 586, 588, 601.

18. A History of the Special Section, Office of Inspector General (29 June 1941 to 16 November 1944), n.d., item 90.

19. Osur, *Blacks in the Army Air Forces during World War II*, pp. 97–98.

20. Kenneth P. Werrel, "Mutiny at Army Air Force Station 569: Bamber Bridge, England, June 1943," *Aerospace Historian*, vol. XXII (Winter/December 1975), pp. 203–204, 206–208.

21. Memorandum, John J. McCloy, Assistant Secretary of War, for the Chief of Staff, July 3, 1943, subject: Negro Troops, item 73.

22. Memorandum, General George C. Marshall, Chief of Staff, for the Commanding Generals, Army Air Forces, Army Ground Forces, Army Service Forces, July 3, 1943, item 74.

23. Memorandum, Truman K. Gibson, Jr., Acting Civilian Aide to the Secretary of War, May 14, 1943, item 71.

24. Osur, *Blacks in the Army Air Forces during World War II*, pp. 84–85.

25. *Ibid.*, pp. 55–59.

26. The account of the conflict over admission to the officers' club is based upon Osur, *Blacks in the Army Air Forces during World War II*, pp. 114–119, and Alan L. Gropman, *The Air Force Integrates* (Washington, 1978), pp. 20–31.

27. Thomas R. Brooks, *Walls Come Tumbling Down: A History of the Civil Rights Movement* (Englewood Cliffs, New Jersey, 1974), p. 46.

28. Hasdorff, "An Interview with Brig. Gen. Noel F. Parrish," pp. 178–179.

29. Osur, *Blacks in the Army Air Forces during World War II*, pp. 104–105.

Chapter 11. INTEGRATING THE FIGHTING, THOUGH NOT THE ARMY

1. Lee, *The Employment of Negro Troops*, pp. 202–204, 210–212.

2. *Ibid.*, pp. 303, 328–330.

3. *Ibid.*, pp. 314–315.

4. *Ibid.*, pp. 278–286.

5. *Ibid.*, pp. 296, 349.

6. Memorandum, John J. McCloy, Assistant Secretary of War, for the Chief of Staff, July 3, 1943, subject: Negro Troops, in MacGregor and Nalty, *Blacks in the Armed Forces*, vol. V, item 73. All documents cited by item number in the chapter are reproduced in this volume.

7. Lee, *The Employment of Negro Troops*, pp. 351, 368–369.

8. *Ibid.*, pp. 323–324.

9. Memorandum, George C. Marshall, Chief of Staff, to the Commanding Generals, Army Air Forces, Army Ground Forces, Army Service Forces, July 3, 1943, subject: Negro Troops, item 74.

10. War Department Pamphlet No. 20-6, *Command of Negro Troops*, February 29, 1944, item 83.

11. Lee, *The Employment of Negro Troops*, pp. 400–401.

12. *Ibid.*, pp. 428–431, 497–498.

13. Stetson Conn, Rose C. Engelman, and Byron Fairchild, *The U.S. Army in World War II: The Western Hemisphere: Guarding the United States and Its Outposts* (Washington, 1964), pp. 436–441.

14. Annette Palmer, "The Politics of Race and War: Black American Soldiers in the Caribbean Theater during the Second World War," *Military Affairs*, vol. XLVII (April 1983), pp. 59–61.

15. Minutes of Meeting of Advisory Committee on Negro Troop Policies, April 26, 1944, item 87.

16. "Colored Troops in Combat," *Congressional Record: House*, February 23, 1944, pp. 2007–2008.

17. Memorandum, Truman K. Gibson, Jr., Civilian Aide to the Secretary of War, to the Assistant Secretary of War, November 3, 1943, item 78.

18. Letter, with enclosure, Eleanor Roosevelt to Mr. McCloy, November 23, 1943, item 81.

19. Lee, *The Employment of Negro Troops*, pp. 497–498; Dalfiume, *Desegregation of the U.S. Armed Forces*, pp. 94–95, 124–126.

20. Memorandum, John J. McCloy for the Secretary of War, March 2, 1944, (with notations), item 86.

21. Lee, *The Employment of Negro Troops*, pp. 498–499.

22. *Ibid.*, pp. 500–501, 504–512, 527; John Miller, Jr., *The United States Army in World War II: The War in the Pacific: Cartwheel: The Reduction of Rabaul* (Washington, 1959), pp. 109, 121–122.

23. Memorandum, Major General Virgil L. Peterson, Acting Inspector General, for the Deputy Chief of Staff, May 14, 1945, subject: Exemplary Conduct of the 24th Infantry at Saipan, item 95.

24. Lee, *The Employment of Negro Troops*, pp. 536–552.

25. Memorandum, Truman K. Gibson, Acting Civilian Aide to the Secretary of War, to the Assistant Secretary of War, August 23, 1943, item 76.

26. Lee, *The Employment of Negro Troops*, pp. 334–335.

27. Memorandum, Major O. J. Magee, Intelligence Division, Army Service Forces, for Colonel Roamer, December 6, 1944, subject: Remarks on the 92nd Infantry Division, item 92.

28. Lee, *The Employment of Negro Troops*, pp.552–553.

29. Memorandum, Truman K. Gibson, Jr., Civilian Aide to the Secretary of War, December 20, 1944, item 94.

30. Lee, *The Employment of Negro Troops*, pp. 580–588.

31. *Ibid.*, pp. 335, 446, 644–660.

32. *Washington Star*, January 25, 1976; 761st Tank Battalion, Combat Highlights [a unit history], Center of Military History; Major Gerald K. Johnson, "The Black Soldier in the Ardennes," *Soldiers*, vol. XXXVI (February 1981), pp. 18–19.

33. Russell F. Weigley, *Eisenhower's Lieutenants: The Campaign of France and Germany, 1944–1945* (Bloomington, Indiana, 1981), p. 568.

34. Message, Headquarters, Communications Zone, European Theater of Operations, to Commanders of Colored Troops, Communications Zone, December 26, 1944, subject: Volunteers for Training and Assignment as Reinforcements, item 98.

35. Weigley, *Eisenhower's Lieutenants*, pp. 569, 660.

36. Message, Headquarters, Communications Zone, European Theater of Operations, to Commanding General, Southern Line of Communications; Commanding General, United Kingdom Base; Section Com-

manders, Communications Zone, December 26, 1944, subject: Volunteers for Training and Assignment as Reinforcements, item 99.

37. Lee, *The Employment of Negro Troops*, pp. 693–695.

38. Weigley, *Eisenhower's Lieutenants*, pp. 660–662.

39. Information and Education Division, Army Service Forces, Opinions about Negro Infantry Platoons in White Companies of Seven Divisions, July 3, 1945, item 102.

40. Lee, *The Employment of Negro Troops*, pp. 406–407, 414–415.

41. *Ibid.*, pp. 609–613, 632–633, 636–637, 641.

42. Foner, *Blacks and the Military*, p. 165–166.

43. War Department Pamphlet no. 20-6, *Command of Negro Troops*, February 29, 1944; Army Service Forces Manual M5, *Leadership and the Negro Soldier*, October, 1944; A History of a Special Section, Office of Inspector General; items 83, 89, and 90; Lee, *The Employment of Negro Troops*, pp. 387–389.

44. Memorandum, Truman K. Gibson, Jr., Acting Civilian Aide to the Secretary of War, to the Assistant Secretary of War, June 2, 1943, and A History of a Special Section, Office of Inspector General, items 72 and 90.

45. Lee, *The Employment of Negro Troops*, pp. 331–332.

46. Brooks, *Walls Come Tumbling Down*, p. 37.

47. John Morton Blum, *V Was for Victory: Politics and American Culture during World War II* (New York, 1976), pp. 199–207.

Chapter 12. THE NAVAL SERVICE IN WORLD WAR II: POLICY AND REALITY

1. Memorandum, Chairman of the General Board, Walton R. Sexton, for the Secretary of the Navy, September 17, 1940, subject: Enlistment of Colored Persons in the U.S. Navy, with enclosure, in MacGregor and Nalty, *Blacks in the Armed Forces*, vol. VI, item 2. Unless otherwise noted, all documents cited by item number in the chapter are reproduced in this volume.

2. Letter, Frank Knox to Senator Arthur Capper, August 1, 1940, item 1.

3. Walter White, *A Man Called White: The Autobiography of Walter White* (Bloomington, Indiana, paperback edition, 1948), pp. 190–191.

4. Memorandum, Chief of the Bureau of Navigation to the Chairman, General Board, January 22, 1942, subject: Enlistment of men of the colored race in other than the messman branch, with enclosures, item 11.

5. Foner, *Blacks and the Military*, p. 172–173; Gordon W. Prange, in collaboration with Donald M. Goldstein and Katherine V. Dillon, *At Dawn We Slept: The Untold Story of Pearl Harbor* (New York, 1978), pp. 514–515.

6. Historical Section, Bureau of Naval Personnel, *The Negro in the Navy in World War II*, pp. 4–5, item 101; Morris J. MacGregor, Jr., *Defense Studies: Integration of the Armed Forces, 1940–1965* (Washington, 1981), pp. 62–63.

7. Bureau of Naval Personnel, *The Negro in the Navy in World War II*, p. 5.

8. Hearing before the General Board of the Navy, January 23, item 12.

9. Memorandum, Vice Admiral W. R. Sexton, Chairman, General Board, to the Secretary of the Navy, February 3, 1942, subject: Enlistment of men of the colored race in other than the messman branch, item 13.

10. Memorandum, Frank Knox for Vice Admiral W. R. Sexton, February 14, 1942, item 14.

11. Memorandum, Chairman, General Board, to the Secretary of the Navy, March 30, 1942, subject: Enlistment of men of the colored race in other than the messman branch, item 23.

12. Memorandum, F. D. R. [Franklin D. Roosevelt] for the Secretary of the Navy, March 31, 1942, item 25.

13. Navy Department press release, April 7, 1942, Navy to Accept Negroes for General Service, item 26; Bureau of Naval Personnel, *The Negro in the Navy in World War II*, pp. 8–9.

14. Bureau of Naval Personnel, *The Negro in the Navy in World War II*, pp. 9, 54; MacGregor, *Integration of the Armed Forces*, pp. 68–69.

15. MacGregor, *Integration of the Armed Forces*, p. 70.

16. Bureau of Naval Personnel, *The Negro in the Navy in World War II*, pp. 10–13.

17. Memorandum, F. D. R. for the Secretary of the Navy, February 22, 1943, item 43.

18. MacGregor, *Integration of the Armed Forces*, p. 71.

19. *Ibid.*, pp. 75–77.

20. *Ibid.*, pp. 67, 72–75, 80.

21. Letter, Secretary of the Navy Frank Knox to Mr. Algernon D. Black, City-Wide Citizens Committee on Harlem, April 23, 1943, item 33.

22. Memorandum, Rear Admiral Randall Jacobs for the Secretary of the Navy, April 27, 1943, item 34.

23. Memorandum, the Secretary of the Navy for Rear Admiral Randall Jacobs, April 29, 1943, Item 35.

24. Memorandum, Secretary of the Navy James V. Forrestal for the President, July 28, 1944, item 36.

25. MacGregor, *Integration of the Armed Forces*, p. 87; Navy Department press release, Negro Women to Be Accepted in Women's Reserve, U.S. Navy Reserve, October 19, 1944, item 38.

26. MacGregor, *Integration of the Armed Forces*, p. 88.

27. Bureau of Naval Personnel, *The Negro in the Navy in World War II*, p. 98; Foner, *Blacks and the Military*, p. 174. The official count of black WAVES is seventy-two officers and enlisted women, though a total of fifty-seven has appeared in secondary works.

28. Letter, Frank Knox to Senator David I. Walsh, May 21, 1942, item 32.

29. MacGregor, *Integration of the Armed Forces*, pp. 80–82.

30. *Ibid.*, pp. 77–78; Bureau of Naval Personnel, *The Negro in the Navy in World War II*, pp. 42–43, 92; Memorandum, Captain Louis E. Denfeld,

Assistant Chief of Naval Personnel, to Commander in Chief, U.S. Fleet, December 1, 1943, subject: Plans for the Assignment of Negro Enlisted Personnel to One DE [destroyer escort] and One PC [submarine chaser], item 78.

31. Memorandum, James Forrestal for the President, May 20, 1944, item 79; MacGregor, *Integration of the Armed Forces*, p. 84.

32. Memorandum, Captain L. E. Denfeld, the Assistant Chief of Naval Personnel, to Commander in Chief, United States Fleet, and Chief of Naval Operations, July 4, 1944, subject: Negro Enlisted Personnel—Assignment to Large Auxiliary Vessels of the Fleet, item 80.

33. Memoranda, Admiral Randall Jacobs, Chief of Naval Personnel, to Commanding Officers, USS *Antaeus . . . Vega*, August 9, 1944, subject: Negro Enlisted Personnel—Assignment of, to Ships of the Fleet, item 83; Captain L. E. Denfeld, Assistant Chief of Naval Personnel, to Commanding Officers, USS *Antaeus . . . Vega*, January 9, 1945, subject: same, item 84; Admiral Jacobs to Commander in Chief, United States Fleet, and Chief of Naval Operations, March 6, 1945, subject: Negro Personnel—Expanded Use of; F. J. Horne, Vice Chief of Naval Operations, for Commander in Chief United States Fleet and Chief of Naval Operations, March 9, 1945, subject: same; First Memorandum Endorsement for Vice Chief of Naval Operations, March 28, 1945, subject: same, the last three in item 85.

34. White, *A Man Called White*, p. 273.

35. MacGregor, *Integration of the Armed Forces*, p. 92.

36. Henry I. Shaw, Jr., and Ralph W. Donnelly, *Blacks in the Marine Corps* (Washington, 1973), pp. 44–45.

37. White, *A Man Called White*, pp. 282–285.

38. Lieutenant Dennis D. Nelson, *The Integration of the Negro into the United States Navy, 1776-1947*, with a Brief Historical Introduction (Washington, 1948), p. 178.

39. Dalfiume, *Desegregation of the U.S. Armed Forces*, p. 102.

40. Memorandum, Chief of Naval Personnel to Commandants, All Recruit Training Commands, June 11, 1945, subject: Negro Recruit Training—Discontinuance of special program and camps for, item 95.

41. Message, Secretary of the Navy to ALNAV [a dissemination list for message traffic], December 12, 1945, ALNAV, no. 423, item 100.

42. Mary and Albert Cocke, "Hell Roaring Mike: A Fall from Grace in the Frozen North," *Smithsonian*, vol. XIII (February 1983), p. 120; Linda E. Townsend and Dupree Davenport, *A History of Blacks in the Coast Guard from 1790* (Washington, n.d.), pp. 1–17, 26–27.

43. Hearings before the General Board of the Navy, January 23, 1942, item 12.

44. Memorandum, with attached plan, Rear Admiral R. R. Waesche, Commandant of the Coast Guard, for Admiral Sexton, February 2, 1942, subject: Enlistment of colored men in the Coast Guard in ratings other than mess attendant, included with item 12.

45. MacGregor, *Integration of the Armed Forces*, pp. 115–117.

46. Appearance of Mr. Carlton Skinner, Director of Information, Department of the Interior, before the President's Committee on Equality of Treatment and Opportunity in the Armed Forces, April 25, 1949, in MacGregor and Nalty, *Blacks in the Armed Forces*, vol. X, pp. 930–934.

47. MacGregor, *Integration of the Armed Forces*, pp. 121–122.

48. Memorandum, Commandant of the Marine Corps to the Chairman, General Board, February 27, 1942, subject: Enlistment of men of the colored race in other than the messman branch, item 21.

49. Shaw and Donnelly, *Blacks in the Marine Corps*, pp. 3–8.

50. *Ibid.*, pp. 16–23.

51. Memorandum, Commandant of the Marine Corps to Distribution List [a dissemination list], March 20, 1943, subject: Colored Personnel, item 106.

52. U.S. Marine Corps Historical Division, "The Negro in the Marine Corps," draft MS, n.d., item 112; MacGregor, *Integration of the Armed Forces*, pp. 107–108, 267.

Chapter 13. A Postwar Transition

1. Brooks, *Walls Come Tumbling Down*, pp. 88–89; Richard H. Kluger, *Simple Justice: The History of Brown v. Board of Education and Black America's Struggle for Equality* (New York, 1976), p. 298.

2. White, *A Man Called White*, pp. 330–331.

3. Kluger, *Simple Justice*, pp. 297, 299–300.

4. Brooks, *Walls Come Tumbling Down*, p. 58.

5. *Ibid.*, pp. 88–89.

6. Kluger, *Simple Justice*, pp. 234–238.

7. Brooks, *Walls Come Tumbling Down*, pp. 47–48, 62–67.

8. Minutes of a Press Conference held by Mr. Lester B. Granger, November 1, 1945, in MacGregor and Nalty, *Blacks in the Armed Forces*, vol. VII, item 13. All documents cited by item number in the chapter are reproduced in this volume.

9. Letter, Lester Granger to Secretary of the Navy James Forrestal, August 4, 1945, item 11.

10. MacGregor, *Integration of the Armed Forces*, pp. 167–168; Bureau of Naval Personnel Circular Letter No. 48–46, February 27, 1946, item 32.

11. Memorandum, Director, Division of Plans and Policies, to the Commandant of the Marine Corps, May 13, 1946, subject: Negro Personnel in the Post-War Marine Corps, item 34; MacGregor, *Integration of the Armed Forces*, pp. 173–174.

12. Memorandum, The Adjutant General to the Commander in Chief, Southwest Pacific Area, the Commanding Generals, U.S. Army Forces in the other theaters, and the Commanding Generals, Alaskan Depart-

ment, Northwest Service Command, and Caribbean Defense Command, May 23, 1945, subject: Participation of Negro Troops in the Post-War Military Establishment, item 4.

13. Memorandum, Truman Gibson, Jr., Civilian Aide to the Secretary of War, for Mr. John J. McCloy, Assistant Secretary of War, August 9, 1945, item 5.

14. Enclosure to memorandum, Colonels Waldo Shumway, J. S. Leonard, et al., Office of Commanding General, Army Service Forces, for Director of Plans and Operations, Army Service Forces, September 27, 1945, subject: Participation of Negro Troops in the Postwar Military Establishment, item 6.

15. Special Planning Division, Office of Assistant Chief of Air Staff–1, Air Staff Summary Sheet, October 12, 1945, subject: Participation of Negro Troops in the Post-War Military Establishment, item 7.

16. Enclosure to Memorandum, Colonel E. F. Olson, Ground Adjutant General, Army Ground Forces, for the Chief of Staff, U.S. Army, November 28, 1945, subject: Participation of Negro Troops in the Postwar Military Establishment, item 8.

17. Letter, Colonel Noel Parrish to Brigadier General William E. Hall, Deputy Assistant Chief of Air Staff, Personnel, Headquarters, U.S. Army Air Forces, August 5, 1945, item 19.

18. MacGregor, *Integration of the Armed Forces*, pp. 153–154.

19. War Department Circular No. 124, Utilization of Negro Manpower in the Postwar Army Policy, April 27, 1946, item 28.

20. Memorandum, J. J. McC. [John J. McCloy] for Judge Patterson, November 24, 1945, item 25.

21. Memorandum, Truman K. Gibson, Jr., Civilian Aide to the Secretary of War, for Mr. Robert P. Patterson, the Secretary of War, November 28, 1945, included in item 27; MacGregor, *Integration of the Armed Forces*, p. 163.

22. First Indorsement, Lieutenant General Ira C. Eaker, Deputy Commander, Army Air Forces, to the Chief of Staff, War Department, n.d., subject: War Department Special Board on Negro Manpower, included in item 27.

Chapter 14. FAILED POLICIES

1. Letter, Representative Stephen Pace to Secretary of the Navy James Forrestal, July 22, 1946, in MacGregor and Nalty, *Blacks in the Armed Forces*, vol. VIII, item 70. All documents cited by item number in the chapter are reproduced in this volume.

2. Letter, Lester B. Granger to Secretary of the Navy John L. Sullivan, March 15, 1948, item 75.

3. MacGregor, *Integration of the Armed Forces*, p. 243.

4. Letter, Lieutenant Dennis D. Nelson, II, to Secretary of the Navy John L. Sullivan, January 7, 1949, item 82.

5. MacGregor, *Integration of the Armed Forces*, p. 248.

6. *Ibid.*, pp. 245–246.

7. *Ibid.*, p. 242; Memorandum, Lieutenant Dennis D. Nelson, USNR, to Rear Admiral R. F. Hickey, Deputy Director, Office of Public Relations, March 26, 1948, subject: Problems of the Stewards' Branch, item 76; Memorandum, with enclosure, Lieutenant D. D. Nelson to the Chief of Naval Personnel, via Commander L. B. Cook, Director of Public Information, Office of the Chief of Naval Personnel, November 29, 1948, subject: Complaint of Navy Enlisted Man Made to PITTSBURGH COURIER and Delivered by Washington Correspondent and Representative, item 80; Letter, with attachment, E. S. Hope to Secretary of Defense James Forrestal, May 17, 1948, item 78.

8. Letter, Under Secretary of the Navy for the Honorable Clyde Doyle, Member of Congress, August 21, 1949, item 83.

9. MacGregor, *Integration of the Armed Forces*, pp. 250, 252.

10. Memorandum, Director, Division of Plans and Policies, to the Commandant of the Marine Corps, September 25, 1946, subject: Post-War Negro Personnel Requirements, item 119; Additional reference to cited memorandum, item 120.

11. Memorandum, the Commanding Officer, 52nd Defense Battalion, to the Commandant of the Marine Corps, via the Commanding General, Fleet Marine Force, Pacific, January 15, 1946, subject: Employment of Colored Personnel as Antiaircraft Artillery Troops, Recommendations on, item 113.

12. Memorandum, Division of Plans and Policies for the Commandant, January 6, 1947, subject: Negro Requirements, item 125.

13. Letter, the Commanding Officer, Marine Barracks, Naval Ammunition Depot, McAlester, Oklahoma, to Commandant of the Marine Corps, via the Commanding Officer, Naval Ammunition Depot, McAlester, Oklahoma, November 5, 1946, subject: Assignment of colored marines, item 122.

14. Endorsement, J. F. Goodwin, Commanding Officer, Naval Ammunition Depot, McAlester, Oklahoma, November 13, 1946, subject: same, item 122; Letter, Commandant of the Marine Corps to the Chief of Naval Operations, December 3, 1946, subject: Assignment of Negro Marines to MB, Naval Magazine, Port Chicago, California, and MB, NAD, Earle, N.J., item 123; Letter, the Chief of Naval Operations to the Commandant of the Marine Corps, January 6, 1947, subject: Assignment of Negro Marines to Marine Barracks, Naval Magazine, Port Chicago, California, and Marine Barracks, Naval Ammunition Depot, Earle, New Jersey, item 124.

15. MacGregor, *Integration of the Armed Forces*, pp. 255–256.

16. Memoranda, Division of Plans and Policies for the Commandant, April 16, 1947, subject: First Enlistments of Negro Personnel, item 130; Division of Plans and Policies for the Commandant, May 7, 1947, subject:

General Policy Governing Negro Reservists, item 132; Division of Plans and Policies for the Commandant, May 11, 1948, subject: Appointment to commissioned rank in the regular Marine Corps, case of Midshipman John Earl Rudder, item 144; Department of the Navy Press Release, August 25, 1948, First Regular Marine Corps Negro Officer Undergoes Training at Quantico, Virginia, item 146.

17. MacGregor, *Integration of the Armed Forces*, pp. 177–179.
18. Letter, the Adjutant General to the Commanding Generals, Army Air Forces, Ground Forces, and Service Forces, and Theater Commanders, February 4, 1946, item 1.
19. MacGregor, *Integration of the Armed Forces*, pp. 179, 182–188.
20. *Ibid.*, pp. 191–193.
21. *Ibid.*, pp. 201–202.
22. *Ibid.*, p. 210; Report of the Negro Newspaper Association to the Honorable Secretary of War, Judge Robert P. Patterson, on Troops and Conditions in Europe, July 18, 1946, item 9: Marcus H. Ray, Civilian Aide, Report to the Secretary of War, Mr. Robert P. Patterson, of Tour of European Installations, November 16–17, 1946, item 25; Historical Division, European Command, Negro Personnel in the European Command, 1 January 1946–30 June 1950, item 43.
23. MacGregor, *Integration of the Armed Forces*, p. 209; Gropman, *The Air Force Integrates*, pp. 64–67.
24. Memorandum, Commanding General, Army Air Forces, to Chief of Staff, April 1946, item 85.
25. Memorandum, Lieutenant General I. H. Edwards, Deputy Chief of Staff, Personnel and Administration, December 5, 1947, subject: Air Force Negro Troops in the Zone of Interior, item 86.
26. Gropman, *The Air Force Integrates*, pp. 89–90.
27. *Ibid.*, pp. 78–80.
28. *Ibid.*, pp. 74–75, 81–83.
29. Minutes of the Air Board Conference, January 6–7, 1948, p. 40, Records Group 340, Box 17, National Archives.
30. Minutes of the Air Board Conference, May 4–5, 1948, pp. 155–160, Records Group 340, Box 17, National Archives.
31. Letter, General Carl Spaatz to Mr. Lemuel E. Graves, Washington correspondent, *The Pittsburgh Courier*, April 7, item 94.

Chapter 15. POLITICS AND PRINCIPLE

1. Minutes of the Air Board Conference, May 4–5, 1948, p. 174, Records Group 340, Box 17, National Archives.
2. Merle Miller, *Plain Speaking: An Oral Biography of Harry S. Truman* (New York, 1973), p. 183.

3. Brooks, *Walls Come Tumbling Down*, pp. 59–60; Barton J. Bernstein and Allen J. Matusow, eds., *The Truman Administration: A Documentary History* (New York, 1966), pp. 87–94.

4. Robert Ferrell, ed., *Off the Record: The Private Papers of Harry S. Truman* (New York, 1980), p. 147.

5. Donald R. McCoy and Richard T. Ruetter, *Quest and Response: Minority Rights and the Truman Administration* (Lawrence, Kansas, 1973), pp. 87–95.

6. Excerpt from *To Secure These Rights: The Report of the President's Committee on Civil Rights* (Washington, 1947), in MacGregor and Nalty, *Blacks in the Armed Forces*, vol. VIII, item 150. Unless otherwise indicated, all documents cited by item number in the chapter are reproduced in this volume.

7. MacGregor, *Integration of the Armed Forces*, pp. 298–304.

8. Transcript, National Defense Conference on Negro Affairs, April 26, 1948, morning session, pp. 49–51, 58–59, item 153.

9. *Ibid.*, afternoon session, pp. 18–19, 44–45.

10. Dalfiume, *Desegregation of the U.S. Armed Forces*, pp. 167, 169.

11. *Ibid.*, pp. 170–171; MacGregor, *Integration of the Armed Forces*, pp. 309–312.

12. Executive Order 9981, July 26, 1948, item 164.

13. The President's News Conference of July 29, 1948, item 165.

14. Letter, Bayard Rustin, Secretary of the Working Committee, Campaign to Resist Military Segregation, to Secretary of Defense Forrestal, August 20, 1948, item 166.

15. Letter, Lester Granger to Secretary of Defense Forrestal, August 26, 1948, item 167.

16. MacGregor, *Integration of the Armed Forces*, pp. 332–333.

17. Shaw and Donnelly, *Blacks in the Marine Corps*, pp. 54–55.

18. MacGregor, *Integration of the Armed Forces*, pp. 317–318; William C. Berman, *The Politics of Civil Rights in the Truman Administration* (Columbus, Ohio, 1970), pp. 119–120.

19. Gropman, *The Air Force Integrates*, pp. 91–92.

20. Unpublished interview, Major Alan L. Gropman with Lieutenant General Idwal H. Edwards, February 10, 1973, Office of Air Force History.

21. Gropman, *The Air Force Integrates*, pp. 82–84.

22. Unpublished interview, Major Alan L. Gropman with General William F. McKee, May 1973, Office of Air Force History.

23. MacGregor, *Integration of the Armed Forces*, pp. 313–314.

24. *Ibid.*, pp. 343–344.

25. Memorandum, Clark Clifford for the President, August 17, 1948, subject: The 1948 Campaign, item 163.

26. U.S. Department of Commerce, Bureau of the Census, *Historical Statistics of the United States, Colonial Times to 1970*, 93rd Congress, 1st Ses-

sion, House document no. 93–78 (Washington, 1975), part 1, pp. 25–33; part 2, pp. 1073, 1075, 1077–1078.

27. Lawrence H. Suid, *Guts and Glory: Great American War Movies* (Reading, Massachusetts, 1978), pp. 47–51. The author emphasizes the subordinate role of the black character, a corporal compared to the higher-ranking white heroes, rather than the contrast in loyalty and decency between African and Nazi.

28. "Rosie the Riveter Remembers: Interviews by Mark Jonathan Harris, Franklin D. Mitchell, and Steven J. Schechter," *American Heritage*, vol. XXXV (February–March 1984), p. 97.

29. Jules Tygiel, "Beyond the Point of No Return," *Sports Illustrated*, vol. LVIII (June 20, 1983), pp. 66, 68–69, 74–75.

30. MacGregor, *Integration of the Armed Forces*, pp. 349–350.

31. Gropman, *The Air Force Integrates*, pp. 86–88, 116.

32. Department of the Air Force Letter no. 35–3, Military Personnel: Air Force Personnel Policies, May 11, 1949, Appendix B to *Freedom to Serve, Equality of Treatment and Opportunity in the Armed Services: A Report by the President's Committee*, vol. XI, item 37.

33. *Ibid.*

34. Gropman, *The Air Force Integrates*, pp. 120–121; National Military Establishment, Office of Public Information, Press Release, May 11, 1949, Secretary Johnson Approves Air Force Policies for Equality of Treatment and Opportunity, vol. XI, item 8.

35. National Military Establishment, Office of Public Information, Press Release, April 20, 1949, Secretary Johnson Directs Services to Review Personnel Practices, vol. XI, item 2; MacGregor, *Integration of the Armed Forces*, pp. 346–347; Arnold A. Rogow, *James Forrestal: A Study of Personality, Politics, and Policy* (New York, 1963), pp. 312–319.

36. Memorandum, Dan A. Kimball, Acting Secretary of the Navy, for the Secretary of Defense, May 23, 1949, subject: Equality of Opportunity and Treatment in the Armed Forces, vol. XI, item 10.

37. Shaw and Donnelly, *Blacks in the Marine Corps*, pp. 55–58.

38. Memorandum, Secretary of the Army Kenneth C. Royall for the Secretary of Defense, April 21, 1949, subject: Equality of Treatment and Opportunity in the Armed Forces, vol. XI, item 5.

39. MacGregor, *Integration of the Armed Forces*, pp. 352–355.

40. *Ibid.*, p. 360; *Freedom to Serve*, p. 61, vol. XI, item 37.

41. Memorandum, President's Committee on Equality of Treatment and Opportunity in the Armed Services for the Secretary of the Army, September 8, 1949, subject: Substitution of a GCT Quota for a Racial Quota, vol. XI, item 22.

42. Memorandum, Secretary of the Army Gordon Gray for the Secretary of Defense, September 30, 1949, subject: Equality of Treatment and Opportunity in the Armed Services, vol. XI, item 25.

43. Department of Defense, Office of Public Information, Press Release no.

256–49, September 30, 1949, Army Program for Racial Equality Approved by Secretary of Defense, vol. XI, item 26.

44. MacGregor, *Integration of the Armed Forces*, pp. 364–365.

45. Memorandum with attached report, Charles Fahy for the President, October 11, 1949, vol. XI, item 27.

46. Department of Defense, Office of Public Relations, Press Release no. 64-50, January 16, 1950, Army Revises Policy Governing Utilization of Negro Manpower, vol. XI, item 29.

47. Memorandum, Charles Fahy for Secretary Gray, February 9, 1950, subject: Recapitulation of the Proposal of the President's Committee for the Abolition of the Racial Quota, vol. XI, item 32.

48. Letter, with notations, Secretary of the Army Gordon Gray to the President, March 1, 1950, vol. XI, item 33.

49. Memorandum, H. S. T. [Harry S. Truman] for the Secretary of the Army, March 27, 1950, vol. IX, item 35.

50. MacGregor, *Integration of the Armed Forces*, pp. 377–378; Message, Department of the Army, G-1, to Chief of Army Field Forces and Army Commanding Generals, March 27, 1950, vol. XI, item 36.

51. *Freedom to Serve*, p. 61, vol. XI, item 37.

Chapter 16. THE KOREAN WAR:
RACIAL INTEGRATION AFFIRMED

1. Roy E. Appleman, *The U.S. Army in the Korean War: South to the Naktong, North to the Yalu (June–November 1950)*, (Washington, 1961), pp. 21, 36–38, 46–38, 193–195.

2. Memorandum, Lieutenant General Stephen J. Chamberlain, through the Chief of Staff, to the Secretary of the Army, February 9, 1950, subject: Report of Board of Officers on the Utilization of Negro Manpower in the Army, in MacGregor and Nalty, *Blacks in the Armed Forces*, vol. XII, item 37. All documents cited by item number in the chapter are reproduced in this volume.

3. MacGregor, *Integration of the Armed Forces*, pp. 437, 440; Office of Deputy Assistant Secretary of Defense for Equal Opportunity and Safety Policy, *Black Americans in Defense of Our Nation* (Washington, 1982), pp. 62–63.

4. MacGregor, *Integration of the Armed Forces*, pp. 436–439; Thurgood Marshall, "Summary Justice in Korea," *The Crisis*, May 1951, item 39.

5. Matthew B. Ridgway, *The Korean War* (New York: 1967), p. 193.

6. MacGregor, *Integration of the Armed Forces*, pp. 442–443.

7. Disposition Form, with attachments, Assistant Chief of Staff, G-1, for the Chief of Staff, May 23, 1951, subject: Utilization of Negro Manpower; Memorandum, Acting Chief Staff for the Secretary of the Army, May 28, 1951, subject: same; Message, Assistant Chief of Staff, G-3, Department of the Army, to Commander in Chief, Far East Command, n.d., subject: Integration of Negroes in FEC; items 42, 43, and 44.

8. Extract from advance draft, Utilization of Negro Manpower in the Army, a study prepared by the Operations Research Office, Johns Hopkins University, July 1951, item 46.

9. Assistant Chief of Staff, G-1, Letter of Evaluation, ORO Report on Utilization of Negro Manpower in the Army, n.d., item 47.

10. MacGregor, *Integration of the Armed Forces*, pp. 434, 450–452.

11. Shaw and Donnelly, *Blacks in the Marine Corps*, p. 59.

12. Memorandum, G-1, Division of Plans and Policies, Headquarters, U.S. Marine Corps, to Assistant Director of Public Information, June 4, 1951, subject: Article in Pittsburgh Courier of 26 May 1951, item 20.

13. Shaw and Donnelly, *Blacks in the Marine Corps*, p.59.

14. *Ibid.*, p. 61.

15. *Ibid.*, pp. 61–64.

16. Letter, Commander Durward W. Gilmore, Lieutenant Commander Robert Poor Roper, and Lieutenant Commander William H. Robertson, Jr., to Vice Admiral J. L. Holloway, Jr., Chief of Naval Personnel, August 31, 1953, item 30.

17. Memorandum, Lieutenant D. D. Nelson for Mr. Charles Durham, [Staff] Member, Fahy Committee, June 17, 1949, subject: Implementation of Proposed Navy Racial Policy, item 13.

18. *Ibid.*; Letter, Secretary of the Navy Dan A. Kimball to Lester B. Granger, November 19, 1952, item 28.

19. Bureau of Naval Personnel, Memorandum on Discrimination of the Negro, January 24, 1959, item 32, MacGregor, *Integration of the Armed Forces*, p. 416.

20. Malcolm W. Cagle and Frank A. Manson, *The Sea War in Korea* (Annapolis, Maryland, 1957), pp. 176–177; John E. Weems, "Black Wings of Gold," *U.S. Naval Institute Proceedings*, vol. CIX (July 1983), pp. 38–39.

21. Gropman, *The Air Force Integrates*, pp. 125–127, 145–147, 221–223; Thurgood Marshall, "Summary Justice in Korea," item 39.

22. Memorandum, G-1, Division of Plans and Policies, Headquarters, U.S. Marine Corps, to Assistant Director of Public Information, June 4, 1951, subject: Article in Pittsburgh Courier of 26 May 1951, item 20.

23. MacGregor, *Integration of the Armed Forces*, p. 409.

24. Unpublished interview, Major Richard H. Emmons with Lieutenant General Fred M. Dean, February 25–26, 1975, pp. 159–161, Office of Air Force History.

25. MacGregor, *Integration of the Armed Forces*, pp. 488–500.

Chapter 17. BLACK AMERICANS FORCE THE ISSUE

1. U.S. Department of Commerce, Bureau of the Census, *Historical Statistics of the United States, Colonial Times to 1970*, 93rd Congress, 1st Session, House document 93-78, part 2, p. 1143.

2. Kluger, *Simple Justice*, pp. 377–379, 392–395, 702–710, 744–755.

3. Brooks, *Walls Come Tumbling Down*, pp. 95–96, 113–114, 117–119.

4. MacGregor, *Integration of the Armed Forces*, pp. 480–481.

5. Dwight D. Eisenhower, *The White House Years: Waging Peace, 1956–1961* (New York, 1965), pp. 151–153; Berman, *The Politics of Civil Rights in the Truman Administration*, pp. 224–231.

6. Thomas J. Noer, "The New Frontier and African Neutralism: Kennedy, Nkrumah, and the Volta River Project," *Diplomatic History*, vol. VIII (Winter 1984), pp. 62–63, 78–79.

7. Brooks, *Walls Come Tumbling Down*, p. 131.

8. Eisenhower, *Waging Peace*, pp. 155–162; Stephen E. Ambrose, *Eisenhower*, vol. II, *The President* (New York, 1984), pp. 406–413.

9. Eisenhower, *Waging Peace*, pp. 162–165; Brooks, *Walls Come Tumbling Down*, p. 128; Ambrose, *Eisenhower*, vol. II, *The President*, p. 409.

10. MacGregor, *Integration of the Armed Forces*, pp. 496–498; Ambrose, *Eisenhower*, vol. II, *The President*, p. 410.

11. Brooks, *Walls Come Tumbling Down*, pp. 146–148, 155–158; Carl M. Brauer, *John F. Kennedy and the Second Reconstruction* (New York, 1977, pp. 10–11, 47–51.

12. MacGregor, *Integration of the Armed Forces*, pp. 505–506, 508; Theodore Sorenson, *Kennedy* (New York, 1965), pp. 473–475.

13. Memoranda, Robert S. McNamara for Assistant Secretary of Defense (Manpower), March 13, 1961, and Carlisle P. Runge for the Secretary of Defense, March 14, 1961, subject: Ceremonial Units and Honor Guard Details, both in MacGregor and Nalty, *Blacks in the Armed Forces*, vol. XII, items 96 and 98. Unless otherwise indicated, all documents cited by item number in the chapter are reproduced in this volume.

14. Letter, Representative Charles C. Diggs, Jr., to President John F. Kennedy, June 27, 1962, item 117.

15. MacGregor, *Integration of the Armed Forces*, pp. 511–512.

16. Memoranda, Adam Yarmolinksy, the Special Assistant, for Assistant Secretary Runge, March 13, 1961; Carlisle Runge for Adam Yarmolinsky, March 24, 1961; Robert S. McNamara for the Secretaries of the Military Departments, Director, Defense Research and Engineering, Chairman, Joint Chiefs of Staff, et al., March 24, 1961, subject: Non-Discrimination in Employment; Robert S. McNamara for all employees, March 24, 1961, subject: same; items 97, 100, 101, 102.

17. MacGregor, *Integration of the Armed Forces*, p. 517; Lewis J. Paper, *John F. Kennedy: The Promise and the Performance* (New York, paperback edition, 1975), pp. 243–244, 590.

18. MacGregor, *Integration of the Armed Forces*, pp. 511–512; Memorandum, Robert S. McNamara for the Secretaries of the Military Departments, Chairman, Joint Chiefs of Staff, Director, National Security Agency, April 28, 1961, subject: Military and Civilian Employee Recreational Organizations, item 104.

19. MacGregor, *Integration of the Armed Forces*, pp. 513–515.

20. *Ibid.*, pp. 536–537.

21. Letter, President John F. Kennedy to Gerhard A. Gesell, June 22, 1962, attachment to press release, Office of White House Press Secretary, June 24, 1962, vol. XIII, item 1.

22. MacGregor, *Integration of the Armed Forces*, pp. 535–536.

23. *Ibid.*, p. 540.

24. Initial Report of the President's Committee on Equal Opportunity in the Armed Forces, *Equality of Treatment and Opportunity for Negro Personnel Stationed within the United States*, pp. 27–29, vol. XIII, item 10.

25. *The Negro in the Armed Forces: 1963 Report of the U.S. Commission on Civil Rights*, item 121.

26. Office of Public Affairs, Department of Defense Directive no. 5120.36, July 26, 1963, subject: Equal Opportunity in the Armed Forces, attachment to Department of Defense Press Release, July 26, 1963, vol. XIII, item 20.

27. Office of Public Affairs, Department of Defense Press Release, July 29, 1963, Alfred B. Fitt named Deputy Assistant Secretary of Defense (Civil Rights), vol. XIII, item 21.

28. Department of Defense Directive 5120.36.

29. Anthony Lewis, ed., *Portrait of a Decade: The Second American Revolution* (New York, 1964), pp. 190–191.

30. Sorenson, *Kennedy*, pp. 494–497; Brauer, *John F. Kennedy and the Second Reconstruction*, pp. 290–292; Stephen B. Oates, *Let the Trumpet Sound: The Life of Martin Luther King, Jr.* (New York, 1982), pp. 261–262.

31. Excerpt from *The Congressional Record*, July 3, 1963, vol. XIII, item 22.

Chapter 18. FROM NONVIOLENCE TO VIOLENCE

1. Merle Miller, *Lyndon: An Oral Biography* (New York, 1980), p. 345.

2. Lyndon B. Johnson, *The Vantage Point: Perspectives of the Presidency, 1963–1968* (New York, 1971), pp. 156–166; Brooks, *Walls Come Tumbling Down*, pp. 234–236.

3. Brooks, *Walls Come Tumbling Down*, pp. 243–246; Len Holt, *The Summer That Didn't End* (New York, 1965), pp. 28, 30, 74. See also Milton Viorst, *Fire in the Streets: America in the 1960s* (New York, 1979), pp. 258–259.

4. MacGregor, *Integration of the Armed Forces*, pp. 556–558, 573.

5. Attachment to memorandum, Cyrus Vance, Secretary of the Army, for the Assistant Secretary of Defense (Manpower), August 15, 1963, subject: Equal Opportunity in the Armed Forces; Attachment to memorandum, James P. Goode, Deputy Secretary of the Air Force for Manpower, Personnel, and Organization, for the Assistant Secretary of Defense

(Manpower), August 15, 1963, subject: Implementation of DOD Directive 5120.36; Memorandum, Paul B. Fay, Jr., Under Secretary of the Navy, for the Assistant Secretary of Defense (Manpower), n.d., subject: Outline Plan for Implementing Department of Defense Directive 5120.36, "Equal Opportunity in the Armed Forces," dtd 26 July 1963; all in MacGregor and Nalty, *Blacks in the Armed Forces*, vol. XIII, items 28, 29, and 30. All documents cited by item number in the chapter are reproduced in this volume.

6. Final Report of the President's Committee on Equal Opportunity in the Armed Forces: Military Personnel Stationed Overseas and Membership and Participation in the National Guard, November 1964, item 14.

7. Stephen B. Oates, *Let the Trumpet Sound: The Life of Martin Luther King, Jr.* (New York, 1982), pp. 310–322, 325–327, 336–337, 343–349, 353–354, 362–365.

8. Stanley Karnow, *Vietnam: A History* (New York, 1983), pp. 368–376, 411–416, 419–420.

9. Oates, *Let the Trumpet Sound*, pp. 364–365.

10. The Civil Rights Policies of the Department of Defense, a speech by Stephen N. Schulman, Deputy Assistant Secretary of Defense (Civilian Personnel, Industrial Relations, and Civil Rights), May 4, 1965, item 40; Department of Defense Instruction no. 5525.2, July 24, 1964, subject: Processing of Requests by Military Personnel for Action by the Attorney General under the Civil Rights Act, item 39.

11. Oates, *Let the Trumpet Sound*, pp. 373–375, 394–395.

12. *Ibid.*, pp. 185–187, 437–438.

13. Brooks, *Walls Come Tumbling Down*, pp. 265–266, 273–274.

14. Viorst, *Fire in the Streets*, pp. 311, 330–332, 337, 339.

15. Martin Luther King, Jr., *Where Do We Go from Here: Chaos or Community?* (Boston, 1968), pp. 92–93.

16. Letter, Governor Otto Kerner and Mayor John V. Lindsay to the President, August 10, 1967, item 53.

17. National Guard Bureau, talking paper, July 25, 1967, subject: Legal Aspects of Integration of Negroes in the National Guard, item 52.

18. Memorandum, Robert S. McNamara for the Secretary of the Army, August 12, 1967, item 54; Department of the Army, Proposal to Increase Negro Participation in Army Reserve Components, n.d., item 55.

19. History and Analysis of Negro Participation in the National Guard, May 22, 1970, item 58.

20. Adam Yarmolinsky, *The Military Establishment: Its Impacts on American Society* (New York, 1971), pp. 341–342.

21. Charles C. Moskos, Jr., "Racial Integration in the Armed Forces," *American Journal of Sociology*, vol. LXXII (September 1966), p. 138.

22. Foner, *Blacks and the Military*, p. 203; Jack Beatty, "Vietnam: Sorrow, Rage, and Remembrance," a review of *Long Time Passing: Vietnam and The Haunted Generation* by Myra MacPherson, *Washington Post Book*

World, June 3, 1983, pp. 1, 14; Myra MacPherson, *Long Time Passing: Vietnam and the Haunted Generation* (Garden City, New York, 1984), pp. 32, 74–75, 406, 640–643.

23. MacGregor, *Integration of the Armed Forces,* pp. 601–605.

24. *Ibid.,* pp. 620–623.

25. *Time,* vol. LXXXIX (May 26, 1967), pp. 15–19.

26. Wallace Terry, *Bloods: An Oral History of the Vietnam War by Black Veterans* (New York, 1984), pp. 40–41.

27. Brooks, *Walls Come Tumbling Down,* p. 264.

28. Oates, *Let the Trumpet Sound,* pp. 469–470, 490–491, 494; *Public Papers of the Presidents of the United States: Lyndon Johnson, 1968–1969* (Washington, 1970), book I, pp. 509–510.

Chapter 19. TURBULENCE IN THE ARMED FORCES

1. *Time,* vol. XCVIII (November 29, 1971), p. 24.

2. Terry, *Bloods,* p. 172.

3. *Ibid.,* p. 116; Foner, *Blacks and the Military,* p. 213.

4. Terry, *Bloods,* p. 103.

5. Charles Moskos, Jr., *The American Enlisted Man: The Rank and File in Today's Military* (New York, 1970), pp. 118, 122–123.

6. *Newsweek,* vol. LXXII (September 30, 1968), p. 35.

7. C. V. Glines, "Black vs. White—Trouble in the Ranks," *Armed Forces Management,* vol. XVI (June 1970), pp. 20–22; Millett, *Semper Fidelis,* pp. 598–599; Terry, *Bloods,* pp. 156–158.

8. Glines, "Black vs. White," pp. 20, 23.

9. William L. Hauser, *America's Army in Crisis: A Study in Civil-Military Relations* (Baltimore, 1973), pp. 98–102; Millett, *Semper Fidelis,* p. 599.

10. Colonel Harold W. Hobbs, Commander, 377th Combat Support Group, July 1970–July 1971, End of Tour Report, December 18, 1971, Office of Air Force History.

11. Commander Jack M. White, "Seven Days in July," *U.S. Naval Institute Proceedings,* vol. XCVIII (January 1972), pp. 38–40.

12. "Air Force Jim Crow," *The Crisis,* June-July 1970, in MacGregor and Nalty, *Blacks in the Armed Forces,* vol. XIII, item 59. All documents cited by item number in the chapter are reproduced in this volume.

13. The Search for Military Justice: Report of the NAACP Inquiry into the Problems of Negro Servicemen in West Germany, item 60.

14. Foner, *Blacks and the Military,* p. 222.

15. *Ibid.,* p. 216.

16. Department of Defense Human Goals, August 16, 1969, educational material issued by the Defense Race Relations Institute provided by Captain RitaVictoria DeArmond, USAF.

17. Foner, *Blacks and the Military*, pp. 216–217; Office of Deputy Assistant Secretary of Defense for Equal Opportunity and Safety Policy, *Black Americans in Defense of Our Nation* (Washington, 1982), p. 46; Memorandum, Office of Assistant Secretary of Defense (Manpower), Policy Formulation Planning and Action in the Office of Deputy Assistant Secretary of Defense (Civil Rights), September 21, 1965, item 41.

18. Carl Rowan, *Just Between Us Blacks* (New York, 1974), pp. 37–39.

19. *Ibid.*, p. 38.

20. Elmo Zumwalt, Jr., *On Watch: A Memoir* (New York, 1976), pp. 190–195, 198.

21. Foner, *Blacks and the Military*, pp. 240–241.

22. Zumwalt, *On Watch*, pp. 210–211.

23. Major Alan M. Osur, "Black and White Relations in the U.S. Military, 1940–1972," *Air University Review*, vol. XXXIII (November–December 1981), p. 76.

24. Gropman, *The Air Force Integrates*, p. 216; Unpublished interview, Lieutenant Colonel Robert G. Zimmerman with Colonel John E. Blake, July 24, 1974, Office of Air Force History.

25. Department of Defense Directive no. 1322.11, June 24, 1971, subject: Department of Defense Education in Race Relations for Armed Forces Personnel, item 63.

26. Osur, "Black and White Relations," p. 76.

Chapter 20. EMPHASIS ON EDUCATION

1. Unpublished interview, Shelby E. Wickham with Lieutenant Colonel Thomas J. Sizemore, Chief, 2750th Air Base Wing Social Actions Office, March 3, 1977, Office of Air Force History.

2. Robert C. Seamans, Jr., "The Air Force and Equal Opportunity," *Air University Review*, vol. XXIII (September-October 1972), pp. 4–5.

3. Osur, "Black-White Relations," p. 77; *New York Times*, September 21, 1972, p. 54.

4. Zumwalt, *On Watch*, pp. 217–219; Report by the Special Subcommittee on Disciplinary Problems in the U.S. Navy of the Committee on Armed Services, House of Representatives, 92nd Congress, 2nd Session, January 2, 1973, in MacGregor and Nalty, *Blacks in the Armed Forces*, vol. XIII, item 67. All documents cited by item number in the chapter are reproduced in this volume.

5. Zumwalt, *On Watch*, p. 222.

6. Report by the Special Subcommittee on Disciplinary Problems in the Navy, item 67.

7. Foner, *Blacks and the Military*, pp. 245–248, 251.

8. *Ibid.*, pp. 256–257.

9. *Ibid.*, p. 249; Zumwalt, *On Watch*, pp. 235–239.

10. Report by the Special Committee on Disciplinary Problems in the U.S. Navy, item 67; F. Edward Hebert with John McMillan, *"Last of the Titans": The Life and Times of Congressman F. Edward Hebert of Louisiana* (Lafayette, Louisiana, 1976), p. 325.

11. Zumwalt, *On Watch*, pp. 245, 271–272; Foner, *Blacks and the Military*, p. 249; *Hartford Courant*, December 30, 1984, p. B1.

12. Foner, *Blacks and the Military*, pp. 251–258.

13. *Ibid.*, pp. 229–233.

14. Attachment to letter, the Adjutant General, U.S. Army, Europe, and Seventh Army for Commanders of USAREUR Major Commands and Assigned Units and Activities (to Battalion Level), Heads of Staff Offices, This Headquarters, July 20, 1973, subject: USAREUR Race Relations: Attitude Trends, item 68.

15. Foner, *Blacks and the Military*, pp. 236–237.

16. Report of the Task Force on the Administration of Military Justice in the Armed Forces, November 30, 1972, letter of transmittal, item 66.

17. *Ibid.*, pp. 24–36.

18. *Ibid.*, pp. 38–48, 59–66.

19. *Ibid.*, pp. 112–126.

20. *Ibid.*, pp. 106–108.

21. *Ibid.*, addenda.

22. Matt Glasgow, "Changing Times," *Soldiers*, vol. XXXIV (July 1979), p. 39; Office of Deputy Assistant Secretary of Defense for Equal Opportunity and Safety Policy, *Black Americans in Defense of Our Nation* (Washington, 1982), p. 42.

Chapter 21. VOLUNTEERS, RACIAL REPRESENTATION, AND THE TIPPING POINT

1. Statement Announcing the Appointment of the President's Commission on an All-Volunteer Armed Force, March 27, 1969, *Public Papers of the Presidents of the United States: Richard Nixon, 1969* (Washington, 1971), p. 258.

2. Special Message to the Congress on Reforming the Military Draft, May 13, 1969, *Public Papers of Richard Nixon, 1969*, pp. 365–369.

3. Stanley Karnow, *Vietnam: A History* (New York, 1983), p. 601; *Washington Post*, May 21, 1969, p. A24.

4. *New York Times*, May 21, 1969, p. 1.

5. *Ibid.*

6. Address to the Nation on the War in Vietnam, November 3, 1969, *Public Papers of Richard Nixon, 1969*, p. 906.

7. Karnow, *Vietnam*, pp. 595–596; Statement on United States Troops in Vietnam, September 16, 1969, *Public Papers of Richard Nixon, 1969*, p. 718.

8. *Report of the President's Commission on an All-Volunteer Armed Force* Washington, 1970), pp. 15–17, errata sheet.

9. Charles C. Moskos, Jr., "The Emergent Army," *Parameters: The Journal of the U.S. Army War College*, vol. IV (1974), p. 22.

10. *Ibid.*, pp. 24, 27; Zumwalt, *On Watch*, p. 210; Millet, *Semper Fidelis*, pp. 619–620; Osur, "Black and White Relations," p. 76.

11. Morris Janowitz and Charles C. Moskos, Jr., "Racial Composition in the All-Volunteer Force," *Armed Forces and Society: An Interdisciplinary Journal*, vol. I (Fall 1974), pp. 110–113; Jonathan Schell, *The Time of Illusion* (New York, 1976), pp. 39–44, 215–216.

12. Morris Janowitz and Charles C. Moskos, Jr., "Five Years of the All-Volunteer Force, 1974–1978," *Armed Forces and Society: An Interdisciplinary Journal*, vol. V (Winter 1979), p. 197.

13. Martin Binkin and Mark J. Eitelberger with Alvin J. Schnexnider and Marvin M. Smith, *Blacks and the Military* (Washington, 1982), pp. 42, 106–107.

14. *Ibid.*, table A–1; Seamans, "The Air Force and Equal Opportunity," p. 4.

15. Patricia M. Shields, "Enlistment during the Vietnam Era and the 'Representation' Issue of the All-Volunteer Force," *Armed Forces and Society: An Interdisciplinary Journal*, vol. VII (Fall 1980), p. 144.

16. Janowitz and Moskos, "Five Years of the All-Volunteer Force," pp. 193–196.

17. *Ibid.*, pp. 199–200; Binkin, Eitelberg, et al., *Blacks and the Military*, pp. 52–54.

18. Binkin, Eitelberg, et al., *Blacks and the Military*, pp. 51–52.

19. Shields, "The 'Representation' Issue," p. 147.

20. Binkin, Eitelberg, et al., *Blacks and the Military*, pp. 75–78.

21. *Ibid.*, p. 81.

22. Clifford L. Alexander, Jr., "In the Army Now," a review of *Blacks and the Military* by Martin Binkin and Mark J. Eitelberger with Alvin J. Schnexnider and Marvin M. Smith, *Washington Post Book World*, August 22, 1982, p. 3.

23. *Chicago Tribune*, October 9, 1983, p. 1.

24. *Washington Post*, November 3, 1983, p. A18.

25. *Ibid.*, October 13, 1983, p. B7; November 3, 1983, p. A18.

26. *Ibid.*, January 30, 1985, p. B4, January 31, 1985, p. C4.

27. Shields, "The 'Representation' Issue," p. 147.

28. Janowitz and Moskos, "Five Years of the All-Volunteer Force," pp. 196, 198.

29. Seamans, "The Air Force and Equal Opportunity," p. 8.

30. Report of the Task Force on the Administration of Military Justice in the Armed Forces, pp. 106–108.

31. Glasgow, "Changing Times," pp. 39–40.

32. Office of Deputy Assistant Secretary of Defense for Equal Opportunity

and Safety Policy, *Black Americans in Defense of Our Nation* (Washington, 1982), pp. 42–45.

33. Craig Pugh and Robert K. Ruhl, "Up Front—Where the Action Is," *Airman*, vol. XXV (February 1981), p. 38.

34. Defense Manpower Data Center, Distribution of Active Duty Forces by Service, Rank, Sex, and Ethnic Group, June 1983, in Office of the Deputy Assistant Secretary of Defense for Equal Opportunity and Safety Policy.

35. *Ibid.*; *Washington Post*, November 24, 1983, p. A20. The Office of the Assistant Secretary of Defense, Manpower, Installations, and Logistics, supplied revised statistics.

36. *Washington Post*, February 27, 1983, p. A14.

37. *Ibid.*, November 24, 1983, p. A20.

38. *Ibid.*, March 10, 1984, p. A16.

39. Defense Manpower Data Center, Distribution of Selected Reservists by Reserve Components, Pay Grades, Sex, and Ethnic Group, December 1982, in Office of the Deputy Assistant Secretary of Defense for Equal Opportunity and Safety Policy.

Afterword

1. Robert F. Lockman and Aline O. Quester, "The AVF: Outlook for the Eighties and Nineties," *Armed Forces and Society: An Interdisciplinary Journal*, vol. XI (Winter 1985), pp. 176–177, 179–180.

2. Lorenzo D. Harris, "The 'Blue' in Bluford," *Airman*, vol. XXVIII (February 1984), pp. 7–14.

3. *Newsweek*, vol. CIII (January 9, 1984) pp. 20–21, vol. CIII (January 16, 1984), pp. 14–15; *Ebony*, vol. XXXIX (March 1984), pp. 155–161.

Bibliography

Any investigation of the status of blacks in the armed forces of the United States profits from three collections of documents. The most recent of these, *The Black Military Experience*, published in 1982 by the Cambridge University Press, is the second of six segments that will constitute *Freedom: A Documentary History of Emancipation, 1861–1867*. The editors—Ira Berlin and two associates, Joseph P. Reidy and Leslie S. Rowland—have mined the resources of the National Archives of the United States to produce an illuminating collection of documents dealing with black soldiers in the Civil War. Especially interesting are letters written by soldiers and by members of their families—some letters simply exchanging information and offering gestures of affection, other letters speaking of injustice, seeking redress, or describing life in the service. The introduction to one chapter, dealing with the struggle for equal pay, and a few of the more important documents form the basis for an article in the Fall 1982 issue of *Prologue: The Journal of the National Archives*.

A second collection, upon which Berlin and his colleagues have drawn, is *The Negro in the Military Service of the United States, 1639–1886*. Broader in chronological coverage than *The Black Military Experience*, this body of documents—some 5,000 pages of original items, copies, and extracts—was assembled under the direction of Elon A. Woodward, chief of the Colored Troops Division of the Office of the Adjutant General. Originally intended as the raw material for an official documentary history, the compilation is now available on microfilm from the National Archives.

A third collection, which treats briefly the years covered by the other two but emphasizes more recent times, is *Blacks in the United States Armed Forces: Basic Documents*, published in 1977 by Scholarly Resources of

Wilmington, Delaware. These thirteen volumes, edited by Morris J. Mac-Gregor, Jr., with my assistance, draw upon *The Negro in the Military Service of the United States* but also include official documents dealing with such diverse subjects as the Brownsville incident, the Houston riot, racial integration during World War II, the Fahy and Gesell committees, and racial friction in the services at the time of the Vietnam conflict. The thirteen volumes have been abridged into one, *Blacks in the Military: Essential Documents,* published by the same firm in 1981.

Several books and monographs published under official auspices deal with the subject of the racial policies of the armed forces. Ulysses Lee's *The Employment of Negro Troops,* a special study in the Army's history of World War II, helped earn the Office of Chief of Military History (now the Center of Military History) a deserved reputation for candor. Aptly described by a reviewer as "magisterial," Morris MacGregor's *Integration of the Armed Forces* helps preserve that reputation. The Air Force may be proud of the two monographs that recount the formation of racial policy from the onset of World War II until the 1960s. Both Alan M. Osur's *Blacks in the Army Air Forces during World War II* and Alan L. Gropman's *The Air Force Integrates, 1945–1964* are thoroughly researched, ably written, and objective. *Blacks in the Marine Corps* by Henry I. Shaw, Jr., and Ralph W. Donnelly, is especially valuable for its treatment of World War II and the Korean conflict. The Coast Guard monograph *A History of Blacks in the U.S. Coast Guard,* by Linda Townsend and Dupree Davenport, focuses on the normal activities of that service—rescue, maritime safety, and the like—rather than wartime contributions as part of the Navy Department. The Navy has produced a monograph by Dennis D. Nelson, *The Integration of the Negro into the United States Navy, 1776–1947,* whose treatment of the subject ends with 1947 and concentrates upon World War II.

BOOKS, MONOGRAPHS, AND COLLECTIONS OF DOCUMENTS

BARBEAU, ARTHUR E., and FLORETTE HENRI. *The Unknown Soldiers: Black American Troops in World War I.* Philadelphia: Temple University Press, 1974.

BERLIN, IRA, ed., with JOSEPH P. REIDY, and LESLIE S. ROWLAND. *Freedom: A Documentary History of Emancipation, 1861–1867;* series II, *The Black Military Experience.* Cambridge: Cambridge University Press, 1982.

BERMAN, WILLIAM C. *The Politics of Civil Rights in the Truman Administration.* Columbus, Ohio: Ohio State University Press, 1970.

BINKIN, MARTIN, and MARK J. EITELBERG, with ALVIN J. SCHNEXNIDER and MARVIN M. SMITH. *Blacks and the Military.* Washington: Brookings Institution, 1982.

BRAUER, CARL M. *John F. Kennedy and the Second Reconstruction.* New York: Columbia University Press, 1977.

BROOKS, THOMAS R. *Walls Come Tumbling Down: A History of the Civil Rights Movement, 1940–1970.* Englewood Cliffs, New Jersey: Prentice-Hall, 1974.

BULLARD, ROBERT LEE. *Personalities and Reminiscences of the War*. Garden City, New York: Doubleday, Page, 1925.

CARROL, JOHN M., ed. *The Black Military Experience in the American West*. New York: Liveright, 1973.

CASHIN, HERSCHEL V., CHARLES ALEXANDER, et al. *Under Fire with the Tenth Cavalry, Being a Brief, Comprehensive Review of the Negro's Participation in the Wars of the United States*. New York: The Arno Press and *The New York Times*, 1969.

CHACE, WILLIAM C., and PETER COLLIER, eds. *Justice Denied: The Black Man in White America*. New York: Harcourt, Brace and World, 1970.

CLENDENEN, CLARENCE C. *Blood on the Border: The United States Army and the Mexican Irregulars*. New York: Macmillan, 1969.

CORNISH, DUDLEY TAYLOR. *The Sable Arm: Negro Troops in the Union Army, 1861–1865*. New York: Longmans, Green, 1956.

DALFIUME, RICHARD M. *Desegregation of the U.S. Armed Forces: Fighting on Two Fronts, 1939–1953*. Columbia, Missouri: University of Missouri Press, 1969.

DIERKS, JACK CAMERON. *A Leap to Arms: The Cuban Campaign of 1898*. Philadelphia: Lippincott, 1970.

FISHEL, LESLIE H., and BENJAMIN QUARLES, eds. *The Black American: A Documentary History*. Glenview, Illinois: Scott, Foresman, 1970.

FLETCHER, MARVIN E. *The Negro Soldier and the United States Army, 1891–1917*. University of Wisconsin, doctoral dissertation, 1968. (Published at Columbia, Missouri: University of Missouri Press, 1974.)

FONER, ERIC. *Politics and Ideology in the Age of the Civil War*. New York: Oxford University Press, 1980.

FONER, JACK D. *Blacks and the Military in American History*. New York: Praeger, 1974.

FOWLER, ARLEN. *The Black Infantry in the West, 1869–1891*. Westport, Connecticut: Greenwood, 1971.

FRANCIS, CHARLES E. *The Tuskegee Airmen: The Story of the Negro in the U.S. Air Force*. Boston: Bruce Humphries, 1955.

GREENE, LORENZO JOHNSTON. *The Negro in Colonial New England*. New York: Atheneum, 1974.

GROPMAN, ALAN L. *The Air Force Integrates, 1945–1964*. Washington: Office of Air Force History, 1978.

HARROD, FREDERICK S. *Manning the New Navy: The Development of a Modern Naval Enlisted Force, 1899–1940*. Westport, Connecticut: Greenwood, 1978.

HART, ROBERT A. *The Great White Fleet: Its Voyage around the World, 1907–1909*. Boston: Little, Brown, 1965.

HAUSER, WILLIAM L. *America's Army in Crisis: A Study in Civil-Military Relations*. Baltimore: Johns Hopkins University Press, 1973.

HAYNES, ROBERT V. *A Night of Violence: The Houston Riot of 1917*. Baton Rouge, Louisiana: Louisiana State University Press, 1976.

HEYWOOD, CHESTER D. *Negro Troops in the World War: The Story of the 371st Infantry.* Worcester, Massachusetts: Commonwealth Press, 1928.

JOHNSON, BARRY C. *Flipper's Dismissal: The Ruin of Lt. Henry O. Flipper, U.S.A., First Coloured Graduate of West Point.* London: privately printed, 1972.

KARSTEN, PETER. *The Naval Aristocracy: The Golden Age of Annapolis and the Emergence of American Navalism.* New York: The Free Press, 1972.

KLUGER, RICHARD. *Simple Justice: The History of Brown v. Board of Education and Black America's Struggle for Equality.* New York: Knopf, 1976.

LANE, ANN J. *The Brownsville Affair.* Port Washington, New York: National University, 1971.

LANGLEY, HAROLD D. *Social Reform in the United States Navy, 1798–1862.* Urbana, Illinois: University of Illinois Press, 1967.

LECKIE, WILLIAM H. *The Buffalo Soldiers: A Narrative of the Negro Cavalry in the West.* Norman, Oklahoma: University of Oklahoma Press, 1967.

LEE, ULYSSES. *The United States Army in World War II, Special Studies: The Employment of Negro Troops.* Washington: Office of Chief of Military History, 1966.

LEWIS, ANTHONY, and *The New York Times. Portrait of a Decade: The Second American Revolution, a First-Hand Account of the Struggle for Civil Rights.* New York: Random House, 1964.

LEWIS, FRANCIS, E. *Negro Army Regulars in the Spanish-American War: Smoked Yankees at Santiago de Cuba.* University of Texas, master of arts report, 1969.

LITTLE, ARTHUR W. *From Harlem to the Rhine: The Story of New York's Colored Volunteers.* New York: Covici Friede, 1936.

LITWACK, LEON F. *Been in the Storm So Long: The Aftermath of Slavery.* New York, Knopf, 1980.

_____. *North of Slavery: The Negro in the Free States, 1790–1860.* Chicago: University of Chicago Press, 1970.

LOVELL, JOHN P., and PHILIP S. KRONENBERG, eds. *New Civil-Military Relations: The Agonies of Adjustment to Post-Vietnam Realities.* New Brunswick, New Jersey: Transition Books, 1974.

LYNK, MYLES V. *The Black Troopers or the Daring Heroism of the Negro Soldiers in the Spanish-American War.* New York: AMS, 1971.

MACGREGOR, MORRIS J. *Defense Studies: Integration of the Armed Forces.* Washington: Center of Military History, 1981.

_____, and BERNARD C. NALTY, eds. *Blacks in the United States Armed Forces: Basic Documents,* 13 vols. Wilmington, Delaware: Scholarly Resources, 1977.

MACPHERSON, MYRA. *Long Time Passing: Vietnam and the Haunted Generation.* Garden City, New York: Doubleday, 1984.

MARSZALEK, JOHN F., JR. *Court Martial: The Army vs Johnson Whittaker, an Account of the Ordeal of a Black Cadet at West Point.* New York: Scribner, 1972.

McCONNELL, ROLAND. *Negro Troops of Antebellum Louisiana: A History of the Battalion of Free Men of Color.* Baton Rouge, Louisiana: Louisiana State University Press, 1968.

McCOY, DONALD R., and RICHARD T. RUETTEN. *Quest and Response: Minority Rights and the Truman Administration.* Lawrence, Kansas: University of Kansas Press, 1973.

McGOVERN, JAMES R. *Black Eagle: General Daniel "Chappie" James, Jr.* Tuscaloosa, Alabama: University of Alabama Press, 1985.

MILLETT, ALLEN R. *The General: Robert L. Bullard and Officership in the United States Army, 1881-1925.* Westport, Connecticut: Greenwood, 1975.

_____. *Semper Fidelis: The History of the United States Marine Corps.* New York: Macmillan, 1980.

MOORE, GEORGE H. *Historical Notes on the Employment of Negroes in the American Army of the Revolution.* New York: Charles T. Evans, 1862.

MOSKOS, CHARLES C., JR. *The American Enlisted Man: The Rank and File in Today's Military.* New York: Russell Sage Foundation, 1970.

NASH, GARY B. *Red, White, and Black: The Peoples of Early America.* Englewood Cliffs, New Jersey: Prentice-Hall, 1974.

NELSON, DENNIS DENMARK. *The Integration of the Negro into the United States Navy, 1776-1947, with a Brief Historical Introduction.* Washington: Department of the Navy, 1948.

NICHOLS, LEE. *Breakthrough on the Color Front.* New York: Random House, 1954.

OSUR, ALAN M. *Blacks in the Army Air Forces during World War II.* Washington: Office of Air Force History, 1977.

PATTON, GERALD W. *War and Race: The Black Officer in the American Military, 1915-1941.* Westport, Connecticut: Greenwood, 1981.

POST, CHARLES JOHNSON. *The Little War of Private Post.* Boston: Little, Brown, 1960.

PRINGLE, HENRY F. *Theodore Roosevelt: A Biography.* New York: Harcourt, Brace, 1931.

PURDON, ERIC. *Black Company: The Story of Subchaser 1264.* Washington–New York: Robert B. Luce, 1972.

QUARLES, BENJAMIN. *The Negro in the American Revolution.* Chapel Hill, North Carolina: University of North Carolina Press, 1961.

_____. *The Negro in the Civil War.* Boston: Little, Brown, 1953.

SCOTT, EMMETT J. *Scott's Official History of the American Negro in the World War.* Chicago: Homewood Press, 1919.

SHAW, HENRY I., JR., and RALPH W. DONNELLY. *Blacks in the Marine Corps.* Washington: History and Museums Division, Headquarters, U.S. Marine Corps, 1975.

SINGLETARY, OTIS A. *The Negro Militia and Reconstruction.* Austin, Texas: University of Texas Press, 1971.

SMYTHE, DONALD. *Guerrilla Warrior: The Early Life of John J. Pershing.* New York: Scribner, 1973.

STILLMAN, RICHARD J., II. *Integration of the Negro in the U.S. Armed Forces.* New York: Praeger, 1968.

TERRY, WALLACE. *Bloods: An Oral History of the Vietnam War by Black Veterans.* New York: Random House, 1984.

THOMAS, ROBERT S., and INEZ ALLEN. *The Mexican Punitive Expedition under Brigadier General John J. Pershing, U.S.A., 1916–1917.* Washington: Center of Military History, unpublished manuscript.

TOULMIN, HARRY A. *With Pershing in Mexico.* Harrisburg, Pennsylvania: Military Service, 1935.

TOWNSEND, LINDA, and DUPREE DAVENPORT. *A History of Blacks in the U.S. Coast Guard.* Washington: Department of Transportation, U.S. Coast Guard, n.d.

TRASK, DAVID. *The War with Spain in 1898.* New York: Macmillan, 1981.

UTLEY, ROBERT M. *Frontier Regulars: The United States Army and the Indian, 1866–1890.* New York: Macmillan, 1973.

UYA, OKON EDET. *From Slavery to Public Service: Robert Smalls, 1839–1915.* New York: Oxford University Press, 1971.

WEAVER, JOHN D. *The Brownsville Raid.* New York: Norton, 1970.

WHITE, WALTER. *A Man Called White: The Autobiography of Walter White.* Bloomington, Indiana: Indiana University Press, 1970.

WHITE, WILLIAM B. *The Military and the Melting Pot: The Army and Minority Groups, 1865–1924.* University of Wisconsin, doctoral dissertation, 1968.

WOLFF, LEON. *Little Brown Brother: How the United States Purchased and Pacified the Philippine Islands at the Century's Turn.* Garden City, New York: Doubleday, 1961.

WOODWARD, C. VANN. *The Strange Career of Jim Crow.* New York: Oxford University Press, 1966.

YARMOLINKSY, ADAM. *The Military Establishment: Its Impacts on American Society.* New York: Harper Colophon, 1971.

ARTICLES

APTHEKER, HERBERT. "The Negro in the Union Navy," *Journal of Negro History,* vol. XXXII (April 1947), pp. 168–200.

BERLIN, IRA, BARBARA J. FIELDS, JOSEPH REIDY, and LESLIE S. ROWLAND. "Writing *Freedom's* History," *Prologue: The Journal of the National Archives,* vol. XIV (Fall 1982), pp. 129–139.

BLASSINGAME, JOHN W. "Negro Chaplains in the Civil War," *Negro History Bulletin,* vol. XXXVII (October 1963), pp. 1, 23.

BOWMAN, LARRY G. "Virginia's Use of Blacks in the French and Indian War," *Western Pennsylvania Historical Magazine,* vol. LIII (January 1970), pp. 57–63.

BOYD, GEORGE M. "A Look at Racial Polarity in the Armed Forces," *Air University Review*, vol. XXI (September-October 1970), pp. 42–50.

BRYANT, WILLIAM CULLEN, II. "A Yankee Soldier Looks at the Negro," *Civil War History*, vol. VII (June 1961), pp. 132–148.

BULLARD, ROBERT LEE. "The Negro Volunteer: Some Characteristics," *Journal of the Military Service Institution of the United States*, vol. XXIX (July 1901), pp. 29–39.

CASSELL, FRANK A. "Slaves of the Chesapeake Bay Area and the War of 1812," *Journal of Negro History*, vol. LVII (April 1972), pp. 144–155.

DYE, IRA. "Seafarers of 1812: A Profile," *Prologue: The Journal of the National Archives*, vol. V (Spring 1973), pp. 1–13.

EVERETT, DONALD E. "Ben Butler and the Louisiana Native Guards, 1861–1862," *Journal of Southern History*, vol. XXIV (May 1958), pp. 202–217.

FIELD, R.L. "The Black Midshipman at the U.S. Naval Academy," *U.S. Naval Institute Proceedings*, vol. CXIX (April 1973), pp. 28–36.

FLETCHER, MARVIN. "The Black Volunteers in the Spanish-American War," *Military Affairs*, vol. XXXVIII (April 1974), pp. 48–53.

_____. "The Negro Volunteer in Reconstruction," *Military Affairs*, vol. XXXII (December 1968), pp. 124–131.

GATEWOOD, WILLARD B., JR. "Alabama's 'Negro Soldier Experiment,' 1898–1899," *Journal of Negro History*, vol. LVII (October 1972), pp. 333–351.

_____. "Black Americans and the Quest for Empire, 1898–1903," *Journal of Southern History*, vol. XXXVIII (November 1972), pp. 545–566.

_____. "Kansas Negroes and the Spanish-American War," *Kansas Historical Quarterly*, vol. XXXVII (Autumn 1971), pp. 300–313.

_____. "Negro Troops in Florida, 1898." *Florida Historical Quarterly*, vol. XLIX (July 1970), pp. 1–15.

_____. "North Carolina's Negro Regiment in the Spanish-American War," *North Carolina Historical Review*, vol. XLVIII (October 1971), pp. 370–387.

GLASGOW, MATT. "Changing Times," *Soldiers*, vol. XXXIV (July 1979), pp. 37–40.

GLINES, C.V. "Black vs. White—Trouble in the Ranks," *Armed Forces Management*, vol. XVI (June 1970), pp. 20–27.

GREENE, LORENZO J. "The Negro in the Armed Forces of the United States, 1619–1783," *Negro History Bulletin*, vol. XIV (March 1951), pp. 123–127, 138.

_____. "The Negro in the War of 1812 and the Civil War," *Negro History Bulletin*, vol. XIV (March 1951), pp. 133–137.

_____. "Some Observations on the Black Regiment of Rhode Island in the American Revolution," *Journal of Negro History*, vol. XXVII (April 1952), pp. 142–172.

HARRIS, LORENZO D. "The 'Blue' in Bluford," *Airman*, vol. XXVIII (February 1984), pp. 8–14.

HASDORFF, JAMES C. "Reflections on the Tuskegee Experiment: An Interview with Brig. Gen. Noel F. Parrish, USAF (Ret.)," *Aerospace Historian*, vol. XXIV (Fall/September 1977), pp. 173–180.

HELLER, CHARLES E. " 'Between Two Fires,' the 54th Massachusetts," *Civil War Illustrated*, vol. XI (April 1972), pp. 32–41.

JAMES, DANIEL, JR. "Rapping with Chappie," *Air University Review*, vol. XXIII (July-August 1972), pp. 12–21.

JANOWITZ, MORRIS and CHARLES C. MOSKOS, JR. "Five Years of the All-Volunteer Force: 1973–1978," *Armed Forces and Society: An Interdisciplinary Journal*, vol. V (Winter 1979), pp. 171–218.

_____. "Racial Composition in the All-Volunteer Force: Policy Alternatives," *Armed Forces and Society: An Interdisciplinary Journal*, vol. I (November 1974), pp. 109–123.

JOHNSON, CHARLES. "The Army, The Negro, and the Civilian Conservation Corps: 1933–1942," *Military Affairs*, vol. XXXVI (October 1972), pp. 82–88.

JOHNSON, GERALD K. "The Black Soldier in the Ardennes," *Soldiers*, vol. XXXVI (February 1981), pp.16–19.

LANGLEY, HAROLD. "The Negro in the Navy and Merchant Marine, 1789–1860," *Journal of Negro History*, vol. LII (October 1967), pp. 273–286.

LOCKMAN, ROBERT F., and ALINE O. QUESTER. "The AVF: Outlook for the Eighties and Nineties," *Armed Forces and Society: An Interdisciplinary Journal*, vol. XI (Winter 1985), pp. 169–182.

LOGAN, RAYFORD W. "The Negro in the Quasi War, 1798–1800," *Negro History Bulletin*, vol. XIV (March 1951), pp. 128–132.

McGUIRE, PHILLIP. "Judge William H. Hastie and Army Recruitment, 1940–1942," *Military Affairs*, vol. XLII (April 1978), pp. 75–79.

MOSKOS, CHARLES C., JR. "The Emergent Army," *Parameters: The Journal of the U.S. Army War College*, vol. IV, no. 1 (1974), pp. 17–30.

_____. "Racial Integration in the Armed Forces," *American Journal of Sociology*, vol. LXXII (September 1966), pp. 132–148.

_____, JOHN SIBLEY BUTLER, ALAN NED SABRONSKY, and ALVIN J. SCHNEXNIDER. "Symposium: Race and the United States Military," *Armed Forces and Society: An Interdisciplinary Journal*, vol. VI (Summer 1980), pp. 586–613.

OSUR, ALAN M. "Black-White Relations in the U.S. Military, 1940–1972," *Air University Review*, vol. XXXIII (November-December 1981), pp. 69–78.

PALMER, ANNETTE. "The Politics of Race and War: Black American Soldiers in the Caribbean Theater during the Second World War," *Military Affairs*, vol. XLVII (April 1983), pp. 59–62.

PASZEK, LAWRENCE J. "Negroes and the Air Force, 1939–1949," *Military Affairs*, vol. XXI (Spring 1967), pp. 1–9.

_____. "Separate but Equal? The Story of the 99th Fighting Squadron," *Aerospace Historian*, vol. XXIV (Fall/September 1977), pp. 135–145.

PUGH, CRAIG, and ROBERT K. RUHL. "Up Front: Where the Action Is," *Airman*, vol. XXV (February 1981), pp. 37–40.

RACKLEFF, ROBERT. "The Black Soldier in Popular American Magazines, 1900–1971, *Negro History Bulletin,* vol. XXXIV (December 1971), pp. 185–189.

REDDICK, L.D. "The Negro Policy of the American Army since World War II," *Journal of Negro History,* vol. XXVIII (Ap;ril 1953), pp. 194–215.

_____. "The Negro Policy of the United States Army, 1775–1945," *Journal of Negro History,* vol. XXXIV (January 1949), pp. 9–29.

ROBINSON, MICHAEL C., and FRANK N. SCHUBERT. "David Fagen: An Afro-American Rebel in the Philippines, 1899–1901," *Pacific Historical Review,* vol. XLIV (February 1975), pp. 68–83.

ROSE, ROBERT A. "The Lonely Eagles," *Journal of the American Aviation Historical Society,* part 1, vol. XX (Summer 1975), pp. 118–127, part 2, vol. XX (Winter 1975), pp. 240–252.

RYAN, PAUL B. "USS Constellation Flare-up: Was It Mutiny?" *U.S. Naval Institute Proceedings,* vol. CII (January 1976), pp. 46–53.

SCHUBERT, FRANK N. "Black Soldiers on the White Frontier: Some Factors Influencing Race Relations," *Phylon,* vol. XXXII (Winter 1971), pp. 410–415.

_____. "The Fort Robinson Y.M.C.A., 1902–1907," *Nebraska History,* vol. LV (Summer 1974), pp. 165–179.

_____. "The Suggs Affray: The Black Cavalry and the Johnson County War," *Western Historical Quarterly,* vol. IV (January 1973), pp. 57–68.

_____. "The Violent World of Emanuel Stance, Fort Robinson, 1887," *Nebraska History,* vol. LV (Summer 1974), pp. 203–219.

SEAMANS, ROBERT C., JR. "The Air Force and Equal Opportunity," *Air University Review,* vol. XXIII (September-October 1972), pp. 2–8.

SHIELDS, PATRICIA M. "Enlistment during the Vietnam Era and the 'Representation' Issue of the All-Volunteer Force," *Armed Forces and Society: an Interdisciplinary Journal,* vol. VII (Fall 1980), pp. 133–151.

SINGLETARY, OTIS A. "The Negro Militia during Radical Reconstruction," *Military Affairs,* vol. XIX (Winter 1955), pp. 177–186.

WEEMS, JOHN E. "Black Wings of Gold," *U.S. Naval Institute Proceedings,* vol. CIX (July 1983), pp. 35–39.

WERRELL, KENNETH P. "Mutiny at Army Air Force Station 569: Bamber Bridge, England, June 1943," *Aerospace Historian,* vol. XXII (Winter/December 1975), pp. 202–209.

WHITE, JACK M. "Seven Days in July," *U.S. Naval Institute Proceedings,* vol. XCVIII (January 1972), pp. 37–41.

Index